Strategic Value Chain Management

Models for competitive advantage

Qeis Kamran

KoganPage

First published in Great Britain and the United States in 2021 by Kogan Page Limited

2nd Floor, 45 Gee Street
London
EC1V 3RS
United Kingdom
www.koganpage.com

122 W 27th St, 10th Floor
New York, NY 10001
USA

4737/23 Ansari Road
Daryaganj
New Delhi 110002
India

Kogan Page books are printed on paper from sustainable forests.

ISBNs

Hardback 978 1 78966 041 8
Paperback 978 0 7494 8442 2
eBook 978 0 7494 8443 9

British Library Cataloguing-in-Publication Data

A CIP record for this book is available from the British Library.

Library of Congress Cataloging-in-Publication Data
Names: Kamran, Qeis, author.
Title: Strategic value chain management : models for competitive advantage / Qeis Kamran.
Description: London ; New York, NY : Kogan Page, 2021. | Includes bibliographical references and index. |
Identifiers: LCCN 2020013983 (print) | LCCN 2020013984 (ebook) | ISBN 9780749484422 (paperback ; alk. paper) | ISBN 9781789660418 (hardback; alk. paper) | ISBN 9780749484439 (ebook)
Subjects: LCSH: Business logistics. | Strategic planning. | Value.
Classification: LCC HD38.5 .K34 2020 (print) | LCC HD38.5 (ebook) | DDC 658.7–dc23

Typeset by Integra Software Services, Pondicherry
Print production managed by Jellyfish
Printed and bound by CPI Group (UK) Ltd, Croydon CR0 4YY

CONTENTS

PREFACE

The research and practice of globally operating firms – especially those that are hidden champions (HC), based on the German avant-garde foundation of *Unternehmertum* of highly unique niche positions and diverse multinational corporations (MNCs) – underpin the dimension of a model-based management steering of firms, which is still based on a linear conceptualization of the notion of globalization. What I refer to here is the late 1970s notion of a linear understanding of globalization. Thus, the globalization of goods put into containers and shipped from China to the West and the globalization of capital sent back in return to finalize the transaction is not sufficient to justify the term *containerization* within the contemporary logic of logistics, supply chain management (SCM) and global value chains (GVCs).

There is a vital need to actualize this notion from a linear observation of globalization towards a new term coined here as the *globalization of totality*. This notion requires a new and yet-to-be-designed model of a holistic navigation of the firm within the turbulent waters of the *globalization of totality* that embraces additional perspectives essential for the management of HCs and MNCs facing highly complex and turbulent environments challenging the resilience of their GVCs on an unprecedented scale and rate of change, even after the 2008 'management crisis', to which some still refer as 'the financial crisis'. However, we must observe that management crises would always result in some sort of financial crisis, and not the other way around – financial crises are always a result of bad and linear management models and doctrines.

There are five essential foundations of the globalization of totality:

1. **The globalization of capital:** for example, capital movement has shifted from being purely from the West to the East. In 2015, China invested more FDI in Germany than the other way around.
2. **The globalization of connectivity:** the world has become one. While geographical boundaries may exist, the world of digital connectivity and ubiquitous computing is a new story of the world in concert.
3. **The globalization of pandemics:** the Corona virus is a prime example that has changed the world; we are able to see the visible hands of countries'

helmsmen within a functioning socio-economic system, in comparison with those countries that choose to hide behind reductionist walls of economic nationalism applied towards a global high-stakes problem.

4 **The globalization of fundamentalism:** for example, it was populism in the UK that resulted in Brexit, and in the US the rise of Trumpocracy; likewise we have the rise of radical Islamism in terms of non-state-actor terrorism by groups such as ISIS. The ubiquitous transmission of information does not provide a filter between a good or a bad idea.
5 **The globalization of migration:** the refugee crisis in the European Union (EU) has challenged the very fabric of the EU and its traditional values. This trend has even challenged the raison d'être of the American constitution and melting-pot society, which once welcomed and was built by immigrants.

In the era of ubiquitous and real-time management, the notion of internal operations of the firm and how it communicates with the outside world has been the major frontier of academic research and practical thinking, and above all pivotal to managerial success in times of turbulence. Therefore, the essence of the book is to design a general navigator model (GNM) – the Six Forces Model (SFM) – for the global management and value chain design of HCs and MNCs and furthermore to put communication at the locus of innovation, over the next few decades, in globally operating firms.

The book uses the science of cybernetics to embark on a journey of aligning all fields within the notion of communication and the possibilities of the digital economy (artificial intelligence, etc), which innovative models of ubiquitous communication and organizational steering can provide. The aim is to deliver answers to the diverse questions that the management of HCs and MNCs have in times of global disruption and turbulence from a non-biased external point of view beyond the industrial 'illusio' in a 'Bourdieuian sense'. Simultaneously, these answers must provide a foundation for coping with the external challenges, global discontinuities and internal structural dynamics of firms' systems, based on contemporary technological advances, in times of ubiquitous computing and pandemics. In this particular time of global pandemic and 'black swans', the author (as a global consultant and academic scholar to HCs and MNCs) has had the privilege of applying these models successfully in diverse firms.

The structural shifts in diverse industries and diffusion of power are felt in all industries, not only from a pure growth perspective but also within the established models that made global operations possible. While from the applied Friedmanian lens since the late 1970s until today, notions of outsourcing and off-shoring have made the greatest sense to advance the bottom lines of firms, we must now add the dimension of changing the limitation of what business administration (BA) has put on firms based on specially coined terminologies. Hence, marketing calls its spectrum of dominance 'the market', strategic management has been occupied with the logic derived from the *weltanschauung* of 'the industry', and the natural scientific method borrowed for BA is still occupied with the notion of *reductionism* of actually dismantled systems, whereupon the 'quantification of dismantalism' has been extended to absurdity within the field to navigate organizations, which in reality are productive social systems that ought to be operating as viable and systemic wholes. The notion of *'reductio ad absurdum'* has not served BA well. This has enhanced its normative crisis coming from the very word *'administration'*, which actually is as much a *'core rigidity'* as the word 'soft' was to the Microsoft Corporation, which has been bypassed by Apple Inc. and Samsung, who had no challenges making hardware from their meta-structural configurations. Furthermore, the very term 'business administration' was coined in the post-First and Second World War US market, wherein the only major complexity was to manage growth via tools such as 'diversifications' within a large single market, a single currency, one major language and all united by the dominated ideologies of the Cold War era.

The book is about the management of complex systems beyond the shallowness of administration, better defined by the German word *'Verwaltung'* in terms of public and municipal management. Within this state of multidimensionality of challenges faced by the management of firms, the book seeks to find some adequate and solid strategies and to navigate possibilities within the turbulence of the challenges that lie ahead. The foundation of why all these challenges need to be dealt with, via the power and possibilities within the scientific discourse in this book, and why a framework of control is needed, is based on the author's understanding that management is a field of professional and applied sciences, wherein solid answers for practical and pragmatic solutions for solving the challenges managers are globally facing are created and designed for practitioners.

Gutiérrez and Penuel (2014)

> ...argue for a reconceptualization of rigor that requires sustained, direct, and systematic documentation of what takes place inside programs to

document how students and teachers change and adapt interventions in interactions with each other in relation to their dynamic local contexts.

They close by describing how this new criterion – 'relevance to practice' – can ensure the longevity and efficacy of educational research. Hence, it is within the new criteria that the discrepancy, especially within management research, may close as the major criteria for rigour within the field is indeed the dimension of relevance to a practical and contemporary challenge that firms' navigators face. As professional schools, business schools especially need to aspire to construct research rigour with practical relevance. While there have been concerns that business schools are increasingly uncoupled from practice and that business school research lacks real-world relevance, this failed assumption ought to be changed. The relevance–rigour gap affects the quality of teaching as well as the institutional legitimacy of business schools (Simon, 1969; O'Reilly and Tushman, 2011); therefore, solid practical problems are in severe need of being brought to management research so that adequate responses for practitioners can be designed to create a better functioning world. The book has been created within the framework of relevance to practice for today's knowledge workers and, therefore, it is essential to establish a historical account of strategy and cybernetics *avant la lettre*, and then to proceed to the dimension of precise literature reviews in science and in practice, and to design solid methodological frameworks for further research and practice that can actually carry the weight that is on the shoulders of globally operating managers.

References

Gutiérrez KD and Penuel WR (2014) Relevance to practice as a criterion for rigor, *Educational Researcher*, **43** (1), pp 19–23, doi: 10.3102/0013189X13520289

O'Reilly CA and Tushman ML (2011) Organizational ambidexterity in action: how managers explore and exploit, *California Management Review*, **53** (4), pp 5–22, doi: 10.1525/cmr.2011.53.4.5

Simon HA (1969) *The Sciences of the Artificial*, MIT Press, Cambridge, MA

ACKNOWLEDGEMENTS

I want to express my sincere appreciation to the team at Kogan Page, especially to Julia Swales, Head of Publishing, for her patience and constant support, Adam Cox, Development Editor, who was always able to find a solution to all the challenges with me, and to Philippa Fiszzon for her perceptiveness, which has given the book the highest quality.

I also want to thank Andres Ruiz, Saskia Topp and Maryam Sezavar Keshavarz, my three Masters students at ISM International School of Management from the University's International Management MSc Programme. They have made many valuable contributions to the quality and the editing, and in helping me meet the publication deadlines. I have learned through the practice of teaching as a serious learner that the best teachers are your own students. I also want to express my especial thanks to Sebastian Bahr for his support in reading and constant feedback during the production of the manuscript.

I want especially to thank my wonderful wife and my children, whose lives were quite complicated during the time I was finalizing the manuscript of the book. I promise to give them all a break at least until my next project.

I also thank my family members, friends and colleagues, whose encouragement made a huge difference during the time I was researching, writing and constantly talking to them about this book.

This book is dedicated to my wonderful Doktorvater Prof. Dr. habil. Klaus Kellner, in friendship and great admiration.

– 'Philosophy is the universal unity of science on a rising absolute foundation.' Martin Heidegger

... so is strategy...

Introduction

The nature of competition has been shifted from the pure economic boundaries of organizations, industrial structures and mere linear understanding of strategy as financial predictions, top–down calculations, linear planning and forecasting methods. Strategic thought for the contemporary era needs to embrace structural design of the firm and its web of networks, configurations and intelligence of the organizations' systems that ought to be structured in a way that displays viability and a holistic embeddedness within the complexity of the global markets. This book is designed for scholars of strategy and organizational design, especially for managers of global value chains that are looking for a robust model upon which a global value chain design and configuration from a strategic world-view can be constructed. A weak value chain based on linear models will endanger not only the resilience of organizational operations and the firm's agility, but, moreover, it will endanger the firm's survival. The diverse pressures of cost-leadership models, green operations and customer preference for sustainability, regulatory restrictions and boundaries, the rise of global competition with obscured business models and financial backup from Asia, and the much amplified technological disruption and acceleration require firms to apply new and robust models of science into their practice that can absorb the shocks and complex perturbations hitting firms and their value chains globally.

Readers are given a holistic model that will help them to integrate their web of diverse suppliers and stakeholder networks with much better precision and strategic foresight to configure and reconfigure a robust design of global operations from a global value chain perspective that goes beyond the notion established by Porter (1985) – the linear understanding of value chains being a set of activities that firms perform in terms of primary and secondary dimensions. Sustainable competitive advantage today is based on firms' ability to apply a solid model of global ambidexterity that embraces the notions of dynamic capabilities of the firm as a whole to address the changing global and dynamic business environment.

The book is written as a set of scholarly papers, which are designed as diverse interrelated articles, wherein the whole notion of the book's raison d'être is embedded. The book is intended to deliver much needed value for scholars and practitioners of strategic management and competitive strategy, organizational design and behaviour, logistics, supply chain management, as well as for navigators of global value chains to understand the notion of structural conditioning and design as a solid and robust strategy beyond the Chandlerian dimension of structure following some linear and predictable benchmarked strategies. Structure therefore does not follow strategy; it follows the dynamics of the interrelated and systemic complexities that can only be absorbed via such robust means as cybernetics and systems sciences by delivering a new reconfiguration of the pure economic lens of organizational realities. Economics world-view and performance is thus not denied, but only highlighted as a single regime within the diverse layers of firms' global structural fitness, which is observed as competition for viability once the constraints of economic KPIs are met. In order to achieve a more in-depth understanding of the notion of economics for the mode-based management (MBM) methodology, this book provides a solid treatment of the field of economics, which is provided in Chapter 5. This establishes a solid foundation for the strategic thinking beyond the economic constraints a firm navigating the turbulent waters of the global interconnected world needs to achieve.

By reading the book, organizational designers will observe the field of strategy from a holistic, cybernetics and system thinking perspective for all types of organizations under their control. Indeed, cybernetics is the science of effective organization, while management is the profession of effectively controlled organizations (Beer, 1972, 1985). The laws of the sciences of cybernetics are universally valid and relevant, and deal with the most difficult problems of this century, coined as 'the century of complexity' (Hawking, 2000). It is the first attempt ever to establish strategy on the basis of the sciences of cybernetics, 'the science of control and communication in the animal and the machine' (Ashby, 1956; Wiener, 1948). Cybernetics as the scientific vital pillar has been the base and forefather for numerous scientific pursuits and accomplishments. Two major advancements derived from cybernetics that are also presented in this book are bionics and complexity sciences, which could be used as means of strategic management.

The field of competitive strategy and its inception, which is a cornerstone of the mainstream practised strategy around the globe, was founded by Michael Porter with his legendary article, 'How competitive forces shape strategy' (Porter, 1979a). The model has received proclaimed fame and far-reaching dominance in the field of strategy and competitiveness. It is widely taught and practised in all MBA programmes, business studies and consulting projects around the globe, even 40 years after its publication. Although strategic management as a field is still young, scholars can reflect upon its essence and what models, theories, concepts, frameworks and methods have gathered to give a solid view of the field.

Indeed, 40 years is a long time in a field with no general agreement of universally accepted scientific base or proven laws. Hence, strategic management cannot be limited to the next fashionable book or short-term recipes, all promising sustainable competitive advantage; a word, which to the author's best knowledge and maybe the current reader's, has been an impossibility to achieve. If sustainability means seeing the real world with all its diverse problems based on a land-locked industry – in view of the Porter doctrine and considering the dimensions of every organizational problem within the boundaries of an economical lens – no wonder the word crisis has become a familiar term which seems to be normal. The author has often visited the European capital and its essential institutions. During these stays he has seen many scholars and practitioners, who have backgrounds in law or at best in economics. Not a single time was the author a subject of an acquaintance with a strategist professional or a person with a long-term experience of running a high-stakes organization exposed to the dynamics of complexity and turbulence. If the European Union (EU) itself sees the realities of the world merely from a legal perspective and at best from an economic dimension, then one does not need to wonder why they are failing and are desperately keeping ill-fared members alive on temporary emergency stabilization and rescue packages and umbrellas, while their doses of mercy are dependent on the sacrifices of their people. These types of crises also happened to Porter's co-founded consulting firm The Monitor Group LLC, which filed for US Chapter 11 bankruptcy on 7 November 2012.

As the author's publications reveal (Kamran, 2011a, 2011b, 2012a, 2012b, 2012c, 2013a, 2013b, 2014a, 2014b, 2014c, 2014d, 2014e, 2017a, 2017b, 2018a, 2018b, 2018c), this demise of the US management and strategy doctrine led by Porter was foreseen. The foreseen and predicted crises of the mainstream managerial and strategic doctrines led by the US Ivy League universities were based on fundamental cybernetic analysis and logic, which is the science of control. The Monitor Group's collapse was one of the last shaky pillars that was blown out of its roots, wherein many of the contemporary management strategy doctrines are embedded, thus this was the top consultancy firm co-founded by Michael Porter.

Porter's work (1979a), and later much revised and rewritten versions (Porter, 2008b), is still observed by the mainstream as an unfalsified work, and above all the whole spectrum of the Porter doctrine has been examined in this book and is the chief *terminus a quo* of the author's work. To the author's knowledge, this work embodies the most in-depth analysis of the Porter mindset.

This book looks into the field of strategic management from a multi-dimensional and holistic perspective and is a contribution to the field of strategy beyond the sash of reductionism. Indeed, strategy deals with the most vital problems of the contemporary era and needs a much wider and broader grasp of world-view than it has currently been given whereupon to see the world.

Another highly acclaimed strategy doctrine – the Chandlerian dictum and credo, 'structure follows strategy' (Chandler, 1962) – is thoroughly discussed and analysed. The author postulates that 'structure IS strategy', which fits more accurately to the current Zeitgeist of strategic thought. Indeed, it is the structure that unchains strategy from the repression of wishful thinking and the pure planning school. Strategy is a conglomerate of goal (an objective, a vital position to be acquired or a crisis to be outmanoeuvred), a solid plan of 'how to' (a road map) and action (execution and feedback), which embodies the alignment of the cognitive and the physical activity based on course-correcting feedback. Thus, the book reveals that organizational intelligence, eigen behaviour and eigen dynamic (culture and internal dynamics), in addition to the relation and interrelation of its parts, capabilities, cognitive and physical boundaries are sub-systems (units) which construct the whole structure of the firm once combined. Structure is strategy; thus, it captures the essence of the strategy.

The Soviet Union did not collapse because of US supremacy in strategic foresight; the collapse was due to the unproductive and dysfunctional structure of the whole Soviet empire. Even the US was surprised when it collapsed. Its $800 billion worth of military, industrial and intelligence complex could not even foresee the collapse. It was the same with the cases of the Shah of Iran (Jervis, 2012), the collapse of capitalism's cauldron Wall Street in 2008, and the collapse of the Middle East's most suppressive regimes holding their dictatorial sash over their people for over 40 years, which happened in

2011–2012, as well as the war in Syria, which is still ongoing. It was the crash of their systemic structures from within.

Structure does not follow strategy; it follows its own laws and its interrelated complex chains of systemic dynamics. The strategist's vocation is based on 'jujitsuing' these dynamics to the organization's favour and juggling between diverse views and tools of science and practice to bestow the organization with the first objective of strategy, which the author has coined after Mintzberg's notion and contextualization of the 'Ten Schools of Strategy' (Mintzberg *et al*, 1998) as the 'Eleventh School of Strategy' (Kamran, 2011a, 2011b, 2012a). I have coined this school 'The Immunity School of Strategy'. Thus, the immunity school deals with problems of survival, and survival is the main, fundamental and the first foundational objective of strategy.

Strategy's main dimension of thought and its overall doctrine must embed and aim at survival as its main priority, thus organizational survival is the ethos of strategy – profits always come second. The foreseen and predicted crises of the mainstream managerial and strategic doctrines led by the US Ivy League universities were based on fundamental cybernetic analysis and logic, which is the science of steering or control. There is no escape for the strategist from answering the most vital question for what strategy longs for, namely the question of how to control a complex, social productive system in an era of turbulence and complexity. Speaking of sustainability, what about finding it in the holism of the question above? Via this work, the strategist knows, according to Stafford Beer, that there is cybernetics:

> the science of effective organization [after Beer],... the science of communication and control in the animal and the machine [Wiener, 1948],... the science of understanding [Maturana],... a science concerned with the study of systems of any nature which are capable of receiving, storing, and processing information so as to use it for control [after Kolmogorov],... cybernetique = the art of growing [after Ampere],... [and] the ability to cure all temporary truth of eternal triteness [after Brun] (ASC, 2019).

Powered by the laws of cybernetics the strategist is able to act and explore, thus the strategist is the helmsman at the steering wheel of the organization and its future direction... how much freedom this is and how much is at stake!

This book also provides – based on the aforementioned MBM methodology – a foundation upon which managers and scholars can take an interdisciplinary approach by bridging diverse fields of science and practice and furthermore to cybernetically connect the fields of strategic management and supply chain management (SCM) towards delivering a solid foundational ground upon which the field of value chain management (VCM) can be founded within a fresher and more timely outlook. While the dimension of technicity is overwhelming for firms competing in a global and interconnected world to absorb, understanding the role of the firm's structure within the dimensions of the resource-based view (RBV) of the firm and the notions of dynamic capability, and ambidexterity, which establish a transcendental leverage for the firm's overall competitive position, is more essential than ever. Systems and cybernetics sciences thus deliver a robust scientific clarity, whereupon a new path for observing VCM within the field of holistic management could be pursued. Furthermore, designing structural dynamics of high variety generation and foresight are powerful strategic advantages that firms ought to be competing for within the century of complexity.

This book provides a path for a much richer managerial capacity, but above all to embrace the notion of control in terms of steering the firm within a design for an end-to-end value chain across cultures, national borders, industrial boundaries and scientific limitations and focal points of diverse fields. This book is at the hand of the reader for closing the gap between science and practice and thus acting on a new mantra of understanding relevance to practise as a solid criteria for rigour.

Structure of the book

Maintaining viability is the essence of this work. Additionally, a scientific/theoretical and practical attempt should be made to base and embed the author's findings and research results within the framework of Porter's five forces model (FFM), while maintaining the ability of the sixth force model developed in this book to be applied as a stand-alone model. Therefore, Beer's 'viable system model' (VSM) (Beer, 1972, 1979b, 1981, 1984, 1985) is a prerequisite of this work's logic to enhance Porter's FFM (Porter, 1980, 1998, 2008a).

In Chapter 1, the theoretical concepts, their practical relevance and a general, holistic and thorough treatment of Porter's FFM is undertaken. To the author's knowledge, this treatment of the FFM embodies one of the most in-depth analyses of the model from diverse perspectives. In addition, the reader is well advised to see the chapter as a solid and profound general introduction into the Porter strategic mindset and Porter's large volume of substantial work in the strategy of competitiveness. This chapter will enable a solid understanding of Porterian logic.

Chapter 2 introduces the reader to the science of complexity, cybernetics, chaos theory and system sciences. This chapter is also a general introduction and an establishment of the notion and essentiality of seeing and observing strategy from a system sciences point of view. The chapter, furthermore, establishes an observation of natural organisms from a bionics perspective whereby it establishes a fundament for a future research field in accordance with the Popperian logic of scientific work, which encourages intellectual audacity, and not intellectual cowardice.

According to Sowell (2009):

> An intellectual's work begins and ends with ideas... Animal life also varies with environmental differences and, while animals like humans (and unlike vegetation) have thought and volition, that thought and volition are not always the decisive factors in the outcomes. In short, between individual volition and general outcomes are systemic factors which limit or determine what will survive, creating a pattern, rather than chaos.

Ansoff *et al* (1976) account for the wider flux and transition of the strategic problem in the 20th century – which they define as the 'holistic positioning' of a system in its environment with respect to all links and relations and under the integration of formation and development of the internal capabilities of the firm – to ubiquitously adapt to new realities and conditions (Malik, 1984, 1993, 1994, 1996, 1997, 2000, 2007, 2008). The strategic conceptual framework of the book constructs and synthesizes on the foundation as Ansoff and Hayes describe and furthermore on the works of Beer, Ashby, Malik, von Foerster, Ulrich, Simon and Mintzberg. Thus, organization as an organism must cope with all the applicable forces and situational challenges which create complexities for the organization that it has to cope with. Complexity can be attenuated via:

1. a systemic structure (order); and
2. problem-solving (steering, navigating) capacity of the organization.

In Chapter 3, the work concentrates on analysing, finding and extending established and assessed strategic models for the purpose of finding and constructing an accurate and appropriate model, whereof the essential attributes can be applied and used for constructing a holistic model, dealing with the multiple challenges by the power of Kamran's sixth forces model.

The book coins **complexity** as the vital sixth force, which is among the most vital problems strategists have in this era. Furthermore, these models are used to construct the final management model and management cockpit, whereby the strategist is actually able to encounter and attenuate environmental perturbations and mobilize internal sub-systems by delivering a complex response according to Ashby's Law. Thus, only variety – which is the number and sets of a system's behaviour and the sum of the state of its parts – can attenuate complexity.

Chapter 4 also substantiates the claim on the meaning of strategy for the future of strategic work in enterprise ventures, thus the chapter establishes and delivers substantial evidence on how to define a new strategy, especially for this much needed and deluded term in business. Hence, the notion of strategy is separated from its militaristic past and bridges managerial, strategic and systems-biologic sciences to establish strategy theory and its application for the era of complexity. Complexity has already knocked on the door of strategists, who still analyse the world via linear tools that can only measure the tail of what Mintzberg so beautifully calls the 'strategy beast'.

Chapter 5 gives a solid introduction to the developments and history of logistics, supply chain management and global value chains (GVCs), thus establishing a foundation for designing GVLs based on the author's six forces model (SFM), wherein each layer constructs a vital aspect of a robust GVC. In addition, the chapter explores a case on how the model was applied to reinvigorate a firm in the turbulent environment of the Iranian market.

Furthermore, a practical application of the economic layer of the FFM and the authors' designed fourth generic strategy extending the Porterian generic strategies dimension of the firm and clarified on solid examples, have been demonstrated within the Appendix part of the book.

This book is a foundation for strategic thought in terms of constructing business models and GVCs for firms operating in complex and turbulent environments. While the model is a new and original construction based on Ashby's Law of requisite variety, whereby only organizations can cope with the amplifying external perturbations, where this complexity has been reflected and mirrored form an inner self-cultivation of organizational habitus and eigen behaviour establishing the status of homeostasis and autopoiesis.

Management and strategy as tools of organizational functionality

The world of tomorrow will be dominated by different types of problems and challenges. Understanding and coping with them is vital for the strategist.

However, the main tools of the strategists' handcraft have not only been looked into very narrowly in terms of the questions, objectives and problems, which have been addressed, but moreover they have lost their actuality in these complex and turbulent times. By observing the condition of the current organizational realities and the state of world affairs thoroughly, one can clearly see that the pillars on which the strategist has stood so proudly are not sufficient to carry the weight that rests on the strategist's shoulders today. The book's main emphasis is on the narrow, compartmentalized notion of academia and the reductionism approach of scientific pursuits, which at best can deliver temporary pain-relieving prescriptions without curing the causes of the disease. A mere finance-mathematical view of the field of strategy, or seeing real strategic problems just from an economic perspective and the main scientific approach of *'reductio ad absurdum'* on conducting research and analysis on such complex matters as managing a country, a multinational corporation (MNC), a hospital, a university, an NGO or other complex organizational phenomena such as an economy by simplistic tools and mindsets is, although to some extent a narrow and partially correct view, but it is just a single view, and it needs an overhaul.

Judt (2011) captures the zeitgeist of the contemporary era in the following manner:

> For thirty years my students have been complaining to me that 'it was easy for you': your generation had ideals and ideas, you believed in something, you were able to change things. 'We' (the children of the 80s, 90s, 00s) have nothing. In many respects my students are right.

Judt's observations highlight that in these times of manufactured consent, the world-view of young students is shaped by indoctrinated questions such as 'Is it sufficient?', 'How do we exploit resources for business opportunity?', 'How do we cut jobs based on a case study trained logic?', while questions such as 'Is it just?', 'Is it right?', 'Is it fair?' and 'Will it contribute to a better world?' are hardly asked. According to Judt, the first set of questions are those to be taught over and asked once more. As a matter of fact, the training that the strategist has enjoyed so far, which has been mainly fashioned by the US-dominated business schools and their myopic doctrines of the delusion of endless growth, over-privatization and additionally the military-dominated inheritance of the field of strategy, from which strategy has been retrieved, has only been able to make the monetarist strategist navigate their organization in the era, where calculability, continuity and simplicity are the domains and major foundational spectrums and strategists can show their talents. But if a systemic crisis, an unforeseen event, a complex problem or a butterfly effect occurs, the best managerial and strategic doctrines fall apart and the best remedy out of the misery is coined the bailout of capitalism by a socialist public funding method.

However, the one-sided view has its advocates and the supply chain of top talent is highly successful. According to NPR (2012): 'At some Ivy League schools last year, up to half of the graduates went into finance or consulting, a move that could have a profound effect on the economy in the years to come.' The top brainpower of the US has been drained out to the finance industry and analyst vocations, thus they are drawn solely to commit themselves to the finance industry to design more 'complex financial models' that actually have not worked – this explains the crises and the mess the world is actually in. Stephen Haber, in his introduction essay, observes: 'Since the Asian economic collapse of 1997 scholars and policymakers have grown increasingly interested in the phenomenon of crony capitalism. Indeed, much of the surprisingly rapid meltdown of the East Asian economies is often attributed to widespread cronyism' (Haber, 2002: xi). According to White (2004: 389): 'Crony capitalists were "private-sector businessmen who benefited enormously from close relations" with leading officials and politicians, obtaining "not only protection from foreign competition, but also concessions, licenses, monopoly rights, and government subsidies".' According to President Obama:

> And by the way, if we don't have an economy that's built on bubbles and financial speculation, our best and brightest won't all gravitate towards careers in banking and finance. Because if we want an economy that's built to last, we need more of those young people in science and engineering. This country should not be known for bad debt and phony profits. We should be known for creating and selling products all around the world that are stamped with three proud words: Made in America (*The Guardian*, 2011).

The 'West' with its incredible richness has been overwhelmed daily by more news of crises of states and countries' bankruptcies. The rating agencies are issuing their guilty verdicts of rating thumbs down on the ones who fall short of the grace according to ancient Rome's oath of '*Sacramentum Gladiatorium*' (Barton, 1995), regardless of the consequences for a land, its people and country's long-term perspectives. In this advanced state of 'strategy crises', no wonder strategists' performance, the resulting chaos and crises the world faces on a daily basis, its breadth, length, depth and spectrum, make the strategist look like a third-rate showmaster performing some acrobatics on a unicycle. The author objects to the mainstream understanding or observation of the 'capitalism crises of 2008' being downplayed as mere financial crises. Some scholars such as Malik have observed the crisis as a management crisis and subsequently also as a 'systems crisis', which more accurately embraces the nature of the crisis. The author wants to establish an additional notion to Malik's observation; hence the crisis resembles a vital strategic failure of governance, control and the 'total collapse of the American management doctrines', which ought to be coined as the 'advanced systems and strategic crisis'.

It is high time that strategists' education, understanding, vocation in general, perception of reality, handicraft, doctrines and tools are examined, since strategists must be regarded as the most effective safeguards of tomorrow (Drucker, 1954). The main question a strategist needs to ask today is how the complex organization under their control can achieve the capability to design its freedom. According to Beer (1973):

> I am a scientist, but to be a technocrat would put me out of business as a man. Yet I was eighteen months ago, intent on creating a scientific way of governing. And here today, proud of the tools we have made. Why? Because I believe that cybernetics can do the job better than bureaucracy – and more humanely too. We must learn how to expunge technocracy, without rejecting science – because the proper use of science is really the world's brightest hope for stable government. Some people in Chile share that view; and they reject technocracy as strongly as do I. All of us have already been misrepresented in that respect, just as the scientific work we have done has already been misrepresented as analogous to other management control systems that have failed. Both comments miss out the cybernetics (Beer, 1973: 3).

In essence, the job of the strategist is to design a favourable future for their organization. This shift in thinking requires the strategist to look beyond the notion of strategy observed and deluded by the common junk on management and strategy filling the shelves of management and strategy bookstores, which are promising more short-term profits and easier to absorb models for so-called strategists, who are actually themselves misguidedly trained to only function in the 'vanished world' (Beer, 1975), which was dominated by simplicity. A big flaw is especially to solely rely on the analysis of data describing reality based on a rearview mirror (Hetzler, 2008). For strategists, however, the world of today and precisely tomorrow carries different types of problems beyond the measures of financial wizardry, engineering and portfolio-balancing alchemy. These problems and the resulted chaos cannot be solved and controlled by the traditionally dominated schools of strategic thought. The author claims that the problems with which strategists will be confronted in the near future may not even be solvable via the general strategic, managerial and scientific lens developed to observe problems, understand them and cope with them.

The need for a transformation from the reductionist to the holistic world is sensed everywhere. This change creates crises and opportunities that have the potential to carry people to the new world, which has already been created for the strategist to enter and navigate their organization. The real problems that strategists need to observe and cope with are the problems of survival, control and function. These problems require a different lens and the integration of various sciences into the world of strategic management by the mainstream academia in business administration (BA). These sciences are holistic and deal with problems of causes, connectivity and relations, function, structure and behaviour and, above all, they deliver answers to the ultimate question in strategy, which is how to remain immune and to control a complex and adaptive organization in the century of complexity (Hawking, 2000), the era of transformations and big turbulences (Malik, 1993), explosive change (Beer, 1966, 1975, 1979a, 1988, 1994) and far-reaching system and control crises (Malik, 2011).

Although the strategist has always dealt with making decisions in uncertainty, the times of stability had more structure and some predictions could be made. Today's fast-paced world denies the strategist of this privilege, by not only making their job more vital to the organization's security but also, more importantly, to the well-being of general society. According to Porter and Kramer (2011):

> Companies must take the lead in bringing business and society back together. The recognition is there among sophisticated business and thought leaders, and promising elements of a new model are emerging. Yet we still lack an overall framework for guiding these efforts, and most companies remain stuck in a 'social responsibility' mind-set in which societal issues are at the periphery, not the core.

Businesses as the true creators of wealth must become a craft for societal and environmental well-being and not a part of the problem, as they have become over the last three decades. This puts the strategist in a unique and interesting position. This book is specifically written for the audience who is interested in strategy and ready for a theoretical and practical journey with the author to solve their many organizational problems by applying a holistic view of science and, above all, to dissolve emerging problems, hence their success and survival will surely depend upon them.

'Everything said is said by an observer.'

(FOERSTER, 2003)

The contemporary undertaking of strategic thought

The best place to begin applying science to the practical problems of strategists and practitioners is Heinz von Foerster's First Theorem, which Stafford Beer coined as 'Heinz Von Foerster's Theorem Number One' (Foerster, 2003). The theorem states: 'The more profound the problem that is ignored, the greater are the chances for fame and success' (Foerster, 2003). As a corollary to von Foerster's Theorem Number One is 'Heinz von Foerster's Theorem Number Two', which describes a vital scientific and strategic dilemma: 'The hard sciences are successful because they deal with the soft problems; the soft sciences are struggling because they deal with the hard problems' (Foerster, 2003). It is the success of reductionist thinking and its scientific application that von Foerster is pointing to. Thus, the world finds itself more and more modelled to live in the so-called 'Schrödinger's cat paradox.'

According to Foerster (2003):

> It is known that 'Quantum Mechanics',... could be regarded more as a 'mathematical theory' rather than a physical theory. It is wave mechanics allowing a corpuscular duality... the Schrödinger's cat paradox is defined as a state where the cat can be dead, or can be alive, or it is undecided (i.e. we don't know if it is dead or alive), then herein the Neutrosophic Logic, based on three components, truth component, falsehood component, indeterminacy component, works very well. In Schrödinger's cat problem the Neutrosophic Logic offers the possibility of considering the cat neither dead nor alive, but undecided, while the fuzzy logic does not do this. Normally indeterminacy is split into uncertainty and paradox (conflicting).

However, what von Foerster is underpinning here is the notion that systems and complexity sciences deliver holistic lens and control tools. In comparison, reductionism is not capable of understanding, describing or modelling systems and their dynamics, thus, it fails to describe complex phenomena and organisms in biology and cannot steer complex social systems in turbulence or model their behaviour. Von Foerster substantiates his claim by stating:

> This will become obvious when we contemplate for a moment the method of inquiry employed by the hard sciences. If a system is too complex to be understood it is broken up into smaller pieces. If they, in turn, are still too complex, they are broken up into even smaller pieces, and so on, until the pieces are so small that at least one piece can be understood. The delightful feature of this process, the method of reduction, 'reductionism', is that it inevitably leads to success (Foerster, 2003).

Table 0.1 establishes the essential differences between the holistic and systemic lens and the reductionist view.

Therefore, the author is concentrating on the strategic problem of stability and survival in social systems. Stability and survival are strategy's first priority. Stability should not be lowered to the level of mere analytical quantifications done by analysts trained in a very reductionist method and occupied with a reductionist mindset. It lies within the laws of nature and environment. It depends on the state of organizational internal functions and their capability of coping with the ever-growing environmental complexity (Beer, 1975–1994; Pagels, 1988; Malik, 2011; Kamran, 2011a, 2012a) and systemic dynamics. To survive in a world dominated by complexity is the 'meta strategic objective' (MSO), thus the strategist must achieve and maintain control over the organization's immunity. MSOs embrace the normative objectives of strategic

TABLE 0.1 A comparison between the reductionist and systems approach

Reductionist Approach	Systems Approach
Focus on parts	Focus on wholes
Linear causality A causes B	Circular causality A causes B causes C causes D
Observer status objective	Observer status subjective
Context not very relevant	Context highly relevant
One truth, lens of best answer	Multiple truths and best answer
Externalities not important	Externalities very important
Problems solved	Problems dissolved

Based on Leonard and Harnden (1994)

thinking and are a term that the author introduces to be integrated to the sciences of strategy. They are identity-transforming and identity-preserving goals, which are vital to survival.

According to Ross W. Ashby in his ground-breaking book *Introduction to Cybernetics* (Ashby, 1956):

> The word 'stability' is apt to occur frequently in discussions of machines, but is not always used with precision. Bellman refers to it as '... stability, that much overburdened word with an unsterilized definition'. Since the ideas behind the word are of great practical importance, we shall examine the subject with some care, distinguishing the various types that occur. Today's terminology is unsatisfactory and confused; I shall not attempt to establish a better.

The author's definition of stability in strategy and controlling a complex system for the purpose of this book is:

> the state of equilibrium, where the balance between the system's internal recursive control within the sub-systems and the system as a whole is maintained and thus to balance the internal varieties with the environment's perturbations in a biological organism, a social organization, a firm or enterprise and an economy as a whole is preserved.

Thus, stability of homeostasis is the complexity which cannot be attenuated via a partial view of the whole as the mere economic or additional lenses.

Science is in crisis, for being itself about separation, thus this very scientific thinking actually dismantles a functioning system constituted of a set of complex parts and their sub-systems to understand it. According to Kauffman (2008):

> The Galilean spell that has driven so much science is the faith that all aspects of natural word can be described by such laws... Perhaps the most radical scientific claim I shall make is that we can and must break the Galilean spell. Indeed, this is the heart of reductionism.

Since the times of Descartes, Galileo, Newton and the additional founders of the methodology of science, the pivotal objective has been to understand the world via reductionism (cf. Mitchell, 2009). It is precisely here that the question must be raised on how to understand and manage, but above all how to control, such a complex phenomenon as a social organization, firm, culture, language, religion, human-conscious, man, machine and animal's behaviour and their inter-connectedness in the ever complex-growing environment. According to Beer (1973):

> I am trying to display the problem that we face in thinking about institutions. The culture does not accept that it is possible to make general scientific statements about them. Therefore, it is extremely difficult for individuals, however well intentioned, to admit that there are laws (let's call them) that govern institutional behaviour, regardless of the institution. People know that there is a science of physics; you will not be burnt at the stake for saying that the earth moves round the sun, or even be disbarred by physicists for proposing a theory in which it is mathematically convenient to display the earth as the centre of the universe after all. That is because people in general, and physicists in particular, can handle such propositions with ease. But people do not know that there is a science of effective organization, and you are likely to be disbarred by those who run institutions for proposing any theory at all. For what these people say is that their own institution is unique; and that therefore an apple-growing company bears no resemblance to a company manufacturing water glasses or to an airline flying aeroplanes. The consequences are bizarre. Our institutions are failing because they are disobeying laws of effective organization which their administrators do not know about, to which indeed their cultural mind is closed, because they contend that there exists and can exist no science competent to discover those laws. Therefore, they remain satisfied with a bunch of organizational precepts which are equivalent to the precept in physics that base metal can be transmuted into gold by incantation – and with much the same effect.

As already stated above, the success of the Newtonian universe has blessed the world with its current development and the rise of Western dominance over the world, but then one wonders how such powerful nations and economies are doomed to be internally collapsing and their debt ceilings reaching astronomical numbers that can never be repaid. Thus, strategists occupied by some sort of a hard-science mindset are, as the word 'strategy' itself resembles its militaristic-historic past, mere militant quantificationists. The evolution of BA concentrates on reducing costs and enhances BA's biblical doctrine of 'the shareholder value', which uncomfortably rests on the shoulders of reductionism and is responsible for some of the severest crises and value destructions of the contemporary era.

Now is the need to revisit von Foerster again and observe his 'Theorem Number Two', wherein he brings it to the point by stating:

> Unfortunately, the soft sciences are not blessed with such favorable conditions. Consider, for instance, the sociologist, psychologist, anthropologist, linguist, etc., if they would reduce the complexity of the system of their interest, i.e., society, psyche, culture, language, etc., by breaking it up into smaller parts for further inspection they would soon no longer be able to claim that they are dealing with the original system of their choice. This is so, because these scientists are dealing with essentially nonlinear systems whose salient features are represented by the interactions between whatever one may call their 'parts' – whose properties in isolation add little, if anything, to the understanding of the workings of these systems when each is taken as a whole. Consequently, if he wishes to remain in the field of his choice, the scientist who works in the soft sciences is faced with a formidable problem: he cannot afford to lose sight of the full complexity of his system, on the other hand it becomes more and more urgent that his problems be solved (Foerster, 2003).

Occupied with von Foerster's wisdom on understanding organizational failures, the strategist needs to turn to an organization and system, having a history of management and strategic thinking that has been out-competed and out-smarted by all the forces combined, namely by nature itself. Ashby (1958) states:

> Let us start at the beginning. The most basic facts in biology are that this earth is now two thousand million years old, and that the biologist studies mostly that which exists today. From these two facts follow a well-known deduction, which I would like to restate in our terms. ... if a dynamic system is large and composed of parts with much repetition, and if it contains any property that is autocatalytic, i.e. whose occurrence at one point increases the probability that it will occur again at another point, then such a system is, so far as that property is concerned, essentially unstable in its absence. This earth contained carbon and other necessary elements, and it is a fact that many combinations of carbon, nitrogen, and a few others are self-reproducing. It follows that though the state of 'being lifeless' is almost a state of equilibrium, yet this equilibrium is unstable, a single deviation from it being sufficient to start a trajectory that deviates more and more from the 'lifeless' state. What we see today in the biological world are these 'autocatalytic' processes showing all the peculiarities that have been imposed on them by two thousand million years of elimination of those forms that cannot survive. The organisms we see today are deeply marked by the selective action of two thousand million years' attrition. Any form in any way defective in its power of survival has been eliminated; and today the features of almost every form bear the marks of being adapted to ensure survival rather

than any other possible outcome. Eyes, roots, cilia, shells and claws are so fashioned as to maximize the chance of survival. And when we study the brain we are again studying a means to survival.

Indeed, the history of nature's balance sheet tells a success story of more than 2 billion years of sustainability, continuity and managerial mastery. Challenges of energy, noise, waste, wars and conflicts, efficiency, social and ecological responsibility, and mass unemployment are themes of a longer past that nature has already solved with perfection. Human beings still need to learn much from the nature; for example, a firefly can produce light with 95 per cent efficiency, while the best light bulbs waste three-fourths of the energy produced as unnecessary thermal energy. This, admittedly slightly exaggerated, example and comparison should reveal that people have a long way to go to absolute productivity and efficiency – and it is not well constituted with the way people are managing resources and, moreover, how we have structured and constructed our social systems, organizations and economic-political doctrines.

The shaky pillars on which the strategist stands today must be revised and rebuilt. The holistic view and tools of scientific application must be re-doctrinated and rewritten to embrace problems in their entirety, since strategists must understand that real problems do not respect the departmentalization of science and cannot be solved via a narrow view and with the boundary of myopia. One lives in a systemic world with a vast proportion of complexity. There is no alternative of ever coming back to simplicity. All matters that management strategy hold so dear, such as production, logistics, distribution, finance, HR, procurement, accounting and R&D – also as described by Beer (1985) as managing men, materials, machinery and money – are systems embedded in their systemic governed industry clusters. These social systems, clusters, joint ventures, interconnected organizations and alliances are systems and sub-systems that require a holistic approach to map and understand them and their dynamics and behaviours, but above all to develop the ability to control and navigate them in turbulent waters.

To model and observe living systems and organisms in order to learn from them for strategic management is a complicated subject matter. It is difficult to think, to learn and to talk about. So why does the strategist need this complex subject matter instead of just going to the simple stuff? The answer lies in 'Ashby's Law of requisite variety', which is the basis for the inception of the science of managerial cybernetics. It states: 'only variety can absorb variety' (Beer, 1985). Ashby's Law is fundamental to management and gives the strategist the ultimate answer to the problems of how to control and absorb complexity. In terms of managerial cybernetics, it means that complex problems require a complex response and an organizational structure that is capable of carrying out that response to destroy the complexity brought on the organization through measures and engineering of the amplified variety.

It is therefore high time that a different approach to strategic management and organizational studies is introduced and insights from additional sciences are integrated, which are embedded under the umbrella of cybernetics and complexity and are made practicable for the most vital vocation and profession of society: strategizing. The duty of a strategist is to cope with society's pivotal problems, namely absorbing the ever-increasing complexity, to assure the survival and longevity of the organization and to design its immunity.

This book will investigate and examine the field of strategy via four dimensions:

1 from the Porterian point of view, which is the starting point in competitive strategy (Porter, 1977, 1979a, 1979b, 1980, 1981, 1985, 1986, 1987, 1993, 1996, 1998, 2007, 2008a, 2008b);
2 from a cybernetic, complexity, bionic and systems sciences point of view, which are interdisciplinary sciences concerning understanding and controlling complex and interrelated systems and organizations;
3 from a scientific and practical perspective by examining the 'top strategy models' (TSM) of the current management and strategy field by making their essence applicable in this book;
4 from a design thinking perspective by exploring its philosophical foundations and extending the field's implications for strategic management by incorporating the notion of meaning and 'dasein' thinking.

The main objectives of the book are outlined below:

1 Dissolving organizational and environmental complexity lies at the heart of strategic management. The interconnected, globalized and turbulent world of today requires the strategist to have at their disposal more favourable and useful models, new patterns of thought, better and real-time-based information, strong forecasting capability, decision environments, and high sensory connection to the environment, its 'eigen' systems and sub-systems.

2 Business models are ways of communication and they are designed and developed to resolve business problems and challenges. Some contemporary models in business are useful, but some apply only to certain narrow challenges or situations in the past, and some need to be developed further to cope with the challenges of the 21st century.

3 Strategic success means having a holistic applicable model which can handle the challenges strategists face via proactive capability.

4 According to Ashby's Law, complex problems require complex responses. Deep environmental complexity requires complex models, organizational structures and adequate strategists' handicraft for it to be controlled and absorbed. Contemporary organizational structures resemble a family tree-based model that only shows which unit or person is to blame. An organizational structure must describe and model viability. Thus, according to Beer (1979a), 'the purpose of a system is what it does'. Conant and Ashby (1970), in their theorem, observe: 'Every good regulator of a system must be a model of that system.' The current organizational models applied to organizations work to the contrary. They embody the chain of blame, instead of being models that actually work. Conant and Ashby (1970) conclude:

> The developing knowledge of regulation, information processing, and control is building similar criteria for the brain. Now that we know that any regulator (if it conforms to the qualifications given) must model what it regulates, we can proceed to measure how efficiently the brain carries out this process. There can no longer be question about whether the brain models its environment: it must.

5 Porter's five forces model (FFM) is solely a positioning school based on a strategic view of a specific organization in a specific industry. Therefore, it is narrow and limited. Although the model as already stated is right and generally observed as unfalsified, it still fails to cover a vital strategic matter which this book sets forth – that organizational reality requires a holistic view beyond the industry boundaries in which the organization is embedded. The greatest disruption comes into being via forces and phenomena outside of the industry. In the globalized world of today, forces that actually threaten an organization do not only lie within the borders of an industry; it can be the very strategy the organization applies to communicate with its environment and its rivals that could develop into a force that causes a collapse (for example The Monitor, Enron,

WorldCom, Lehman Brothers, Merrill Lynch, Bear Stearns, Freddie Mac, Fannie Mae). Thus, the strategic complexity a strategist faces is to find what truly threatens the organization's competitive advantage and, above all, its survival.

6 The best resource of an organization in the ever-globalizing and interconnected world of today is information and well-trained and able 'human capital' (HC). HC are self-organizing and complex adaptive agents organized to work in unison for the larger organizational goal. According to Heinz von Foerster's revolutionary statements, 'Everybody is a manager' (Beyes, 2005); the law that governs from an evolutionary perspective in nature is 'self-organization'. It is the most powerful method and law of people management as well. There are no CEOs and controllers in nature, but the functioning of nature as a complex system is one of the best management and strategic schools one can observe. Making this law applicable for organizational management will give organizations a vital competitive advantage. The vital resource that is needed in the contemporary era is a unique set of capabilities and value chain activities by trained and informed people.

7 'Structure follows strategy', Chandler's (1962) doctrine, has been the contemporary strategic insight and the scientific-practical understanding of the structure vs. strategy debate. The book puts the thesis to the test of theory; it is high time to revise Chandler's observation and thesis (Hall and Saias, 1980; Kamran, 2011a, 2011b, 2012a; Miles *et al*, 1974; Weick, 1969). The book suggests a newer and fresher view and challenges Chandler's approach, since the author believes that Chandler's observations are incomplete. The author suggests the thesis: 'Structure is strategy' (Kamran, 2011a, 2012a). That means, without the proper and viable structure, strategists will not be able to execute and apply the best strategies for the goals to be achieved. Strategy formation, application and control are a dynamic and ever-changing organizational capability and intelligence, therefore they require a viable systems structure based on real-time information management capability, to ensure that the organization under control can operate and adapt to situations not yet known or unknowable at the time of launching the strategy.

8 An additional debate between structure and the resource-based view (RBV) shows strategists that organizational structure cannot be left to a narrow and mere financial view of costs and resources. Viability, in terms of financial or resource viability, limits all organizational problems to an economic dimension. The strategist of tomorrow should see the organizational challenges beyond the above-mentioned notion and should proactively make their organization immune, adaptive and viable against environmental disruptions and financial constraints (Beer, 1985). The strategist's question in the new world of complexity is: '*Can the organization actually survive — assuming that the financial constraints are met?*' (Beer, 1985). Knowledge is more essential than time and energy, information more essential than money, and the purposive ability of self-organization more essential than power.

9 In the scientific discourse in this book, the author follows the 'Popperian doctrine' towards research and knowledge enhancement. Popper's doctrine requires scientists to show intellectual bravery, boldness and audacity. Intellectual cowards cannot survive the contemporary era. Popper challenges the method of induction, which is based on observations and theory formed by generalization. In the development of his theory, the author maintains this spirit, stated by Popper in his book on the philosophy of science (Popper, 2002). The author therefore suggests that strategists need to test new methods and be a proponent of an interdisciplinary scientific approach. Current problems have a holistic nature; thus, they require holistic problem-solving methods. Scientists should enable strategists to have more than Maslow's hammer at their disposal, since all problems are not 'nails', just like 'liquidity and shareholder value' is not the only measure of organizational fitness and viability. Complexity science and cybernetic-based views are more appropriate ways to look at problems and matters. The Newtonian lens leads one to reduce all matters to *ad absurdum*, and while it deals with such concepts as position, velocity, motion, dynamics and philosophy, it has led humans to a clockwork world-view. In contrast, the sciences of complexity and cybernetics deliver a foundation for analysing and profiting by ubiquitous information, control, communication, and the relations and interrelations among the environment and the systems and sub-systems. Additionally, organizations built out of diverse parts and sub-structures are more than the sum of their parts. They tend to develop eigen behaviours, eigen dynamics, eigen functions and eigen values (cf. Foerster, 2003). The sole jettisoning of data and its analysis is not an adequate method to ensure organizational survival and immunity to collapses, which is the first purpose and foundational pillar of strategy.

Practical applicability

Purely from a practical perspective of strategic management, this work will contribute to the deeper understanding and coping with the force of complexity, apart from that for enhancing strategists' ability to identify, proactively control, effectively absorb and cope with strategic challenges. In addition, by the demonstration of the book's practical relevance for the strategist, it intends to transfer and translate the demands and insights gained by the theoretical view and perspective into practice.

Concretely, from the practical view, the following objectives must be achieved:

1. The sixth force should be made applicable into the framework of Porter's FFM and additionally as a standalone strategy model. The sixth force must be understandable and applicable for the practising manager and strategist. However, it is not the prior knowledge of the manager that is essential here and that can be trained, but it is moreover the actual mindset regarding applying science, based on the notion of rigour that includes the major criterion of relevance to practice into the managerial work in general that matters the most. It is the author's aim to bring this notion to the awareness of practitioners, wherein via the application of science into the domain, practical problems can be thoroughly addressed and that scientific application is not a luxury but a necessity if survival and longevity are the primary yardsticks against which the strategist sees the fitness of their organization.
2. Insights from diverse scientific fields must be integrated based on a practical approach for effectively absorbing and recommending a final model of complexity as the sixth force and how to cope with it.
3. Applicable suggestions, models and recommendations for managing and coping with complexity must be forwarded.
4. The integration and application of information and communication technology and brain-like environments such as the strategy cockpit (SC) must be demonstrated and made useful for a practical application and real-time control.
5. Cybernetics is the science of effective organization, of which management is the vocation, according to Beer; subsequently, the author describes strategy as the immune system of effective organization. This pursuit of organizational immunity must be turned into practicable and applicable tools. Strategy is the immunity-regulator of the organization. An illustration of this pursuit is described in Figure 0.1.

FIGURE 0.1 Onwarding crises threaten organization survival

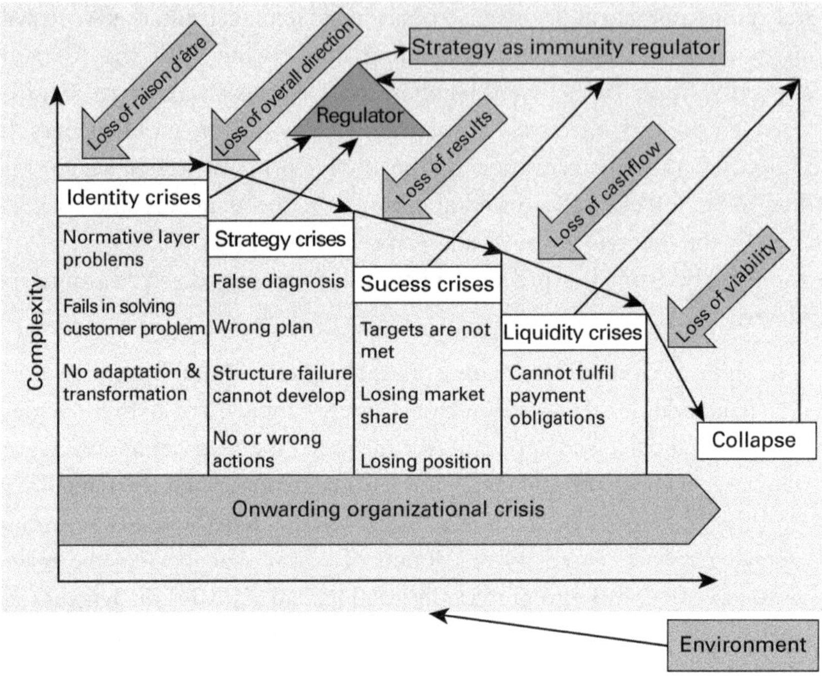

Based on Kamran (2013a).

Scientific theoretical positioning

It is the purpose of this book to position itself amid its scientific and theoretical nature in the field of applied theoretical sciences, enabling strategists to cope effectively with complexity in the field of strategic management. Furthermore, to construct, with the support of the gained insights of theoretical and fundamental sciences, practical-scientific models and realities, applied epistemologies are developed based on the notion of scientific practice.

The book establishes and distinguishes itself from an applied (practical) scientific view primarily in the following ways:

1. The scientific-practical problem emerges in coherence and is related to its practical relevance and its foundation in reality.
2. The strategist-observed reality creates additional, more favourable realities, thus diagnosing the problem by observing it is a major step in applying and constructing the right set of scientific tools, models and theories to resolve the strategic challenge at hand.

3 Practicability of application is essential, a vital and constitutive element, whereupon this work is based.

4 Enhancing the state of practical knowledge and contributing to the development and advancement of applied science and applied theoretical science is pursued.

5 Reducing complexity for the job of strategist/manager is the core of the work, thus a bridge between Porter's work in strategy and competitiveness and the works of the founding fathers of cybernetics, system sciences and other views in strategy is established.

6 To the author's knowledge, this work is the first ever attempt to observe Porter's models, the Porterian mindset and the scientific-practical lens from the perspective of creating a holistic strategy model by cybernetic and system-theoretical sciences, wherewith the author addresses the core issues of contemporary thinking in strategic thought.

The book distinguishes itself in scientific and theoretic perspectives in the following ways:

1 Observation of natural and evolutionary/theoretical phenomenon through literature scanning is conducted and an attempt to bring evolutionary sciences into a theoretical/scientific discourse for solving strategic problems in strategy theory is established and constructed.

2 A bridge between diverse theories is established to enhance the field of strategy as a theory.

3 The author's work challenges some established notions and attempts to falsify some long preserved scientific views and theories, whereby it stays truthful to the Popperian logic of scientific discovery, which, according to Popper (1957), must demonstrate the following attributes:

   - 'Once a hypothesis has been proposed and tested, and has proved its mettle, it may not be allowed to drop out without "good reason". A "good reason" may be, for instance: replacement of the hypothesis by another which is better testable; or the falsification of one of the consequences of the hypothesis.' The same logic is applied on the validity of the author's theses.
   - 'The way in which one answers these questions will largely depend upon one's attitude to science. Those who, like the positivists, see empirical science as a system of statements which satisfy certain logical criteria, such as meaningfulness or verifiability, will give one answer. A

very different answer will be given by those who tend to see (as I do) the distinguishing characteristic of empirical statements in their susceptibility to revision – in the fact that they can be criticized, and superseded by better ones; and who regard it as their task to analyze the characteristic ability of science to advance, and the characteristic manner in which a choice is made, in crucial cases, between conflicting systems of theories.'

- 'A system such as classical mechanics may be "scientific" to any degree you like; but those who uphold it dogmatically – believing, perhaps, that it is their business to defend such a successful system against criticism as long as it is not conclusively disproved – are adopting the very reverse of that critical attitude which in my view is the proper one for the scientist. In point of fact, no conclusive disproof of a theory can ever be produced; for it is always possible to say that the experimental results are not reliable or that the discrepancies which are asserted to exist between the experimental results and the theory are only apparent and that they will disappear with the advance of our understanding. (In the struggle against Einstein, both these arguments were often used in support of Newtonian mechanics, and similar arguments abound in the field of the social sciences.) If you insist on strict proof (or strict disproof) in the empirical sciences, you will never benefit from experience, and never learn from it how wrong you are.'

4. Knowledge and scientific theories, which the author via this work has created, are falsifiable, whereby, according to Popper (1957), the work is considered a part of the logic of scientific discovery. Thus, via the quality of observations, the theoretical claims it makes and the features it puts to empirical test and experiential evidence, an advance towards pushing the boundary of knowledge and science is achieved.
5. The author's theories fulfil and fall within the essential conclusions made by Popper (1957), namely an attempt at confirmation of the theories is conducted, whereby:
   a. They are refutable.
   b. An uneasy attempt is made to establish a further, better and more accurate theory to solve strategic problems. According to Popper (1957): easy confirmations and verifications are always possible, when we look for them.

6 The author's theories deliver methods to cope with the force of complexity, which has created vital and fundamental challenges for the strategist. The work aims to give practitioners a vital tool, model and framework to sharpen the strategist handicraft. This, according to Popper's prohibition doctrine (1957), resembles a theory of high quality.

Positioning a scientific work, especially in the field of applied science, has the vital characteristic that the generated knowledge must be or be able to be immediately applied, corrected by trial and error in solving practical problems while it ubiquitously contributes to its own advancement. Complexity as a force, which the author is pursuing to unfetter and extricate from its state of being a mere buzzword, requires holistic treatment; therefore, it must be handled by an interdisciplinary approach (Hetzler, 2008).

Strategic management and competitive strategy – an advanced introduction

According to Magretta (2012) in her latest book, *Understanding Michael Porter*, 'Strategy is an antidote to competition', and moreover, 'a dangerous concept in business'. According to Ghemawat (2002):

> Strategy is a term that can be traced back to the ancient Greeks, for whom it meant a chief magistrate or a military commander in chief. The use of the term in business, however, dates only to the twentieth century, and its use in a self-consciously competitive context is even more recent.

According to Mintzberg (1987):

- in the military: Strategy is concerned with 'drafting the plan of war... shaping the individual campaigns and within these, deciding on the individual engagements.'
- in Game Theory: Strategy is 'a complete plan: a plan which specifies what choices the player will make in every possible situation.'
- in management: Strategy is 'a unified, comprehensive, and integrated plan... designed to endure that the basic objectives of the enterprise are achieved.'
- in the dictionary: Strategy is (among other things) 'a plan, method, or series of manoeuvres or strategies for obtaining a specific goal or result.'

According to the author, strategy is based on the essential pillars as described below. Thus strategy is:

1. an objective, goal, a position to be achieved or a problem, a competition dilemma to be addressed and solved;
2. the process of creating and designing a plan and the 'how-to' of achieving the above;
3. action and execution via a self-correcting and self-organizing system of feedback;
4. a solid and ubiquitous feedback system of information based on the actions applied to correct errors; however, the chief objective of the strategy is primarily in dissolving problems before they become crises.

However, before we further outline the notion on strategy, it is essential to establish a wider theoretical notion of the field. Thus, at the beginning a fundament is laid down for the strategist and practitioner on what strategy is not:

1. Strategy is not operational effectiveness (Porter, 1996). Strategy is not a mere operational activity, although operations are embedded in it in a wider sense (Gälweiler, 2005).
2. Strategy is not a trend or a fashion.
3. Strategy is not liquidity and temporary successes (Gälweiler, 2005).
4. Strategy is not hyper-competition (Porter, 1996).
5. Strategy is not an undynamic and static activity or random set of activities.
6. Strategy is not an outcome or a mere document (Ference and Thurman, 2009).
7. Strategy is not the application of pure force against the rivals and competition (Schelling, 2005).
8. Strategy is not a single and standalone activity; it's a set or system of activities (Porter, 2008a).
9. Strategy is not just an approach (Gälweiler, 2005).
10. Strategy is not tactics; strategy is actively doing something, manoeuvre, course and a way to differentiate (Gälweiler, 2005).
11. Strategy (in management and for the purpose of this book) is not military strategy; these two approaches differ in the statement of the problem

they intend to cope with, to resolve and how these problems can be tackled. The objectives of military strategies do not coincide with the strategies of managing an enterprise.

12 Strategy is not always and from the outset a zero-sum-game (Gälweiler, 2005).

13 Strategy is not a success guarantee and does not answer this unsolvable problem (Malik, 1984, 2008).

14 Strategy is not a temporary project.

15 Strategy is not a yearly, nice-to-have plan or once-in-a-while method of doing something for the long run.

16 Strategy is not solely defined by and aimed at economic and financial targets (Beer, 1985).

Porter (1980, 1998) gives business (competitive) strategy a profound notion, which he underpins in the following manner:

> The essence of formulating a competitive strategy is relating a company to its environment. Although the relevant environment is very broad encompassing social as well as economic forces, the key aspect of the firm's environment is the industry or industries in which it competes. Industry structure has a strong influence in determining the competitive rules of the game as well as the strategies potentially available to the firm. Forces outside the industry are significant primarily in a relative sense; since outside forces usually affect all firms in the industry, the key is found in the differing abilities of firms to deal with them.

In another study, derived from a large sample, McGahan and Porter (1997) observed: 'Industry proves to have a powerful direct and indirect influence on profitability.' However right this view and notion may be, its effects are possibly true in a linear environment, but other factors and the wider and more in-depth observation of additional factors, forces and organizations' structures and their dynamics are necessary to deal with today's problems and more holistic strategic challenges. However, at this part of the book, the above two observations fit the framework, and the author generally agrees with the researchers. A good example is *The Blue Ocean Strategy* by Kim and Mauborgne (2005), which demonstrates concentration on a better organizational structure, attracting a different type of customer or addressing the wants of until now unsatisfied or non-considered customer groups. This is also a valid analogy for a particular industry, the redesigning of a business model of an established industry, the gaining of additional capabilities by concentrating on customer value as a new strategic doctrine substituting the shareholder value and differentiation by a unique value delivery to the customer, which would result in vastly superior achievements and successfully challenge industry-held myopic beliefs.

The author wants to establish the claim that strategy primarily must be aimed at positioning an organization in its most advantageous position against the strongest forces. The forces may differ from organization to organization or industry to industry; however, the essential point is that strategy must target the most vital forces that threaten the organization's survival by proactive measures in advance of the crises and the problems' occurrence. The strongest forces, which played the main role in the dismantling of many financial institutions, starting with Lehman Brothers' bankruptcy, were not primarily economic or financial threats. They were more the sum of systemic mismanagement, strategic and regulatory failures over a long period of time that started the 2008 global crises of capitalism. Furthermore, influenced by the latest crises and read and heard daily in the media, the author wants to initiate a serious scholarly debate on the definition of what the notion of 'structure' means for 'strategic immunity and strategic control' of organizations. Having large sums of bad and unworthy financial portfolios under management, which especially in the financial industry must be regarded as the vital part of the organizational structure of those institutions, and the hyper-rivalry among the big players for more profits and over-leveraging for more risk substantiates the author's claim. Granted, profitable performance is essential for overall health and organizational existence; however, the author wants to enhance the debate on the structure's importance as a vital strategic concern and objective. It is also essential that non-tangible and non-quantifiable elements such as the notions of trust, culture, reputation and organizational intelligence, organizational eigen behaviour and interrelations, which play an essential role in strategy-making, ought to be regarded as the organization's structure. According to Hall and Saias (1980): 'An organization decides and acts in accordance with its perception of changes in the environment or in its own capabilities.' Miles *et al* (1974) observe: 'The organization whose managerial talent is fully employed in the operation of the existing technology and process is unlikely to perceive new environmental threats or opportunities.'

Strategy is a large and complex field of study with almost no agreement or general observation on the common-held belief; thus, to challenge the only pillars, whereupon some agreement is held, such as the widely accepted 'resource-based view', the Porterian doctrines (starting with the five forces model (FFM) known as competitive strategy (CS)) or the Chandlerian thesis of 'strategy follows structure', is a difficult undertaking. But it is essential to question these notions as the globally interconnected world asks for it.

Thus, the following observations deliver a conceptual framework on what strategy means for the purpose of the work and what strategy must resolve so that the organization can survive and thrive:

1. Strategy is a highly focused and coherent combination of diagnosis, policies and actions for the best results.
2. Strategy is a set of coherent actions, which result in a vital change of the future by the actions taken today.
3. Strategy is dissolving organizational complexity.
4. Strategy is a hypothesis of what is going to succeed in the future.
5. Strategy is a set of proactive and dynamic course-correcting actions for the achievement of the highest organizational objective.
6. Strategy is the most essential part of organizational survival. Before any organizational collapses, the strategist must fail in advance.
7. Strategy's main problem is organizational immunity.
8. The strategist's activity field takes place in the future, by connecting it to the present.
9. Strategy's main task is maintaining the unconditional supremacy over the strongest force.
10. Strategy is an identity-preserving and identity-transforming organizational capability.
11. Strategy is designing an intelligent and viable organizational structure to cope with emergent and unforeseen phenomena.
12. Strategy, according to Ashby's fundamental law of management ('Only variety can absorb variety'), is ensuring the sufficient amount of variety is provided at the disposal of the strategist at all times.
13. 'Strategy rests on unique activities.' 'Competitive strategy is about being different. It means deliberately choosing a different set of activities to deliver a unique mix of value' (Porter, 1996).

14 Strategy is the creation of the right sort of crises in advance so that the organization can adapt to them and proactively dismantle their effects.

15 According to Porter (2008a), 'Strategy can be viewed as building defences against the competitive forces or finding a position in the industry where the forces are weakest.'

16 Mintzberg *et al* (1998) divide strategy into 10 different schools:

1. The Design School: strategy formation as a process of conception
2. The Planning School: strategy formation as a formal process
3. The Positioning School: strategy formation as an analytical process
4. The Entrepreneurial School: strategy formation as a visionary process
5. The Cognitive School: strategy formation as a mental process
6. The Learning School: strategy formation as an emergent process
7. The Power School: strategy formation as a process of negotiation
8. The Cultural School: strategy formation as a collective process
9. The Environmental School: strategy formation as a reactive process
10. The Configuration School: strategy formation as a process of transformation.

The author intends to establish an additional school of thought in the field of strategy; the claim of this school of thought will be substantiated throughout the book. Thus, an additional school of strategic thought is introduced:

> The Immunity School: Strategy formation as a proactive problem-detecting and problem-solving process, whereby the pre-problem phase of strategic immunization of organizational problems and crises is the key part. Thus, before the organization is endangered, the strategist has to fail in advance (see also Figure 0.2.).

Maintaining organizational viability and organizational fit lies at the heart of strategic management. Any actions contrary to this claim must be regarded as non-strategic activities. Indeed, some of our managerial actions originating from an economic dimension are dangerous to the organization. According to Malik (1998) the biggest fallacy and delusion is the notion of maximizing profits, the shareholder value doctrine, value appreciation and increase, which are regarded as the highest organizational objectives. Another false notion is quitting strategy at all, since according to a contrary view; it is impossible to plan and develop it, which is also a dangerous fallacy (Gälweiler,

2005). Müller-Stewens and Lechner (2011) of the University of St Gallen give the following six objectives to strategy:

1 strategy as a position;
2 strategy as performance-oriented actions;
3 strategy as the pursuit of uniqueness;
4 strategy as the ability to be adaptive;
5 strategy as management of initiatives;
6 strategy as resource allocation.

What a strategy should achieve in ultimate consequence is to ensure that sufficient time is available in order to identify, analyse and act and to absorb complexity (internal and external environmental disturbance and perturbation, and the diverse states of the systems) and incalculable and unforeseen developments and occurrences (Gälweiler, 2005; Hetzler, 2008).

Whittington (1993), as shown in Figure 0.2, enables us to see a broad and concise basis to discuss divergent views on the formation and implementation of strategies. Houchin (2003) defines four basic conceptions of strategy as:

1 rational;
2 fatalistic;
3 pragmatic; and
4 relativist.

The above conceptions have very different implications for how organizations go about 'doing strategy'.

> The rational or classical approach is the oldest, underpinning the planning methods dominant in textbooks. It is still the most influential. The evolutionary approach is fatalist and has strong links with Darwinian evolutionary theory. Processualists are pragmatists who emphasized that organizations and markets are unreliable. They advocate an incremental approach. The Systemic approach is relativistic regarding the ends and means of strategy. Strategy is inescapably linked to the cultures and powers of the social systems in which it takes place. Whittington's basic conceptions are, in my view, a usefully structured way of understanding and separating out the variety of approaches that exist in the strategy field (Houchin, 2003).

Figure 0.2 describes the four dimensions of strategic thinking according to Whittington (1993):

1 classical;
2 evolutionary;
3 processual; and
4 systemic.

Wit *et al* (1998) account for the following reasons to look at strategy from two different perspectives. These views are:

1 content (Ansoff, 1984);
2 process (Porter, 1980; Chandler, 1962; Quinn *et al*, 1988; Hannan and Freeman, 1988; Granovetter, 1985; and Cyert and March, 2006).

'There are strongly differing opinions on most of the concepts of strategy. These run so deep that even a common definition of the term is scarcely possible' (Houchin, 2003). According to Mintzberg *et al* (1998), concepts such as strategy formation cannot be reduced to a single definition.

According to Houchin (2003):

> The word is generally used in different ways suggesting that implicitly we accept various definitions even though formally we tend to quote only one. The variety of conflicting views means that strategy cannot be reduced to a number of models or flow diagrams which can simply be followed like an instruction manual. In order to study strategy a structured process has to be followed so that the various approaches can be viewed separately, compared and contrasted.

FIGURE 0.2 Generic perspectives on strategy

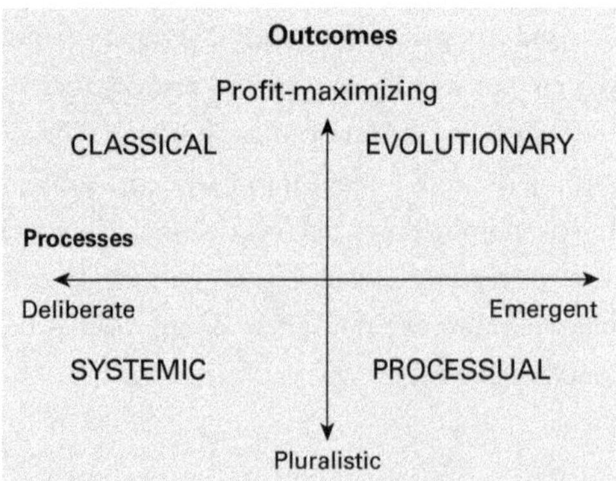

Adapted from Whittington (1993)

Observation as stated above is fundamental for the job of the strategist.

What robust strategy models can accomplish

Models are a way of communication for the organization: internally, with itself and its sub-systems, and externally, with the forces and dynamics of the organizational milieu. Strategy models have diverse control objectives ensuring a healthy and functional organizational whole. Thus, they fulfil a very solid and profound task and are essential for the handicraft of strategists, their daily operations and the real-time strategy cockpit, enabling an accurate and quick overview of the land. A strategy model constructs a reality wherein an organization can achieve an organizational/strategic goal or maintain its control over a disturbance regarding a dangerous situation. According to Ashby's Law of Requisite Variety, the demand we can put on a strategic model is to deliver proliferating variety (Ashby, 1958). Above all, strategy models must embed and display the following attributes:

1 Viability, which is the foundation upon which any strategic model must be based. While a catastrophic event may at a particular instant throw the viable organization into systemic chaos, the fundamental characteristic of viability embedded in a model's system lessens its vulnerability to the surprise, making it more adaptive to change (Espejo, 2003). An organization can proclaim to be viable if and only if it can maintain a separate, autonomic and self-organizing existence. Thus, for the purpose of this book, viability is a vital pillar of modelling an organizational structure.

2 Transparency, which is vital to the strategy. The strategist must ensure they are provided with the highest level of transparency and clarity regarding the situation. Is the strategist in desperate need of freeing themselves from some of the arbitrary decisions they are following? Indeed, if one puts the same yardstick and scale on the decisions of the crew of an aeroplane as one puts on the management of organizations, no one would fly; every flight would be an instrumental flight on the basis of the data of the previous month's average. The crew would not have an actual plan and picture of the current situation. Early-warning systems and real-time information would not be needed (Hetzler, 2008). This high level of communication and information is required so the crew can prepare and respond to turbulence and disturbance in real time and before it can spread

to the wider architecture of the system. Therefore, the essence of strategic modelling is to ensure that an accurate state of affairs is generated, and a quick response is possible, which in itself can be corrected via a solid feedback system. High transparency enhances the currency of the strategist, which is the time the strategist has to cope with a forthcoming challenge. This currency of the strategist in Gälweilerian spirit is time. Time is the trade commodity of the strategist, and it is precisely and exactly here that the strategist must maintain full control of their resources, thus time is the currency of the strategist.

References

Ansoff HI (1984) *Implanting Strategic Management*, Prentice/Hall International, Englewood Cliffs, NJ

Ansoff HI, Declerck RP and Hayes RL (1976) From strategic planning to strategic management, in *International Conference on Strategic Management 1973: Vanderbilt University*

ASC (2019) *Defining Cybernetics*, http://asc-cybernetics.org/?s=defining+cybernetics (archived at https://perma.cc/HHE7-VCE6) (accessed 24 November 2019)

Ashby WR (1956) *Introduction to Cybernetics*, Chapman & Hall, London

Ashby WR (1958) Requisite variety and its implications for the control of complex systems, *Cybernetica,* **1** (2), pp 83–99

Barton CA (1995) *The Sorrows of the Ancient Romans: The gladiator and the monster,* Princeton University Press, Princeton, NJ

Beer S (1966) *Decision and Control: The meaning of operational research and management cybernetics*, Wiley, London

Beer S (1972) *Brain of the Firm: A development in management cybernetics*, Lane, London

Beer S (1973) *Designing Freedom: The future that can be demanded now*, Center for Cassette Studies, Portland, OR

Beer S (1975) *Platform for Change*, Wiley, Chichester

Beer S (1979a) *Decision and Control: The meaning of operational research and management cybernetics*, Wiley, Chichester

Beer S (1979b) *The Heart of Enterprise*, Wiley, London/New York

Beer S (1981) *Brain of the Firm: The managerial cybernetics of organization*, Wiley, Chichester

Beer S (1984) The viable system model: its provenance, development, methodology and pathology, *Journal of the Operational Research Society*, **35** (1), pp 7–25

Beer S (1985) *Diagnosing the System for Organizations*, Wiley, Chichester

Beer S (1988) *Decision and Control: Meaning of operational research and management cybernetics*, Wiley, Chichester

Beer S (1994) *Decision and Control: The meaning of operational research and management cybernetics*, Wiley, Chichester

Beyes TP (2005) Observing observers: Von Foerster, Luhmann, and management thinking, *Kybernetes*, **34** (3/4), pp 448–459

Chandler AD (1962) *Strategy and Structure Chapters in the History of the Industrial Enterprise*, MIT Press, Cambridge, MA

Conant RC and Ashby WR (1970) Every good regulator of a system must be a model of that system, *International Journal of Systems Science*, **1** (2), pp 89–97

Cyert RM and March JG (2006) *A Behavioral Theory of the Firm*, Blackwell, Malden, MA

Drucker PF (1954) *The Practice of Management*, Harper & Row, New York

Espejo R (2003) Social systems and the embodiment of organisational learning, in *Complex Systems and Evolutionary Perspectives on Organisations: The application of complexity theory to organisations*, ed E Mitleton-Kelly, pp 53–70, Pergamon, Amsterdam

Ference TP and Thurman PW (2009) *MBA Fundamentals: Strategy*, Kaplan, New York

Foerster H (2003) *Understanding Understanding: Essays on cybernetics and cognition*, Springer-Verlag, New York

Gälweiler A (2005) *Strategische Unternehmensführung*, Campus-Verl, Frankfurt/ Main, New York

Ghemawat P (2002) Competition and business strategy in historical perspective, *Business History Review*, **76** (1), pp 37–74

Granovetter M (1985) Economic action and social structure: The problem of embeddedness, *American Journal of Sociology*, **91** (3), pp 481–510

Haber S (2002) Introduction: the political economy of crony capitalism, in *Crony Capitalism and Economic Growth in Latin America: Theory and evidence*, Hoover Institution Press, Stanford University, Stanford

Hall DJ and Saias MA (1980) Strategy follows structure!, *Strategic Management Journal*, **1** (2), pp 149–163

Hannan MT and Freeman J (1988) The ecology of organizational mortality: American labor unions, 1836–1985, *American Journal of Sociology*, pp 25–52

Hawking S (2000) I think the next century will be the century of complexity, *San Jose Mercury News*

Hetzler S (2008) *Brain-supporting-environments für Entscheide in komplexen Systemen: ein kybernetischer Ansatz für die Gestaltung wirksamer Entscheidungsumfelder*, Dissertation, Rosch-Druck, Schesslitz, Germany

Houchin K (2003) *Applying Complexity Theory to the Strategic Development of an Organisation*, Dissertation, University of Glasgow, Glasgow

Jervis R (2012) *Why Intelligence Fails: Lessons from the Iranian revolution and the Iraq war*, Cornell University Press, Ithaca, NY

Judt T (2011) *Ill Fares the Land*, Penguin Books, London

Kamran Q (2011a) *Complexity of Negotiation and Negotiation of Complexity: Getting to trust*, Available at: https://papers.ssrn.com/sol3/papers.cfm?abstract_id=2137877 (archived at https://perma.cc/6XYD-9NT6) (accessed 22 November 2018)

Kamran Q (2011b) Management by deception (MBD): the need for designing a viable strategy, *SSRN Electronic Journal*, Available at: http://dx.doi.org/10.2139/ssrn.2137880 (archived at https://perma.cc/6Y7J-UC4X) (accessed 4 December 2018)

Kamran Q (2012a) *'Complexity', the 6th Competitive Force that Shapes Management Strategy: A cybernetic approach to 'Porter's Five Forces that Shapes Industry Strategy' in Turbulent and Complex Environments*, Available at: https://papers.ssrn.com/sol3/papers.cfm?abstract_id=2137853 (archived at https://perma.cc/F4LS-Z2WF) (accessed 22 November 2018)

Kamran Q (2012b) Running multinational corporations (MNC) in China: A survival-kit to Western CEOs, in *Aktuelle Entwicklungen des europäischen und internationalen Wirtschaftsrechts,* ed C Baudenbacher, pp 249–317, Helbing et Lichtenhahn, Basel, München

Kamran Q (2012c) *The Transformation of Porter's Strategic Mind from 'Shareholder Value' to 'Shared Value': Bridging the sciences of economics, strategy and cybernetics*, Available at: https://ssrn.com/abstract=2219284 (archived at https://perma.cc/8AYU-A8JJ)

Kamran Q (2013a) *Complexity, the Sixth Competitive Force That Shapes Strategy: A cybernetics approach to 'Porter's FFM' in turbulent and complex environments*, Lambert Academic Publishing, Saarbrücken

Kamran Q (2013b) *Reinvigorating Antitrust Enforcement in Obama's Second Term*, LAP LAMBERT Academic Publishing, Saarbrücken

Kamran Q (2014a) *An Argument of Organisational Functionality in the World of Tomorrow*, Available at: https://papers.ssrn.com/sol3/papers.cfm?abstract_id=2475864 (archived at https://perma.cc/GQB9-MR5Y) (accessed 22 November 2018)

Kamran Q (2014b) *Conceptualizing Complexity as the Sixth Competitive Force that Shapes Strategy in Complex and Turbulent Environments*, Available at: https://papers.ssrn.com/sol3/papers.cfm?abstract_id=2476277 (archived at https://perma.cc/BW6Q-W6TQ) (accessed 22 November 2018)

Kamran Q (2014c) *Defining Complexity for Organizations and its Implication for Strategy*, Available at: https://papers.ssrn.com/sol3/papers.cfm?abstract_id=2475953 (archived at https://perma.cc/FT5N-5QRS) (accessed 22 November 2018)

Kamran Q (2014d) Model safari in strategy: Scanning the landscape of the essential strategy models, *O&M: Structures & Processes in Organizations eJournal,* **6** (44) (accessed 22 November 2018)

Kamran Q (2014e) *Observing, Understanding and Revisiting Porter as the Fundament of the Research in Strategy*, Available at: https://papers.ssrn.com/sol3/papers.cfm?abstract_id=2475915 (archived at https://perma.cc/7SH2-C2LA) (accessed 22 November 2018)

Kamran Q (2017a) An Empirical Case Study of Applying the Sixth Force Model on a German Hidden Champion, *SSRN Electronic Journal*

Kamran Q (2017b) Cybernetics and Strategy: A necessary synergy for strategic models – complexity, the sixth competitive force that shapes strategy in turbulent and complex environments – a cybernetics approach to Porter's FFM: in turbulent and complex environments, in *Academy of Business Administration (ABA) Year Book*, Yapsilanti, MI, pp 1–65, *Innovation Law & Policy eJournal*, 5 (25) (accessed 22 November 2018)

Kamran Q (2018a) Da-Sein Thinking: A phenomenological epistemology for design thinking, *SSRN Electronic Journal,* Available at: https://papers.ssrn.com/sol3/papers.cfm?abstract_id=3273883 (archived at https://perma.cc/L4UD-56BQ) (accessed 22 November 2018)

Kamran Q (2018b) *The History of Design Thinking: From pragmatism to phenomenology*, Available at: https://papers.ssrn.com/sol3/papers.cfm?abstract_id=3273872 (archived at https://perma.cc/R9GQ-JRGB) (accessed 22 November 2018)

Kamran Q (2018c) The service-dominant perspective to create value in the maritime business, in *Container Logistics: The role of the container in the supply chain*, ed R Neise, pp 346–373, Kogan Page, London

Kauffman SA (2008) *Reinventing the Sacred: A new view of science, reason, and religion*, Basic Books, New York

Kim WC and Mauborgne R (2005) *Blue Ocean Strategy: How to create uncontested market space and make the competition irrelevant*, Harvard Business School Press, Boston, MA

Leonard, A and Harnden, R (1994) in *How Many Grapes Went into the Wine: Stafford Beer on the art and science of holistic management*, Wiley

Magretta J (2012) *Understanding Michael Porter: The essential guide to competition and strategy*, Harvard Business Review Press, Boston, MA

Malik F (1984) *Strategie des Managements komplexer Systeme*, Haupt, Bern & Stuttgart

Malik F (1993) *Systemisches Management, Evolution, Selbstorganisation: Grundprobleme, Funktionsmechanismen und Lösungsansätze für komplexe Systeme*, Haupt, Bern & Stuttgart

Malik F (1994) *Management-Perspektiven: Wirtschaft und Gesellschaft, Strategie, Management und Ausbildung*, Haupt, Bern

Malik F (1996) *Strategie des Managements komplexer Systeme: Ein Beitrag zur Management-Kybernetik evolutionärer Systeme*, Haupt, Bern

Malik F (1997) *Wirksame Unternehmensaufsicht: Corporate governance in Umbruchzeiten*, Frankfurter Allgemeine, Zeitung für Deutschland, Verl.-Bereich Buch, Frankfurt am Main

Malik F (1998) Die Welt des Peter Drucker, *Malik Letter,* **98** (12)

Malik F (2000) *Strategie des Managements komplexer Systeme: Ein Beitrag zur Management-Kybernetik evolutionärer Systeme*, Haupt, Bern

Malik F (2007) *Management: Das A und O des Handwerks*, Campus-Verl, Frankfurt/Main

Malik F (2008) *Strategie des Managements komplexer Systeme: Ein Beitrag zur Management-Kybernetik evolutionärer Systeme*, Haupt, Bern

Malik F (2011) Die große Transformation, *Malik on Management m.o.m.-Letter*, **11** (2)

McGahan AM and Porter ME (1997) How much does industry matter, really?, *Strategic Management Journal*, **18** (S1), pp 15–30

Miles RE, Snow CC and Pfeffer J (1974) Organization-environment: Concepts and issues, *Industrial Relations: A Journal of Economy and Society,* **13** (3), pp 244–264

Mintzberg H (1987) *Crafting Strategy*, Harvard Business School Press, Boston, MA

Mintzberg H, Ahlstrand BW and Lampel J (1998) *Strategy Safari: A guided tour through the wilds of strategic management*, Free Press, New York

Mitchell M (2009) *Complexity: A guided tour*, Oxford University Press, Oxford

Müller-Stewens G and Lechner C (2011) *Strategisches Management: Wie strategische Initiativen zum Wandel führen*, Schäffer-Poeschel, Stuttgart

NPR (2012) *Stopping the 'Brain Drain' of the US Economy*, Available at: https://www.npr.org/2012/02/05/146434854/stopping-the-brain-drain-of-the-u-s-economy (archived at https://perma.cc/AU5R-8AGD) (accessed 24 November 2019)

Pagels HR (1988) *The Dreams of Reason: The computer and the rise of the sciences of complexity*, Simon & Schuster, New York

Popper KR (1957) Philosophy of science: A personal report, in *British Philosophy in the Mid-Century*, ed CA Mace, Allen & Unwin, London

Popper KR (2002) *The Logic of Scientific Discovery*, Routledge, London

Porter ME (1977) From entry barriers to mobility barriers: Conjectural decisions and contrived deterrence to new competition, *Quarterly Journal of Economics,* **91** (2), pp 241–261

Porter ME (1979a) How competitive forces shape strategy, *Harvard Business Review*, March, **57** (2), pp 137–145

Porter ME (1979b) The structure within industries and companies' performance, *The Review of Economics and Statistics,* **61** (2), p 214

Porter ME (1980) *Competitive Strategy: Techniques for analyzing industries and competitors*, Free Press, New York

Porter ME (1981) The contributions of industrial organization to strategic management, *Academy of Management Review*, **6** (4), pp 609–620

Porter ME (1985) *Competitive Advantage: Creating and sustaining superior performance*, Free Press, New York

Porter ME (1986) *Competition in Global Industries*, Harvard Business School Press, Boston, MA
Porter ME (1987) From competitive advantage to corporate strategy, *Harvard Business Review*, **65** (3), pp 43–59
Porter ME (1993) *Competition in Global Industries*, Harvard Business School Press, Boston, MA
Porter ME (1996) What is strategy?, *Harvard Business Review*, **73** (6) (accessed 22 November 2018)
Porter ME (1998) *The Competitive Advantage of Nations: With a new introduction*, Free Press, New York
Porter ME (2007) *Clusters and Economic Policy: Aligning public policy with the new economics of competition*, ISC White Paper (Institute for Strategy and Competitiveness, Harvard Business School) (accessed 21 November 2018)
Porter ME (2008a) *On Competition: Updated and extended edition*, Harvard Business School Press, Boston, MA
Porter ME (2008b) The five competitive forces that shape strategy, *Harvard Business Review*, **86** (1), pp 78–93
Porter ME and Kramer MR (2011) Creating shared value, *Harvard Business Review*, **89** (1/2), pp 62–77
Quinn JB, Mintzberg H and James RM (1988) *The Strategy Process: Concepts, contexts, and cases*, Prentice Hall, Upper Saddle River, NJ
Schelling TC (2005) *The Strategy of Conflict: With a new preface*, Harvard University Press, Boston, MA
Sowell T (2009) *Intellectuals and Society*, Basic Books, New York
The Guardian (2011) Full text of Barack Obama's speech in Osawatomie, Kansas: US president reprises themes of Theodore Roosevelt, decrying the 'you're on your own' economics of Republicans, Available at: https://www.theguardian.com/world/2011/dec/07/full-text-barack-obama-speech (archived at https://perma.cc/PY72-EZTK) (accessed 24 November 2019)
Weick KE (1969) *The Social Psychology of Organizing*, Addison-Wesley, Reading, MA
White NJ (2004) The beginnings of crony capitalism: Business, politics and economic development in Malaysia, c. 1955–70, *Modern Asian Studies*, **38** (2), pp 389–417
Whittington R (1993) *What Is Strategy: And does it matter?* Routledge, London
Wiener N (1948) *Cybernetics: Or control and communication in the animal and the machine*, MIT Press, Cambridge, MA
Wit Bd, Meyer R and Heugens P (1998) *Strategy: Process, content, context an international perspective*, International Thomson Business Press, London

01

Michael Porter – the founder of competitive strategy

The reason for choosing Porter's work to embed the author's model into that framework is admittedly a very daring and audacious one, but it was an easy decision. Thus, no other strategy scholar has proclaimed that level of justified popularity and status in the field of strategic management literature and its practice, but above all in the last four decades. As a matter of fact, starting the understanding of strategy and competition in business administration (BA) begins with Porter's work and the five forces model (FFM) (Magretta, 2012). His mission to go after the biggest and most consequential problems in strategy and asking why some firms are generating more profits than others (Magretta, 2012), and delivering ground-breaking insights to that question, gives Porter a special place in the Olympus of business strategy. According to Porter in his collected articles published under the topic of 'On competition' (Porter, 2008a), Porter advises the reader: to begin and to seriously understand his work, the reader ought to begin their research with the FFM. One of the essential reasons why his work has endured for decades and still has not lost its utility and usefulness is that unique interdisciplinary approach he applies from his background in economics and BA. In the fashionable world of BA literature, gurus come and go (Magretta, 2012), but Porter's legacy has withstood the test of time. Not only is he, from a scientific and academic perspective, the most-cited author in economics and BA, but his ideas and insights are among the most widely applied in the real world by practitioners around the globe. The FFM is the fundamental curriculum of all MBA programmes and, above all, is still an unfalsified model. Embedding a business to its environment (industry) and making it viable against the industry force was a major breakthrough and is still an essential part of strategy in BA. However, it is the objective of the author to make this model more holistically applicable to the current era of complexity and interconnectedness. This chapter will give a brief but precise introduction to the work of Porter and is concluded by an in-depth literature review on the FFM's inception and its pathology.

A further, widely known attribute of this work is in the author's conceptual design and enhancement of the introduced models and theories. This is essential, since the reader can be a companion of the author from the start and they can follow the author developing ideas from their inception and throughout the book. It is essential that the insights are applied by practitioners, thus a key attribute of a scientific work ought to be its ability to stay interesting, to arouse questions and critique, which is a necessary part of scientific discourse, but above all to not twiddle its thumbs on the dusty shelves of an almost never consulted library.

Porter's generic strategies

Generic strategies defined by Porter (1986–1998) deliver the ground, where the battle for gaining a competitive advantage is fought. These three pillars of competitive advantage are:

Cost leadership

Cost leadership is the strategy whereby a company establishes itself, according to Porter, as 'below the industry price actor' in the market. This means the company is a low-cost producer and a cost leader in its industry.

Differentiation

Differentiation enables a company to position itself along the most valued dimensions in the industry for customers. However, the research work of Kim and Mauborgne (2005), which will be discussed later, challenges the commonly held view of Porter, where a company can be attractive for customers, who are not the general target group, for which the general differentiation was created but moreover by the combination of the value proposition and breaking industry boundaries. Nevertheless, being a high and above-average performer is the key to differentiation, and a company must decide how it will differentiate itself and how it can maintain this against its rivals in the market.

According to Burke (2009):

> Blue ocean strategy seeks to turn strategic management on its head by replacing 'competitive advantage' with 'value innovation' as the primary goal where firms must create consumer demand and exploit untapped markets. Empirical analysis has been focused on case study evidence and so lacks generality to resolve the debate. We provide a methodological synthesis of the theories enabling us to bring statistical evidence to the debate. Our analysis finds that blue ocean and competitive strategies overlap, and managers do not face a discrete either/or decision between each strategy. Our evidence for the Dutch retail industry indicates that blue ocean strategy has prevailed as a dominant long-term viable strategy.

Focus

The focus strategy differs from the above, since by this strategy a company optimizes its strategy by excluding other rivals (Porter, 1985, 1998).

These optimizations are:

1. Cost focus: seeking and establishing a cost focus in the target segment.
2. Differentiation focus: seeking and establishing a difference for usual needs of the customers or having service and products that better serve the needs of the target of segment.

Thus, the breadth of a target is clearly a matter of degree, but the essence of focus lies in the exploitation of a narrow target's difference from the rest of the industry (Porter, 1985, 1998). Figure 1.1 displays Porter's 'generic strategies' revealed by the above ideas.

FIGURE 1.1 Porter's 'generic strategies'

1. Cost leadership	2. Differentiation
3A. Cost focus	3B. Differentiation focus

Based on Porter (1985–1998)

Establishing a difference that a company can preserve and fine-tuning it with the rate of focus the firm decides to establish its product/service attractively to the customer (also observed as market segment) requires making trade-offs in respect of choices. Thus, trade-offs on behalf of the focus the organization wants to make and the difference it wants to preserve are the remedy against mediocrity (Porter, 1985, 1998).

Viable structure

An additional perspective is given by the author, as shown in Figure 1.2. Thus, an organization that can adapt and sense change ubiquitously by having a structure that can cope with these environmental turbulences in terms of fluidity, flexibility and self-organization delivers a generic strategy. This claim is substantiated by the author's theory that strategy, whether generic or advanced, needs an organizational structure that can actually carry it, reshape, refocus and ubiquitously recreate itself until the objective is achieved. Figure 1.2 describes this reality.

FIGURE 1.2 Porter's 'generic strategies' with fourth generic strategy of structure added

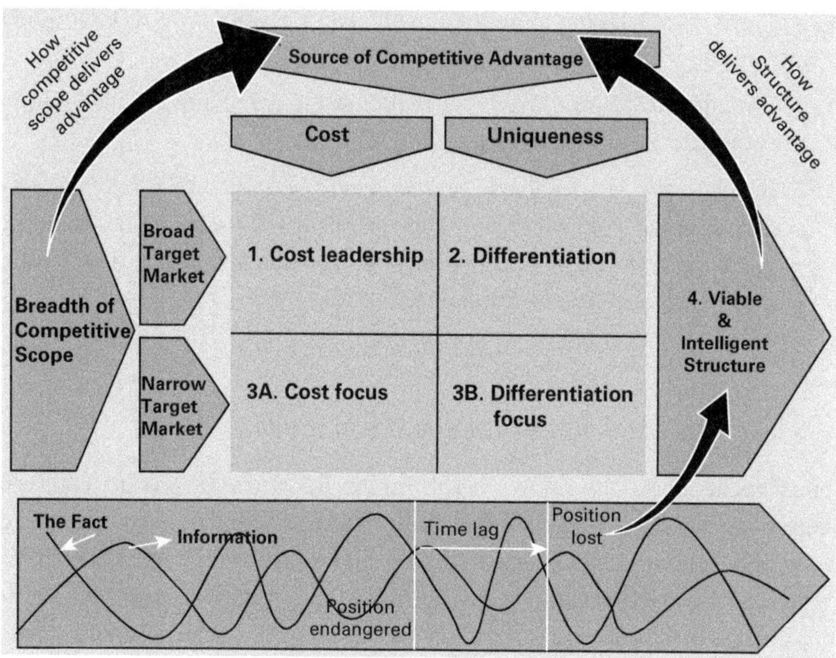

Based on Porter (1985–1998), extended by the author

The author bases his theory on the following works:

- from the 'military sciences' perspective, see: the works of Boyd in Houchin (2003) and Greene (2010);
- from the 'management and strategy sciences' perspective, see: Porter (1974–2013); Mintzberg *et al* (1998); Malik (1974–2008); Schwaninger (1984a, 1984b, 1985, 1987, 1998, 2000, 2001a, 2001b, 2004a, 2004b, 2006a, 2007, 2009b, 2010);
- from the 'management cybernetics' perspective, see: Beer (1959, 1972, 1973, 1979, 1984, 1985, 1988, 2002, 2008, 2011);
- from the 'business administration and management' perspective, see: Ulrich (1968), Ulrich and Krieg (1972);
- from 'bionics, management and management cybernetics' perspective, see: Malik (1981, 1984, 1993, 1994, 1996, 1997, 2000a, 2000b, 2007, 2015).

Thus, every strategic move requires four essential pillars to succeed. These pillars are:

1. a goal, a position to acquire, a problem and a crisis to solve (dissolve);
2. a plan, a map, which is embodied by the set of actions it needs to conduct and apply;
3. action and execution – without it, every strategy remains hostage within the boundaries of 'nice to haves';
4. feedback – it's via feedback that course and policy-relating, mission-accomplishing, goal-achieving and problem-solving activities can be corrected within due process without dangerous and costly time losses, reaction gaps and organizational inabilities.

Porter's value chain model

The sequence of activity a firm is performing as R&D, design, procurement and supply chain, HR, operations, sales and marketing, planning, execution and additional support activities are understood as a firm's value chain. The basic 'value chain model' (VCM) (Porter, 1985, 1998) is described in Figure 1.3. It explains in three sections the spectrum of the model. In section 1 are the inter-dependent activities that firms engage in first to build a system of activities and later to divide these activities into further smaller activities and/or sub-systems.

FIGURE 1.3 The value chain model and the advantage a company creates

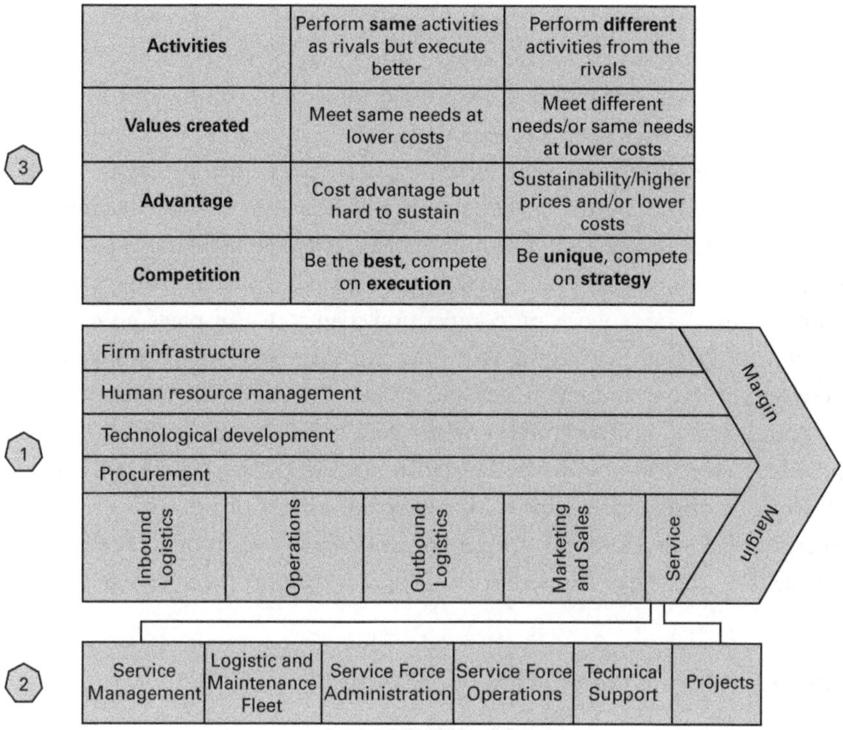

Author's interpretation, based on Porter (1985, 1998) and Magretta (2012)

In section 2, an organization creates its holistic structure. An organization is a system of dynamic activities and not a static departmentalization. An organization ought to deliver superior performance on the need it has created for the customer or the need it fulfils, which defines its success. According to Drucker (1954), the purpose of a business is to create a customer or a need. The choices a firm makes, the strategies it designs, the quality of its execution applied via feedback (see section 3) and how the firm chooses to differentiate itself and, as a result, determines its profitability, attractiveness and superiority over competition is vital to its success and survival.

The competitive advantage is a model that is under the direct command of the strategist. One may not be able to shape the industry in a short time, although the first sign of a good strategy is that the market plays the industry leader's game, as the rise of Apple has shown. Thus, the value chain is a set of activities that can bring competitive advantage that is not easy to copy – if a firm chooses to differentiate in terms of business model, execution and customer satisfaction, while maintaining profit leadership (Kim and Mauborgne, 2005). Below I outline the FFM, which is the foundational pillar of the book.

Porter's five forces model (FFM)

Strategists are professionals that distinguish themselves from general managers by their main focus on the organization's competitive position towards rivals, the market and external or internal forces known or as yet unknown via scientific knowledge, professional training, solid research and application base. This specialization on the subject of strategy and competition –initiated and dominated by Porter in the late 1970s and early 1980s – has been the chief academic interest of the author. My strategic thinking was mainly shaped – and my interest in pursuing an academic career was essentially ignited – by Porter's work on competition. Figure 1.4 displays an extended version of the FFM, whereby from the Porterian lens one can distinguish between the major and much weaker competition within the industry.

Porter started his work on the wider held belief that generalizations were possible in the field of industrial organizations (IO) (Kiechel, 2010). Porter's strategic mindset started by challenging the beliefs of his business policy Professor Kenneth Andrew at Harvard, which was the cutting-edge belief in the field at the time. Thus, Porter declared them as 'very stylized' views

FIGURE 1.4 Porter's five forces that shape strategy

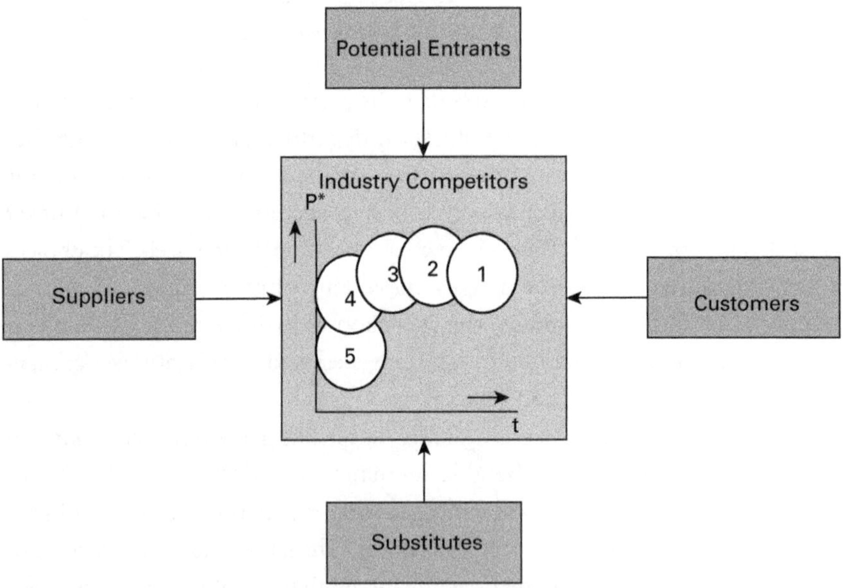

P* = Performance and place in the marketplace; t = time to customers need/market need/creating a want
Author's interpretation, based on Porter (1974, 1980, 2008a, 2008b)

(Kiechel, 2010). There he saw his big chance and 'to turn things on its head', as he emphasized, by focusing instead on what structural factors created opportunities in an industry that a company could exploit to its competitive advantage (Kiechel, 2010). Porter, although to this day a proponent of the uniqueness attribute of every individual business (Kiechel, 2010), addressed two major problems in his later works, which delivered the foundation for his legacy up until today. First, IO economists focused on issues of public policy instead of the business policy: 'they concerned themselves with the minimization rather than the maximization of "excess" profits' (Ghemawat, 2002). Second, conduct within the IO paradigm – emphasized by Joe Bain, another professor from Harvard's economics department, and his successors – focused on using a limited list of structural variables to explain industry profitability and short-changed the richness of modern industrial competition (Ghemawat, 2002). Both of the challenges were addressed by Porter, starting with his paper 'Note on the Structural Analysis of Industries' (1975). His later ground-breaking book, *Competitive Strategy* (Porter, 1980, 1998), established the field of competitive strategy in its own right, with its core disciplines of industry analysis, competitor analysis, and strategic positioning of the firm. Porter's FFM was a breakthrough in strategic thinking, namely shifting the commonly held view from competition mainly focused on 'extended rivalry' with a direct competitor to a 'value generating' approach within the industry. Although 'import competition and multimarket contact' (Ghemawat, 2002) have been introduced into additional determinants to intensify the FFM and framework, additional force integration has been denied by Porter with respect to the wider strategic management literature. According to Porter (1980), 'the essence of formulating competitive strategy is relating a company to its environment.' However, under environment, Porter widened and translated the key aspect of environment to the industry, where the organization is directly embedded in the industry's structure, wherein it competed for more value (Kiechel, 2010). According to Porter, the FFM encompasses the following five forces:

1. powerful customers;
2. powerful suppliers;
3. substitute products;
4. new entrants; and
5. rivalry among existing competitors.

The forces are described in more detail below.

Force 1: powerful customers

Bargaining power of buyers is basically the demand of delivering the highest quality for the lowest price possible. Porter (1980, 1998, 2008b) argues that:

> powerful customers can capture more value by forcing down prices, demanding better quality or more service (thereby driving up costs), and generally playing industry participants off against one another, all at the expense of industry profitability. Buyers are powerful if they have negotiating leverage relative to industry participants, especially if they are price sensitive, using their clout primarily to pressure price reductions.

Customer power is better described in Figure 1.5.

Although Porter generally observes customers as buyers, the author's notion regarding the buyer as a force differs from Porter's observation, thus buyers as a force are not always after the most low-price items. The author suggests a wider and more holistic understanding of the customer value concept and its integration into the FFM. Thus, the ultimate objective of a business is to create a customer and to solve a customer problem or to satisfy the customer's want (Drucker, 1954).

FIGURE 1.5 The power of customers, according to Porter

Powerful customers

Bargaining power of the customer:

Customer concentration
Customer volume
Switching costs
Customer information
Customer profits
Substitute products
Pull-through
Price sensibility
Price/total purchase
Product differences
Brand identity
Ability to backward integrate
Impact on quality/performance
Decision-makers' incentives

Author's interpretation, based on Ghemawat (2002)

Force 2: powerful suppliers

Suppliers' power is the flip side of the coin. Powerful suppliers are more concentrated than the industry it sells to. Microsoft's near monopoly in operating systems – which led to many competition lawsuits against it, coupled with the fragmentation of PC assemblers – exemplified this situation precisely (Porter, 2008b). The supplier concentration, which does not depend heavily on the industry or the individual customer for its revenues, and suppliers serving many industries, will not hesitate to absorb maximum profits from each customer. Powerful suppliers and their implications are exemplified and displayed in Figure 1.6.

Force 3: substitute products

Substitutes are ever present to create a new sensation, industry customers and customer behaviours. When Apple launched its iPod, it not only revolutionized the typical mp3 industry of digital music, but moreover it shaped the way customers observe and enjoy music in general. Above all, iPod made CDs irrelevant for the music industry, just as did CDs by replacing cassettes and LPs. The same dimension is observed from the disruption by technology within the print media industry, to the music industry, and now to the whole

FIGURE 1.6 The power of suppliers, according to Porter

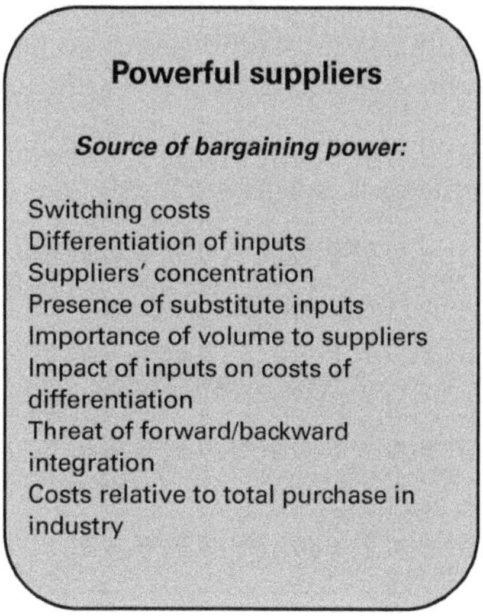

Author's interpretation, based on Ghemawat (2002)

product lifecycles of movies and visual entertainment, with the example of Netflix disrupting not only video rentals, but movie theatres, TV and the retail purchase of DVDs. These new business models of innovation within the direct consumer design–search spaces are disrupting industries that could defend themselves for many decades. Amazon, Apple and now also Disney entered these models, which created many vertical and horizontal disruptions to many businesses.

In Afghanistan and other emerging economies, for example, the surge in demand for wired telephone lines has been capped as many customers, from private consumers to industry and public officials, opt to make a mobile phone their main phone line (Porter, 2008a). In the interconnected world of today, IT and artificial intelligence (AI) have replaced not only how the typical postal industry (email vs. postal mail) works, but moreover the way we communicate and what we understand under communication. iPads, mobile devices and post-PC devices, computers, books, cameras, and watches are among the vital powers of the substitute products.

Figure 1.7 describes the power of substitute products that can be a major force according to Porter.

Force 4: new entrants

> When industry structure is in flux, new and promising competitive positions may appear. Structural changes open up new needs and new ways to serve existing needs. Established leaders may overlook these or be constrained by past strategies from pursuing them. Smaller competitors in the industry can capitalize on such changes, or the void may well be filled by new entrants (Porter, 2008b).

FIGURE 1.7 Substitute products, according to Porter

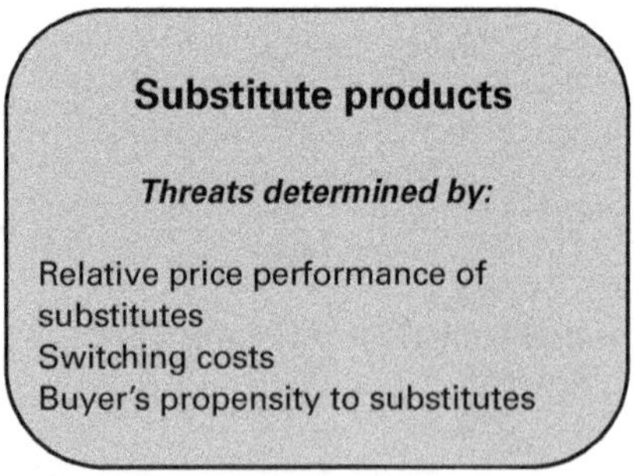

Author's interpretation, based on Ghemawat (2002)

New entrants to an industry bring new capacity and new dynamics. They can change the game, decrease prices to a very low level, even below the industry's low-price provider, and redefine the competition in that industry. New entrants can also provide more value and/or different value to the customer and even revolutionize or challenge an unattractive industry, as André Rieu and Andrea Bocelli have revolutionized the classical music industry. Figure 1.8 describes the shifting power of new entrants that can disrupt an industry structure and its share of the market between the existing rivals.

Force 5: rivalry among existing competitors

Intensive rivalry is the typical jockeying for better market position, eg more creative and effective advertisement campaigns, extended warranty, zero per cent or lower-rate credits on purchases, low-price insurance services in connection with a car or boat, etc, purchase and other service (Porter, 2008b). Figure 1.9 describes the rivalry between existing competitors within an industry.

FIGURE 1.8 The power of new entrants, according to Porter

Author's interpretation, based on Ghemawat (2002)

FIGURE 1.9 The power of industry competitors, according to Porter

Powerful industry competitors

Factors affecting rivalry:

Industry growth
Concentration and balance
Fixed costs/value added
Intermittent overcapacity
Product differences
Brand identity
Switching costs
Informational complexity
Corporate stake
Exit barriers

Author's interpretation, based on Ghemawat (2002)

According to Porter's McKinsey Foundation award-winning paper (Porter, 1980), he attributes intense rivalry to the presence of the following factors:

1. Competitors are numerous or are roughly equal in size and power. In many US industries, of course, foreign contenders have become part of the competitive picture in recent years.
2. Industry growth is slow, precipitating fights for markets share that involve expansion-minded members.
3. The product or service lacks differentiation or switching costs, which lock in buyers and protect one combatant from raids on its customers by another.
4. Fixed costs are high, or the product is perishable, creating strong temptation to cut prices. Many basic materials businesses, like paper and aluminum, suffer from this problem when demand slackens.
5. Capacity is normally augmented in large increments. Such additions, as in the chlorine and vinyl chloride businesses, disrupt the industry's supply–demand balance and often lead to periods of overcapacity and price cutting.
6. Exit barriers are high. Exit barriers, like very specialized assets or management's royalty to a particular business, keep companies competing even though they may be earning low or even negative returns on investment. Excess capacity remains functioning and the profitability of the healthy competitors suffers as the sick ones hang on. If the entire industry suffers from overcapacity, it may seek government help – particularly if foreign competition is present.

7 The rivals are diverse in strategies, origins and 'personalities'. They have different ideas about how to compete and continually run head-on into each other in the process.

Porter's wheel of competitive strategy, which drew strongly from the work of Andrews (1971) and Christensen *et al* (1987), was coined as the complete articulation of a competitive strategy and a firm's key operating policies, referring to the spokes of the wheel (Porter, 1980). This was designed to show a complete overview of how a firm competes and by which yardsticks the company measures its success and where a superb competitive position must be seen.

FIGURE 1.10 Porter's 'wheel of competitive strategy'

Based on Porter (1980)

According to Porter's wheel of competitive strategy, as described in Figure 1.10, firms compete with each other by fulfilling the portfolio of activities and pursuing economic and non-economic objectives. Porter's approach on the extensive rivalry among competitors outlined that the higher the intensity, the more value will be subtracted to the customers. Porter's main objectives were to substantiate this claim, thus shifting strategists' basic notion from a high concentration on each other to a better approach to competition, namely competing for more value generation instead of extensive rivalry with each other.

The FFM – a scientific analysis

Porter's models have revolutionized the nature of competition and competitive strategy, in practice and among academics. Porter's insights – coming from his interdisciplinary background in economics and business administration – have shaped the way managers and consultants think and how they navigate their organization in their respective industries. Figure 1.11 describes the economic heritage and embedded notion of Porter's FFM.

FIGURE 1.11 How Porter's theory derived from economics

Attractive industry	
Porter's five forces	Areas of microeconomics
Powerful supplier	Supply and demand theory, cost of production theory, price flexibility
Powerful customers	Supply and demand theory, customer behaviour, price
Power of substitute products	Effects of substitution
Threat of new entrants	Market entry barriers
Extensive rivalry	Number of competitors, market size, growth
Profitability	

Author's interpretation, based on Recklies (2008)

According to Recklies (2008):

> Porter's Five Forces model is simple. It is nothing but microeconomics. This man had locked himself in a library for a few years, had analyzed some companies and then he managed to summarize nearly the whole science of microeconomics in one single simple model. – That is the reason why all other economists hate him: they are envious because they did not see something so obvious themselves.

The FFM has been the subject of much critique and its actuality, effectiveness for strategy and its strength have been questioned by many practitioners, consultants and scholars. Among them are Mintzberg *et al* (1998), Miller (1992), Recklies (2008), Narayanan and Fahey (2005), Foss (2007), Powell *et al* (1996), Kraaijenbrink *et al* (2010), and Alvesson and Willmott (2003). Recklies (2008) observes: 'Evidence from emerging economies indicates that FFF's assumptions about the qualifiers are not met in these economies. Indeed, firms in these economies adopt strategies not derivable from FFF to tackle their unique institutional contexts.' Foss (2007) underpins:

> In contrast to most of the proponents and opponents of economics in strategy thinking, a balanced pluralist perspective is adopted. According to this, a discipline should strike a balance between the generation of new theoretical alternatives and the selection among them. Applying this general idea, I argue that the strategy field is too pluralistic, and that the unfortunate consequences of excessive pluralism and eclecticism may be remedied by economics playing a larger role in the conversation of strategy researchers. This does not necessarily mean standard neoclassical economics or new industrial organization economics; evolutionary economics, for example, is a serious contender, too. The evolution of Michael Porter's thinking is used as a case for demonstrating some of the advantages and some of the dangers of economics in the strategy field, and for illustrating points about eclecticism and pluralism.

Powell *et al* (1996) observe:

> Although Porter's competitive strategy (1980) is by far the most widely cited publication in the strategy literature (Finkelstein and Hambrick, 1990), the book's central feature – the industry framework – has attracted little empirical attention. ..., Porter's five factors reduced empirically into three independent factors – industry maturity, entry barriers, and competitive power, with rivalry, the threat of substitutes, power relative to customers and power relative to suppliers collapsing into a single variable. Only the entry barrier and competitive power main effects explain significant performance variance, with

> industry maturity impacting performance through its statistical interaction with industry barriers. The classical focus on industry analysis is mistaken because these industries are too heterogeneous to support classical theory. It is also mistaken because the most important impediments to the equilibration of long-run rates of return are not associated with industry, but with the unique endowments, position, and strategies of individual business.

Kraaijenbrink *et al* (2010) state:

> The resource-based view (RBV) of the firm has been around for over 20 years – during which time it has been both widely taken up and subjected to considerable criticism. Inasmuch as the RBV's original impulse was to critique Porter's five-force analysis (Spender, 1996; Wernerfelt, 1984), we must conclude his real estate metaphor of sustained superior positioning has done its valuable work but should now give way to the postmodern innovator's anxiety about the never-ending race against the market's own clock.

According to Alvesson and Willmott (2003):

> Some scholars firmly established in the field of strategy have critiqued the perspective, technocratic, approach represented by the work of Porter (1980, 1985), Andrews (1971) and Chandler (1962), for its reliance on a rational, logical and linear model of analysis and planning.

Grundy (2006) accounts for:

> number of important opportunities for using Porter's model in an even more practical way, including: mapping the competitive forces, which can vary significantly over market and competitive terrain and within the same industry; understanding its dynamics; prioritizing the forces; doing macro analysis of the sub-drivers of each of the five forces; exploring key interdependencies, both between and within each force.

Moore *et al* (2011) describe their experiences, which are based on the intellectual rivalry between Porter and Mintzberg, in the following way:

> Emergent strategy is the view that strategy emerges over time as intentions collide with and accommodate a changing reality. Emergent strategy is a set of actions, or behavior, consistent over time, 'a realized pattern [that] was not expressly intended' in the original planning of strategy. Emergent strategy implies that an organization is learning what works in practice. Given today's world, I think emergent strategy is on the upswing. Here's why. But first, in

> the interest of transparency, I have worked closely with Henry co-directing and co-teaching on Leadership Programs at McGill, where we are both on the faculty, for more than a decade. In fact, many times, I have presented key parts of Porter's ideas on strategy for a couple of hours and then Henry presents his ideas as a contrast to Michael's. We started doing this tag team effort about 11 years ago and it has become increasingly easy for Henry to shoot me down in the last few years. And the executives in the class agree with Henry.

Grundy (2006) further establishes the notion that:

> Michael Porter's five competitive forces model has been a most influential model within business schools but has perhaps had less appeal to the practicing manager outside of an MBA and certain short business school course..., it is argued that whilst there are a number of reasons why the model has not achieved greater currency, most importantly it can be developed a lot further.

Grundy's observations and experiences also reflect not only the author's scientific research interests, which are foundational to this book, but moreover the author's additional interest of making the FFM more practically applicable, wider in its spectrum of strategic grasp and more holistic to the strategist entering their strategy cockpit (SC) to observe the competitive reality they need to deal and cope with.

The strengths, weaknesses, opportunities and threats of the FFM

The 'being-too-static debate' of the FFM (Collis and Montgomery, 1995; Mintzberg *et al*, 2001), the 'structure vs. resources debate' in strategic positioning, planning and thinking, or the holistic views from the organizational and environmental complexity and chaos sciences in strategic and military (Durham, 1997; Glenn, 1996; van Creveld, 1985) and strategic management (Beer, 1959, 1981, 1985; Schwaninger, 1984a, 1985, 1987, 1990, 1998, 1999, 2000, 2001b, 2002, 2003, 2004b, 2006a, 2006b, 2007, 2009a, 2009b, 2010, 2014, 2015a, 2015b; Malik, 1974–2008; Hetzler, 2008) are all still ongoing. As already described in Moore's observations on his position to take Porter's views vs. Mintzberg presenting his mindset to the practitioners in this part of the book, it is essential that we take the reader deeper into the different approaches of the Porter vs. Mintzberg debate. These two scholars, above many, have had a vital impact on the way the world of strategic management has evolved, whereby their views have differed much on the subject. Moore *et al* (2011) underpin the author's claim with the following essential observation:

> There are two people, and only two, whose ideas must be taught to every MBA in the world: Michael Porter and Henry Mintzberg. This was true more than 25 years ago, when I did my MBA at USC. These are two academics who have had real impact for a long time. Part of their success, beyond having big relevant ideas, is due to their clear and concise writing skills (There is certainly a lesson in there for many of us business school academics).

As Moore further emphasizes from first-hand acquaintance with both Porter and Mintzberg, and the way managers and students observe the reality based on their own experiences, the shift in thinking towards an evolutionary and emergent notion of strategy thinking is evident. But before going further, an examination of the forces via a SWOT analysis is essential.

EVOLUTION OF THE FFM

As the author has exemplified, the FFM and its economic origin have contributed into the wider range of managers', scholars' and consultants' understanding and by its application and integration into the pursuits of positioning the organization towards the competitive forces within their industries. The following examination will visualize the forces according to Dosher *et al*'s (1960) SWOT analysis (Friesner, 2011). While Porter advocates a pure economic view black-boxed in an industry, other authors (including myself), although not completely disagreeing with him, have substantiated additional views towards strategic management. Among the most prominent in representing additional views is Richard Rumelt (1974, 1979, 1982, 1991, 1997, 2012).

STRENGTHS OF THE FFM

The strengths of the FFM are formulated, hence the essential contributions of Porter are demonstrated. Shifting the strategists' notion from a sole concentration on rivals towards other major forces that shape strategic behaviour is still a highly original and vital idea. Porter's FFM made the following contributions to strategy:

1. starting the field of strategic management and defining the broader competition in BA;
2. connecting a firm to its economic environment (industry);
3. starting the debate on competing for profits (economic perspective);
4. giving an easy-to-apply and demonstrate model, showing what firms need to do and to avoid based on a single model;
5. representing solid insights from the field of economics and the approaches in BA;

6 giving strategists a vital tool for competition and its understanding in the linear environment;
7 defining industrial structure and the positioning school of strategy;
8 starting the debate and the diagnoses of an industry's structure, the embedded forces therein and how to cope with them.

WEAKNESSES OF THE FFM

The current organizational structures require more holistic, rather than reductionist and linear, thinking to tackle the most vital strategic challenges of our day. The weaknesses of FFM are described below:

1 Representing a still very narrow view of what competition really is.
2 Sole concentration on an industry as a firm's environment, which is a limited understanding of an organization's total environment.
3 A, to some extent, static and linear notion of competition and environmental disruption.
4 No recognizable updates of the model by Porter since its inception some 40 years ago – the notion of delivering a solid response and analysing environmental calculability and predictability cannot be advocated in this era of complexity via only Porter's five forces dimension, thus by assuming that environment will not be dynamic, and competition will only arise from and within the industry.
5 The unwillingness of Porter to allow other forces to be integrated is a major starting point of the FFM doctrine's weakness – according to Krishnamurthy (2010): 'Porter (1996) has defended the model and argued that good positioning still matters. In contrast, Hax and Wilde (2002) have shown with the Delta Model that there is more to strategy than positioning'.
6 The model still represents the understanding of competition during the late 1970s and the 1980s; so much has changed and so much innovation in understanding and being able to cope with the new era is needed.
7 A reductionist lens of the notion of strategy, its spectrum and understanding makes the organization weak and leaves the strategist merely coping with surprises or losing the currency of time. This may also make the strategist deal with secondary forces, while losing focus on the big picture and the most vital force that actually challenges the organization.

8 Avoidance of the integration of other interdisciplinary sciences and models with respect to the school of thought into the FFM.
9 The FFM may be a dangerous model if other models are not integrated in it, since it does not represent viability or demonstrate a viable strategy of survival, but all pursuits are based on mere profits-oriented dimensions.
10 The model does not represent the dynamic behaviour of outside competition, structural forces, culture and adaptability; the FFM actually does not demonstrate any structural-based view of the organization's reality.
11 No internal view of organizational body, eigen behaviours, linkages, and system dynamics and structure, to leave it all to the static dimension of the value chain model, is not sufficient.
12 The FFM fails to give a creative and innovative response not only to customers within the industry but to non-customers, who buy from rivals; the essential pillar of innovative creativity starts with breaking the boundaries of industry walls.
13 The FFM does not represent a wider horizon except defending the market share against other rivals.

The FFM's application field is limited, especially in the emerging new economies. A solid example of this is within the Chinese market, where the government is a major force. This force is absent in the Porterian dimension of the FFM. Whittington (2001) has underpinned the notion in the following way: 'blithely relegates his assumption of profit objectives to a footnote and concentrates his industry analysis on five sets of economic force amongst which government and labor are almost completely lost.'

THREATS OF THE FFM

The threats of the FFM are:

1 Although the FFM explains thoroughly what the structure of the industry is, it still does not tell strategists where the journey of innovation will go beyond industry competition. This situation brings a vital strategic threat, as I have already stated: some vital threats making an industry or a product obsolete come from outside the industry. Some examples are Microsoft threatening Apple in 1996 with the introduction of Windows 95 (Rumelt, 2012), Microsoft bringing about the bankruptcy of Encyclopedia Britannica by including a cheaper version in its software for free. According to Alevizou (2002):

When multimedia technologies were introduced in the late 1980s, they were presented as valuable tools to transform and reinforce the learning potential of large reference works. Effectively, works like encyclopaedias could advance the educational value of the personal computer for home users. As a result, Microsoft grasped the opportunity to extend its influence, and in 1993 offered Encarta, a multimedia product on CD-ROM that was based on the print encyclopaedia Funk and Wagnall's. Arguably Encarta did not have the deep information of Britannica. However, it proposed an alternative value: better search capabilities, portability, entertaining media features, and was much less expensive. Those alternative value propositions and Microsoft's aggressive marketing strategy and distribution power contributed in making Encarta one of the most widely recognisable electronic encyclopaedia brand.

The same pattern can be found in Apple's transformation to challenge not only the music industry but the telecommunications, the PC, post-PC mobile devices and now the watch industry. Apple TV is making the traditional TV business obsolete and would even challenge the whole lifecycle of products, as the examples of Netflix and Amazon are demonstrating.

2. The FFM does not give an overview of what is happening outside of the industry and creation of a new industry. Thus, it reflects a narrow view of reality and strategists must see the iceberg before time runs out and a course-correction is impossible.
3. The FFM is not a holistic view of organizational, environmental and competitive reality; it merely represents, even in strategy, just part of the positioning school.
4. The FFM is an outdated model, since other major forces are shaping competition, which combined can be observed as the force of complexity.
5. The FFM does not make the organization viable nor contribute to its survival, except by balancing the organization towards forces in a perfect market.
6. The FFM lacks a systems-view-based interrelatedness and the forces are not interconnected, so that the effects of one force on the other, as well as the general notion of competing for profits, are absent. All the measurement is based purely on profitability. This notion is also dangerous; hence, some profits are endangering a vital strategic position necessary for the survival of the organization in the future.

7 The model cannot cope with the complexity of the new era, the information age and the interconnected and globalized world. Thus, as emerging economies rise and the globalized world and diverse cultures shape the future of business, a change in interaction within industries and outside of industries will occur – the FFM is not powerful enough to cope with this.
8 The FFM is solely based on the economic pillar of an organizational reality, which is not wrong, but it does not represent everything for which the strategy stands.
9 The FFM is too much a black box view of the industry, thus it does not represent emerging strategic challenges and is a partial map of reality:

> The model assumes competition as a driving force with organizations trying to derive an advantage at the expense of others. This is hardly the case today with coopetition often holding the key, strategic alliances becoming ever more popular, and virtual networks being a reality (Krishnamurthy, 2010).

OPPORTUNITIES OF THE FFM

In essence, the FFM is a solid analysis tool to understand profit-making factors and identify and exploit these forces for economic gain. The opportunities of the FFM are formulated as follows:

1 ability to distinguish and understand the temporary and cyclical changes from vital structural shifts in an industry (Porter, 2008b);
2 ability to generate more bargaining power towards suppliers;
3 ability to generate more bargaining power towards the customers;
4 maintaining an eye on the new entrant with respect to responding to the threat that it exposes;
5 adjusting the organization's product portfolio against substitute products;
6 competing against rivals in the industry, monitoring their actions and products via a systemic five forces view;
7 ability to maintain an industry-in and organization-out view from the economic perspective of an organization.

The strengths of the FFM have vital effects on the costs, market price, and investment essential for competition, thus from an industry-in perspective the profits of industry participants are tied to the forces (Porter, 2008b). Having a better application of an advanced integration of the model, especially with its enhancement to an additional sixth force, would give the strategist a powerful tool to observe not only profitability but moreover the immunization of the organization against other economic and environmental 'black swans' (Taleb, 2007).

THE FFM AND STUCK IN THE MIDDLE

The other side of the coin, namely trying to be anything to anybody, pushes the company into a position coined by Porter as 'stuck in the middle' (Porter, 1985). This means having no vital or sustainable competitive advantage for the firms in their industries. Companies that have fallen into this trap can easily be outperformed. They can only generate profits that can be attractive by being in a high-profit industry (Porter, 1986). According to Porter (1985):

> A firm that engages in each generic strategy but fails to achieve any of them is 'stuck in the middle.' It possesses no competitive advantage. This strategic position is usually a recipe for below-average performance. A firm that is stuck in the middle will compete at a disadvantage because the cost leader, differentiator, or focuser will be better positioned to compete in any segment. If a firm that is stuck in the middle is lucky enough to discover a profitable product or buyer, competitors with a sustainable competitive advantage will quickly eliminate the spoils. In most industries, quite a few competitors are stuck in the middle.

Pursuits of more than one of the above-mentioned differentiation strategies, which differ from each other widely, is vital to be understood and avoided, since otherwise the stuck in the middle fallacy is looming large. Thus, it is essential to observe that a generic strategy by itself does not lead to the sustainable competitive position a company seeks to proclaim. Therefore, a company must unconditionally be able to defend this advantage on which it has focused and has based its unique value proposition to the customer. Stuck in the middle is also considered a position where the firm has no significant advantage with respect to superiority in the previously described three generic strategies of Porter (1980). In addition, if a firm is losing to the five forces described above, it is also stuck between those and losing its ground of profitability to one or many of the forces; therefore, it cannot proclaim a winning or dominant position in responding to customer profitably as others do. Stuck in the middle also describes a position of low profitability with an eventual loss of control over the firm's success. Failing in having a strategy that is viable is the precursor to failing in a business endeavour and the firm is going to collapse sooner or later.

If the navigator of the firm loses control and the stronger position to bargain effectively with the forces, this reduces their 'better alternative to negotiated agreement' (BATNA) with partners and suppliers, hence suppliers may want to force a renegotiation and take sides with rivals (Fisher *et al*, 1991). In addition, suppliers may give competitors better deals, rivals' profits may grow larger, and this can lead to a position where the rival can defend a better low-cost position. Furthermore, the strategist's 'zone of possible agreement' (ZOPA) (Fisher *et al*, 1991) may reduce itself to the strategist's disadvantage.

The fourth generic force that the author has introduced is based on the 'structure is strategy debate', which establishes the notion further that firms that cannot execute well or act in a timely way on the needs of the market may lose their competitive advantages, where execution requires a viable structure that can focus while seeing the big picture and not lose their focus on the detailed tailored strategy.

Limits of the FFM

As has been discussed thoroughly during the book, the FFM has a solely economic view of the strategic landscape, wherein an organization's competition takes place. According to Ghemawat (2002):

> Other strategists have argued that some very limiting assumptions were built into such a framework and the Porter framework made three tacit but crucial assumptions: First, that an industry consists of a set of unrelated buyers, sellers, substitutes, and competitors that interact at arm's length. Second, that wealth will accrue to players that are able to erect barriers against competitors and potential entrants, or, in other words, that the source of value is structural advantage. Third, that uncertainty is sufficiently low that you can accurately predict participants' behavior and choose a strategy accordingly.

Coyne and Subramaniam (1996) argue that strategy in today's world is a demanding, complex and subtle discipline; however, this truth has been widely missing in the contemporary strategic management literature and academia. 'Each season brings a new crop of experts proclaiming that their frameworks – core competencies, customer retention, time-based competition, total quality management, "white spaces", managing chaos and value migration – are definitive' (Coyne and Subramaniam, 1996). The following examples may clarify the point:

1 How should strategists decide, if they need to make a $1 billion 'yes or no' decision on whether they will invest in a certain type of technology or new industry to bring more value to their customers?
2 How should strategists of a software firm position themselves towards their largest supplier or customers, who are also their main and chief competitors?
3 How should strategists in the financial or banking industry position themselves strategically towards a rapid change or product cycles that vary every six months?
4 How can strategists position themselves towards competitors who are outside of the industry? The facts are already revealed to the reader above.
5 How can strategists position themselves towards a competitive force yet unknown to them? How can they respond to an attack and how can they counterattack, while not losing the sight of both the big and small picture?
6 How can a regional banker or retailer position itself for value towards a local competitor if all the vital decisions are met centrally?
7 How can a strategist position itself towards a business environment where the change is the state in the business affairs, in comparison with the times, where there was a state, then came the change, then there was a new state (Bea and Haas, 1997)?
8 How can strategists position themselves towards a rival who actually has a strategic perspective of 30 or 40 years of positioning their organization, in comparison with the contemporary strategic fashion, where they need to deliver on objectives, which are within cycles of three to six months?
9 How can strategists compete for value if the most vital force that distinguishes between winner and loser is the structure, culture and capability to execute of the firm (Coyne and Subramaniam, 1996)?
10 What additionally is not observed by the FFM is whether the industry opportunity is one that can be exploited by the firm in question – that is, does the firm have the structure, the vision and competencies to compete in this market and in the long run?

According to Coyne and Subramaniam (1996) and the author's added scenarios, more than 50 per cent of cases lie outside of Porter's FFM's application and effectiveness and the conditions wherein described, which actually started the competitive strategy field. This substantiates the author's claim that economic and industry-driven strategy is insufficient to cope with the overall strategic challenges a strategist needs to dissolve *avant la lettre*. But this claim can be widened in perspective that no other strategy model so far can embark on all the threats and challenges that the strategist faces (Coyne and Subramaniam, 1996).

These threats combined cause a complex strategic problem that requires a holistic response and understanding of the affairs and their dynamics. It is the chief objective of the book to shed some light and progress towards designing a holistic model that comes closer to understanding complex strategic challenges.

PRACTICAL APPLICATION OF THE FFM

The FFM can be better applied only if all industry structure is based on rational but predictable competitors and actors. Some sets of circumstances where the model can be applied are described below. Thus, the industry is based on a set of unrelated and unconnected groups of buyers, customers, rivals and substitutes acting, reacting and counter-reacting to each other:

1. All of the actors are competing for profits.
2. The rivals view competition from a micro-economic lens by the industry-in lens.
3. The forces of regulation such as government are merely a factor, not a vital force.
4. The market is calm and predictable, as are the competitors.
5. The rate of change, uncertainty and turbulence is calculable; the strategist can make precise predictions of the market and environmental development.
6. The strategist can strongly predict rivals', customers' and suppliers' behaviours, and calculate the number or the option they have, so that they can react strategically to their behaviours.
7. Entry and exit barriers are measurable for all rivals, and positioning the organization into the structure of the industry is vital: 'structure advantage is source of value' (Coyne and Subramaniam, 1996).

In general, the author adheres that the FFM is an industry-locked and partially resource-based view, which the firm's environment and the approach of the strategy is based on. The industry is defined largely as being homogeneous, and competition is seen as occurring via positioning in respective industries. The industry-based view embeds the strategic challenge to see and identify attractive industries and markets, wherein to compete.

The RBV, however, was much popularized by Hamel and Prahalad in their ground-breaking book *Competing for the Future* (Hamel and Prahalad, 1994). Thus, the authors conceptualized the firm as a bundle of resources. Many other scholars agree, such as Malik (2011), who sees management and organization as the transformation of resources into benefits. This view underpins that the way the resources are gained, and the way they are combined, make the firm different from others and in turn allow a firm to deliver products and services in the market. The better they can allocate the resources, the stronger position they can acquire in their industries.

Porter's assumption that markets are a zero-sum game and that all the firms embedded in a certain industry are in pursuit of a perfect game has shifted strategists' attention from customer value to merely a forces-related industry-in environment of competition by seeing the organizational reality solely based on juggling between the forces for more profits. However, the 2008 strategy crisis revealed the vulnerability of firms in diverse industries and the inability of Porter's model to prepare firms for these crises or save them from their abyss.

The author sees the organization as a set of sub-systems, which are viable themselves in terms of autonomy and decisions, structured recursively and acting in unison to achieve a larger objective. This objective must be at first the guarantor of the firm's survival, thus firms are goal-achieving beings. One of the objectives is beyond the notion of seeing customers as buyers, who are a group to squeeze profits from; a solid strategist sees customers not as a force but more as *raison d'être* of the organization. Drucker's words, 'the purpose of a business is to create a customer', must be at the heart of every strategy (Drucker, 1954). Indeed, defining strategy just based on five forces and relating all of them to a land-locked industry-in view may not be the whole story, whereby a firm's survival may be guaranteed and on which the firm's ultimate objectives are founded.

AN ANATOMY OF COMPETITIVE STRATEGY

The firm's inputs and outputs, its behaviour and actions, and how it transforms its structure and preserves its identity or advances it, connects the firm from the present to the future. The strategist can generally adhere that within the set and bundle of activities of the firm lies its future. The strategist's main objective is not only to transform the organization so that it fits in the environment and the challenges of the future, but to see that the future is also designed favourably, so the organization is actually capable of delivering answers, products and solutions based on innovation and the Drucker logic of the 'customer want' (Drucker, 1954).

Distinguishing between strategy and action, as Rumelt (2012) describes, is a vital flaw in understanding strategy:

> Many people assume that a strategy is a big-picture overall direction, divorced from any specific action. But defining strategy as broad concepts, thereby leaving out action, creates a wide chasm between 'strategy' and 'implementation.' If you accept this chasm, most strategy work becomes wheel spinning. Indeed, this is the most common complaint about 'strategy'. Echoing many others, one top executive told me, 'We have a sophisticated strategy process, but there is a huge problem of execution. We almost always fall short of the goals we set for ourselves.'

To demonstrate the author's claim, a solid picture of Apple's struggle for survival and how Steve Jobs transformed it from a bankrupt organization to the Olympus of excellence is given below.

When Steve Jobs took over Apple again in 1997 the organization was actually bankrupt; it could only afford to stay in business for the next two months as its cash reserves had vanished. In 1995 Microsoft released its Windows 95 multimedia operating system; this caused Apple to fall into a death spiral. On 5 February 1996, *Business Week* put Apple's famous trademark on its cover to illustrate its lead story: 'The Fall of an American Icon.' CEO Gilbert Amelio struggled for Apple's viability in a world being rapidly dominated by Windows-Intel-based PCs. He laid off people and reorganized the company's many products into four groups: (1) Macintosh, (2) information appliances, (3) printers, and (4) peripherals and 'alternative platforms'. A new 'Internet Services Group' was additionally added to the 'Operating Systems Group' and the 'Advanced Technology Group'. But the case was lost, and Apple's crisis was serious. The bankruptcy was due in September. Steve Jobs, who had co-founded the company with his friend Steve Wozniak in 1976, agreed to return to serve on a reconstructed board of directors and to be interim CEO without pay (Rumelt, 2012). Many fans of the original Macintosh computer were overjoyed, but the general business world and their analysts were not expecting much (Rumelt, 2012).

What would the strategist need to do if they or their organization has fallen that far? If the reader has followed the line of the book's argument and logic, they can distinguish a clear path on which the author's claims are grounded. Jobs needed to concentrate on one focused but vital notion of strategy, namely a combination of three different sets of actions and activities to ensure the ultimate strategic objective – Apple's survival:

- diagnosing Apple's state of crises, challenges and problems;
- drawing a precise, detailed and diverse set of activities into a dynamic plan for the whole firm;
- executing the plan, taking all the obstacles and challenges from attaining a right-away liquidity to survive to the launch of the iPod, what Jobs called the next big thing (Rumelt, 2012).

According Rumelt (2012):

> A good strategy includes a set of coherent actions. They are not 'implementation' details; they are the punch in the strategy. A strategy that fails to define a variety of plausible and feasible immediate actions is missing a critical component. Executives who complain about 'execution' problems have usually confused strategy with goal setting. When the 'strategy' process is basically a game of setting performance goals – so much market share and so much profit, so many students graduating high school, so many visitors to the museum – then there remains a yawning gap between these ambitions and action.

Organizational crises emerge when an organization fails to attain, transform, and adapt itself to its environment while it navigates the stormy waters of change, turbulence, longevity and unpredictability. Figure 1.12 exemplifies how organizations collapse, and how crises emerge and get stronger in a certain time period. The reader can comprehend how Apple's crises emerged and how Jobs corrected the course of Apple's direction from failing to being a star and the unique company it has become. Another notion that Figure 1.12 displays, which is a vital strategic significance, is that the game of strategy and the uncertain environment that surrounds its decision-making is to some extent traceable and predictable – thus it is the author's chief conviction that before the organization collapses or the organization or firm has a success problem, the strategist's strategy must fail first. Thus, by being able to design and act in the pre-problem phase, many crises can be avoided and many firms saved. It is therefore the purpose of strategy to dissolve problems before having to act in surgical measure to rescue just a part of the firm. Jobs' actions resemble the surgeon who intends to just keep the core alive.

FIGURE 1.12 How crises emerge and organizations collapse

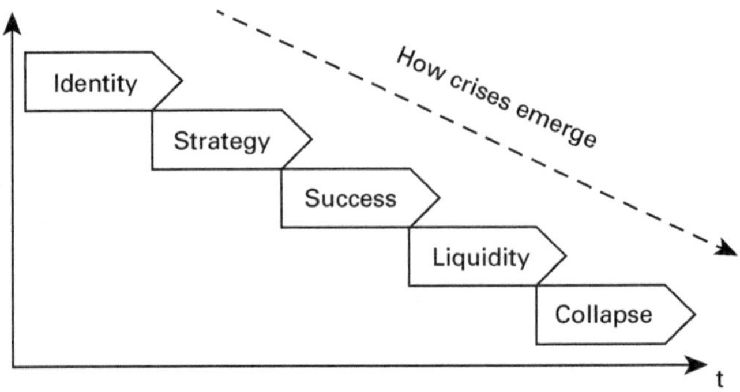

Author's own interpretation

Wired magazine carried an article titled '101 Ways to Save Apple' (Daly, 1997). Analysts' suggestions and comments included:

> Key question: Why save Apple? It isn't entirely obvious why a company whose management has done as much destruction to shareholders, employees, vendors, and customers ought to be saved. More to the point, what does save really mean? Besides why, we need to consider who and what, in addition to the implied how. Having been flamed – mindlessly and sometimes venomously – by Guy Kawasaki's Mac-addict brown shirts, I hesitate to make any formal recommendation. However, emboldened perhaps by a glass of adequate merlot, I will offer this utterly hypothetical speculation as grist for lateral thinking: maybe Apple's shareholders should sell what is left of Apple to Steve Jobs's Pixar for, say, $400 million. (Lewis J. Perelman, president of Kanbrain Institute)

> Apple should: 1. Merge with Nintendo – this moves the brand into the consumer space and under one management team. 2. Buy Gateway – out with the cow spots and in with the Apple logo. 3. License Windows 95 and NT – keep the guts of the OS and work exclusively on making the Windows GUI just like the Mac. (Ann Winblad, principal at Hummer Winblad Venture Partners)

> I'm a Mac lover, but last year I switched over completely to Windows because Apple couldn't build a reasonable laptop. I really want it to succeed, but I think the company's finished. Software vendors aren't turning out enough code to keep the Mac as a really good platform, even for family and school stuff. This whole NeXT decision seems to be a waste of time. It should have been sold to HP for $35 per share a year and a half ago. Maybe if Apple caves in, Windows will get so much market share that the Department of Justice will intervene and

break up Microsoft. I think Windows competition is really the NC- and WebTV-type box. Which is truly sad. (Milo Medin, president of @Home)

Repurpose entirely and sell actual apples – the fruit, that is. It could hybridize in special orchards south of Santa Clara, California, and release Apple 1.0 in time for the fall pie season. (Jon Carroll, newspaper columnist)

At a certain critical point – perhaps five years ago – Apple stopped investing time, effort, brainpower, and money in continuing to make a better product. Instead, it dissipated its energy on everything but the Macintosh – on Newton, Sweet Pea, Kaleida, Taligent. Meanwhile, the rest of the world caught up. The last great engineering task accomplished on the Mac was the switch to PowerPC. However, no new features went in. The company that had been the leader in operating systems found that it could no longer write an operating system – Copland was a disaster that never shipped. It had to suffer the ultimate ignominy of buying one outside. The NeXT purchase is too little too late. The Apple of the past was an innovative company that used software and hardware technology together to redefine the way people experienced computing. That Apple is already dead. Very adroit moves might be able to save the brand name. A company with the letters A-P-P-L-E in its name might survive, but it won't be the Apple of yore. (Nathan Myhrvold, chief technology officer at Microsoft)

The suggestions of *Wired* magazine are too many to display, but the reader is advised to see Daly (1997) for additional views on how to save Apple.

Jobs transformed the firm within a year. Contrary to adding products or introducing advanced technology, which was expected of him, Jobs cut all computers to only one 'the Mac 3'; he cut all of the printers business and additional ballast. According to Jobs:

The product line up was too complicated and the company was bleeding cash. A friend of the family asked me which Apple computer she should buy. She couldn't figure out the differences among them and I couldn't give her clear guidance, either. I was appalled that there was no Apple consumer computer priced under $2,000. We are replacing all of those desktop computers with one, the Power Mac G3. We are dropping five of six national retailers – meeting their demand has meant too many models at too many price points and too much markup (Rumelt, 2012).

According to Rumelt (2012): Jobs convinced Bill Gates of Microsoft – who was suffering from a major anti-trust suit, where Apple's bankruptcy would have enhanced Microsoft's losing position much more in front of the anti-trust commission – to invest $150 million in Apple – giving Apple the ability to survive another six months. As the reader knows, the rest is history:

> Having a coherent strategy – one that coordinates policies and actions. A good strategy doesn't just draw on existing strength; it creates strength through the coherence of its design. Most organizations of any size don't do this. Rather, they pursue multiple objectives that are unconnected with one another or, worse, that conflict with one another. (...) The power of Jobs's strategy came from directly tackling the fundamental problem with a focused and coordinated set of actions. He did not announce ambitious revenue or profit goals; he did not indulge in messianic visions of the future. And he did not just cut in a blind ax-wielding frenzy – he redesigned the whole business logic around a simplified product line sold through a limited set of outlets (Rumelt, 2012).

Apple's rise from the abyss and object of ridicule to the trendsetter – not only in its own industry but being a trendsetter and game changer in additional industries such as music, IT and telecommunications, the way people use and observe computers, the internet, and enjoy, store and distribute music, movies and data – is beyond comparison in the recent history. It transformed many industries and created the best technology brand in contemporary history. What would have happened if Jobs followed the advice of Jon Carroll, a newspaper columnist, who told him: 'Repurpose entirely and sell actual apples – the fruit that is. It could hybridize in special orchards south of Santa Clara, California, and release Apple 1.0 in time for the fall pie season' (Daly, 1997).

The FFM and competitive advantage

The terms 'competitive advantage' (CA) (Porter, 1985) and 'sustainable competitive advantage' (SCA) were both coined by Porter and belong to the two pivotal and to some extent strategic objectives a firm can achieve. According to Porter: 'The strongest competitive force or forces determine the profitability of an industry and become the most important to strategy formulation. The most salient force, however, is not always obvious' (Porter, 2008a). Establishing a position where the organization can maintain a high profit position is vital to the firm for creating a competitive advantage over its rivals. The FFM gives the strategist the ability to create this position by analysing the organization through its five defined forces analysis. However, a competitive advantage can only be created if the firm is able to defend the position in its industry over a long period of time. While maintaining the superior position it can create additional value as economies of scale by leveraging its product performance in the market, negotiating additional or better deals with suppliers and customers. According to Porter (2008a), the point of conducting industry analysis is not to define whether an industry is attractive or not, but to understand the underpinnings of competition and the root causes of profitability. While Porter's definition of competitive advantage rests on the firm's profitability, additional views must be taken under consideration to establish a competitive advantage that cannot be easily copied. The strategist needs to define a clear action path for the organization, where they see the competitive advantage of their firm to be created. This can mean different things for different firms. While for a shareholder-oriented firm, since its model is based on short-term achievements, it can mean good financial data over the last three to six months, and how that organization has performed, for a family business or entrepreneurial-run organization, it can mean how the organization has established a set of actions that actually ensures the viability of the firm for generations. The FFM is a good place to start to understand and differentiate a firm by the set of concentrated actions towards a position of profitability; however, additional models – as it is the objective of this book – are essential to be established and integrated, so a surprise action and threat from an unknown force can be ruled out. The Porterian mindset establishes the notion that prevailing in the five forces within the industry enables the strategist to maintain an advantageous position in that industry. Porter's notion is correct, and as already stated many times the only challenge is that it requires a highly stable market with less disruption and a narrow field of environmental reality shared by predictable rivals and the whole system that constructs the FFM.

The FFM and generic strategies

Above-average and superb performance of a firm comes from its position of being able to maintain and defend an SCA. A firm may have some weaknesses and strengths in comparison with its competitors; however, there are two basic positions of competitive advantage that firms can possess, namely low cost and differentiation (Porter, 1985). Thus, the significance of the weaknesses and strengths comes from the industry structure in which the firm is embedded. But moreover, they result from the firm's ability to better cope and to out-manoeuvre the rivals by the application of the FFM (Porter, 2008b). It's precisely the choices that a firm makes that transform it into a high-performing organization. Thus, a firm in a very poor industry may still be able to outperform competitors in profits, while another firm is actually outsmarted and outperformed by its rivals in a highly profitable industry (Porter, 1985). The industry, its profitability and the position of the firm is embedded regardless if their profitability abruptly changes. The attractiveness of an industry can vary and be dependent on diverse factors and regulations, where the firms do not have vital control over it (Porter, 1985); however, a firm can apply better competitive strategies and choices of things to do or not to do, and establish itself as a top-tier company within the industry. '[A] firm can clearly improve or erode its position within an industry through the choice of strategy. Competitive strategy then not only responds to the environment but also attempts to shape that environment in a firm's favour' (Porter, 1985). It is the purpose of the strategist to shape the environment for a better ability to higher growth and success of the organization; however, this must be based on a long-term view and with minimum damage to the society.

The FFM and blue ocean strategy

A fundamental work on changing the way firms compete was introduced by Kim and Mauborgne (2005): *The Blue Ocean Strategy*. According to Kim and Mauborgne:

> Blue ocean strategy challenges companies to break out of the red ocean of bloody competition by creating uncontested market space that makes the competition irrelevant. Instead of dividing up existing – and often shrinking – demand and benchmarking competitors, blue ocean strategy is about growing demand and breaking away from the competition (Kim and Mauborgne, 2005).

Although this work was strongly criticized by Magretta (2012), Porter's protégé, who described it 'as a misconception worth highlighting' (Magretta, 2012), the fact of the matter is that the blue ocean approach is a newer and more profitable way in how managers, entrepreneurs and existing firms involved in heavy competition can break free to change the industry, but moreover to achieve higher values over the long run. However, scholars such as Burke (2009), in his research paper *Blue Ocean versus Competitive Strategy: Theory and Evidence*, examines these two models and underpins the view:

> existing blue ocean literature does not provide distinction between short-term and long-term strategic time horizons. This means that managers choose either blue ocean or competitive strategy irrespective of any time horizon. We construct

> a model capable of investigating this time horizon and find that the short term (i.e., the period during which equilibrium-restoring forces are at work) appears dominated by competitive strategy (red ocean) effects while the long term appears consistent with blue ocean. As a result, the analysis provides a level of synthesis between blue ocean and competitive strategy uncovering a more complex environment where managers implement an inter-temporal strategic blend of blue ocean and competitive strategy. Put differently, a firm which is currently in a competitive (red ocean) market and which aspires to find a blue ocean, will still need to be able to compete in the short term in order to remain viable while it gradually achieves this longer-term blue ocean objective. This evidence is in fact consistent with the innovation strategy outlined by Boston Consulting Group's seminal business portfolio matrix where a firm can use revenue from a 'cash cow' which is gradually becoming a 'dog' (i.e. in an increasingly red ocean market) to fund the development of 'question marks' into 'rising stars' (i.e. to find a blue ocean).

Figures 1.13 and 1.14 describe the author's combination of the two dominated theories of Porter by his vision of competition within the industry for value and the blue ocean competition based on innovation. The author's notion is a much broader definition of competition, thus the author not only combines both doctrines but also represents the notion that the competition of the future takes place based on a viable and high-quality organizational structure, which not only makes immunity possible but moreover the holistic perspective, which is vital to strategy (Kamran, 2011a, 2011b, 2012a).

Kim and Mauborgne (2005), with their strategy approach, did not create a new industry or a new path into the field of strategy. Many companies have developed breakthrough products and ground-breaking innovations. Blue ocean opportunities have always existed. However, their contribution is to establish a systemic analysis of how value for the customers and the firm is and could be innovated, how firms can exploit opportunities outside of their industry or by observing the industry, the industry illusion, the customers and their perceptions of value with a different outside-of-the-industry-box lens. With their approach, opportunities that transform the whole meaning of competition can be achieved:

> As they have been explored, the market universe has been expanding. This expansion, we believe, is the root of growth. Yet poor understanding exists both in theory and in practice as to how to systematically create and capture blue oceans (Kim and Mauborgne, 2005).

FIGURE 1.13 FFM and the industry challenger defining a new market/industry by redefining competition, based on blue ocean strategy

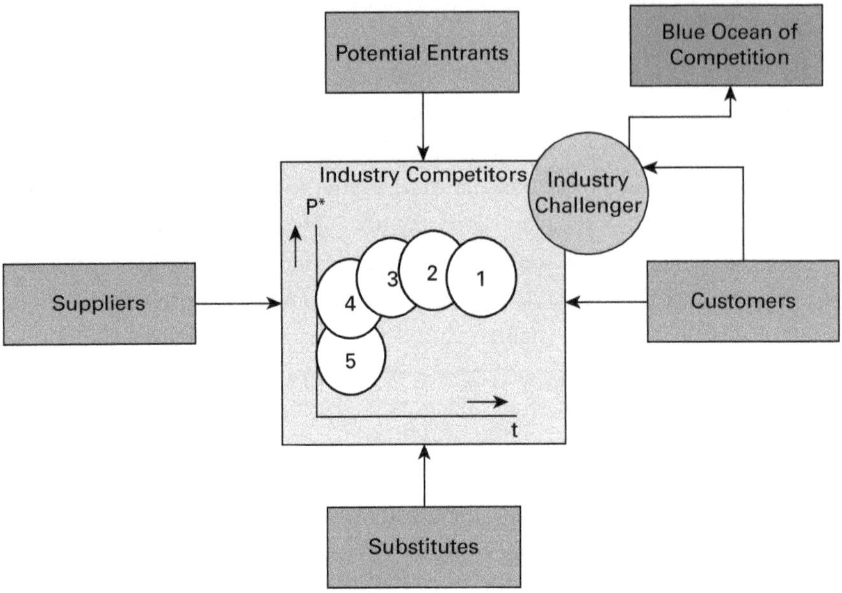

Author's interpretation, based on Porter (1980) and Kamran (2013a)

FIGURE 1.14 FFM and the industry challenger defining a new market/industry by redefining competition beyond the linearity of the five forces

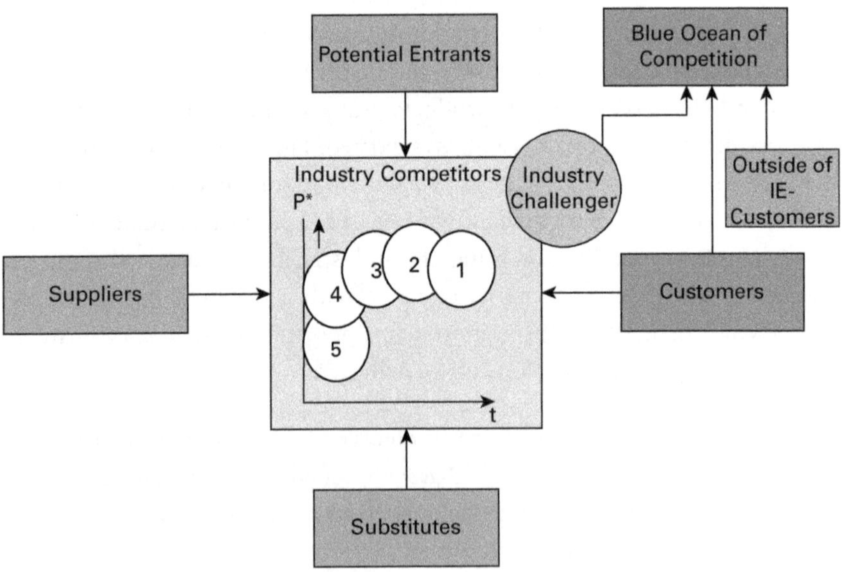

*IE (industry economics)
Author's interpretation, based on Porter (1980)

They argue and criticize the way competition has been established and widely understood, mainly by the Porterian view of strategy of an industry landlocked view, which they have coined the 'red ocean of competition':

> Since the ground-breaking work of Porter (1980, 1985), competition vis a vis a direct rival or between the actors within the industry has occupied the center and core of strategic thinking, and how competition is defined. Unfortunately, this resulted in that blue oceans are largely uncharted. The dominant focus of strategy work over the past twenty-five years has been on competition-based red ocean strategies (Kim and Mauborgne, 2005).

Although a solid and in-depth understanding of how competition in red oceans is carried out – which has been established by Porter via analysing the underlying economic structure of an existing industry and choosing a strategic position of either low cost, differentiation or focus – is vital, the thinking and tools to innovate outside of the industry and make unprofitable industries more profitable have been widely missing. Moreover, there have been little practical insights on how to create these blue oceans and how to give strategists some precise sets of tools to polish their handicraft, to innovate not only the products, but moreover innovate whole industries. 'Without analytic frameworks to create blue oceans and principles to effectively arrange risk, creating blue oceans has remained wishful thinking that is seen as too risky for managers to pursue as strategy' (Kim and Mauborgne, 2005). Figure 1.15 reveals how the FFM as described by many as 'too static, and linear', can be transformed to more creative and trend-setting competitive models and behaviours, where 'the creative destructionist' (Schumpeter, 1942) strategist in the Schumpeterian lens is the true game-changer of industry and innovation. Thus, good examples can be seen by the rise of Apple, Tesla, Space-X, Netflix, Amazon and many more.

Although the author in Figures 1.13 and 1.14 observed both models of competition, which have much in common in terms of the value-based competition or the innovation-based view of competition, Figure 1.16 outlines some of the essential differences in the author's approach to competition.

Schumpeter (1942) observed:

> The opening of new markets foreign or domestic, and the organizational development from the craft shop and factory to such concerns as the US Steel illustrate the same process of industrial mutation – if I may use that biological term – that incessantly revolutionizes the economic structure from within, incessantly destroying the old one, incessantly creating the new one. This process of Creative Destruction is the essential fact about capitalism (Schumpeter, 1942).

FIGURE 1.15 Transition from the FFM, zero-sum, market share-focused and industry-locked competition, to blue oceans of competition

	Head-to-Head Competition		Blue Ocean Creation
Industry	Focuses on rivals within its industry	→	Looks across alternative industries
Strategic group	Focuses on competitive position within strategic group	→	Looks across strategic groups within industry
Buyer group	Focuses on better serving the buyer group	→	Redefines the industry buyer group
Scope of product or service offering	Focuses on maximizing the value of product and service offerings within the bounds of its industry	→	Looks across to complementary product and service offerings
Functional-emotional orientation	Focuses on improving price performance within the functional-emotional orientation of its industry	→	Rethinks the functional-emotional orientation of its industry
Time	Focuses on adapting to external trends as they occur	→	Participates in shaping external trends over time

Author's interpretation, based on Kim and Mauborgne (2005)

FIGURE 1.16 Difference between FFM and the blue ocean strategy

Red Ocean Strategy	Blue Ocean Strategy
• Compete in an existing marketplace • Beat the competition • Exploit existing demand • Make the value/cost trade-off • Align the whole system of a firm's activities with its strategic choice of differentiation or low cost	• Create an uncontested marketplace • Make the competition irrelevant • Create and capture new demand • Beat the value/cost trade-off • Align the whole system of a firm's activities in pursuit of differentiation and low cost

Author's interpretation, based on Kim and Mauborgne (2005)

The blue ocean strategy fits well into the Schumpeterian economics – as the Porterian economic view constructed the FFM, so does the blue ocean strategy deliver a different notion, where innovation and creative destruction bring a better strategic foresight and ability. Schumpeter (1942) stated:

> The first thing to go is the traditional conception of the modus operandi of competition. Economists are at long last emerging from the stage in which price competition was all they saw. As soon as quality competition and sales efforts are admitted into the sacred precincts of theory, the price variable is

> ousted from its dominant position. However, it is still competition within a rigid pattern of invariant conditions, methods of production and forms of industrial organization in particular, that particularly monopolizes attention. But in capitalist reality as distinguished from the textbook picture, it is not that kind of competition which counts but competition from the new commodity, the new technology, the new source of supply, the new type of organization (the largest-scale of control for instance) – competition which commands a decisive cost or control quality advantage and which strikes at the margins of the profits and of outputs of the existing firm but at their foundations and their lives.

This does not mean that via the industry-based and competitive advantage lens of Porter's FFM no innovation is possible; however, if you look, for example, at Apple, the most innovative company in our era, its transformation can be clearly traced back to its unique approach to product, industry and value innovation. Apple is today appealing to old and young, to professionals, to universities and to private people, thus it has challenged diverse industries and disrupted many. The move to enter the TV and entertainment business to compete with Netflix, Amazon Prime and Disney – even though Apple developed a long-term solid business relationship with the latter – is another reminder that the firm does not neglect new industries and is entering many industries with a synergy to the original Apple business model.

Figure 1.17 reveals value innovation radically increases the appeal of a good, transforming the demand curve from (D1) to (D2). The price policy is applied strategically and is shifted from (P1) to (P2) to capture mass customization in the newly created and expanded market. The resulting enhancement of the product's sales volume from (Q1) to (Q2) and the creation of strong brand recognition are further features for unprecedented value and its innovation. Thus, the firm engages here in target costing to simultaneously reduce the long-run average cost curve from (LRAC1) to (LRAC2) to expand its ability to profit and to prevent free-riding and imitation. This result is a win-win situation: buyers receive a leap in value, transforming the consumer surplus from (axb) to (eyf), while the company earns a leap in profit and growth, game-changing the profit zone from (abcd) to (efgh) (Kim and Mauborgne, 2005).

Figure 1.18 shows how Cirque du Soleil has achieved a vital strategic position and customer attraction by applying the blue ocean strategy. The main sequence of how blue ocean strategy is created consists of four steps:

1. buyer's utility;
2. price;

FIGURE 1.17 How innovation shapes dynamic markets

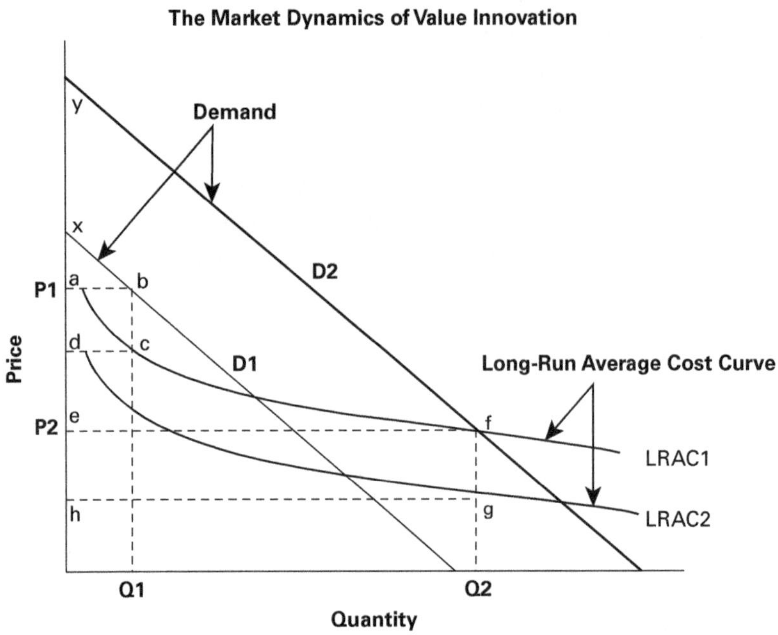

Author's interpretation, based on Kim and Mauborgne (2005)

FIGURE 1.18 How Cirque du Soleil innovated company and customer value via the blue ocean strategy

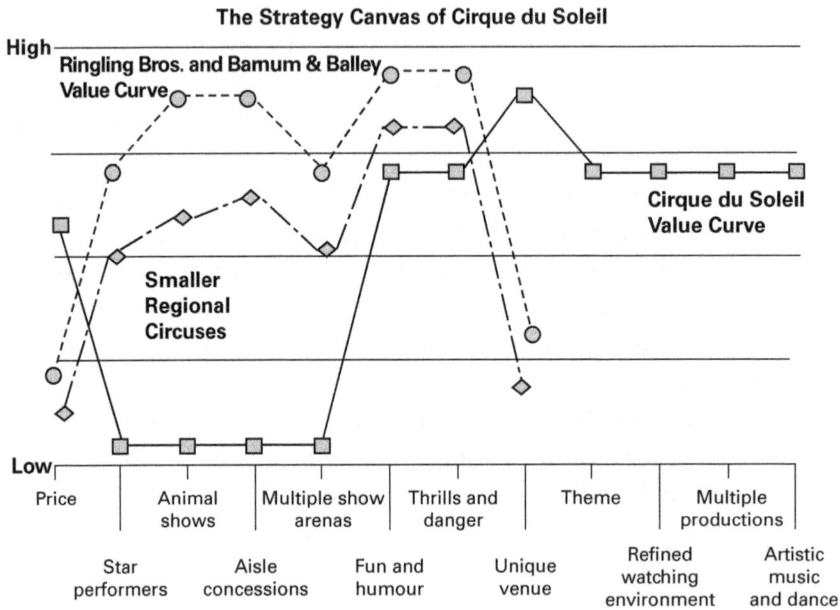

Author's interpretation, based on Kim and Mauborgne (2005)

3 cost;

4 adaptation.

To display for the reader how blue ocean strategy is applied based on the four pillars described above, Figure 1.19 outlines the fundamentals of blue ocean thinking. This model has a very well-functioning system of analysis, whereby customer value engineering is at the centre of model generation. The starting point is buyer utility:

> Does your offering unlock exceptional utility? Is there a compelling reason for the mass of people to buy it? Absent this, there is no blue ocean potential to begin with. Here there are only two options. Park the idea or rethink it until you reach an affirmative answer (Kim and Mauborgne, 2005).

FIGURE 1.19 How ideas are created

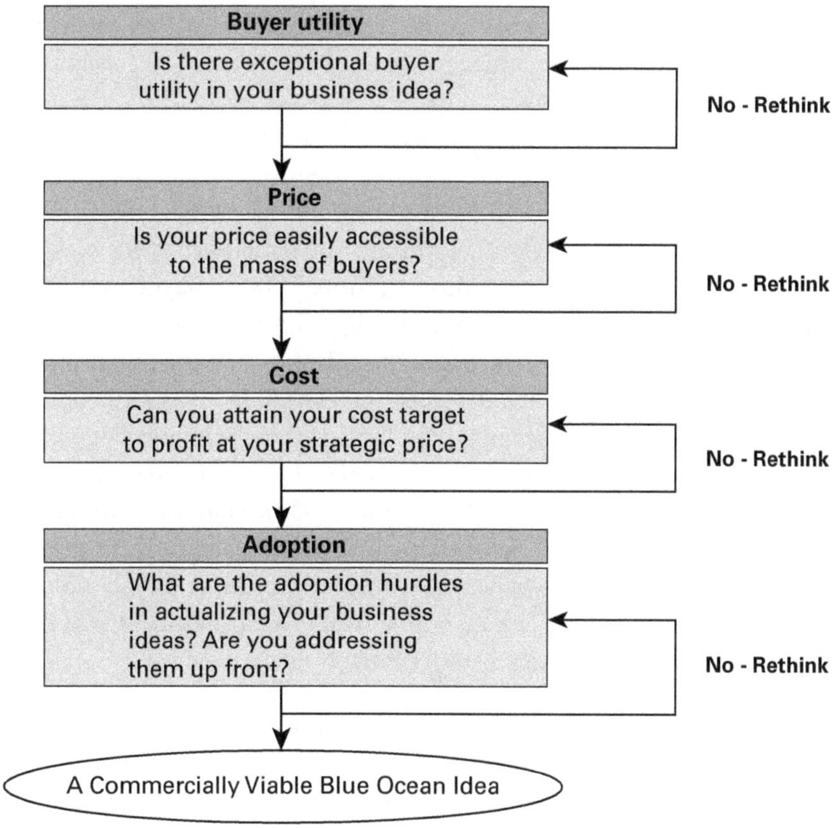

Author's interpretation, based on Kim and Mauborgne (2005)

Burke (2009) concludes his research by stating: 'To investigate the prevalence of either strategic school of thought in reality, a theoretic model is outlined illustrating how blue ocean and competitive strategies are not necessarily discrete choice substitutes but may co-exist as short and long-term strategic priorities.' Hence, the comprehensive empirical evidence that corroborated their investigation based on the Dutch retail industry displayed the prevalence of the blue ocean model vs. the competitive strategy drawing back to Porter. While over the long term the blue ocean strategy dominates, in the short term the Porterian red ocean has also displayed visible merits. However, blue ocean dominates clearly from the period of 1982–2000 via the sample, delivered by Burke, which resembles a useful scholarly laboratory for the investigated debate between both oceans. While the results show that blue ocean does not make the competition irrelevant, it still takes approximately 20–25 years to resonate back to 10 per cent deviation between the actual and the equilibrium number of firms back to equilibrium. This dimension corroborates that in the wider sense the blue ocean would become a red ocean within the period stated above, but between this state of back to equilibrium much long-term profits could be generated.

The FFM and competitive moves

The FFM detects threats from the rival from the firms' two typical vulnerabilities, namely the threat of new entrants or established rivals seeking to reposition themselves in the industry (Porter, 1985). According to Porter (1980), the first place to start in considering competitive moves is the general degree of instability in the industry or the industry-wide conditions that may mean a move will ignite a widespread retaliation. Industry structure has a strong influence on the position of the rivals within the industry; it pressures competitors to make aggressive moves, and influences the degree to which their interests may create a conflict (Porter, 1980). Thus, the starting point, whether a firm is considering offensive or defensive moves, is the degree of instability or the industry-wide condition and the firm's position within the industry (Porter, 1980). The ease or difficulty of competitive moves is a result of the industry structure wherein the firm is embedded.

> In most industries a central characteristic of competition is that firms are mutually dependent: firms feel the effects of each other's moves and are prone to react to them. In this situation, which the economists call an oligopoly, the outcome of a competitive move by one firm depends at least to some extent on the reaction of

> its rival. 'Bad' or 'irrational' reactions by competitors (even weaker competitors) can often make 'good' strategic moves unsuccessful (Porter, 1980).

Although firms' severe rivalry with each other generally squeezes out the profits to the disadvantage of the industry and more towards the customers, it can in some circumstances result in the improvement of one of the rivals' market position, provided the price war or the competitive moves are calculated based on the knowledge or pre-knowledge of the other rivals' possible retaliation alternatives. Thus, entering into a price war with a competitor without having a sustainable low-cost position is a clear recipe for disaster. According to Porter (1996):

> In many industries, however, what some call Hypercompetition is a self-inflicted wound, not the inevitable outcome of a changing paradigm of competition. The root of the problem is the failure to distinguish between operational effectiveness and strategy. The quest for productivity, quality, and speed has spawned a remarkable number of management tools and techniques: total quality management, benchmarking, time-based competition, outsourcing, partnering, reengineering, change management. Although the resulting operational improvements have often been dramatic, many companies have been frustrated by their inability to translate those gains into sustainable profitability. And bit by bit, almost imperceptibly, management tools have taken the place of strategy. As managers push to improve on all fronts, they move farther away from viable competitive positions.

Copying and benchmarking every rival's moves eliminates the difference that a company actually wants to preserve as an asset. Furthermore, these moves are easily reproducible, as everybody can outsource and implement total quality management (TQM), constant improvement, kaizen, etc. An obsession with constant improvement is not a strategy (Porter, 1996). The essence of competitive strategy, however, is to choose a set of activities that makes the firm unique. Going to war with a rival must be in the first instance for attaining or gaining a difference of position that sets the firm apart from its rivals in terms of low-cost position or differentiation. Figure 1.20 describes a solid example of Japanese companies that had the edge of competition and dominated the world of automotive and electronics, but finally lost the game of competition for not recognizing that strategy requires more than just re-inventing and improving organizations' processes. This notion, however, is different in terms of firms' overall structures, which not only lead to process optimizations, but contribute to the holistic approach

FIGURE 1.20 How the curve of constant improvement leads to reducing margin and value in an industry

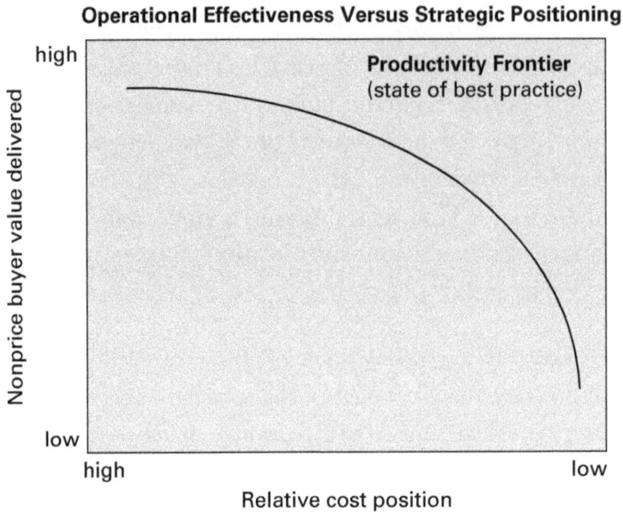

Based on Porter (1996–2008)

of products, processes and business model innovation, agility in terms of quick and adequate responses to the emerging changes and shifts within the dynamics of the markets, leading them to shape the whole dimension of the game of competing, which is played within the diverse industries.

Offensive or defensive moves are risky endeavours, if the generally calculated response is in favour of a harsh retaliation by rivals. The favourable conditions for rivalry are reduced if more players in the market are involved that share a strong position. This results in them having equal powers, types and qualities of products, implemented strategies and even the ease to calculate the competitive moves which are likely to be found out. Having a solid history of competing or interacting with the actors in the market may cause a stability or mutual respect among them. However, breaking interaction may lead to response and competitive moves by the rival, hence they may think there is a need for an action, since the rival is planning something or has a hidden agenda. Starting competition within an industry but rewarding the rival for its losses if both players are represented in additional markets, industries and countries may reduce the severity of the response expected by the firm's rival. The fundament of competitive moves is to not start a costly retaliation or an industry's destabilization with poor results and lower the general profits of the industry regardless of whether it outperforms the rival or not.

The fundamental point is to shift the strategic mindset of competition away from severe rivalry resulting in poor and destructive results to competition mainly focused for value generation. Under value a strategist must understand creating value for the firm and for their customers, which paves the way to sustainable competitive advantage. According to Porter (1980), even if a firm enjoys a considerable amount of strength, a war of attrition is still costly. It is costly to the conqueror as well as the loser and is best avoided. Thus, Porter underpins his claim, by stating that competitive moves are also games of finesse and a combination of brute force that a firm can muster. However, Porter goes further and claims that the best strategy is for the battles of retaliation to never begin at all. A good example here would be the airline industry, where the overall profits of the industry have been decreased much to the benefit of the customers, but not towards the profitability of the industry, wherein almost all airlines are very much struggling.

The FFM and competitive intelligence and forecasting

When Steve Jobs was once asked in 1982 if he wanted to do market research, he said, 'No, because the customers don't know what they want until we've shown them' (Isaacson, 2011). When Microsoft CEO Steve Balmer was interviewed by David Liebermann of *USA Today* and asked about the iPhone launch, he replied by laughing at Jobs' invention and saying:

> $500.00 for a fully subsidized phone with a plan, that is the most expensive phone in the world and it does not appeal to business customers because it does not have a keyboard, which makes it not a very good email machine.... We have our own strategies; we have our own devices in the market today. You can get a Motorola Q phone now for $99.00, it is a very capable machine, it will do music, it will do internet, it will do email, it will do instant messaging, so I kind of look at that and... well I like our strategy..., I like it a lot (Hruska, 2007).

He concluded by saying: 'there is no chance that the iPhone is going to get any significant market share. No chance' (Hruska, 2007). Microsoft had launched 'the Zune' as a product to compete with Apple's iPod – no one today has even heard of such a device. As the reader knows, the rest is history. On the day Jobs introduced the iPhone, he started by saying, 'This is a day that I have been looking forward to for the last 2 1/2 years. Every once in while a revolutionary product comes along that changes everything' (YouTube, 2009).

> iPhone is a revolutionary and magical product that is literally five years ahead of any other mobile phone.... We are all born with the ultimate pointing device – our fingers – and iPhone uses them to create the most revolutionary user interface since the mouse (Apple Inc., 2007).

And it did. Apple's invention truly transformed this generation's understanding and dealing with technology. Apple even transformed the way technology is observed, namely as a luxury retail item the customer can buy as he combines a Hugo Boss suit with a nice shirt at the mall. This competitive mindset was one of the major reasons why Apple became what it represents and what it stands for today – namely, the embodiment of innovation and strategy, a game-changer not just for its own, but for other industries as well. Was Jobs focused on the products of rivals and copying them? Was he interested in their design or marketing tools and data? The research shows that he was not, and the world is happy that he was not. He was focused on some features, namely the features he did not like and what he wanted to be transformed in addition to the game-changing and revolutionizing features he brought to the market by introducing the iPhone to the masses. Jobs thought outside of the box and the boundaries of the industry.

At this point, however, taking again the industry-based competition view is needed to turn to the FFM, where industry and competition's analysis is vital to the success the firm is going to have within the red ocean path. Here information is a crucial aspect to both the offensive and defensive competitive moves. However, regardless of the market locked view or blue ocean strategy in dealing with information, the need to know how to connect the dots in the market is essential:

> ... information is crucial to both offensive and defensive competitive moves. Sometimes selective release of information can serve very useful purposes, in the market signaling communicating commitment, and the like; but often information about plans or intentions can make it a great deal easier for competitors to formulate a strategy. For example, if an impending new product is disclosed in detail competitors will be able to focus their resources in preparing a response (Porter, 1980).

Collecting and processing detailed information about rivals, their capacities and capabilities, and that of the industry and where the journey may lead, from new environmental regulations, antitrust and competition law, to what is happening outside of the industry, are essential for the strategist in order to position the organization on the right path to cope with these multiple challenges. While regulatory factors apply to the whole industry equally – depending on market position, etc – having information about rivals' behaviours and next moves is an essential part of competitive intelligence:

> Forecasting potential competitors is not an easy task, but they can often be identified from the following groups:
>
> - firms not in the industry but who could overcome entry barriers particularly cheaply;
> - firms for whom there is obvious synergy from being in the industry;
> - firms for whom competing in the industry is an obvious extension of the corporate strategy;
> - customers or suppliers who may integrate backward or forward (Porter, 1980).

In today's turbulent environment it is very hard to exactly predict the future, but having a set of solid scenarios on hand to apply as conditions change and signals of weakness are sensed so that a solid pre-established strategy could be applied is a necessity for strategists. Since no one has a crystal ball to foresee how things might turn out or which events may shake the fundaments of the business world, we just need to remember what happened nearly 10 years ago, which started with the Lehman Brothers' collapse, resulting in the meltdown of the global capital system.

The events in the Middle East caught the world off guard and the future of that region is still not known. The very world of Western-backed dictators, from Gaddafi to Ben Ali of Tunisia and Mubarak of Egypt, who stood without any kind of serious disruption for so long, covering many decades of stability, was disrupted within weeks and months. These events caught the world's sole super power, the United States, so off guard that they had to develop some sort of tactics substituted for strategies based on everyday occurrences of the week and as the mood in the media and the demonstrators in the Middle East grew towards toppling the regimes. Because of President Obama's inexperience in foreign affairs, the administration spoke with diverse messages by each of its members on a daily basis. The very rosy tourist business to the land of the Pharaohs in Egypt and the greater Middle East was and still is massively reduced. The events that followed in Syria tell a bloody story of extremely bad forecasting. But above all, the Iranian response to Western aggression by failing to respect a country's sovereignty, the joint treaty on atomic enrichment and for a walkout strategy from negotiating with Iran, while threatening it on a daily basis, has started another global destabilization process that can turn the world of a small business owner in Oklahoma or a mid-size business in Garmisch–Partenkirchen in Germany or a corporation in Mumbai and Zurich totally around. Based on the examples given, the FFM is not an adequate model to deal with the threats and uncertainties described above in a globalized and interconnected world like today's by only analysing the industry and partially the rivalry of the players embedded within it with a linear world-view.

According to Porter (1980) one approach in formulating a strategy is to look for positions in the market, where the firm can achieve its goals without causing a serious threat to the rival's market security resulting in a severe retaliation. Here Porter applies one of Sun Tzu's doctrines, which states:

> Know your enemy and know yourself – if you know the enemy and know yourself, you need not fear the results of a hundred battles. If you know yourself but not the enemy, for every victory gained you will also suffer a defeat. If you know neither the enemy nor yourself, you will succumb in every battle (Sun, 2002).

Porter called Sun Tzu's wisdom in business language 'assumptions':

> The… crucial component in competitor analysis is identifying each competitor's assumptions. These fall into two major categories:
>
> - The competitor's assumption about itself
> - The competitor's assumption about the industry and the companies in it (Porter, 1980).

See Table 1.1 and Figure 1.21 for a detailed checklist on how to analyse the customer. Being able to answer the question and the data is an essential way to calculate to some extent the behaviour of rivals and the changes that may occur in the industry.

Table 1.1 and Figure 1.21 describe how the organization can establish a superb understanding of the market and especially how to use this information for installing a ubiquitous adaptation system, which enables the firm to be changing at the same rate as the environment. This will reduce the gap of understanding the market and the firm's ability to respond to it.

TABLE 1.1 Area of competitor's strengths and weaknesses

Products
Standing of products, from the user's point of view, in each market segment
Breadth and depth of the product line
Dealer/Distribution
Channel coverage and quality
Strength of channel relationships
Ability to service the channels
Marketing and Selling
Skills in each aspect of the marketing mix
Skills in market research and new product development
Training and skills of the sales force
Operations
Manufacturing cost position – economies of scale, learning curve, newness of equipment, etc
Technological sophistication of facilities and equipment
Flexibility of facilities and equipment
Proprietary know-how and unique patent or cost advantage
Skills in capacity addition, quality control, tooling, etc
Location, including labour and transportation cost
Labour force climate; unionization situation
Access to and cost of raw materials
Degree of vertical integration
Research and Engineering
Patents and copyrights
In-house capability in the research and development process (product research, process research, basic research, development, imitation, etc)
R&D staff skills in terms of creativity, simplicity, quality, reliability, etc
Access to outside sources of research and engineering (eg suppliers, customers, contractors)
Overall Costs
Overall relative costs
Shared costs or activities with other business units
Where the competitor is generating the scale or other factors that are key to its cost position
Financial Strength
Cash flow
Short- and long-term borrowing capacity (relative debt/equity ratio)

FIGURE 1.21 Function of a competitor's intelligence system

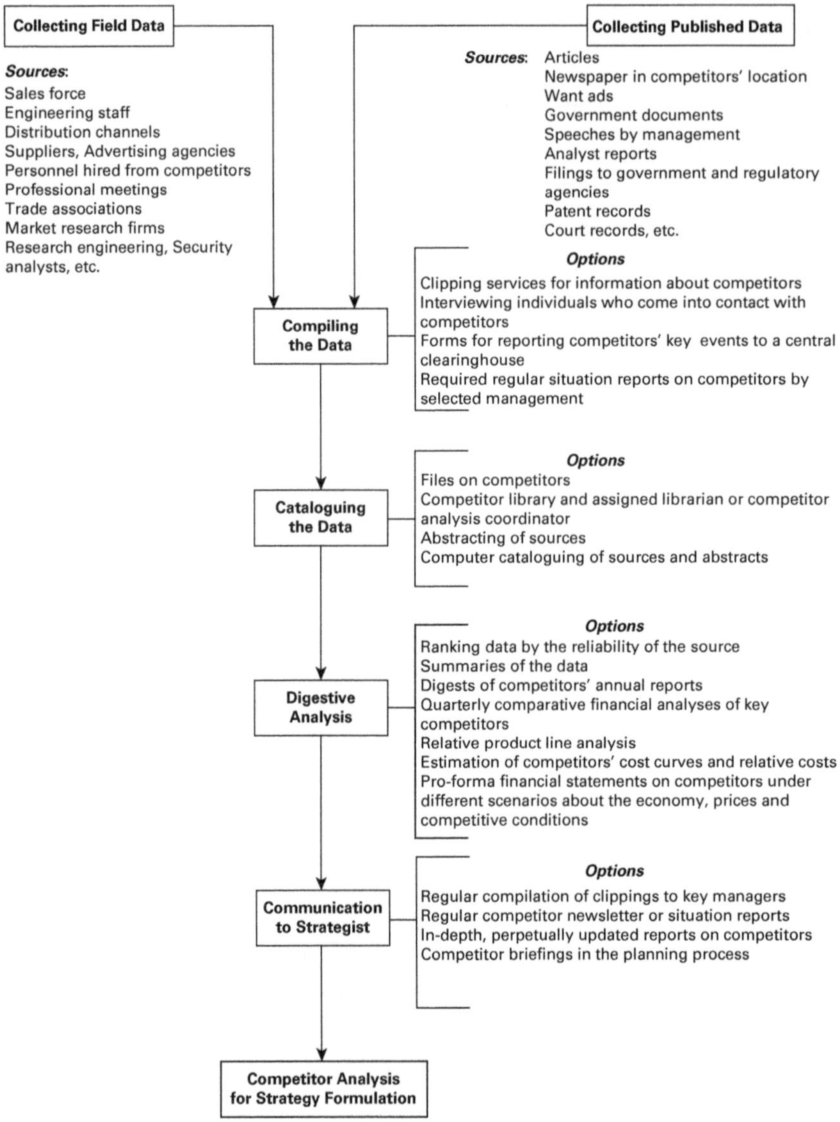

Author's interpretation, based on Porter (1980)

The FFM and clusters, regional competition and Porter's diamond model

In regional micro-economics empirical evidence verifies the importance of competition to raising and maintaining the standard of living in that particular region (Porter, 1998). According to Porter (1998): 'Companies, not countries are in the front line of international competition.' Porter and Rivkin (2012a) define competitiveness as the extent to which firms are operating in a country or region and are able to compete successfully in the global economy while supporting high and rising living standards. Competition really matters now more than ever; it is essential in the new economy, the old economy, and in all types of regions and countries. In the 1980s the US faced severe competition from Japanese companies, since they had mastered efficiency in production to the highest standards possible and led the world by 'just-in-time production' (JIT), kaizen, TQM, etc. These challenges, although of vital significance to American productivity suffering from the generation of the post-Cold War dominance, were still coming just from one major economy and country – Japan. However, the threats that the US economy and its uni-polarity faces today bears much more complexity in its nature and it has approached within today's zeitgeist from multiple sources, directions and diverse nations, which are growing rapidly (Porter and Rivkin, 2012b). Not only is this complexity a major challenge for diverse industry sectors of business and across all party lines, but moreover it has challenged the very notion of democracy in the West. The rise of populism and right-wing movements across the EU and the whole of the West are symptoms of ill-defined and inadequate strategies being applied.

Milton Friedman's doctrines have been applied for far too long. He wrote: 'Few trends could so undermine the very foundations of our free society as the acceptance by corporate officials of a social responsibility other than to make as much money for their stockholders as possible' (Friedman, 1962). His doctrines have brought the demise of Western capitalism, where the world, from Asia to the Middle East, Turkey, Russia and Australia, is bending towards the Chinese block and leaving a Western-led leadership model. The worst-case scenario is also that the US is giving its long-fought and justifiably earned leadership away. The latest examples are the sudden retreat from Turkey, the lone walkouts from the Paris climate accord and from the Iranian nuclear deal.

Coming back to the notion of business competition, in Figure 1.22 Sakakibara and Porter (2001) display the difference of how to measure success in the local and the international market.

FIGURE 1.22 Competition and international competitiveness: evidence from Japanese industry

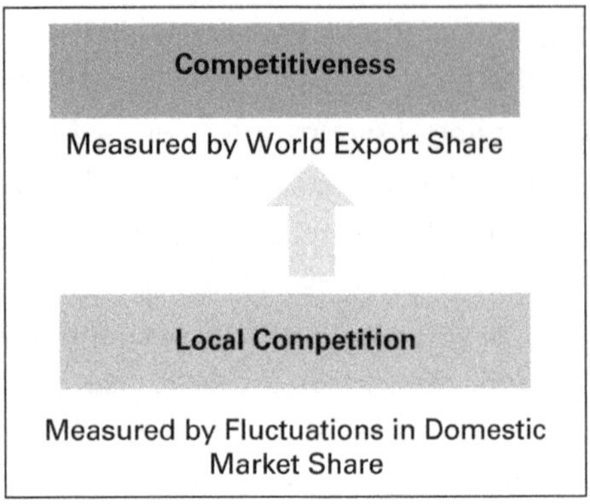

Sakakibara and Porter (2001)

Figure 1.22 describes the difference in measuring success in competition from a local perspective and from the international perspective. According to Sakakibara and Porter (2001):

> We find a positive and highly significant relationship between the extent of market share fluctuations [a measure of local rivalry] and trade performance. Contrary to some popular views, our results suggest that Japanese competitiveness is associated with home market competition, not collusion, cartels, or government interventions that stabilize it.

Reduced to a single phrase, Porter's thesis states: high-intensity competition breeds international success. But this paradigm for international competitive advantage is best revealed in Porter's 'national diamond model' (see Figure 1.23), explaining the key elements that are the foundations for domestic competitive advantage. The below conditions are the key elements which foster domestic competitiveness, according to Porter:

- company strategy, structure and rivalry;
- factor conditions;
- demand conditions;
- related and supporting industries as industry clusters.

Figure 1.23 describes Porter's diamond model, which is one of the most essential models for regional and country policymakers to apply in order to increase a region's or country's attractiveness for capital and the overall well-being of

FIGURE 1.23 National diamond model

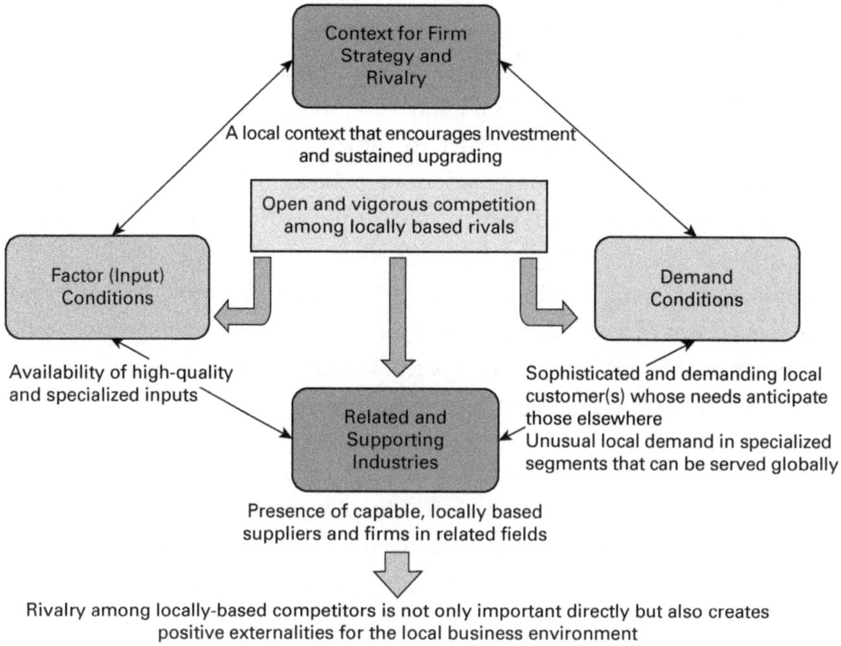

Author's interpretation, based on Porter (1990)

the community. As Porter has seen his work's fundament mainly in economics and himself as an economist (Porter, 2007), he is also the first scholar ever to put economic theory to the field of business strategy (Kamran, 2012d), by bridging both fields. The doctrines of Porter have been established, where he asked the fundamental questions, based on how firms compete. This has led him to a very closed-in view (industry-locked perspective) of competition, which he has been regarding as a complementary approach to top–down economic development by claiming that such environmental factors as institutional development, trade liberalization, privatization and macro-economic stabilization are the bedrock of a country's prosperity. Thus, they have taken him to the concepts and the theories of cluster and competition, and national diamond. As it turns out, according to Porter (2007), with some adjustments one can also apply these theories to nations, regions and cities. The Californian cluster is a clear example of how economic prosperity in a region can lead to international leadership in wine-making (Kamran, 2012b). Today Californian wines are even sold in the highly traditional European wine markets of France and Italy. The quality of Californian wines can match the top European brands, thus they contribute to the US economy and its exports, while at the same time creating a highly successful regional industry employing bankers specializing in winery finance to bottle manufacturers, university professors specializing in wine marketing, alcohol and beverages law and wine business management to wine growers and wine-making machinery producers.

According to Porter: 'So when I started mulling this over and over in my mind it became clear that in order to understand the competitiveness of nations it would be necessary to adopt a bottom-up or microeconomic approach' (Stonehouse and Snowdon, 2007). The FFM, which can embed both kinds of rivalry, as Figure 1.22 describes, would only contribute to the regional and national development if the yardstick, whereby the firm measures the notion of productivity, from a micro-economic perspective is the resemblance of being based on prosperity for the region, the country and the firm itself. In the words of Porter from an interview in 2004:

> National prosperity is strongly affected by competitiveness, which is the productivity with which a nation uses its human, capital, and natural resources. Competitiveness is rooted in a nation's microeconomic fundamentals, manifested in the sophistication of its companies and the quality of its microeconomic business environment.... The central challenge to the world economy is now micro-economic reform (Stonehouse and Snowdon, 2007).

FIGURE 1.24 Californian wine cluster

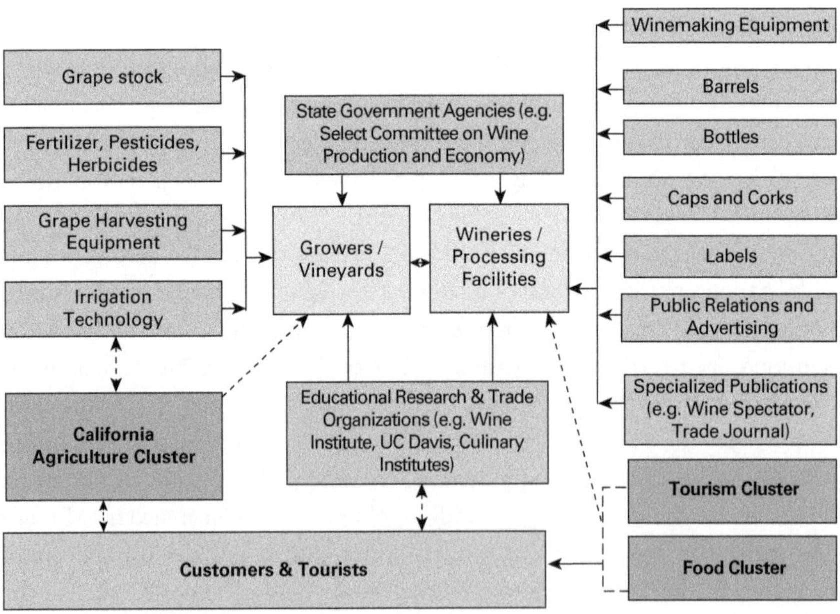

Author's interpretation, based on Porter (2008a)

FIGURE 1.25 Rivalry and value creation as productivity growth

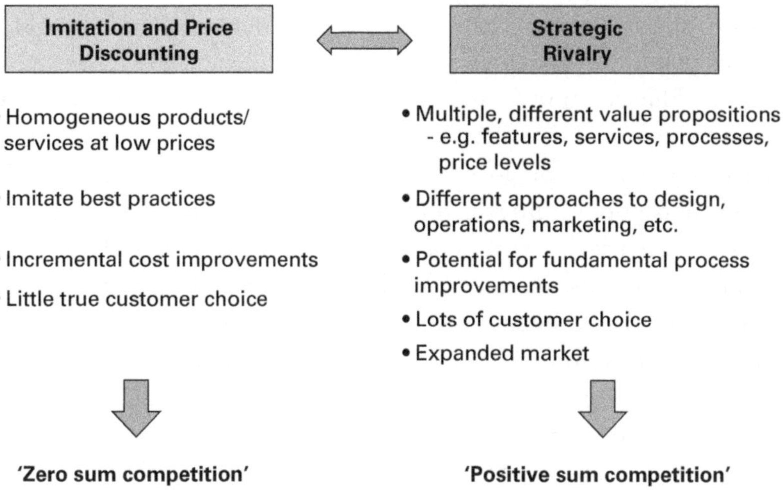

Author's interpretation, based on Sakakibara and Porter (2001)

Figure 1.25 describes the two basic views on how competition within an industry is conducted.

The FFM is a purely economic view of an organization's reality. The notion that Porter created does not have an identifiable basis by seeing the world of business from any other essential perspective. In addition, there is no systemic link that it can embed such an approach to see the world with different eyes. As Porter describes, the FFM is a model to compete for profits, not productivity:

> Awareness of the five forces can help a company understand the structure of its industry and stake out a position that is more profitable and less vulnerable to attack. In essence, the job of the strategist is to understand and cope with competition. Often, however, managers define competition too narrowly, as if it occurred only among today's direct competitors. Yet competition for profits goes beyond established industry rivals to include four other competitive forces as well: customers, suppliers, potential entrants, and substitute products. The extended rivalry that results from all five forces defines an industry's structure and shapes the nature of competitive interaction within an industry (Porter, 2008b).

However, some research displays a shift in Porter's thinking; this shift is strongly sensed in his 2011 article, 'How to fix capitalism and unleash a new wave of growth' (Porter and Kramer, 2011b).

Porter goes further and uncrowns the beast of 'shareholder value' as the ultimate business and capitalist doctrine, observed and applied globally by using substitute terminology of the new and highly overdue approach, namely 'shared value' (Porter and Kramer, 2011a). The concept of shared value creation focuses on the connection between societal and economic progress. It has the power to unleash the next wave of growth. Porter's recommendation goes as far as stating: 'Every firm should look at decisions and opportunities through the lens of shared value. This will lead to new approaches that generate greater innovation and growth for companies – and also greater benefits for society' (Porter and Kramer, 2011a). While the author welcomes these new prospects in the Porterian doctrine of competition, it is important to note and observe that these prospects have been a major shift in Porter's managerial and strategic mindset. It is the purpose of this book to fill this gap and give the five forces a systemic, interrelated and recursive application (Kamran, 2011a, 2011b, 2012a, 2012c, 2012d, 2013a, 2013b, 2014a, 2014b, 2014c, 2014d, 2017, 2019).

In 2012, the news of Porter's consulting firm's bankruptcy was spread across the global news networks. If the reader wants to see the currency and actuality of the points that the author has discussed so far, which embody vital practical significance, the new case of the Monitor Company Group LP, the Cambridge, Massachusetts consulting firm partially owned by Porter, delivers a vital example on how Porter's ideas are a partial view in strategy and that the ideas need a holistic rethinking and re-engineering to cope with the ever-growing complexity.

It is essential to understand what Monitor Group's bankruptcy means for the world of BA, and the MITs and Harvards of the world, as well as the future of the MBA programmes generally. According to Cohan (2012):

> Porter is well-known among business students who must memorize and apply two of his earliest ideas – five forces and value chain analyses – in order to earn their degrees. However, as I pointed out in the preface to my new book, Hungry Start-up Strategy, published November 5, those students are rebelling against Porter... The *New York Journal of Books* concluded that 'while Porter advocates a highly structured, even dispassionate approach to an already established business, Mr. Cohan promotes personal passion and customer connection to creating the business.'

According to Steve Denning:

> What killed the Monitor Group, the consulting firm co-founded by the legendary business guru, Michael Porter?... Why didn't the highly paid consultants of Monitor use Porter's famous five-force analysis to save themselves? Why go through the hassle of actually designing and making better products and services, and offering steadily more value to customers and society, when the firm could simply position its business so that structural barriers ensured endless above-average profits?... Why not call this trick 'the discipline of strategy'? Why not announce that a company occupying a position within a sector that is well protected by structural barriers would have a 'sustainable competitive advantage'?... Why not proclaim that finding these El Dorados of unending excess profits would follow, as day follows night, by having highly paid strategy analysts doing large amounts of rigorous analysis? Which CEO would not want to know how to reliably generate endless excess profits? Why not set up a consulting firm that could satisfy that want? (Denning, 2012).

The answer may be that 'the want' that Porter's co-founded firm offered may be good in times of simplicity and predictability. But as the complexity of doing business rises, so an innovation in the very models deployed to cope with these complexities must occur, as the major conditions of strategic pre-control. Thus, if there is no innovation in the tools, models and frameworks that were used to serve the markets in the late 1970s and early 1980s under the umbrella of competitive strategy, one can predict what may happen to the long-established firms. A good example here is the latest bankruptcy of Thomas Cook in the UK and its subsidiaries worldwide.

This was not just the 2008 crises that brought down the revenues of the Monitor Group, Nokia, Motorola, Research in Motion, Kodak, etc; it was being stuck in the myopic vision. This situation is termed by the author as 'stuck in the middle of the pure profit mindset', which is a threatening assumption on steering the organizations in today's complex world – hence profits on the cost of viability is a highly dangerous and myopic vision.

The force that the author wants to address via this book is 'complexity' – what exactly this means and which spectrum it will cover is established in the next part of the book. Introducing the force of complexity to strategy is needed precisely because of the challenges, crises and disruptions the author has observed and highlighted throughout the book so far. It is a new perspective in the field, but it is not new to operation research and managerial effectiveness. Scholars such as Beer, Malik, Schwaninger, Vester and Gälweiler have published widespread publications and books in this regard. It is, though, the chief objective of this book to conceptually align these insights for the practice of strategy in the new world dominated by complexity.

References

Alevizou P (2002) To wire or not to wire? Encyclopaedia Britannica versus Microsoft Encarta, *Journal of Educational Technology and Society*, **5** (1)

Alvesson M and Willmott H (2003) *Studying Management Critically*, Sage Publications Ltd, London

Andrews KR (1971) *The Concept of Corporate Strategy*, Dow Jones-Irwin, Homewood, IL

Apple Inc. (2007) *Apple Reinvents the Phone with iPhone*, Press Release, Available at: https://www.apple.com/newsroom/2007/01/09Apple-Reinvents-the-Phone-with-iPhone/ (archived at https://perma.cc/75WD-LWVW) (accessed 19 March 2020)

Bea FX and Haas J (1997) *Strategisches Management*, Lucius & Lucius, TestOrt

Beer S (1959) *Cybernetics and Management*, Wiley, New York

Beer S (1972) *Brain of the Firm: A Development in Management Cybernetics*, Lane, London

Beer S (1973) *Designing Freedom: The future that can be demanded now*, Center for Cassette Studies, Portland, OR

Beer S (1979) *The Heart of Enterprise*, Wiley, New York

Beer S (1981) *Brain of the Firm: The managerial cybernetics of organization*, J. Wiley, Chichester

Beer S (1984) The viable system model: Its provenance, development, methodology and pathology, *Journal of the Operational Research Society*, **35** (1), pp 7–25

Beer S (1985) *Diagnosing the System for Organizations*, Wiley, New York

Beer S (1988) *Decision and Control: Meaning of operational research and management cybernetics*, Wiley, Chichester

Beer S (2002) What is cybernetics?, *Kybernetes*, **31** (2), pp 209–219

Beer S (2008) *Diagnosing the System for Organizations*, Malik Management Zentrum, St. Gallen

Beer S (2011) *Designing Freedom*, House of Anansi Press, Concord

Burke A (2009) *Blue Ocean versus Competitive Strategy: Theory and evidence*, Report Series Research in Management, Available at: https://pdfs.semanticscholar.org/ff7d/25cfa568ecb323e293e0fefb3eb176777139.pdf (archived at https://perma.cc/YZA5-3597) (accessed 21 November 2018)

Christensen CR, Andrews KR, Bower JL, *et al* (1987) *Business Policy: Text and cases*, Richard D. Irwin, Homewood, IL

Cohan P (2012) *Cobbler's Shoes: Strategy guru Michael Porter's Monitor Group bankrupt*, Available at: http://www.forbes.com/sites/petercohan/2012/11/14/cobblers-shoes-strategy-guru-michael-porters-monitor-group-bankrupt/2/ (archived at https://perma.cc/D4TS-27C3) (accessed 3 October 2018)

Collis D and Montgomery CA (1995) Competing on resources: Strategy in the 1990s, *Harvard Business Review*, **73** (4), pp 118–128

Coyne K and Subramaniam S (1996) Bringing discipline to strategy, *The McKinsey Quarterly*, (4), pp 61–70

Daly J (1997) *101 Ways to Save Apple*, Available at: https://www.wired.com/1997/06/apple-3/ (archived at https://perma.cc/6K85-QCAE) (accessed 21 November 2018)

Denning S (2012) *What Killed Michael Porter's Monitor Group? The one force that really matters*, Available at: http://www.forbes.com/sites/stevedenning/2012/11/20/what-killed-michael-porters-monitor-group-the-one-force-that-really-matters/3/ (archived at https://perma.cc/QUK8-YLCD) (accessed 21 November 2018)

Dosher M, Benepe O, Humphrey A, Stewart R and Lie B (1960) *The SWOT Analysis Method*, Stanford Research Institute, Mento Park, CA

Drucker PF (1954) *The Practice of Management*, Harper & Row, New York

Durham SE (1997) *Chaos Theory for the Practical Military Mind*, Available at: https://www.semanticscholar.org/paper/Chaos-Theory-for-the-Practical-Military-Mind-Durham/6d1b00c95997517c4ddb13358a49845a4fa55119 (archived at https://perma.cc/7877-84PS) (accessed 8 February 2020)

Finkelstein S and Hambrick DC (1990) Top-management-team tenure and organizational outcomes: The moderating role of managerial discretion, *Administrative Science Quarterly*, **35** (3), p 484

Fisher R, Ury W and Patton B (eds) (1991) *Getting to Yes: Negotiating agreement without giving in*, Houghton Mifflin, Boston, MA

Foss NJ (2007) Strategic belief management, *Strategic Organization*, **5** (3), pp 249–258

Friedman M (1962) *Capitalism and Freedom*, University of Chicago Press, Chicago

Friesner T (2011) *History of SWOT Analysis*, Available at: https://www.researchgate.net/publication/288958760_History_of_swot_analysis (archived at https://perma.cc/S7QA-CETV) (accessed 25 November 2019)

Ghemawat P (2002) Competition and business strategy in historical perspective, *Business History Review*, **76** (1), pp 37–74

Glenn JE (1996) Chaos theory: The essential for military applications, *Newport Papers*, 10, Available at: https://digital-commons.usnwc.edu/cgi/viewcontent.cgi?article=1009&context=usnwc-newport-papers (archived at https://perma.cc/M47K-JU2F) (accessed 8 February 2020)

Greene R (2010) *The 33 Strategies of War*, Profile Books, London

Grundy T (2006) Rethinking and reinventing Michael Porter's five forces model, *Strategic Change*, **15** (5)

Hamel G and Prahalad CK (1994) *Competing for the Future*, Harvard Business School Press, Boston, MA

Hax AC and Wilde DL (2002) The delta model: Toward a unified framework of strategy, *MIT Sloan Working Paper No. 4621-02*, Available at: https://papers.ssrn.com/sol3/papers.cfm?abstract_id=344580 (archived at https://perma.cc/VV2C-HHH6)

Hetzler S (2008) *Brain-supporting-environments für Entscheide in komplexen Systemen: ein kybernetischer Ansatz für die Gestaltung wirksamer Entscheidungsumfelder*, Dissertation, Rosch-Druck, Schesslitz, Germany

Houchin K (2003) *Applying Complexity Theory to the Strategic Development of an Organisation*, Dissertation, University of Glasgow, Glasgow

Hruska J (2007) *Ballmer: iPhone has 'no chance' of gaining significant market share: Steve Ballmer talks some smack about the iPhone, saying that it has 'no chance'*, Available at: https://arstechnica.com/information-technology/2007/04/ballmer-says-iphone-has-no-chance-to-gain-significant-market-share/ (archived at https://perma.cc/EAM4-XCHY) (accessed 21 November 2018)

Isaacson W (2011) *Steve Jobs: Die autorisierte Biografie des Apple-Gründers*, Bertelsmann, München

Kamran Q (2011a) *Complexity of Negotiation and Negotiation of Complexity: Getting to trust*, Available at: https://papers.ssrn.com/sol3/papers.cfm?abstract_id=2137877 (archived at https://perma.cc/96H9-LNAC) (accessed 22 November 2018)

Kamran Q (2011b) Management by deception (MBD): the need for designing a viable strategy, *SSRN Electronic Journal*, Available at: http://dx.doi.org/10.2139/ssrn.2137880 (archived at https://perma.cc/QN7C-T9WM) (accessed 4 December 2018)

Kamran Q (2012a) *'Complexity', the 6th Competitive Force that Shapes Management Strategy: A cybernetic approach to 'Porter's Five Forces that Shapes Industry Strategy' in Turbulent and Complex Environments*, Available at: https://papers.ssrn.com/sol3/papers.cfm?abstract_id=2137853 (archived at https://perma.cc/9DVP-V5CL) (accessed 22 November 2018)

Kamran Q (2012b) Opening an Italian winery, spirits and accessories retail business in northern California: Attracting the customer concentration of an established industry cluster based on Michael Porter's 'cluster and competition theory', *Entrepreneurship & Economics eJournal*, (10)

Kamran Q (2012c) Running multinational corporations (MNC) in China: A survival-kit to Western CEOs, in *Aktuelle Entwicklungen des europäischen und internationalen Wirtschaftsrechts,* ed C Baudenbacher, pp 249–317, Helbing et Lichtenhahn, Basel, München

Kamran Q (2012d) *The Transformation of Porter's Strategic Mind from 'Shareholder Value' to 'Shared Value': Bridging the sciences of economics, strategy and cybernetics*, Available at: https://ssrn.com/abstract=2219284 (archived at https://perma.cc/7DED-TVT3)

Kamran Q (2013a) *Complexity, the Sixth Competitive Force That Shapes Strategy: A cybernetics approach to 'Porter's FFM' in turbulent and complex environments*, Lambert Academic Publishing, Saarbrücken

Kamran Q (2013b) *Running Multinational Corporations in China: A survival kit for western CEOs*, LAP LAMBERT Academic Publishing, Saarbrücken

Kamran Q (2014a) An Argument of Organisational Functionality in the World of Tomorrow (4 August), Qeis Kamran (2013), Complexity the Sixth Competitive Force that Shapes Strategy: A Cybernetics Approach to Porter's five forces model in turbulent and complex environments, Lap Lambert Academic Publishing, Saarbrücken, Germany, Available at: https://ssrn.com/abstract=2475864 (archived at https://perma.cc/2L2B-SSNK)

Kamran Q (2014b) *Conceptualizing Complexity as the Sixth Competitive Force that Shapes Strategy in Complex and Turbulent Environments*, Available at: https://papers.ssrn.com/sol3/papers.cfm?abstract_id=2476277 (archived at https://perma.cc/JYC9-ZR9L) (accessed 22 November 2018)

Kamran Q (2014c) Model safari in strategy: Scanning the landscape of the essential strategy models, *O&M: Structures & Processes in Organizations eJournal*, **6** (44) (accessed 22 November 2018)

Kamran Q (2014d) *Observing, Understanding and Revisiting Porter as the Fundament of the Research in Strategy*, Available at: https://papers.ssrn.com/sol3/papers.cfm?abstract_id=2475915 (archived at https://perma.cc/MKZ9-DP53) (accessed 22 November 2018)

Kamran Q (2017) Cybernetics and Strategy: A necessary synergy for strategic models – complexity, the sixth competitive force that shapes strategy in turbulent and complex environments – a cybernetics approach to Porter's FFM: in turbulent and complex environments, in *Academy of Business Administration (ABA) Year Book*, Yapsilanti, MI, pp 1–65, *Innovation Law & Policy eJournal*, **5** (25) (accessed 22 November 2018)

Kamran Q (2019) *Developing a Holistic Model for Competitive Strategic Management*, University of Latvia

Kiechel W (2010) *Lords of Strategy: The secret intellectual history of the new corporate world*, Harvard Business Review Press, Boston, MA

Kim WC and Mauborgne R (2005) *Blue Ocean Strategy: How to create uncontested market space and make the competition irrelevant*, Harvard Business School Press, Boston, MA

Kraaijenbrink J, Spender J-C and Groen AJ (2010) The resource-based view: A review and assessment of its critiques, *Journal of Management*, **36** (1), pp 349–372

Krishnamurthy B (2010) *Five Forces Model: Analysis from an emerging economy*, Available at: http://papers.ssrn.com/sol3/papers.cfm?abstract_id=1577469 (archived at https://perma.cc/APA4-KH7H) (accessed 22 November 2018)

Magretta J (2012) *Understanding Michael Porter: The essential guide to competition and strategy*, Harvard Business Review Press, Boston, MA

Malik F (1981) *Management-Systeme*, Schweizer Volksbank, Bern

Malik F (1984) *Strategie des Managements komplexer Systeme*, Haupt, Bern & Stuttgart

Malik F (1993) *Systemisches Management, Evolution, Selbstorganisation: Grundprobleme, Funktionsmechanismen und Lösungsansätze für komplexe Systeme*, Haupt, Bern

Malik F (1994) *Management-Perspektiven: Wirtschaft und Gesellschaft, Strategie, Management und Ausbildung*, Haupt, Bern

Malik F (1996) *Strategie des Managements komplexer Systeme: Ein Beitrag zur Management-Kybernetik evolutionärer Systeme*, Haupt, Bern

Malik F (1997) *Wirksame Unternehmensaufsicht: Corporate governance in Umbruchzeiten*, Frankfurter Allgemeine, Zeitung für Deutschland, Verl.-Bereich Buch, Frankfurt am Main

Malik F (2000a) *Führen, Leisten, Leben: Wirksames Management für eine neue Zeit*, Auflage, Stuttgart

Malik F (2000b) *Strategie des Managements komplexer Systeme: Ein Beitrag zur Management-Kybernetik evolutionärer Systeme*, Haupt, Bern

Malik F (2007) *Management: Das A und O des Handwerks*, Campus-Verl, Frankfurt/Main

Malik F (2011) Die große Transformation, *Malik on Management m.o.m.-Letter*, **11** (2)

Malik F (2015) *Navigieren in Zeiten des Umbruchs: Die Welt neu denken und gestalten*, Campus, Frankfurt am Main

Miller KD (1992) A framework for integrated risk management in international business, *Journal of International Business Studies*, **23** (2), pp 311–331

Mintzberg H, Ahlstrand BW and Lampel J (1998) *Strategy Safari: A guided tour through the wilds of strategic management*, Free Press, New York

Mintzberg H, Ahlstrand BW and Lampel J (2001) *Strategy Safari: The complete guide through the wilds of strategic management*, Financial Times Prentice Hall, Harlow

Moore CG, Carter RE, Nietert PJ, *et al* (2011) Recommendations for planning pilot studies in clinical and translational research, *Clinical and Translational Science*, **4** (5), pp 332–337

Narayanan VK and Fahey L (2005) The relevance of the institutional underpinnings of Porter's five forces framework to emerging economies: An epistemological analysis, *Journal of Management Studies,* **42** (1)

Porter ME (1974) Consumer behavior, retailer power and market performance in consumer goods industries, *Review of Economics and Statistics*, 419–436

Porter ME (1975) *Note on the Structural Analysis of Industries*, Harvard Business School Background Note 376-054, September

Porter ME (1976) *Interbrand Choice, Strategy, and Bilateral Market Power*, Harvard University Press, Cambridge, MA

Porter ME (1977) From entry barriers to mobility barriers: Conjectural decisions and contrived deterrence to new competition, Quarterly Journal of Economics, **91** (2), pp 241–261

Porter ME (1979) The structure within industries and companies' performance, The Review of Economics and Statistics, **61** (2), p 214

Porter ME (1980) *Competitive Strategy: Techniques for analyzing industries and competitors*, Free Press, New York

Porter ME (1985) *Competitive Advantage: Creating and sustaining superior performance*, Free Press, New York

Porter ME (1986) *Competition in Global Industries*, Harvard Business School Press, Boston, MA

Porter ME (1990) *The Competitive Advantage of Nations*, Free Press, New York

Porter ME (1996) What is strategy?, *Harvard Business Review*, **73** (6) (accessed 22 November 2018)

Porter ME (1998) *The Competitive Advantage of Nations: With a new introduction*, Free Press, New York

Porter ME (2007) Clusters and economic policy: Aligning public policy with the new economics of competition, *ISC White Paper*, Institute for Strategy and Competitiveness, Harvard Business School (accessed 21 November 2018)

Porter ME (2008a) *On Competition: Updated and extended edition*, Harvard Business School Press, Boston, MA

Porter ME (2008b) The five competitive forces that shape strategy, *Harvard Business Review*, **86** (1), pp 78–93

Porter ME and Kramer MR (2011a) Creating shared value, *Harvard Business Review*, **89** (1/2), pp 62–77

Porter ME and Kramer MR (2011b) How to fix capitalism, *Harvard Business Review*

Porter ME and Rivkin JW (2000) *Industry Transformation*, 10th ed, Harvard Business School Publishing, Boston, MA

Porter ME and Rivkin JW (2012a) *Restoring U.S. Competitiveness: The looming challenge to U.S. competitiveness*, Harvard Business Review, Boston, MA

Porter ME and Rivkin JW (2012b) The looming challenge to U.S. competitiveness, *Harvard Business Review*, **90** (3), pp 54–61

Porter ME, Rivkin JW and Kanter RM (2013) *Competitiveness at a Crossroads: Findings of Harvard Business School's 2012 survey on US competitiveness*, Harvard Business School, Boston, MA

Powell WW, Koput KW and Smith-Doerr L (1996) Interorganizational collaboration and the locus of innovation: Networks of learning in biotechnology, *Administrative Science Quarterly*, **41** (1), p 116

Recklies O (2008) Problems and barriers to strategic planning, *Ekonomika i Organizacja Przedsiębiorstwa czasopismo poświęcone teorii i praktyce ekonomiki i organizacji przedsiębiorstwa*

Rumelt RP (1974) *Strategy, Structure, and Economic Performance*, Division of Research Graduate School of Business Administration, Harvard University, Boston, MA

Rumelt RP (1979) Evaluation of strategies: Theory and models, in *Strategic Management: A new view of business policy and planning*, eds D Schendel and CW Hofer, Little, Brown, Boston, MA

Rumelt RP (1982) Diversification strategy and profitability, *Strategic Management Journal*, **3** (4), pp 359–369

Rumelt RP (1991) How much does industry matter?, *Strategic Management Journal*, **12** (3), pp 167–185

Rumelt RP (1997) Towards a strategic theory of the firm, in *Resources, Firms, and Strategies: A reader in the resource-based perspective*, ed NJ Foss, pp 131–145, Oxford University Press, Oxford

Rumelt RP (2012) Good strategy/bad strategy: The difference and why it matters, *Strategic Direction*, **28** (8)

Sakakibara M and Porter ME (2001) Competing at home to win abroad: Evidence from Japanese industry, *Review of Economics and Statistics*, **83** (2), pp 310–322

Schumpeter JA (1942) *Capitalism, Socialism, and Democracy*, Harper, New York

Schwaninger M (1984a) Management-Entwicklung: Ansätze und Erfahrungen, *Die Unternehmung*, pp 231–243

Schwaninger M (1984b) Zur Marktstrategie einer Nummer 2, *IO Management Zeitschrift*, **53** (3), pp 136–140

Schwaninger M (1985) Methodik der Strategieplanung: Theoretische Neuerungen ermöglichen es, für die Praxis leistungsfähigere Planungssysteme zu gestalten, *Harvard Manager*, 7 (3), pp 54–61

Schwaninger M (1987) A practical approach to strategy development, *Long Range Planning*, **20** (5), pp 74–85

Schwaninger M (1990) Embodiments of organizational fitness: The viable system model (VSM) as a guide, *Systems Practice*, **3** (3), pp 249–264

Schwaninger M (1998) Szenario 2005: Die Organisationen mit den besten Modellen gewinnen, *Management-Szenarien 2005*, **15** (2), pp 136–137

Schwaninger M (1999) Intelligente Organisationen-Grundsätzliches zum Umgang mit Veränderungen, *Agrarwirtschaft und Agrarsoziologie*, pp 151–170

Schwaninger M (2000) Managing complexity: The path toward intelligent organizations, *Systemic Practice and Action Research*, **13** (2), pp 207–241

Schwaninger M (2001a) Intelligent organizations: An integrative framework, *Systems Research and Behavioral Science: The Official Journal of the International Federation for Systems Research*, **18** (2), pp 137–158

Schwaninger M (2001b) System theory and cybernetics: A solid basis for transdisciplinarity in management education and research, *Kybernetes*, **30** (9/10), pp 1209–1222

Schwaninger M (2002) Enhancing organizational cognition, *Seml Radar: Zeitschrift für Systemdenken und Entscheidungsfindung im Management*, **1** (1), pp 71–93

Schwaninger M (2003) A cybernetic model to enhance organizational intelligence, *Systems Analysis Modelling Simulation*, **43** (1), pp 53–65

Schwaninger M (2004a) Long over short term, *Organizational Transformation and Social Change*, **1** (1), pp 11–26

Schwaninger M (2004b) What can cybernetics contribute to the conscious evolution of organizations and society?, *Systems Research and Behavioral Science: The Official Journal of the International Federation for Systems Research*, **21** (5), pp 515–527

Schwaninger M (2006a) Design for viable organizations: The diagnostic power of the viable system model, *Kybernetes*, **35** (7/8), pp 955–966

Schwaninger M (2006b) The evolution of organizational cybernetics, *Scientiae Mathematicae Japonicae*, **13** (2), pp 856–880

Schwaninger M (2007) Optimal structures for social systems, *Kybernetes*, **36** (3/4), pp 307–318

Schwaninger M (2009a) Complex versus complicated: the how of coping with complexity, *Kybernetes*, **38** (1/2), pp 83–92

Schwaninger M (2009b) *Intelligent Organizations: Powerful models for systemic management*, Springer Berlin Heidelberg, Berlin

Schwaninger M (2010) Model-based management (MBM): A vital prerequisite for organizational viability, *Kybernetes*, **39** (9/10), pp 1419–1428

Schwaninger M (2014) Organizing for sustainability, *Systema*, **2** (2), pp 26–42

Schwaninger M (2015a) Model-based management: A cybernetic concept, *Systems Research and Behavioral Science*, **32** (6), pp 564–578

Schwaninger M (2015b) The evolution of models: Uncovering the path of model improvement, in *Computer aided systems theory – EUROCAST 2015: 15th international conference, Las Palmas de Gran Canaria, Spain, February 8-13, 2015 revised selected papers*, eds R Moreno-Díaz, F Pichler and A Quesada-Arencibia, pp 126–132, Springer, Cham

Spender J-C (1996) Making knowledge the basis of a dynamic theory of the firm, *Strategic Management Journal*, **17** (S2), pp 45–62

Stonehouse G and Snowdon B (2007) Competitive advantage revisited: Michael Porter on strategy and competitiveness, *Journal of Management Inquiry*, **16** (3), pp 256–273

Sun W (2002) *The Art of War*, Basic Books, New York

Taleb NN (2007) Black swans and the domains of statistics, *The American Statistician*, **61** (3), pp 198–200

Ulrich H (1968) *Die Unternehmung als produktives soziales System: Grundlagen der allgemeinen Unternehmungslehre*, Haupt, Bern

Ulrich H and Krieg W (1972) *Das Sankt Galler Management-Modell*, Haupt, Bern
van Creveld M (1985) *Command in War*, Harvard University Press, Boston, MA
Wernerfelt B (1984) A resource-based view of the firm, *Strategic Management Journal*, 5 (2), pp 171–180
Whittington R (2001) *What is Strategy – and Does It Matter?*, Thomson Learning, London
YouTube (2009) *Apple's iPhone Introduction (Part 1) – YouTube*, Available at: https://www.youtube.com/watch?v=vZYlhShD2oQ (archived at https://perma.cc/K5ZV-6KWG) (accessed 25 November 2019)

02

A treatise of cybernetics, system sciences and complexity sciences

Underlying organic and social phenomena is a simple but fundamental natural law which is primarily ignored in strategic and management sciences: 'self-organization'. This law is responsible for the markings, and the shapes of those marks, on the bodies of cows and tigers. It is responsible for creating the shapes of sand dunes in the Arabian Sahara. And it is responsible for a flock of birds self-organizing themselves in flight – even though as a whole they do not know what each individual bird's next action will be, they are still able to master the most complex tasks of navigating the planet for thousands of miles for survival without a leader, a strategist. And it is responsible for how the human heart organizes itself and how its cells are coordinated to beat so masterfully that within the span of a human's life of 80–90 years, a disruption rarely occurs.

Imagine giving one of the birds in the flock the position of leader, or giving the affairs of heart-beating to human beings to organize and manage its activities on a daily basis – things might surely turn sour. Figure 2.1 describes an overall holistic view of the sciences of complexity and the wide spectrum it covers. Although covering the whole spectrum is optimal, that is beyond the scope of this book.

Evolution is nothing else but a history of self-organization. Emergence is embedded in its DNA, its atoms, in its structure and how it knows what to do, how to shape itself, for example, how the eye knows to be an eye and a finger knows to be a finger in an embryo. How it is possible that the sole of a newborn's foot knows to be thicker than the skin of its other parts although it has never walked before. Emergence welcomes change and takes its forms by adaptation in an order that it actually can survive. The quest for survival is nature's ultimate doctrine. Survival is embedded in every action and activity of nature. Order and chaos are just as much a natural phenomenon as the shape of a 'fractal' (Mandelbrot, 2003). The notion that complexity arises from complicated matters instead of some simple natural rules and

FIGURE 2.1 Map of complexity as science and these theories are organized

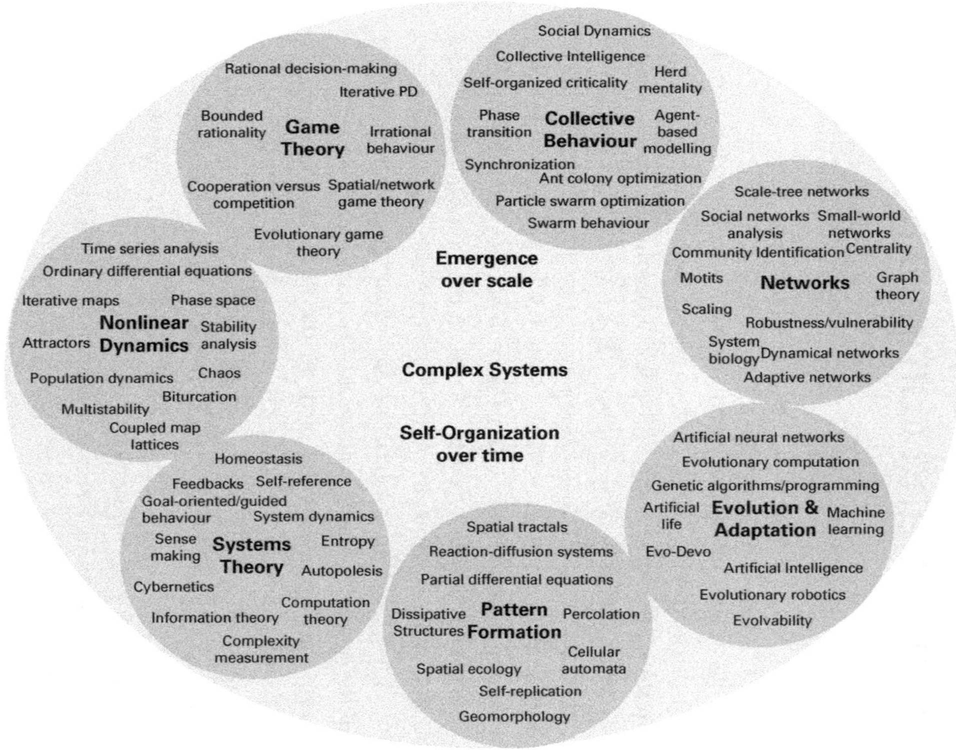

Author's interpretation, based on Sayama (2010)

that these simple natural rules give rise to very complex objects and phenomena is not what is generally observed. Knowing that an object can be complex and simple at the same time does not occur to the observer. They tend to think that complexity must be complicated, and this notion is ever-present. The laws of mathematics reveal that things can be simple and complex, depending on the way the observer sees it. Mandelbrot's is the most powerful and well-known set of simple rules, which are widely recognized and famous outside of mathematics. It is not only known because of its aesthetic appeal, but moreover because of the simple rules that constructs and emerges as the complex structure, and Mandelbrot's model is the best form of displaying mathematics via visualization.

When a set of objects is observed, one sees that it is complex, but knowing and observing the set from a holistic perspective one can see that it is simple. If an object is simple and complex at the same time, or one or the other, it all depends on the quality of the observer's knowing. Thus, self-organization is the most powerful law in nature by an emerging conglomeration of simple rules. Translating insights from the sciences of complexity to organizational behaviour and organizational cybernetics and precisely into the field of strategy is a demanding task, but the resource and time is well invested, thus by this analogy many accomplishments not yet known to the field may give rise to the viability the organization seeks (Beer, 1959, 1966, 1972, 1981, 1985; Foerster, 2003a; Ulrich and Probst, 1984).

There are pioneers of the science that have bridged chaos and complexity sciences into other fields – they have contributed to the scientific and practical understanding and have revealed the power of self-organization as a natural phenomenon, within the context of their fields. It is important to list some vital scholars' observations on self-organization that are essential for management and strategy. Below are some prime examples of this phenomenon and the great contributors:

- **Alan Turing, by his patterns** – 'Under certain not very restrictive conditions (which include a requirement that the sphere be relatively small but increasing in size) the pattern of breakdown of homogeneity is axially symmetrical, not about the original axis of spherical polar co-ordinates, but about some new axis determined by disturbing influences' (Turing, 1952).
- **Belousov, by his chemical reaction** – Boris Belousov is famous for discovering a chemical reaction that spontaneously exhibits temporal periodicity. Zhabotinsky discovered its power and developed it further, calling it the 'Belousov–Zhabotinsky (BZ) reaction' – a chemical clock. Herman Haken used the BZ reaction as a paradigm in his 'synergetics' (Haken and Knyazeva,

2000). 'The philosophical consequences of synergetics, the interdisciplinary theory of evolution and self-organization of complex systems... Synergetics can be considered as one of the modern, most promising research programs. It is oriented towards the research for common patterns of evolution and self-organization of complex systems of any kind regardless of the concrete nature of their elements or subsystems' (Haken and Knyazeva, 2000). This BZ reaction is a prime and standard example of complex behaviour in textbooks on non-linear dynamics.

- **Benoit Mandelbrot, by his fractals** – The term fractals was coined by Mandelbrot (1977) to describe the many phenomena of nature in which small parts resemble the whole. 'The veins in leaves look like branches; branches look like miniatures trees, rocks look like miniature mountains' (Mandelbrot and Taleb, 2010). Similar patterns can be found in economic data and the parts often relate to the whole according to what we can observe as the 'power law'. Fractal finance has not yet earned a place in Ivy League MBA classrooms. Volatility breeds volatility and markets keep the memory of past happenings and moves; it comes in clusters and lumps. Long-run market returns are dominated by a small number of investments. The Mandelbrot set fractals natural principle ($Z \rightleftharpoons Z^2+C$) signposts Mandelbrot's equation and feeds back on itself (Mandelbrot, 1977).
- **Stafford Beer, by his 'first principle of organization'** – 'Managerial, operational and environmental varieties, diffusing through an institutional system, TEND TO EQUATE; they should be designed to do so with minimum damage to people and to cost. The function of management is emerging, as it must finally be understood, as a subsystem of a viable system – and not as some hierarchical overload' (Beer, 1985). The design and creation of Beer's VSM model is one of the most vital and powerful introductions of the power law into social sciences.
- **Ross W. Ashby (1962), by his 'principles of self-organizing systems'** – '..., but it's fundamental and is only too readily forgotten when one comes to deal with organizations that are either biological in origin or are in imitation of such systems. With this in mind, we can now start to consider the so-called "self-organizing" system. We must proceed with some caution here if we are not to land in confusion, for the adjective is, if used loosely, ambiguous, and, if used precisely, self-contradictory... To say a system is self-organizing leaves open two quite different meanings. There is a first meaning that is simple and unobjectionable. This refers to the system that starts with its parts separate (so that the behavior of each is independent of the others' state) and whose parts then act so that they change towards

forming connections of some type. Such a system is "self-organizing" in the sense that it changes from parts separated to parts joined.'

- **Von Foerster, by his 'self-organizing systems and their environments'** – 'Let me briefly summarize...: [...]

  1 By a self-organizing system, I mean that part of a system that eats energy and order from environment.

  2 There is a reality of the environment in a sense suggested by acceptance of the principles of reality.

  3 The environment has structure' (Foerster, 2003a).

What is expected to be called self-organizing from the system is that it develops eigen behaviours to create order out of disorder. The author suggests another complementary definition:

> The system has the attributes of self-meaning out of chaos and a self-transforming but identity-preserving structure out of randomness by a holistic awareness of its environment and itself. One of the chief attributes of a self-organizing social system is the ability to maintain its identity.

Indiscriminate intervention into the system by prerogative means does not possess 'requisite variety' (Ashby, 1958). There we find the reason why state interventions throughout the financial world do not heal the world's economic system. Greece will never become Germany, regardless of the money pumped into its system. Iraq will never become the centre of domino-effect-producing democracy in the Middle East by invasion and advanced military technology; it can only be dismantled as a sovereign country. Thus, once the system is dismantled, all the military might has only produced more chaos instead of order. Why are the US-led forces challenged in Afghanistan, although they possess the most powerful and advanced technology? Because the cure and remedy are not found by the reductionist view of complex affairs and their scientific downward causations, which can only separate top–down by dismantling the systems. The problem of Afghanistan cannot be solved by military means and money-pumping charities; it can only be solved by reinventing and recreating the Afghan identity.

A chief example is charities: to get donations in order to survive, they are shapeable to the desires and wants of the donor, and by the ever-changing donor's list they fail at their identity and their ultimate goal to create a change for which they were created in the first place. Here the author's observation of identity preservation as described above is addressed. Thus, a charity must maintain its identity and create and attract target groups that actually identify themselves with the charity's goals, and not vice versa.

What the world faces today is systems' crises that cannot be ignored nor cured by the methods of reductionist means and how they are applied in separation. These crises must be resolved by a holistic and systemic lens. This requires an interdisciplinary approach, and this chapter substantiates this claim by giving the reader a conceptual tour through the world of chaos, complexity and self-organization. Figure 2.2 describes how the current model of strategic analysis is transformed from 'order to chaos'. Bringing the system in control needs the additional view of other sciences, beyond the Newtonian universe: a strategy that has requisite variety, which is the problem with our contemporary strategy model, a strategic mindset, which is wider in scope and in depth and, according to Ashby's law, by igniting the power of self-organization, which is primarily based on the laws of viability and self-guided mechanisms of eigen behaviour.

The organized society has been established within a short time horizon of approximately 200 years – and this makes society face different types of problems and situations today. Of course, there have been many organizations that existed before and throughout history. There were even very large organizations, eg the construction site and organization of the pharaohs in Egypt and the legendary armies from Napoleon to Genghis Khan, but the research quickly reveals that, although there may have been large organizations in terms of their numbers, they were still very simple and homogeneous organizations. The organization and the numbers with which we have to deal today are complex (Malik, 2000). The large organizations of the past were unfamiliar with problems of communication, because the tasks that they had to perform were apparent and visible, they were observable and tangible.

FIGURE 2.2 The transformation of strategy from stable environments to environments of high velocity and turbulence

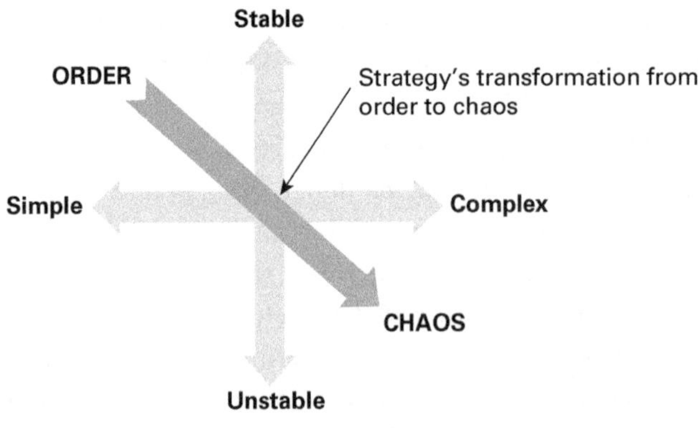

Author's own interpretation

One could see the large construction building sites and experience the enemy. There were still masters and commanders, but the tasks of transporting and breaking stones, transporting water and additional construction tasks or fighting with the enemy from man to man with swords or axes were a numbers game. The organizations of the past were manpowered organizations; the task was simply done by adding people to the task to get the job done, just as a simple act of power. Knowledge and information did not play an essential role (Malik, 2000). Therefore, some very simple and routine rules of how to guide and command were necessary to get the task accomplished. All this simplicity has emerged to become a gigantic complexity in contemporary organizations. The different types of organization and the wider diversity in the tasks of the workforce – almost everyone is hired to perform a different task – have led to complexity of coordination and communication, which is fundamental to the functioning of organizations. Coordination and communication are order-designing and structure-maintaining functions to the organizations (Malik, 2000). Function is the ethos of organization; therefore, it is essential that a shift in thinking about organizations, their structures and parts, systems and sub-systems is established.

Figure 2.2 reveals the challenges the organizations have to master to achieve growth and viability, but above all to be successful in the information and communication era. It is essential that the notion of systems thinking and systems as complex phenomena is established. The reader is invited to a journey in the world of systemic management and strategic thinking via a holistic foresight and understanding that the strategic problems of the contemporary era do not respect the boundaries of academia nor the clockwork Newtonian universe.

Figure 2.3 gives the reader a first glance of the notion of complexity for understanding its significance to strategy and the conceptual framework of the book. The notion of complexity is therefore divided as follows:

- complexity in terms of a holistic view of science for the purpose of scientific discourse with strategy;
- complexity in terms of a newly established field of science with an origin in systems sciences based on a cybernetics lens, thus firms are goal-seeking and goal-achieving entities and organized beings;
- complexity in terms of understanding and navigating complex, adaptive and self-organizing large systems, with many states of behaviour and relations to the environment, other actors and internal interrelations of the parts, which cannot be managed via linear thinking and one-minute manager/management doctrines;

FIGURE 2.3 How 'complex-trategy' tackles complexity, using the power of self-organization

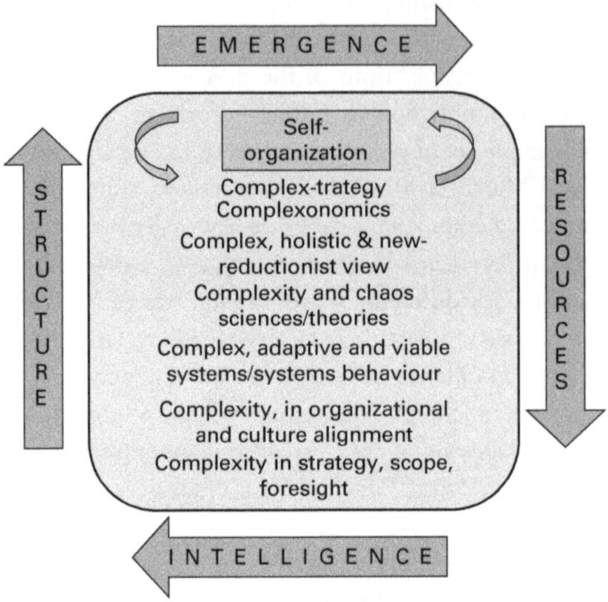

'Complex-onomics' = evolutionary Darwinian economics managed by complex-trategy
Author's own interpretation

- complexity in terms of its understanding from a cultural and eigen behavioural dimension of the complex system;
- complexity in terms of the scope, spectrum and foresight, its applicability, understanding, effectiveness and its immunity against the forces known and unknown regardless of their direction of attack.

This chapter will primarily address the strategic problems of the strategist from the perspective of the complexity sciences and practice notion and will give the reader a solid tool to sharpen their ability to navigate the complex organization in the turbulent waters of tomorrow.

Systems theory and its relevance for strategic management

Systems theory will be thoroughly treated and explained in this section. But first it is essential that an understanding of problem circles, as they are related to the notion of strategic management, is established. Business administration (BA) has always asked via which lens and world-view it ought to approach reality so that it is able to embrace and seize the essentials of business (Ulrich, 1968). The reductionist natural sciences perspective and the essential question from metaphysics – 'what is there?' – is not complete from a management strategic world-view, thus they fulfil only a partial reality. The question that strategists and managers ought to ask is, 'how can?'. This question is the embodiment of all managerial and strategic work; their ethos is to design a better and more favourable future.

To address systems in depth, to understand their dynamics, behaviours, 'eigen behaviours' (Foerster, 2003a), 'eigen values' and their interrelations, it is on the other hand the pivotal task; because of the nature and pace of the world's emerging developments and managerial problems organizations face as a result of these dynamics. But moreover, because of the remedy of the Newtonian 'reductionist' (Kauffman, 2008) and scientific analysis method (Ackoff, 1973), it cannot offer what is needed in a world of holistic and systemic crises.

> System thinking correctly states that while reductionist research strategy was very successful, it underestimates the complexity of it. ... There is no doubt that the superstars of 20th century science are in atomic physics including nuclear and particle physics and molecular (if you wish 'particle' biology). Both disciplines were driven by searching for the constituents of the organized whole. The 'take-home message' of the lessons from the history of science is that methodological reductionism, the analytical decomposition of structures to parts, should be completed by searching for organizational principles, too (Erdi, 2008).

The reader just needs to look outside where the word 'crises' has become a word of familiarity even to schoolchildren and a permanent state of world affairs. These never-ending crisis scenarios are only never-ending because the world treats them by the mindset by which they have been created. One of Einstein's famous quotes states: 'We cannot solve our problems with the same thinking we used when we created them.' By analysing systems, strategists and scientists can observe that a system is part of a larger system and ubiquitously a whole of the interaction of its parts. A brain produces thought (intelligence) or variety, but by taking it out of the human body to analyse it, it will lose its purpose – to create a thought. A car's purpose is to produce speed. Taking the car apart to understand it destroys the property of its behaviour and purpose – to create speed. Going to business school is to become a manager and to understand how an organization is navigated in the larger whole in which it's embedded. However, universities have been organized, by claiming autonomy, by subject and departmentalization. This means concentrating on a single subject such as marketing, accounting, finance, HR, etc, and yet still claiming to create managers. Can this be the reason why financial management has been considered the ultimate manager-producing recipe by the cauldrons of capitalism – the Ivy League business schools, especially in the US?

> As the ... financial crises and the great recession begin to ease, executives may be tempted to heave a sigh of relief and return to the comfort of business as usual. But doing so would constitute a serious mistake to their companies and a grave disservice to capitalism itself. Rising income inequality, high unemployment, and spiraling budget deficits are filling public distrust of business, while the shifting balance of power between East and West exacerbates these tensions. But perhaps the biggest danger is that short-term approaches to investing in and managing companies – the 'quarterly capitalism' that led to the financial meltdown – still persist (Barton, 2011).

Could this be the reason why the US-dominated managerial educational system has produced the kind of manager who only functions in the monetary economy by a myopic vision of only looking backwards at the last three to six months' worth of data, while navigating forward (Kamran, 2011a, 2011b)? 'It's time to fix capitalism's founding principles so that it can deliver the sustainable growth the world needs' (Barton, 2011). Hetzler (2008) underpins the necessity of real-time information early-warning systems, brain-physiological and optimal processing of information as it's expected from the airline industry before a flight takes off. The bigger surprise is that the world is not ready to expect the same level of obviousness and naturalness from the management of social organizations (Hetzler, 2008). The world of mainstream business and academia is too busy to absorb the perturbations of simple problems by analysis and predictions, and this ability could only confirm and be validated in the world of continuity and linearity. There is no graduate school of business that teaches or models nature as the ultimate business model for efficiency and control – understanding how information within the body of an organism is transferred in real time and thereby the notion of control is spread throughout the organism's system. According to Beer: 'The control function is spread through the architecture of the system. It is not a recognizable thing at all, but it exists in some form inferred from the systems behavior' (Malik, 1984). If the body waited a month before raising the alarm of a serious health condition, what would that do to the death rate of the world's population? It's a sad wonder that people run their organizations in exactly this way. Table 2.1 describes some basic differences between system thinking and reductionist thinking.

There are many facets of the systems approach. However, there are two main contributors that need to be distinguished: (1) Ludwig von Bertalanffy and (2) Norbert Wiener (Schwaninger, 2006b).

TABLE 2.1 Scientific reductionist thinking vs. systems thinking approach defined

Analysis (Knowledge)	System thinking (Understanding)
1. Taking something apart and into pieces to analyse it. Asking: what is this made of? To take a car apart cannot answer anything about the speed, which is the purpose of the car.	Asking: What is the system a part of, meaning a larger whole, eg what larger whole is a car a part of? Answer: a transportation system, eg university is a part of the education system, a company is part of a social-productive system.
2. Analysing by focusing on the behaviour of the single parts.	Asking what emergent behaviour may result by the interaction of the whole. The whole is more than the sum of its parts.
3. Separating the whole to focus on what is the single issue, or a part to analyse and focus on that part.	Thinking in a holistic way to understand the whole. What is an educational system, what is a transportation system, what is an economical system?

Author's interpretation

The former will be introduced in this point, for the latter will be thoroughly explained in the section on 'Cybernetics'. Ludwig von Bertalanffy (1901–1972), the Austro-German-Canadian biologist and philosopher, was the creator and chief exponent of 'general system theory' (von Bertalanffy, 1969). Bertalanffy, in the introduction to his book *General System Theory: Foundations, Development, Applications* (von Bertalanffy, 1969, p 3), wrote:

> If someone were to analyze current notions and fashionable catchwords, he would find 'systems' high on the list. The concept has pervaded all fields of science.

Similarly, today we observe that words like 'strategy' and 'complexity' have become the jargon of the day. This fashionable and quick-fix thinking is deeply held within business administration's book-producing industry, and is based on the fallacy that the fancier the title of the book, the more robust the theory behind it. This could not be further from the truth. Managerial sciences need to go much deeper into the field of social and design sciences and bring forth theories based on proven and ground-breaking books that have been written, regardless of their time of publication. Bertalanffy's book belongs to such a category. According to the International Society of Systems Sciences (ISSS), 'Bertalanffy was one of the most important theoretical biologists of the first half of the 20th century…' (Brauckmann, 1999). The notion of the 'whole' or 'holistic' for the purpose of the book and especially according to Bertalanffy's approach is as follows: a whole is a set of, and whereof its lens, the prosperities and phenomenon is constructed. Thus, they embody:

- hierarchy;
- teleology;
- purposefulness of a system;
- differentiation of a system;
- morphogenesis (Turing, 1952);
- stability and ultra-stability;
- emergence;
- evolution;
- immunity.

The above notions are identified, and their structures and mechanisms are understood and described. The basic concept of systems is made up of the following three approaches:

1 The system is a whole that functions by virtue of the interaction of its parts. A system is defined by its elements and the relationship among these elements (Erdi, 2008).
2 The system is the integration of analytic and synthetic methods by taking into account the interaction of the system with its environment (Erdi, 2008).
3 There are two types of systems:
   a) closed systems, which do not interact with other systems;
   b) open systems, which interact with other systems outside of themselves (Erdi, 2008).

Bertalanffy has emphasized:

> 'General system theory' will be an important means to facilitate and control the application of transfer of principles from one realm to another. It will no longer be necessary to duplicate or triplicate the discovery of the same principles in different fields isolated from each other (von Bertalanffy, 1969).

The main points that Bertalanffy underpins are described by Boulding (1956), who emphasized in his ground-breaking paper on 'general system theory':

> General System Theory is a name which has come into use to describe a level of theoretical model-building which lies somewhere between the highly generalized constructions of pure mathematics and the specific theories of specialized

> disciplines. Mathematics attempts to organize highly general relationships into a coherent system, a system however which does not have any necessary connection with the 'real' world around us. It studies all thinkable relationships abstracted from any concrete situation or body of empirical knowledge. It is not even confined to 'quantitative' relationships narrowly defined indeed, the developments of a mathematics of quality and structure is already on the way, even though it is not as far advanced as the classical mathematics of quantity and number.

Boulding (1956) goes further and states:

> Each discipline corresponds to a certain segment of the empirical world, and each develops theories which have particular applicability to its own empirical segment. Physics, Chemistry, Biology, Psychology, Sociology, Economics, and so on all carve out for themselves certain elements of the experience of man and develop theories and patterns of activity (research) which yield satisfaction in understanding and which are appropriate to their special segments.

Beer (1994) in his book on the science of holistic management asks: 'How many grapes went into the wine' (Harnden *et al*, 1994)? This quote by Jan Christiaan Smuts, who was a philosopher, and the first time he wrote the term 'the whole' and referred to its attributes as 'holistic' without the (w) (Smuts, 1926). Beer writes: 'Instead of the animistic, or the mechanistic, or the mathematical universe, we see the genetic, organic, holistic universe' (Smuts, 1952). Additional and fundamental phenomenon of a universal significance to all disciplines and matters is that everything is related to some sort of environment. According to Boulding:

> Every discipline studies some kind of 'individual' electron, atom, molecule, crystal, virus, cell, plant, animal, man, family, tribe, state, church, firm, corporation, university, and so on. Each of these individuals exhibits 'behavior,' action, or change, and this behavior is considered to be related in some way to the environment of the individual that is, with other individuals with which it comes into contact or into some relationship (Boulding, 1956).

Figure 2.4 describes the system's or organization's interaction with its environment.

This interaction of environment and organization, or organism, according to Ashby's Law, however, can only be stable if and only if the O has sufficient capacity to absorb the number of disturbances that the environment produces (O > = E). The notion of 'requisite variety' is as fundamental to strategic management as the 'Second Law of Thermodynamics' is to physics. 'Indeed, a recent article notes that "Ashby's Law" has the same

FIGURE 2.4 Relationship between the environment (E) and the organization (O)

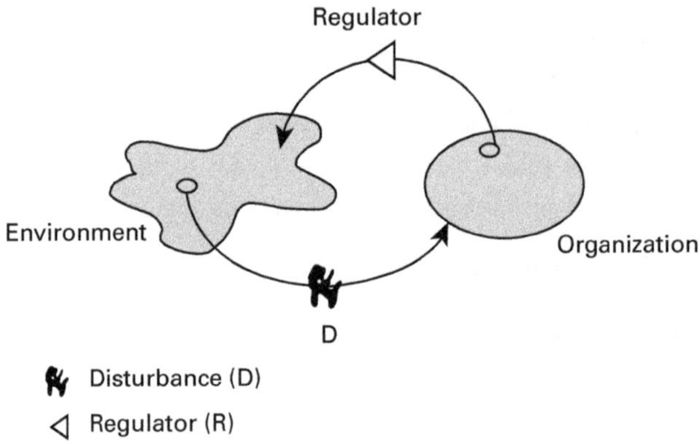

Author's interpretation, based on Christopher (2007)

crucial significance for regulation and control as has the Second Law of Thermodynamics for physics...' (IEEE Systems *et al*, 1979). Systems are everywhere, and system thinking can be applied as the scientific and practical foundation whereupon other sciences can embody a solid unity. In the words of Wolfram (2002):

> The idea of describing the behavior in terms of mathematical equations works well where the behavior is fairly simple. It almost inevitably fails whenever the behavior is more complex. Indeed, there are many common phenomena about which theoretical science has had remarkably very little to say. Degree of difficulty encountered in mathematical representation of a phenomenon increases exponentially by the degree of its complexity.

It is therefore essential and critical to the holistic wellbeing of the systemic world to shift the tools of strategizing from reductionist towards a holistic world-view, thus beginning by changing the strategic lens.

System methodology as a foundation of organizational steering in complex environments

Gharajedaghi (2011) describes the dual shift of paradigms that individuals have been confronted with in the last 50 years:

> Not only has there been a shift in our understanding of nature of the beast from mindless mechanical systems to multi-minded socio-culture system. But,

> there also has been a profound shift in our way of knowing: from analytical thinking, the science of dealing with independent sets of variables, to system thinking the art and science of handling interdependent sets of variables.

Hence, it is precisely the objective of the system methodology to deal with not only the imperative of interdependencies, environmental complexities and varieties of the self-organizing systems and their eigen behaviours, but moreover to deal with the notion of how multi-minded systems, where the interaction of many and diverse agents contributes to the goal and the higher purpose of a larger whole, is controlled and steered (Gharajedaghi, 2011). The contemporary world of BA and its strategy seeks the treatment of single and compartmentalized problems as the general established notion that the problems of the business world appear as single problems separately with no relation to other problems. The strategist is trained to see the problem and the implications of their actions in a dividing lens of its relations. Strategists are even trained to separate a larger problem into pieces in order to deal and cope with it. However, the problems and their causes are related to one another and the remedy prescribed must be also not to just relieve the pain but actually to cure the patient. Von Foerster (1984–1999) emphasizes: 'Act so to always increase the number of total choices' (Foerster, 1984). Von Foerster's proposal, a 'constructive ethical imperative', will serve a strategist very well as one of the most important strategies. This ethical proposal does not lead to reductionist thinking, but to treating problems and their causes. Problems cannot be separated from their causes. It is always better to treat the causes. In economics Boulding (1956) emphasizes:

> When it comes to the theory of economic development, the failure to recognize explicitly the essentially epistemological nature of the problem has led to proliferation of mechanical models of very doubtful value, and, one fears, the giving of a large amount of bad advice.

Beer (1990) predicts a self-fulfilling prophecy on the systemic crises of global economic systems:

> We observe a systemic crisis characterized by regulatory collapse… The soviet bloc under the charismatic leadership of Mikhail Gorbachev has had the nerve to admit to (my words above) systemic crises in regulatory collapse. It is typical of the West to speak of 'victory' at such a moment – which of course becomes vainglorious triumphalism in Britain. We are in fact not far behind. The record-breaking deficits in Britain, the United States, and Canada adumbrate systemic crises, while rates of inflation, unemployment,

> illiteracy, ill health, and poverty signify regulatory collapse. Note that both systems have failed because of various forms of centralization. The difference between them in 1990 is not the degree of failure, but in honesty, courage, and reforming zeal.

According to Gharajedaghi (2006) underpinning his claim, he observes that years of struggle in dealing with the whole by experimentation with different systems at different levels has led him to believe that effective system methodology lies at the interaction of the 'four foundations' (Gharajedaghi, 2006): [...]

1. Holistic Thinking (iteration of structure, function and process)
2. Operational Thinking (dynamic of multi-loop feedback and complexity)
3. Self-organization, movement toward a predefined order (socio-cultural model)
4. Interactive Design (redesigning the future and inventing ways to bring it about) (Gharajedaghi, 2006).

Figure 2.5 explains and substantiates the claim of how the viable and competent systems methodology for 'productive social systems' can be explained. The author has added the four pillars of strategy to the model so the reader can observe the notion of strategic thinking which shifts from the analytic that tries to quantify by numbers, but not the set of behaviours that emerge. Thus, it is the purpose of the author to give a set of concrete application tools whereby the strategist can clearly have a vital advantage when putting the tools into action. However, it is essential to mention and emphasize the point raised by Korn (2011):

> The diversity of speculative thinking about the systemic view of parts of the world, concrete, abstract or imaginary in the natural, artificial, living and in particular human domain, although inspiring and stimulating, has resulted in disagreement regarding the content of the subject matter of the discipline of systems if there is such a thing. The speculative nature of the approach to this subject has produced a vast amount of jargon, difficulties and confusion when trying practical applications.

Ackoff (2006) also observes:

> I frequently talk to groups of managers on the nature of systems thinking and its radical implications to management. In doing so, I use several case studies involving prominent American corporations. At the end of the presentation I am almost always asked, 'If this way of thinking is as good as you say it is, why don't more organizations use it?'.

FIGURE 2.5 The four foundations of system methodology

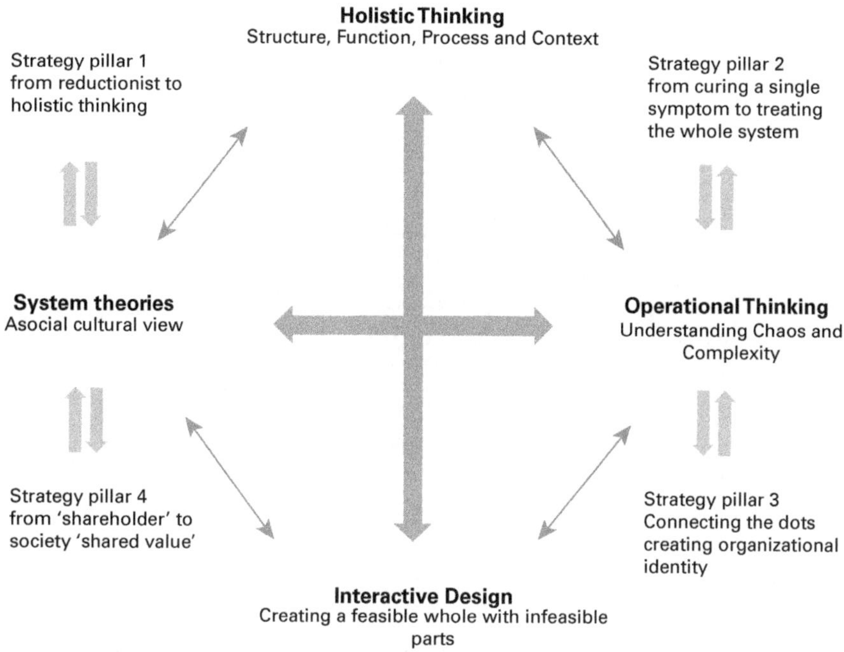

Author's interpretation, based on Gharajedaghi (2004)

Figure 2.5 describes the author's notion of extending Gharajedaghi's model of holistic thinking.

Ackoff's points are essential since they closely correspond to the problems the author has had as a consultant himself explaining the notion of a holistic system thinking methodology and effective way of decision-making. Thus, the reasons why organizations fail to implement the notion are simple:

1 The strategist fails to grasp and recognize a transforming idea, let alone system thinking.

2 The person that has created the failure does not recognize why they have failed and still is busy with over-analysis or trying to hide problems (Ackoff, 2006).

Gharajedaghi (2006) recalls some cases where systems, mega corporations, system-relevant banks, nations, economics systems have failed and categorizes and points out these forces using five hierarchical levels that shift success to failure. Figure 2.6 describes these forces.

FIGURE 2.6 The hierarchy of forces that erode competitive advantage

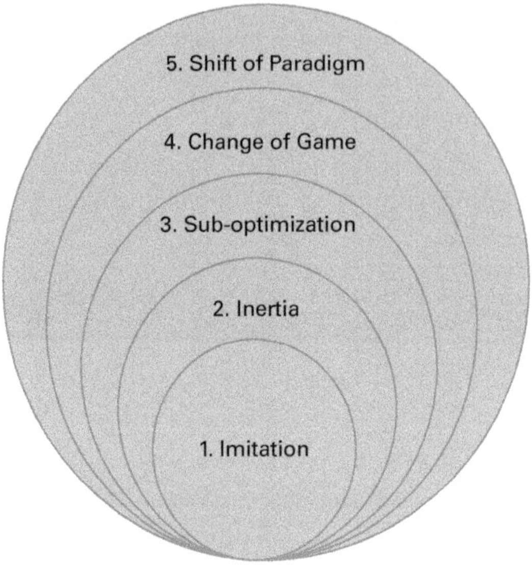

Author's interpretation, based on Gharajedaghi (2004)

1 Benchmarking and hyper-competition is not enough. The system thinking goes beyond pure imitation. For example, General Motors cars became more similar year by year, and instead of competing with rivals, it competed more with itself. The same challenge was responsible in large part for Apple's pre-1996 crises: they had 15 computers, with marginal difference – even Jobs could not tell the difference once when he was asked. Now Microsoft is behind and failing.

2 Inertia is responsible as second-level (supportive) tendencies and behaviours that delay or avoid break-through ideas.

3 Exaggeration – the false assumption that if A is good, the more one does of A, the better. This is the core of the third-level failure. (As the Japanese did with their TQM and over-efficiency and failing to transform this vital competitive advantage into a sustainable competitive advantage, or how the Toyota Way has failed and now the world talks about the VW Way.)

4 Changing of the game or transforming the problem/failure lies at the heart of the counterintuitive process that converts success into failure. The successful player changes the game by playing the game. (See Apple's transformation under Jobs and IBM's transformation under Gershner.)

5 The cumulative master of the forces ultimately manifests themselves in the force of Gharajedaghi, which is the shift in paradigm. This can happen by a dual set of core capabilities that intelligent organizations have in

common: learning and unlearning. According to Beer (1975), 'Acceptable ideas are competent no more and competent ideas are not yet acceptable.' And according to Gharajedaghi (2006), a shift in paradigm requires two possibilities:

a. A change in the nature of reality, and

b. A change in the nature of inquiry. These changes are essential for the scien-trategist. Unfortunately, system thinkers mostly publish for system-thinking scientists or peers. They should transfer this notion to mainstream and publish more for practitioners. The global and simultaneous crises that are on the rise give the systems-thinking strategists the best opportunity, first to make their organizations immune and then to contribute to the well-being of the larger system they are a part of, thus staying loyal to the Ackoffian doctrine of explaining difficult thinking and things with simplicity to others and managing problems the same way as well (Gharajedaghi 2006).

System dynamics and its implications on strategy

Jay Forrester of MIT is the founder of 'system dynamics' (SD), a theory that is the basis for an essential systems movement – the theory of non-linear systems or dynamic systems:

> 'System dynamics' is a professional field that deals with the complexity of systems. System dynamics is the necessary foundation underlying effective thinking about systems. System dynamics deals with how things change through time, which covers most of what most people find important. System dynamics involves interpreting real life systems into computer simulation models that allow one to see how the structure and decision-making policies in a system create its behavior (Forrester, 1999).

'In SD, the main emphasis is on the role of structure, and its relationship with dynamic behavior of systems, modeled as networks of informationally closed feedback loops between stock and flow variables' (Schwaninger, 2006b). SD, according to Forrester, is a very important and popular way of talking and communicating about systems, agreeing that systems are important, and believing that intuition will lead to effective decisions; thus, without a foundation of systems principles, simulation, and experimental approach, systems thinking runs the high risk of becoming superficial, ineffective and prone to arriving at counterproductive conclusions (Forrester,

1999). SD deals with the very complexity of systems. It is the necessary foundation underlying effective thinking about systems and deals with how things change and shift by the passing of time, which covers most of what is considered as essential (Forrester, 1999):

> Our educational, social, and economic systems are far more complex than the technological systems faced by engineers. Even with the simpler systems of chemical refineries and space flight, an engineer would never try to design, and would build prototype systems to demonstrate performance (Forrester, 1999).

SD models business and real-world situations, which are based on observed real conditions and complexities of the firm interacting with its environment and, thus, upon data input. Visualization into a computer simulation model is generated, whereby the strategist and manager are able to see the very structure and consequences of the managerial decision-making process, the later policies created by the system's behaviour and what outcomes are likely to occur as a result of the actions applied.

> The common denominator of the different systems approaches in our day is that they share a worldview focused on complex dynamic systems, and an interest in describing, explaining and a way of thinking ('Systems Thinking' or 'Systemic Thinking') and a methodology for dealing with systemic issues or problems. System Dynamics is a discipline and a methodology for the modelling, simulation and control of complex, dynamic systems. The particular approach of SD lies in representing the issues or systems-in-focus as meshes of closed feedback loops made up of stocks and flows, in continuous time and subject to delays. For this purpose, powerful software is available. The development of the SD methodology, and the worldwide community that applies SD to modelling and simulation in radically different contexts, suggest that it is a 'systems approach' on its own designing or at least influencing them. Therefore, most of the systems approaches offer not only a theory... (Schwaninger, 2006b).

Figure 2.7 describes the way the world is observed by the strategic tools that are designed for a linear and predictable world.

The world does not live in a uni-directional and linear universe in which a problem looks like the one displayed in Figure 2.7, which, once detected, leads to one or two actions, then leads to a foreseeable and calculable solution or situation. Thus, most discussions, reviews and debates, whether in board meetings, at cocktail parties or governmental conferences, are dealt with based on the situation described in Figure 2.7. The world, however, is far more complex and dynamic than the model above is able to absorb. The most profound problems are counter-balanced and counter-attacked, with no relation to the cause of the problems and their origin.

FIGURE 2.7 The world is unidirectional, the problem is static and we need only act to achieve the planned objectives

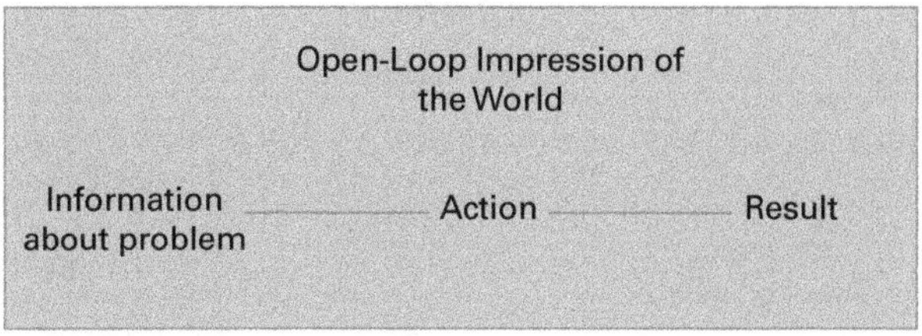

Author's interpretation, based on Forrester (1999)

However, the world lives in an ongoing circular environment, wherein each action is based on present conditions, which are the results of the conditions of the past, actions affect conditions, hence conditions change and the changed conditions become the basis for future actions (Forrester, 1999). There is an identifiable point to begin and no end point in sight, thus social systems and biological agents/systems cannot be phased down or disconnected from other social systems, organizations and other biological systems and their environments, since they are interconnected, and the problems are intertwined in an open or closed loop. Bio-social systems and complex adaptive systems (CAS) cannot be dealt with in separation from the environment, causes of behaviour and their relations and interrelations, thus they cannot be repaired, they can only be given a therapy or treatment, because living and social systems do not have a restart button. This may mean acting indirectly; to change the root causes of the problems the strategist faces or changing the environment where the organization is embedded.

Information is critical; it is the essence of systemic management and relating to the term control in general. In biological systems, information is the foundation, whereby survival is ever possible. Sub-systems embedded in a larger system can only create a viable whole if they are communicating with each other and their environments, based on a recursive organizational structure. According to Heylighen (1991):

> The lower-level elements in this process play the role of building blocks: their stability provides the firmness needed to support the construction, while their variable connections allow several configurations to be tried out. The principle of 'the whole is more than the sum of its parts' is implied by this systemic construction principle, since the system in the present conception is more than a mere configuration of parts, it is a stable configuration, and this entails a number of emergent constraints and properties.

FIGURE 2.8 A closed-loop system and how it reacts to problems and information

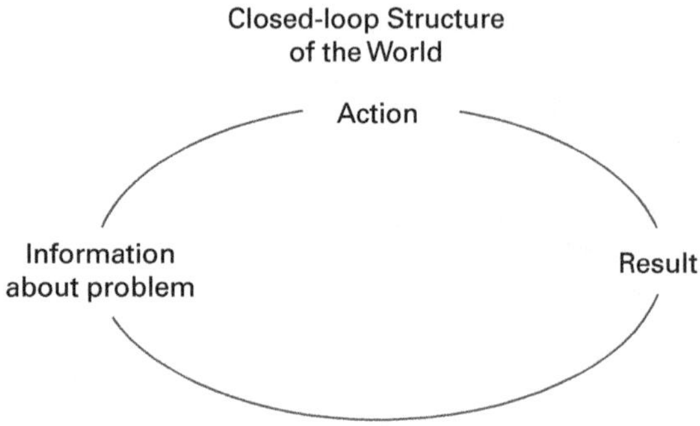

Author's interpretation, based on Forrester (1999)

Figure 2.8 describes Forrester's notion of how a system reacts to problems within a closed-loop system. The more sub-systems, variables, conditions, agents and their behaviours or set of activities are involved, the more complex the system as a whole becomes. Systemic catastrophes cannot be treated, cured or coped with by linear thinking. At the utmost a system may be kept synthetically alive for a while, but problems or organizational cancers not treated by a systemic analysis and method will become bigger and more severe, since not only organizational capabilities and learning grow in time, but so do organizational cancers.

As an example, one can examine the Greek financial crisis. The Greek financial failure has not been due to the problems it has created after Greece joined the EU, but moreover, because of the problems it had successfully hidden before it joined the EU community with the help of the US financial industry, in particular by financial cosmetic surgeries by Goldman Sachs. Moreover, the problems started with the way the structure of Greece's government managed its affairs, social infrastructure, and public facilities and how it controlled and managed the country's larger governmental systems. Before the First World War, Greece had the privilege to run its public systems, such as schools, hospitals, orphanages, and larger public goods, etc, via locally based communities, which was partially due to the Ottoman rule and legacy (Kamaras, 2011). Ottomans were not in the habit of providing public good and governance through a centrally managed government administration. Therefore, when it came to public good, citizens of Greece had to fend for themselves through local and communal organizations (Kamaras, 2011). The system was a very well-functioning system, resulting in Greece becoming a highly successful country. 'That system worked. Through local and communal organization, by the mid to late nineteenth century, the Greeks were one of the most prosperous and dynamic groups in Southeast Europe' (Kamaras, 2011). But matters got worse as Greece modernized and it became centralized in how it managed to execute control over its widening territory.

> So, as the Greek state expanded territorially it also expanded its responsibilities, undercutting old traditions of localism and community action. Herein lies the root of the country's current crisis. Long-established, autonomous local elites were displaced in the 1920s, their place taken by a new group of people adept at managing a rent-seeking relationship with the state. The new local leaders joined national parties and then worked to build up party machines by distributing state largesse. Not a single region or city of note mobilized its resources in pursuit of economic success, based on international competitiveness. Instead all major localities channeled central government resources into patronage. The central government, which was dominated by the same parties, was an energetic accomplice. Once the Greek state was fully formed, however, a central administrative structure took over communal institutions. Powerful new national party machines displaced the local elites who'd successfully served as administrators. In Greece's second largest city, Salonika, this process took a bit more than a decade. Between 1912, when the city was integrated into the Greek Kingdom, and 1925, Salonika's schools, hospitals, and other institutions were nationalized and its local trustees were replaced by centrally appointed bureaucrats. Likewise, the responsibility for funding these institutions passed to the central government. To grasp how dramatic the change was, imagine that Washington nationalized all colleges and universities in the state of Massachusetts, Harvard included, and then ran them through political appointees. (Kamaras, 2011).

Running the government by inefficient and ineffective systems – as revealed by Western capitalism crises being traced back to similar symptoms – Greece already was a financial house of ruins before it entered the EU.

> Wall Street tactics akin to the ones that fostered subprime mortgages in America have worsened the financial crisis shaking Greece and undermining the euro by enabling European governments to hide their mounting debts. As worries over Greece rattle world markets, records and interviews show that with Wall Street's help, the nation engaged in a decade-long effort to skirt European debt limits. One deal created by Goldman Sachs helped obscure billions in debt from the budget overseers in Brussels. Even as the crisis was nearing the flashpoint, banks were searching for ways to help Greece forestall the day of reckoning. In early November – three months before Athens became the epicenter of global financial anxiety – a team from Goldman Sachs arrived in the ancient city with a very modern proposition for a government struggling to pay its bills, according to two people who were briefed on the meeting. The bankers, led by

> Goldman's president, Gary D. Cohn, held out a financing instrument that would have pushed debt from Greece's health care system far into the future, much as when strapped homeowners take out second mortgages to pay off their credit cards (Story *et al*, 2010).

Observing Greece's crises based on a linear system methodology and thinking or by politically motivated tools, the EU will be able to postpone the collapse, but to call it a cure it must be systemically regarded as out of the question. Figure 2.9 displays a business's operation, whereby one can follow the profit stream, how it is conducted and the relations from a sales transaction, which occurs at the normative level of the firm. Regretfully the profit part of the system of operations has been treated with many analytically diverse tools; the latter, which resolves systemic failures, has been ignored even by the grand strategists of business academia.

Figure 2.9 shows the dynamic system of a firm, its operation and how everything is connected internally. The firm is regulated by the three layers of a holistic management view: operations layer, strategic layer and normative layer. Profits are generated directly from the operative layer by possible pre-controlled measures of the strategic layer as the operations higher system, as well as by redesigning some pre-control measures stemming from the normative level of the system as its higher system. The revenues are being modelled as a function of market size and competitiveness (Schwaninger, 2006b). Thus, the change in the market and environment or reductionist interventions by the managers within the system's structure or systemic transformative measures put to work in advance changes the whole game and it is here that a systemic change or different set of turbulences unknown to the strategist, especially when there is a need for a quick response, is there more than ever. The ever-occurring crisis leaves the governmental systems to wonder why all of their efforts do not bring the system under control and, in other words, why the government's actions are not bringing the needed responses and feedbacks of recovery. The notion of system dynamics is hugely important and one to which the author will often return. Thus, the competitive dynamic forces in times of continuity and stability – rather than the manager trained by contemporary tools – have been controlling the stability of the system. How to define and harness those competitive forces has not been effectively treated and addressed by either the business schools or the practising managers in the world of business, and the quick-fix-addicted analysts' understanding, whereby managers have given in totally to the world of financial management and monetary economy (Kamran, 2011a, 2011b).

The feedback structure of the organization can dominate decision-making far beyond the realization of the agents embedded within that system, thus

FIGURE 2.9 Model of a business operation, its strategic and higher normative management model

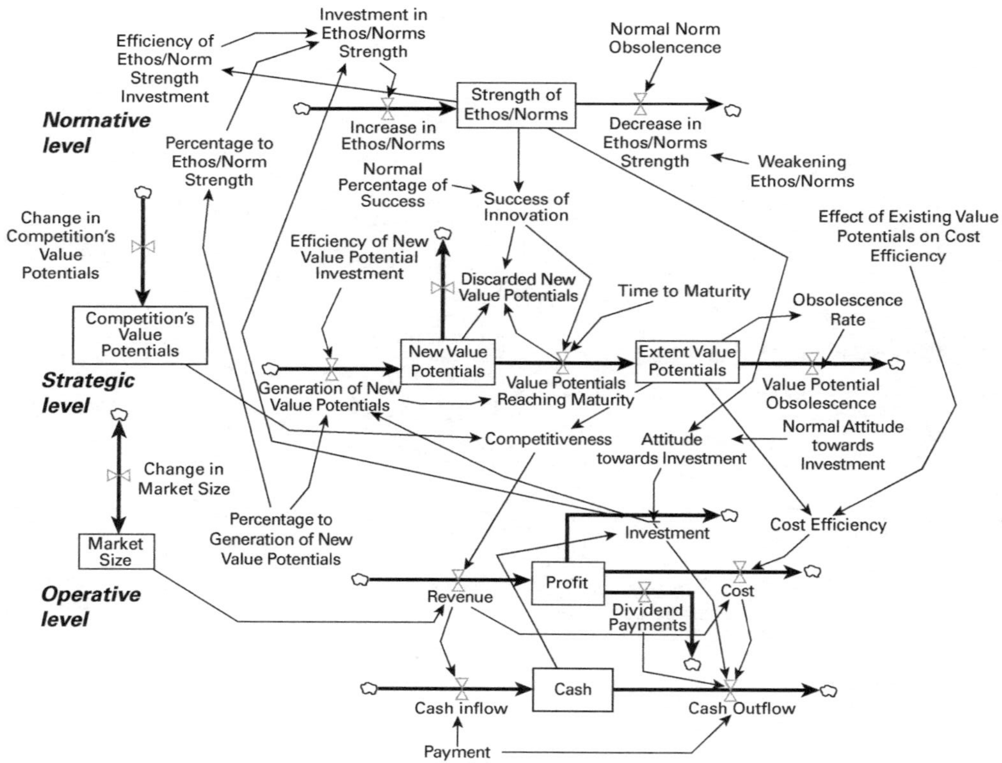

Based on Schwaninger (2006a)

FIGURE 2.10 Counterinsurgency (COIN) dynamics model, a counterinsurgency and strategic plan of the US and coalition forces

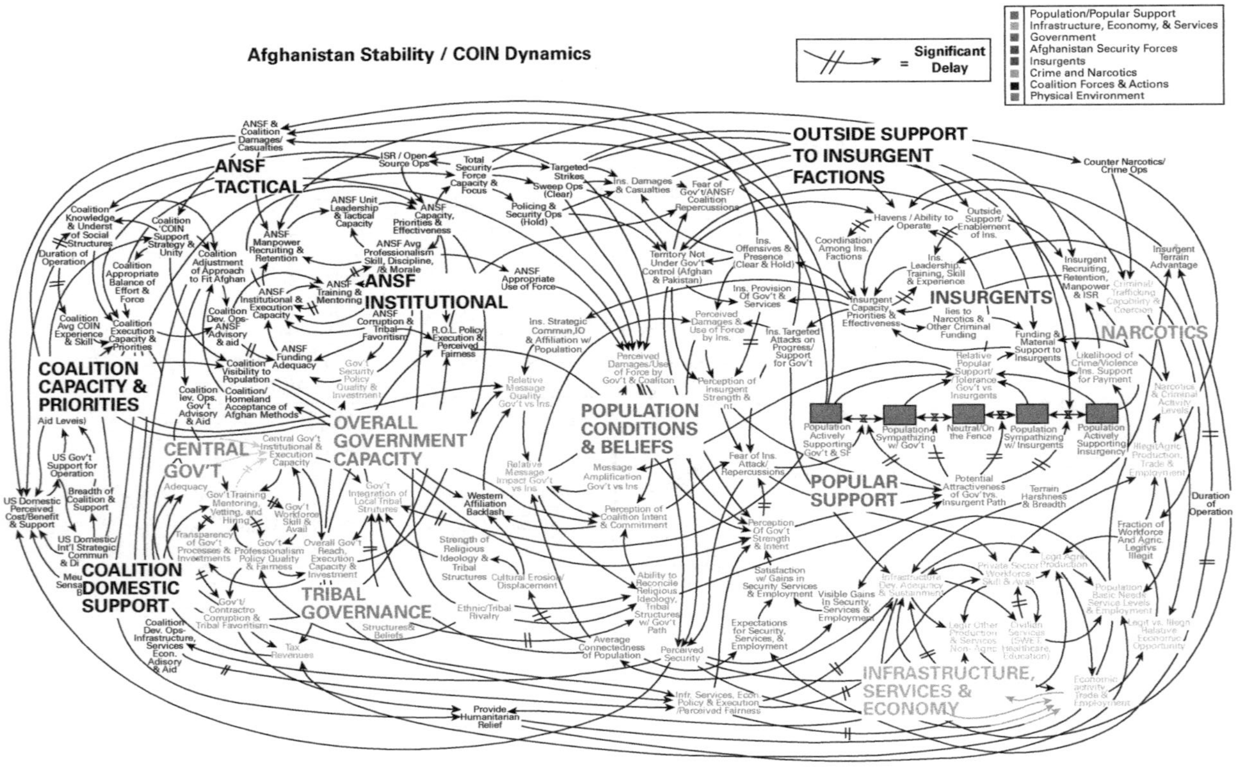

SOURCE http://sdwise.com/2013/07/hey-new-york-times-a-causal-loop-diagram-is-not-a-powerpoint-fail/ (archived at https://perma.cc/7GXL-3635)

NOTE To view Figure 2.10 in full colour, with a full-colour key, go to the URL supplied in the source line.

feedback and interconnectedness are essential empirical facts (Forrester, 1999). Another case to examine is the US-led coalition in Afghanistan. Observing strategic problems of the US and its allies in Afghanistan, especially by the ever-rising counterinsurgency (COIN), the strategy model simulation as described in Figure 2.10 illustrates the complexity, interconnectedness and interrelatedness of the different and diverse sets of actions and their effects. It also demonstrates what happens if a centre of gravity is not found to act upon and bring the chaotic system of COIN under control – the rate of failure looms large.

A simpler but much more effective model is described in Figure 2.11. The model in Figure 2.11 dates back to Boyd and is known as the 'OODA-loop model' or 'The Boyd Cycle'. Boyd called it: 'a compendium of ideas and actions for winning and losing in a highly competitive world' (Osinga, 2005).

Boyd's OODA Model stands for:

1. Observation: Sensing and understanding the world around.
2. Orientation: Orientation requires understanding and setting complex filters to combine cultural predispositions, personal experiences, science and knowledge, and genetic heritage (Osinga, 2005).
3. Decision: At the third part, reserved for decisions, it is to cast the nets of hypotheses upon the decision made and test them; thus, decision is to review all courses of alternative action and to select the most favourable, and understanding and being able to calculate their consequences.
4. Action: Reserved for implementation, which is the vital part of every strategic model.

FIGURE 2.11 John Boyd's OODA model

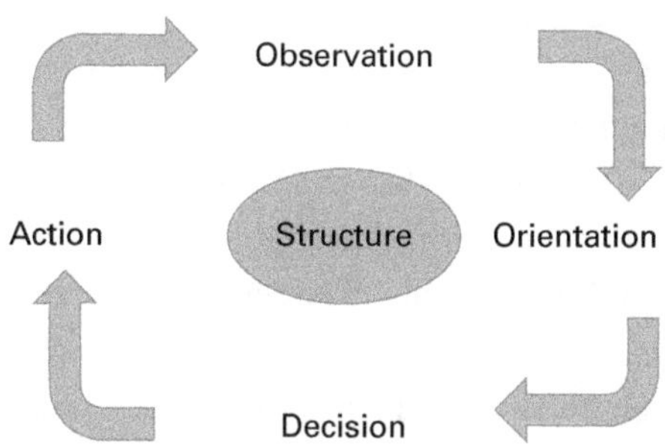

Extended by the author by the integration of 'structure' as a prerequisite to any meta, strategic and operation activity
Based on Osinga (2005)

According to a 'Marine Corps Doctrinal Publication', which is strongly Boydian in influence:

> the essence of maneuver is taking action to generate and exploit some kind of advantage over the enemy... That advantage may be psychological, technological, or temporal as well as spatial. Especially important is maneuver in time – we generate a faster operating tempo than the enemy to gain a temporal advantage. Maneuver warfare is a war fighting philosophy that seeks to shatter the enemy's cohesion through a variety of rapid, focused and unexpected actions which create a turbulent and rapidly deteriorating situation with which the enemy cannot cope (Osinga, 2005).

According to Walby (2007):

> Instead, each social system (whether economy, polity, violence nexus, or civil society) takes all other systems as its environment. Likewise each set of social relations (e.g. gender, ethnicity, class) is a system, taking all others as its environment. Each system, whether domain or set of social relations, can have a different spatial and temporal reach... A system does not necessarily fully saturate the space or territory that it is in. This enables us to think of a set of social relations as not fully saturating an institution or domain – it can overlap with other sets of social relations.

Observing the insurgency and war as a chaotic and complex process, system dynamics indicates that one cannot predict the future reliability of the system, even if one can reduce the system or model dynamics to a set of equations or linear systems. Nevertheless, there are bounds to the unpredictability of a chaotic system. Dynamic, chaotic and complex systems are highly dependent upon their initial conditions but not equally so at all times. It would be false to claim that chaos theory and complexity science can be used alone to derive a theory of warfare. However, a number of authors have argued that war is essentially chaotic or non-linear and they have made efforts to apply 'chaos theory' (CT) to various aspects of warfare. Military students of CT have suggested, for example, that campaign planners can find centres of gravity, where non-linear processes exist in an enemy's political, economic or military system. By identifying the 'attractors' in these non-linear processes, strategists will know where an attack or a concentration of efforts is likely to achieve disproportionately large effects. Therefore, CT and 'complexity science' (CS) provide tools that can predict patterns of system behaviour and define the bounds and patterns within which the system's behaviour is predictable (Gore, 1996).

Elkus (2010) observes:

> As Alan Beyerchen's famous essay on Clausewitz and non-linearity reveals, ideas about complexity and warfare did not begin with the science of complexity itself. Although Clausewitz himself did not invent the inter-related disciplines of complexity science, Beyerchen argues he 'perceived and articulated the nature of war as an energy-consuming phenomenon involving competing and interactive factors, attention to which reveals a messy mix of order and unpredictability. That is why Clausewitz preferred conflict to be studied as a whole rather than in isolation, as a system, composed of many interactive agents, that is highly responsive to initial conditions. The difficulty of reading the more theoretical sections of Clausewitz's book *On War*, in some respects, stems from the difficulty we have in general of visualizing a holistic system given the emphasis on reductionism that predominates in the way we are trained to think about problems. As helpful an analytical device as the 'levels of war' are, they add to the problems of linear categorization that Clausewitz sought to overcome in his writings.

In essence, strategy needs a holistic treatment of the subject but a focus on the centre of gravity. The next section also sees strategy from the lenses of the 'Second Law of Thermodynamics', which is also an essential view of strategy from a holistic perspective.

Entropy and the Second Law of Thermodynamics

Describing thermodynamics (the science of heat) in the field of strategic management is not for an engineer, an accountant, or a mathematician, who are specialists and may feel uneasy outside their fields of expertise, but actually this is a vital point – it ought to be written for them, should the specialist become interested in knowing how man, machines and systems are controlled. While some may generate a substantial amount of advantage from a mechanical or mathematical background, the strategist in times of systemic crises must be a specialist juggler of interdisciplinarity. Strategic problems do not appear and are not treated well in analytically christened case studies. They do not respect the compartmentalized view of the scientifically shared whole, dismantled by *reductio ad absurdum*. Systemic crises require a holistic response; thus, they ask the strategist to be able to navigate stormy waters on a professional basis and to be capable of connecting the dots of diverse symptoms and disturbances to a single larger problem resulting from a systemic failure or crisis. Figure 2.12 describes the Second Law of Thermodynamics.

FIGURE 2.12 The Second Law of Thermodynamics

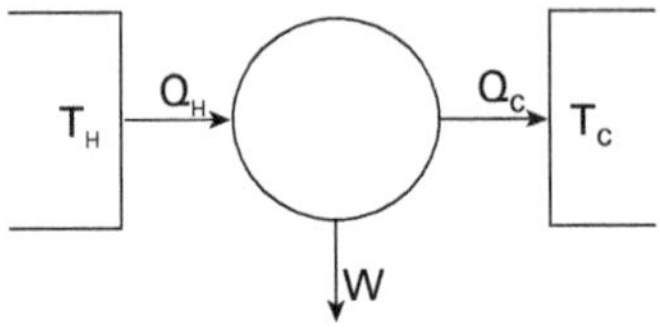

Author's interpretation

According to Pask (1961):

> ... miscegenation of Art and Science which begets inanimate objects that have like living systems. They regulate themselves and survive: they adapt and they compute: They invent. They co-operate and they compete. Naturally they evolve rapidly, pure mathematics, being mere tautology, and pure physics, being mere fact, could not have engendered them; for creatures to live, must sense the useful and the good; and engines to run must have energy available as work: and both, to endure, must regulate themselves. So it is to Thermodynamics and to its brother Σp log p, called Information Theory, that we look for distinctions between work and energy and between signal and noise.

According to Rosnay (1998):

> The principal energy laws that govern every organization are derived from two famous laws of thermodynamics. The second law, known as Carnot's principle, is controlled by the concept of entropy. Today the word entropy is as much a part of the language of the physical sciences as it is of the human sciences. Unfortunately, physicists, engineers, and sociologists use indiscriminately a number of terms that they take to be synonymous with entropy, such as disorder, probability, noise, random mixture, heat; or they use terms they consider synonymous with antientropy, such as information, neguentropy, complexity, organization, order, and improbability.

Rosnay's definition of entropy lies in the following three descriptions:

- as thermodynamics, where the names of Mayer, Joule, Carnot, and Clausius are important;
- as statistical theory, which fosters the equivalence of entropy and disorder – as a result of the work of Maxwell, Gibbs, and Boltzmann;
- and, as information theory, which demonstrates the equivalence of neguentropy (the opposite of entropy) and information – as a result of the work of Szilard, Gabor, Rothstein, and Brillouin (1940–1950) (Rosnay, 1998).

The First Law of Thermodynamics, also described as the 'Principle of Conservation of Energy', states the concentration of energy and how different forms of energy can be converted to each other as mechanical work to heat but cannot be destroyed, while the total energy of an isolated system is constant (Erdi, 2008). 'During any cycle, the cyclic integral of heat added to a system is proportional to the cyclic integral of work done by the system.' The Second Law of Thermodynamics states that while the mechanical work can be converted into heat completely, transforming it reversely cannot be completed unless another change has occurred, as heat cannot be transformed from a cooler to a warmer body without some additional change, thus the Second Law of Thermodynamics is universal (Erdi, 2008). Boyd (1976), a military strategist, states:

> ... when acting within a rigid or essentially a closed system, the goal seeking effort of individuals and societies to improve their capacity for independent action tends to produce disorder towards randomness and death. On the other hand, as already shown, the increasing disorder generated by the increasing mismatch of the system concept with observed reality opens or unstructures the system. As the unstructuring or, as we'll call it, the destructive deduction unfolds, it shifts toward a creative induction to stop the trend toward disorder and chaos to satisfy a goaloriented need for increased order. Paradoxically, then, an entropy increase permits either the destruction, or unstructuring, of a closed system and the creation of a new system to nullify the march toward randomness and death. Taken together, the entropy notion associated with the Second Law of Thermodynamics and the basic goal of individuals and societies seem to work in dialectic harmony driving and regulating the destructive/creative, or deductive/inductive, action – that we have described herein as a dialectic engine. The result is a changing and expanding universe of mental concepts matched to a changing and expanding universe of observed reality. As indicated earlier, these mental concepts are employed as decision models by individuals and societies for determining and monitoring actions needed to cope with their environment – or to improve.

Feedback loops

According to the Merriam Webster Dictionary, feedback is described as: 'the return to the input of a part of the output' (Golec, 2004). This simplicity of description of feedback systems, as shown in Figure 2.13, should not be underestimated. Thus, feedback is essential to the functioning of an organization and an organism. Feedback is a prerequisite to control and in final

FIGURE 2.13 How a simple feedback system operates

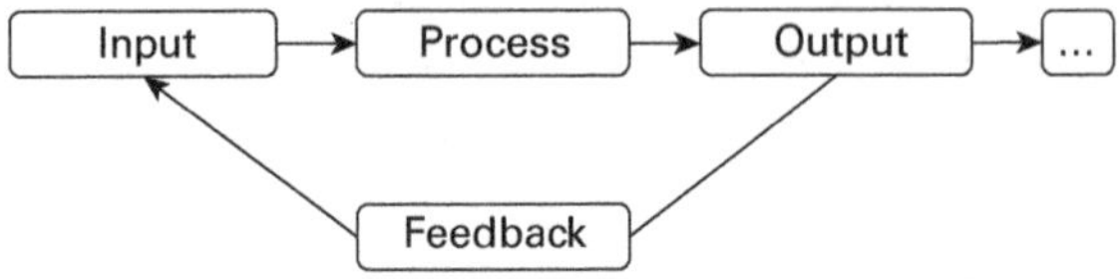

Author's interpretation

consequence vital to survival, hence all control systems are feedback-based systems. Feedback is ubiquitous in all control systems. It is not something imposed on the system; it is a vital part of the system. Figure 2.13 describes how the feedback loop and system works within an organization.

According to Golec (2004): 'This simplicity should however not undermine the importance of feedback mechanisms and their ubiquitousness in our life, both on macro- and micro-scales... Through "feeding back" a part of output again into the system, we obtain a perfect regulatory mechanism.' Strategists ought to implement a systemic feedback control system and an active computable application of feedback control system as a decision-making intervention of a higher order (Golec, 2004). The dynamics of purposefulness whereby control of an agent in nature, in an organization or in a larger society to a productive, constructive and fruitful behaviour is ever possible and can only be maintained by incorporating feedback loops and regulators within the larger body or the system under control. The limits and strength of a control system depends on the foreseeability of the observer as the systems designer and strategist – to what extent they can foresee and calculate challenges that may occur so a systemic preparedness or immunity can be built into the system. Hence challenges and problems are in a flux, change and sometimes more than the sum of the symptoms and obstacles we can foresee and are able to compute; therefore, a dynamic strategy system of control via an intelligent control system ought to be implemented as a vital part of the system. As has been shown, a system is more than the sum of its parts, so there are many challenges that can build a systemic failure, which poses organizational threats larger than to be counterattacked by treating it via single or direct intervention to resolve them. As productive systems generate eigen behaviours, so do systemic problems. This is an essential aspect of computing: the counterbalancing and variety-absorbing strategies and control systems. Strategies of control ought to be designed in an emergent manner while computation of challenges incorporated is still an essential pillar of the system of strategy-building. Mintzberg *et al* (1998) state: 'Thus, emergent strategies are not necessarily bad and deliberate strategies good; effective strategists mix these in ways that reflect the conditions at hand, notably the ability to predict as well as the need to react to unexpected events.' Figure 2.14 describes how a viable strategy is formulated. This combination of strategy formulation as a whole respects the Second Law of Thermodynamics, thus converting and implementing resources into strategy will not be able to reconvert back into its original state. In addition, a strategy must fulfil all three parts of its structure:

1. meta-plan or larger objective (teleology), grand strategy;
2. a plan and map of operations; and
3. execution – there will always be unforeseen conditions upon which the intended strategy must be adjusted (see Figure 2.14), known as 'strategy friction'. According to the author's research, strategy friction is the price of adaptation to the new or unforeseen conditions, based on the prior strategies overthrown. Thus some intended strategies being thrown out is the cost of formulating new and better strategies to get to the desired end. Strategy friction is the resource needed to boost the strategy machine to function, thus it is in accordance with and respects the Second Law of Thermodynamics.

FIGURE 2.14 Dynamic strategy formulation

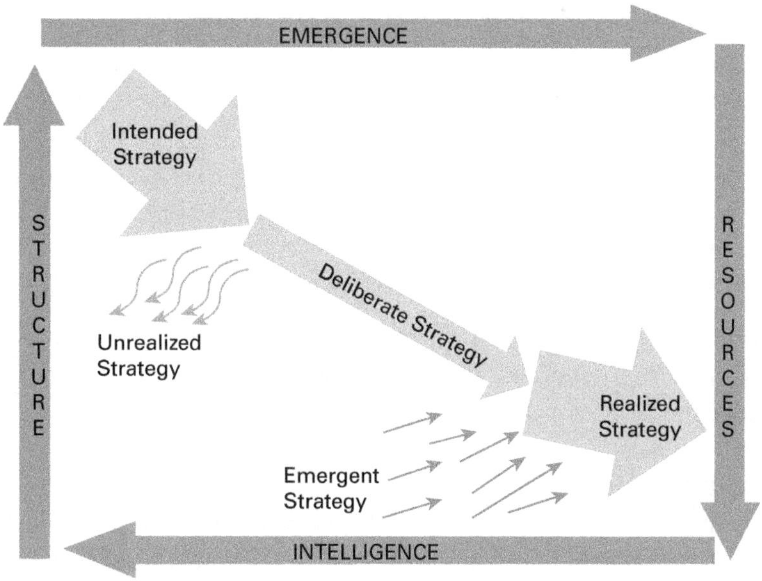

Author's interpretation, based on Mintzberg *et al* (1998)

For the dynamic system to be under control and use the resources with maximum efficiency, two types of feedback systems ought to be implemented into the model. These feedback systems can be distinguished as, namely, positive feedback and negative feedback systems. The author has established a grand strategy model (GSM) (see Figure 2.15) wherein the positive and negative feedback systems described below are integrated. However, it is essential to note and to summarize the understanding of strategy at this point, so that a reasonable and comprehensible understanding is established. According to Osinga (2005), the following description finds common agreement among strategy scholars:

- Strategy concerns both organization and environment: the organization uses strategy to deal with changing environments.
- The substance of strategy is complex: because change brings novel combinations of circumstances to the organization, the substance of strategy remains unstructured, unprogrammed, nonroutine, and non-repetitive.
- Strategy affects overall welfare of the organization: strategic decisions are considered important enough to affect the overall welfare of the organization.
- Strategy involves issues of both content and process: the study of strategy includes both the actions taken, or the content of strategy, and the processes by which actions are decided and implemented.
- Strategies are not purely deliberate: intended, emergent, and realized strategies may differ from one another.
- Strategies exist on different levels: firms have corporate strategy (what business shall we be in?) and business strategy (how shall we compete in each business?).
- Strategy involves various thought processes: strategy involves conceptual as well as analytical exercises. Generally speaking then, in organization and management theory strategy refers to the various ways an organization tries to maintain a strategic fit between an organization's goals (Osinga, 2005).

To maintain the homeostasis of the organization and, as described in the author's GSM, to establish an understanding of the notion of feedback in strategic models, below are descriptions of the feedback systems.

POSITIVE FEEDBACK SYSTEM

A positive feedback system is a regulatory mechanism of a system if the resulting action goes in the same direction as the condition that triggers it (Golec, 2004). According to Golec (2004):

> A good example of positive feedback is a turbo-charger fitted to the engines of vehicles. As we accelerate, increasing revolutions of the engine (after crossing some threshold), set the turbo-charger on, that in fact increases the speed even further. Summarizing, a part of output (acceleration) was "fed back" to the process again, causing action going in the same direction (further acceleration).

NEGATIVE FEEDBACK SYSTEM

A negative feedback system is a regulatory mechanism if the resulting action opposes the condition that triggers it (Golec, 2004). According to Golec (2004):

> To name an example, one might think of the heating systems we use at home. Very often we set our heaters to maintain constant temperature while we are at home. So the heaters turn on and off as a function of the interior temperature. If the temperature drops below some threshold, the heating system is being switched on, compensating and increasing the temperature again. In other words, a part of output (falling temperature) was "fed back" to the system again, causing action going in the opposite direction (increasing temperature).

Applying both of the above control mechanisms as a regulatory whole, the positive response is: do more of the actions initiated by the strategy applied; the negative response is: do less or stop, rethink and re-navigate. This constructs a robust whole in terms of systemic view and modelling of an organizational control system. Thus, this combination of both negative and positive construct into one system, one talks about the negative feedback loop (Golec, 2004). This notion of the author is displayed in Figure 2.15, which models a viable control system from all layers of the organization to execution and thus via a real-time connectivity.

> ... strategy is an adaptive process where piecemeal strategic decisions are taken based on continuous feedback between formulation and implementation in an emergent pattern over time (Osinga, 2005).

BIPOLAR FEEDBACK

According to Sabelli (2003):

> Bipolar feedback is a creative process present in many natural and human systems. Feedback is usually bipolar – that is, positive and negative – in natural

FIGURE 2.15 A 'grand strategy model' as a dynamic system

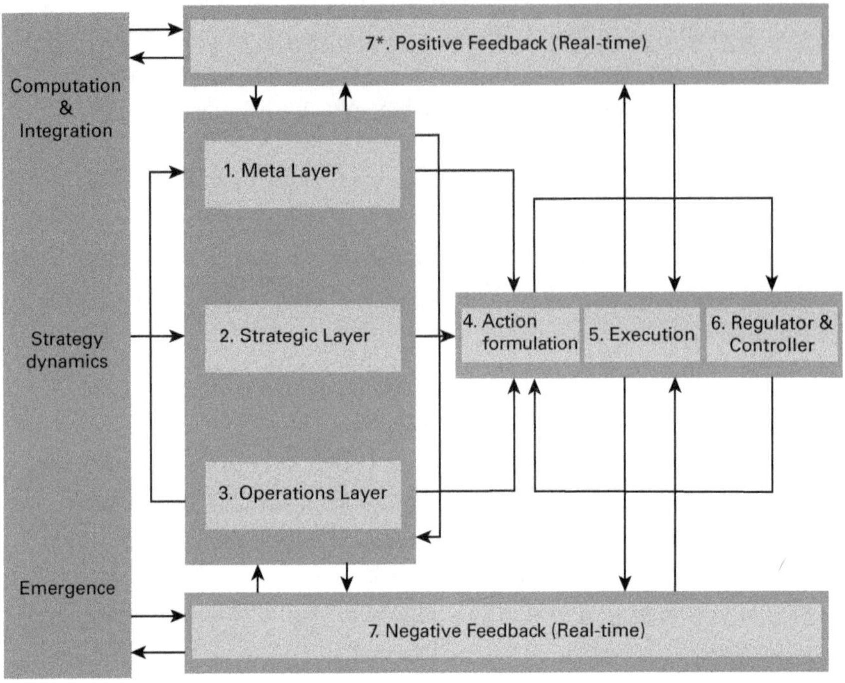

Author's interpretation

> environments, which, in their diversity, furnish synergic and antagonistic responses to the output of any system. Trigonometric models of bipolar feedback generate convergence to a steady state, periodicity, chaos, bios, and leaps. (In contrast, models of unipolar feedback such as the logistic equation generates only steady states, periodicity, and chaos.)

The author's design of integrating the bipolar feedback into the field of strategic management is a solid system of control, whereby the strategist gets the actual and real-time information for the strategies implemented. Thus, the strategist can decide to stop, change, re-plan and execute when the message is negative for the strategies implemented, or if the feedback is positive, to accelerate, since the organization is on course and strategies bear fruits of success.

Designing a grand strategy for management

There is no satisfactory definition or common usage of the term of grand strategy in business management. The Online Business Dictionary describes grand strategy as: 'Comprehensive, long-term plan of essential actions by which a firm plans to achieve its major objectives. Key factors of this strategy may include market, product, and/or organizational development through acquisition, divestiture, diversification, joint ventures, or strategic alliances' (Business Dictionary, 2019). Additionally, the author's research in Google Scholar has revealed 1.1 million search results by searching for the words *Grand+strategy+business* (Google Scholar, 2019); however, only a few results had anything to do with business. The rest of the search was on topics of international relations, politics and on military and security studies.

The roots of strategic problems are that strategists fail to distinguish between operational effectiveness and strategy. The quest for productivity, quality and speed has spawned a remarkable number of management tools, spread throughout the trash of strategic literature in business schools, which still deal with what Beer (1975–1994) calls the 'vanished world' (Beer, 1975). The trendiness of the words and topics used in management and strategy endanger the strategic actions because of their vagueness, imprecision of wording and meaning. How can one distinguish between 15 grand strategies? Which one is essential for survivability? If we ought to have 15 grand strategies, how many strategies should we derive from them? Furthermore, what is then the difference between strategy and grand strategy? Especially, where can strategists distinguish between actions and organizational effectiveness with strategies, as Porter (1996) severely warns of mixing strategies with non-strategies, or what Rumelt (2011) underpins:

> Heavy with goals and slogans, governments have become less and less able to solve problems. Corporate boards sign off on strategic plans that are little more than wishful thinking. The US education system is rich with targets and standards but poor at comprehending and countering the sources of underperformance. The only remedy is for us to demand more from those who lead. More than charisma and vision, we must demand good strategy (Rumelt, 2011).

Strategy coming from military sciences must be treated with precision and searched for within the military and policy literature. The author's research has revealed that there is an established notion of a long-term thinking and observation, what the wording of grand strategy generally reflects in military sciences and 'International Relations' (IR), thus this is an essential and vital topic for managers and strategists of business as well. The best description that the authors saw fit and easy to absorb for these objectives were the works of Barry Posen of MIT. Posen (2008) gives a very precise definition of grand strategy in business. Thus, according to Posen (2008), 'grand strategy' is a state's plan for achieving security. His version of security is rather narrow and exact. Posen gives only four pillars upon which a grand strategy has to rest. These four pillars are described below:

1. safety;
2. sovereignty;
3. territorial integrity;
4. power position.

Power position – being as the means to the end, the threats to the above described points and remedies for those threats. Grand strategy has to set some priorities because resources are scarce, thus grand strategy has to have a certain logic to it. If one claims that these are the threats that the organization faces, here are the priorities and the remedies. One has to ask the question why, and there must be a certain type of understandable and logical story for that why to be answered. Grand strategy is related to foreign policy, but it is not the same. Policy can include some other issues. Grand strategy is about the issues that could hurt badly enough that one will be willing to kill or to die for it. Grand strategy has to be distinguished from security and other issues – issues that have to do with welfare, lifestyle and prosperity, and issues that have to do with philanthropy. Economic issues are security issues when they have to do with these kinds of threats – threats to safety, threats to sovereignty, threats to power position (Posen, 2008). But not all economics issues, just because they are abroad, are necessarily grand strategy issues. So why is it vital to have a grand strategy? Here are three problems that grand strategy has to address in business:

1. The problem of scarcity: resources are always scarce.
2. The problem of coordination: one has to coordinate the action of a vast amount of people by moving them in the same direction. This is a very hard task in terms of orientation, so the people move in that direction.
3. Accountability in democratic and supportive style of management and leadership.

Communication is another vital issue. In grand strategy one is coercing or deterring, convincing people to do things or not to do things. In communication, explaining to the people involved is essential, since they otherwise may not know the importance of the things vital to the grand strategy. It is vital that they do what strategists want them to do and not act otherwise (Posen, 2008).

According to Osinga (2005), 'strategy is a process, a constant adaptation to shifting conditions and circumstances in a world where chance, uncertainty and ambiguity dominate, a view in particular that is very much in line with Boyd's idea.' Translating grand strategy into the world of business by focusing on Posen's insights and work, the author suggests doing it in the following way.

Scarcity of resources

Since the first pillar of Posen (2008) is scarcity of resources, and as some resources will go towards the cost of formulating and acting strategically in the first place according to the Second Law of Thermodynamics – as Drucker (1954) states, 'Profits are the costs of staying in business' – a vital need is still faced on the quality of decisions made and resources wasted, since efficiency and effectiveness in terms of organizational fit have vital strategic consequences. Resources in terms of time also play a vital role, thus time is the currency of the strategist, and therefore the author suggests that the model in Figure 2.16 is taken into account. The model supports the strategist in the quality of decisions, but moreover it reduces strategy friction.

FIGURE 2.16 Model of a control process

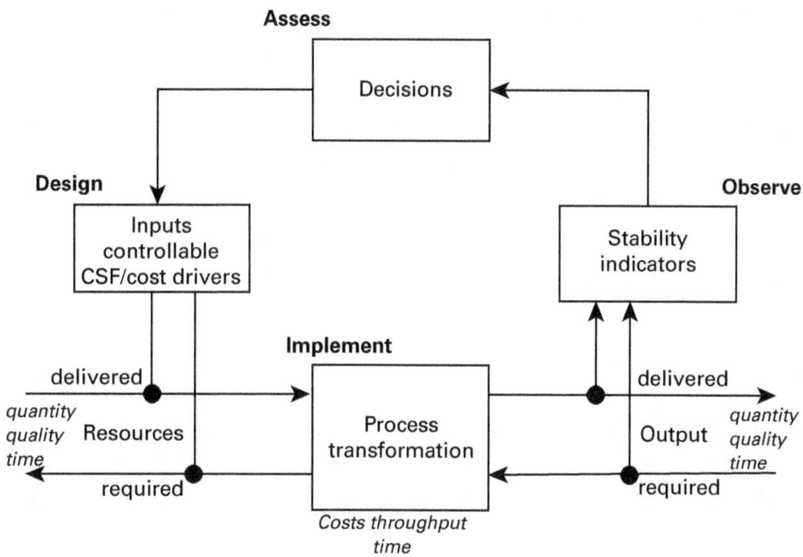

Author's interpretation, based on Espejo *et al* (1996) and Schwaninger (2001)

Feedback and control, as established in the pages above, define cybernetics, since it is via feedback that a system is controlled and regulated. Wiener (1948) gave a vital role to feedback in communication and control and between organizations and society, as well as in technical systems. From a pure decision-making perspective, feedback is specifically defined as 'the transmission of evaluative or corrective information to the original or controlling source about an action, event, or process' (Golec, 2004). Beer states that the most important point about systems is how they are controlled, and the notion that control ought to be imposed on the system is a false way of thinking. Thus, control must be built into the system; it is ever possible via feedback and feedback must be ubiquitous in control systems (Beer, 1959).

> Human decision making is largely based on the concept of feedback. To mention an example on the individual dimension, managers try to estimate the correctness of their past actions by observing the output of these decisions or managerial indicators (like Balanced Score Cards) and introduce necessary corrections. On the group decision making dimension, democratic government is also an example of a controlling body trying to incorporate information from the past into the process of decision-making in the future. Having said that, we have to notice the qualitative change in the weight of the positive and negative feedback. From now on, feedback is not only a piece of information "fed back" to the system again. Critical consequences of feedback must be now included into the system: its role in motivation, consistency and learning (Golec, 2004).

According to Powell *et al* (2001), Figure 2.17 displays a business process using feedback to transform resources into benefits for the customer, thus the management of this process functions on three activities: (1) observation, (2) assessment and (3) design. Therefore, it is essential that strategists establish and specify the stability and control indicators in advance for the processes to be efficient. The additional essential point must be the focus on the decisions that create the most value by the usage of controllable inputs; furthermore, the focus ought to be on the resources needed to affect the process of organizational performance (Powell *et al*, 2001).

Coordination and cohesion

Posen's second pillar of grand strategy tackles the problem of coordination, where the strategist has to coordinate the actions of a large number of people under the umbrella of the larger organizational whole. In order to

FIGURE 2.17 Framework for the design of intelligent organizations

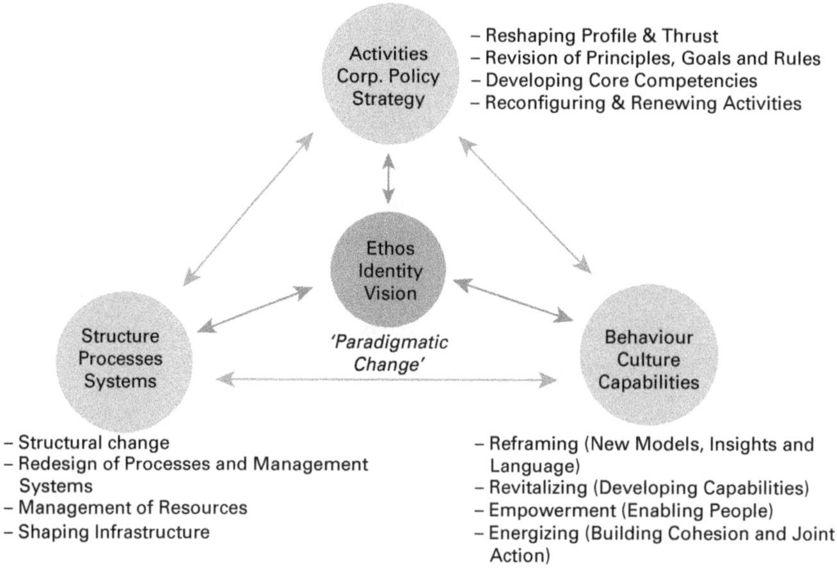

Author's interpretation, based on Schwaninger (2001)

have an effective organization, the structure of an intelligent organization ought to be designed as the prerequisite of a viable organization. Schwaninger (2001) calls this the 'framework for the design of intelligent organizations'. The framework is presented in Figure 2.17, which integrates the three vital aspects of the organization to design an organizational identity and 'ethos', which is transformable, while it preserves the core of the organization.

Schwaninger (2001) proposes the model as an integrative framework, which is in contrast with various other frameworks that emphasize partial aspects of organizations – eg strategy, structure or organization culture. The emphasis in the above framework proposes bringing together the different and most essential components so as to provide a more complete and holistic picture. Integration and composition of an organizational whole is a natural capability of humans, largely based on unconscious inferences (Schwaninger, 2001). The 'Intelligent Organizational Framework' works in defiance of the reductionist thinking and observing of organizational reality, thus it faces the complexity of the real world contrary to the tendency towards reductionism and fragmentation of models that reflect just a small part of reality (Schwaninger, 2001). Thus, Schwaninger's framework is a model to overcome the reductionist limitation. Schwaninger (2001) observes:

> It is made up of an integrated set of essential parameters and their identifiable inter-relationships, which have to be developed in co-alignment, to enhance organizational intelligence. Thereby it does more than merely furnish a list of important aspects. It provides a frame of reference, which is robust, broad enough and sufficiently structured, to enable actors to initiate and catalyse organizational development and transformation more effectively.

Schwaninger's notion is based on five crucial multi-dimensional parts that are combined and interrelated. These parts, as described in Figure 2.17, are listed below (Schwaninger, 2001):

1. activities;
2. structure;
3. behaviour;
4. organizational identity, ethos and vision;
5. time.

The first three dimensions – activities, structure and behaviour – are the dimensions that make up the pillars of the famous *'St Gallen Management Concept'*. Management ought to be based on a multi-level process, thus the normative layer fulfils the foundational function. Schwaninger's framework's dimensions are also typified and incorporated by System 5 in 'Beer's VSM model', strategic management – the orientational function, shown by its System 4 and the interrelationship between Systems 3 and 4 in the VSM; operative management, the function of realization, epitomized by Systems 1, 2 and 3 (including System 3*) and their interrelationships in the VSM (Schwaninger, 2001). Beer's VSM model is one of management's most vital and advanced models ever developed by a management scientist. Schwaninger's model resembles what Posen calls the problem or orientation. Schwaninger (2001) underpins the claim that management is observed as a 'recursive process'. Therefore, the above model applies to any level of recursion of an organization, although some of the terms may contain a certain bias towards the higher levels of recursion. The parts that embody the framework are dynamically interconnected, as shown in Figure 2.17. Thus:

> ... the terms in the diagram give an overview of the domains in which management/leadership can influence the essential parameters and thereby catalyse organizational transformation. The dynamical inter-relationships

between these components call for balanced interventions and a thorough consideration of possible chain reactions and side effects (Schwaninger, 2001).

Accountability

Accountability is the third pillar of a grand strategy according to Posen (2008), which will be illustrated by the author based on the model of the 'meta system evolution' (see Figure 2.18):

> The nature of the metasystem is that it operates as a control impulse domain, which in human systems occurs through the process of 'thinking', and according to De Bono (1977) has come to be associated with beliefs. Without the metasystem, the system would behave with spontaneous responses that are programmed into its structure through what Yolles and Dubois (2001) refer to as strong anticipation. In the context of the human being, like Beer, De Bono relates the concept of the metasystem to the social community when he suggests that without the metasystem a person would act according to its own personal systems, which might be based on immediate gratification, self-indulgence and impulse. Thus, the metasystem lies outside individual systems and overrides these factors in favour of society and a longer time base (Yolles, 2004).

The field of application of the model is very broad and can be widely applied to all organizations, thus it also appeals to NGOs and NPOs.

The meta system evolution model was applied to social system and organizations by:

- Beer (1959) states: 'A control system cannot discuss itself and that the higher order [system] is needed in which to describe the behavior of a system expressed in a given language.'
- Beer (1966) substantiates the claim further and states: 'Since the normal occupation of management is to be expert in using the practical language of the firm's operations, there is the danger that the management will never speak the metalanguage in which its own structure can be discussed.'

Beer called these applications the 'metalanguage' (Yolles, 2004). 'Metalanguage is the language and the logic of the meta-system' (Beer, 1981). Beer (1966) states:

> The point is that managers begin to look at the situation for which they are responsible through descriptions which acknowledge the natural law. They need scientists to help them do this. They need competent models, and the aid of comprehension illuminated by the best thinking-tools that man has yet

FIGURE 2.18 The evolution of the meta system

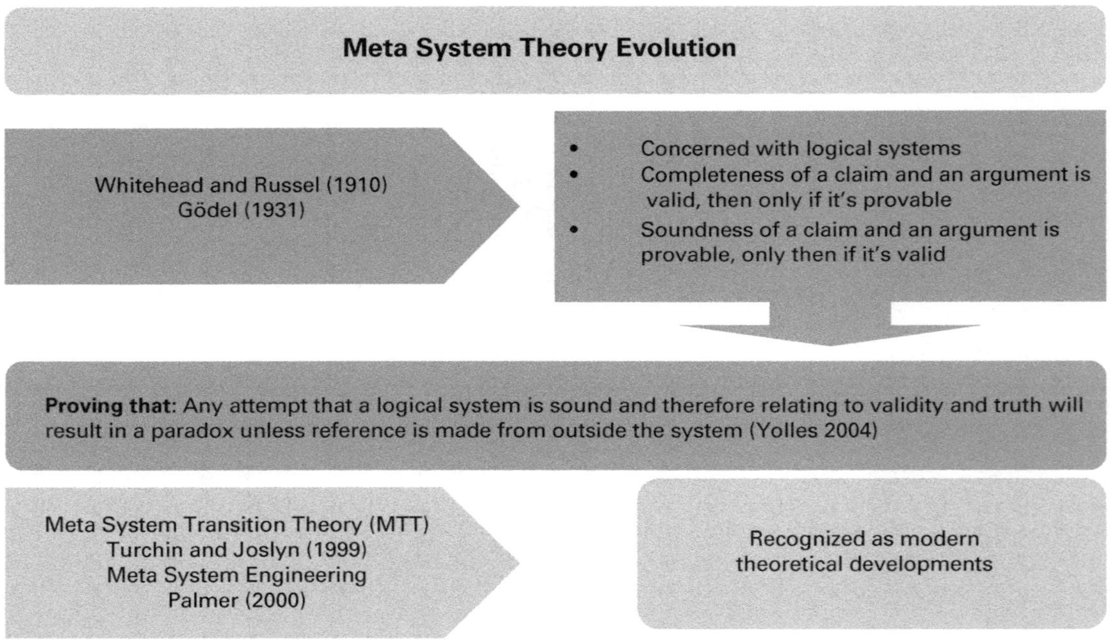

Author's interpretation, based on Yolles (2004)

> discovered for the purpose of dealing with nature; they should quantify those situations if at all possible. It is not the substitution of science for management that is advocated: it is the appeal for a professional rather than an amateur approach to the managerial task.

This appeal is more than justified, thus we ought to look at management in a scientific way. The impenetrable language and models whereby managers are communicating with the firm, with each other, but precisely, wherewith they reflect upon the organizational structure, is insufficient to capture the grasp of the manager/strategist or meta-management's actions and the needed integrity within the information dealt with, whereby the author means the capacity to question one's own action and furthermore transmitting the adequate messages to the firm's middle management and operations. The control function of the organization ought to speak the metalanguage, hence it's the very structure of its survival.

Communication

Posen's fourth pillar of a grand strategy is communication. Cybernetics is the science of real-time communication. Communication in biological systems and organisms is based on the messages received, what the author terms an active and intelligent history – the present message received and the ability or capacity of calculating and pre-determining the next possible incoming message or sub-systems' actions.

In Figure 2.19 the dynamics of an organization's activities from a holistic perspective are demonstrated. At this part the ubiquitous communication of the organization is illustrated as described above. The St Gallen Management Concept was further transformed and developed from its original version in order to enable managers, strategists and students to create what Schwaninger (2001) also calls a 'big bulk of management-relevant-knowledge' coming from diverse and interdisciplinary sciences integrated within a systems framework (Schwaninger, 2001). Communication is better described in terms of recursiveness of the organization's systems, thus communication in cybernetic terms is communication of and within a viable organization.

Figure 2.19 reveals how operative developments are embedded in operations, which is again embedded in its higher level of recursion in strategic management, which then is embedded in its higher system level – the normative level. Finally, the whole organization is embedded and resembles the organizational ethos. Beer (1985) formulates this notion beautifully and precisely in his key aphorism: 'The purpose of a system is what it does. There is,

FIGURE 2.19 Organizational communication, adapted from the 'St Gallen Management Concept'

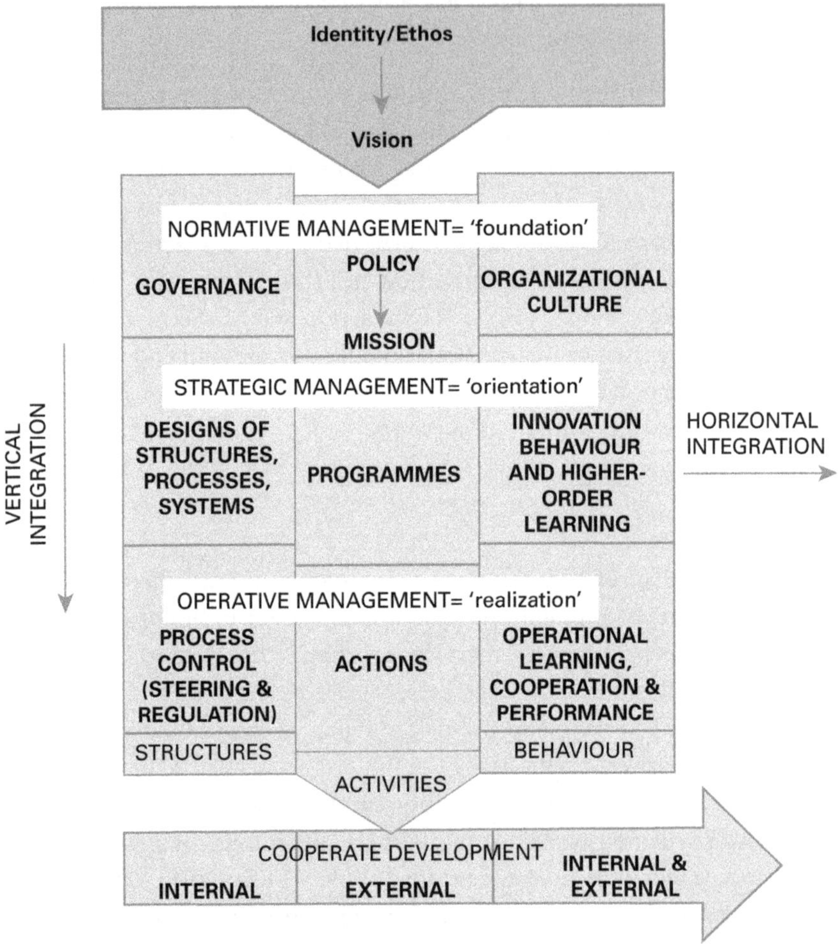

Author's interpretation, based on Schwaninger (2001)

after all, no point in claiming that the purpose of a system is to do what it consistently fails to do.' Beer's (1985) aphorism reflects what the St Gallen Management Concept demonstrates; therefore: 'A comparator, naturally enough, continuously compares the declared purpose with the purpose imputed from the results that the system delivers. This results in the feedback of an error signal (E), which will modify the original statement of purpose' (Beer, 1985).

Therefore, the system will converge on a compromise purpose – it is neither what the higher recursion-systems would most likely do, nor what the viable system itself would most likely indulge in doing, but to manoeuvre and adapt to newer information via high-quality communication channels is vital to purpose and purpose is vital to survival (Beer, 1985).

As soon as strategists see organizations as a larger being built of smaller beings (larger system made of and constructed of smaller sub-systems), then the question of communication is essential. Organizations that have a better communication structure beyond corporate meetings and email trails have a better competitive advantage. This is similar to what Porter means when he says: 'organizational effectiveness is not a strategy….' The strategist seeks and engages their team for uniqueness, and moreover an intelligent organizational structure is the uniqueness that creates a sustainable competitive advantage.

Final thoughts on establishing a grand strategy for business

Naumann *et al* (2007) from the Center for International Strategic Studies (CSIS) describes the complexity of uncertainty in our contemporary era as:

> Certainty in our world is today being eroded by a proliferation of information, knowledge and choice. The erosion of certainty is accelerated by rapid technological, social and cultural change. On occasion, that change occurs too fast for some of our major institutions to cope with. In certain important senses, we are today operating in a mist. Through that current mist a wide range of challenges are appearing. The challenges are acute, and no less so because our certainties are in retreat. If they were stronger, our resolve to address these problems might have stiffened.

In order to deal with uncertainty organizations need a viable strategy and complexity attenuation system. Complexity is not randomly observed, it is merely a state that invites our organizations to take the challenge and start developing.

A study by Shell looking at corporate longevity and companies' lifespans, *The Living Company: Habits for survival in a turbulent business environment* – which is an outstanding piece of research – reveals that, as also defined throughout the book: companies are beings, not things, and there are four characteristics to a living company (Geus, 2002):

1 'Sensitivity to the environment represents a company's ability to learn and adapt.' The author has defined this essential notion under Ashby's Law and via introducing bionics, systems and cybernetics insights to cope with the problem of strategy and design strategic models.

2 'Cohesion and identity, it is now clear, are aspects of a company's innate ability to build a community and a persona for itself.' The notion of identity-transformation and its preservation, cohesion and identity are the foundation for the normative strategy.

3 'Tolerance and its corollary, decentralization, are both symptoms of a company's awareness of ecology: its ability to build constructive relationships with other entities, within and outside itself.' In the concept of systems, cybernetics and Ashby's Law is the principle of recursion (see below) and self-organization.

4 'And I now think of conservative financing as one element in a very critical corporate attribute: the ability to govern its own growth and evolution effectively' (Geus, 2002). The scarcity of resources has been treated by the author as the first pillar of designing the grand strategy (Chandler, 1962).

In a serious debate about seeing a company as a living entity, the 'Shell Study' confirms the author's views that companies are living organisms – and they are not alone representing this notion. Particular attention should also be paid to the works of Maturana, Varela and von Foerster at 'Biological Computer Laboratory' (BCL) (Varela *et al*, 1974). The reader is also advised to see the notions of 'autopoiesis' and 'living system theory' (Maturana, 1975), and also the foundational works of John Holland on 'complex adaptive systems' (CASG, 2019). A clearer understanding of CAS would extend current resources and understanding to exploratory research, especially, which management and strategy sciences need the most.

In the next section the concept of recursion is outlined in detail. This will further establish the foundation for understanding why the integration of system sciences is essential in strategy/management and why biological sciences are the cutting-edge of strategic thinking now and in the future. Thus viable systems maintain the highest level of integrity within the messages that ubiquitously circle in their bodies and which are embodied within the interrelations between their sub-systems.

Recursion – the foundational principle of organizational complexity

The principle of recursion is one of the foundational principles of management in the animal, machine and productive social systems. According to Beer (1985) 'Recursion is a next level that contains all the levels below it'. Malik (1984–2008) underpins this: the principle of recursion is one of the most important principles of systems structuring. Recursion can only be understood in relation to viable organizations and organizational viability. Viability in terms of systemic and cybernetics sciences means: 'able to maintain a separate existence' (Beer, 1989). It derives from bionics and neuropathology. Beer used the science of bionics and neuro-cybernetics by introducing the VSM model into operation research (OR) and management, thus Beer's work is also embedded and referred to as organizational cybernetics. According to Beer (1985):

> The laws of viability in complex organisms are not merely, or even primarily, concerned with the energy (like the metabolism of money) that propels them, but with the dynamic structure that determines the adaptive connectivity of their parts. Can the organization actually survive – assuming that the financial constraints are met? As to managerial problems: these are no respecters of financial boundaries, nor of the territorial preserves of any other professional function or geographic domain. They grow like cancers; and 'secondaries' may appear anywhere. The organization as a viable system has to become immune to infection, adaptive to environmental change, and – somehow – to extirpate its cancers.

Beer has signified two principles of recursion in viable systems:

1 'If a viable system contains a viable system, then the organizational structure must be recursive' (Beer, 1981).

2 'If we decide to define a social system by recursion, we shall find that every viable system contains a viable system' (Beer, 1981).

Figure 2.20 models a whole industry's system according to Beer (1985). The reader can clearly observe therein how the recursive systems of a total industry are embedded in each other:

> The total system contains two systems which are identical with it. Like the one on focus mentioned earlier, these two embedded systems are themselves viable systems. They are RECURSIONS OF THE VIABLE SYSTEM. We shall make use of this mathematical term because, while its meaning in context is evident, it reminds us that we are not talking loosely about any kind of system contained inside another – but about an absolutely precise definition of viability (Beer, 1985).

Figure 2.21 demonstrates that the viability of the cluster's specific conditions, where the innovative orientation of the company and the overall common innovation infrastructure are embedded, reflect via the principles of recursion the very viability of this part of the cluster and, further, the whole cluster's viability.

FIGURE 2.20 An industry with its recursive sub-systems

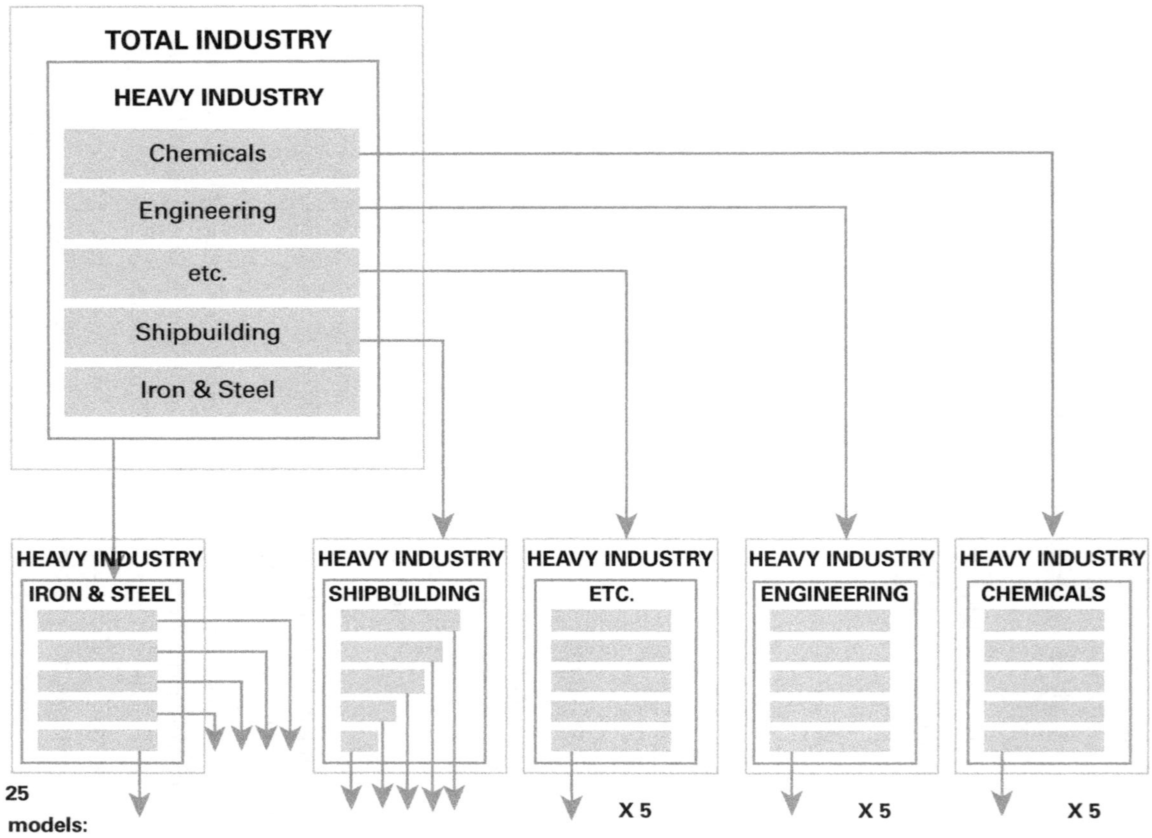

Author's interpretation, based on Beer (1995)

FIGURE 2.21 How innovation in a cluster can be seen in terms of viability and recursion

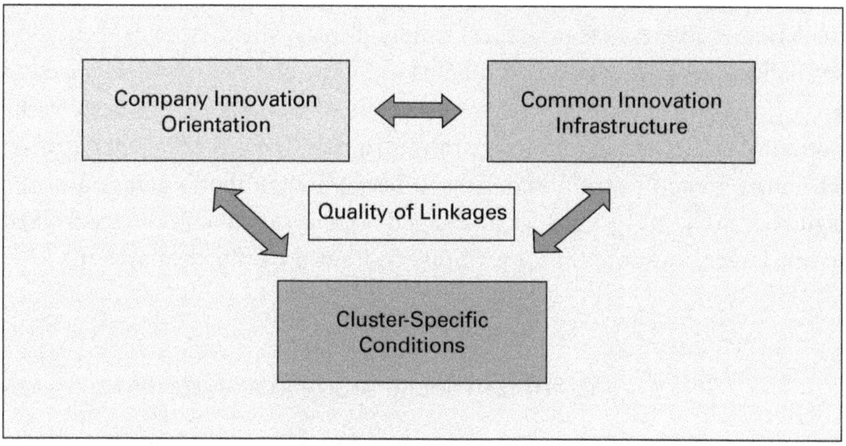

Author's interpretation, based on Porter (2008)

FIGURE 2.22 A simple display of the principle of recursion

The cluster conditions based on diverse interrelated firms work recursively in favour of each other. The concentration here is not only on the notion of model-building, but moreover to understand how a complex and hierarchical organization can be simplified, explained and controlled. It fosters a decentralized control function and enhances the variety of the next higher system to maintain stability, thus achieving organizational objectives efficiently and functioning on the basis of homeostasis within their individual environment. VSM and recursion discovers new guidelines for leaders that will simplify management and its objectives (Christopher, 2007). If the question arises that if one viable system is contained in another viable system, as the Russian dolls (see Figure 2.22) simply display, where in each larger doll a smaller one is contained. With this analogy, another justified question arises, which may state: how is the principle of viability that underpins the notion of 'able to maintain a separate existence' (Beer, 1979a) manifested? The answer can be given according to Beer (1979a): the foundation of the claim lies in the word 'able', as diversified organizational units are contained in one larger unit until they are wholly contained by the meta system.

Self-organization in social productive systems

The notion of 'self-organization' was coined in the 1940s to label processes in which systems become more highly organized over time, without being ordered by outside agents or by external programmes, thus it has become one of the leading revelations to management from the study of non-linear science, without ever having been properly defined and integrated widely (Ashby, 2004):

> Formally, the basic mechanism underlying self-organization is the (often noise-driven) variation which explores different regions in the system's state space until it enters an attractor. This precludes further variation outside the attractor, and thus restricts the freedom of the system's components to behave independently. This is equivalent to the increase of coherence, or decrease of statistical entropy, that defines self-organization (Heylighen, 2001b).

The spontaneous emergence of order and adaptive behaviour in social systems on a day-to-day basis to achieve equilibrium, and of new structures in the laboratory, is easily observed. The most widely known examples are snow crystallization, the appearance of a beautifully symmetric pattern of dense matter in a solution of randomly moving molecules (Heylighen, 2001b). As already stated, the best example of self-organization is the 'Belousov-Zhabotinsky (BZ)' reaction. The BZ:

> ... reaction is an intriguing experiment that displays unexpected behavior. When certain reactants are combined, an "induction" period of inactivity is followed by sudden oscillations in color from red to blue. In spatially nonhomogeneous systems (such as a simple petridish), the red and blue oscillations propagate as spiral wave fronts. The oscillations last about one minute and are repeated over a long period of time. Eventually, the reaction stops oscillating and approaches an equilibrium state (Gray, 2002).

Another very famous example of self-organization was delivered by Turing (1952) in his paper on morphogenesis. According to Turing (1952):

> Morphogenes, reacting together and diffusing through a tissue, is adequate to account for the main phenomena of morphogenesis. Such a system, although it may originally be quite homogeneous, may later develop a pattern or structure due to an instability of the homogeneous equilibrium, which is triggered off by random disturbances. Such reaction-diffusion systems are considered in some detail in the case of an isolated ring of cells, a mathematically convenient, though biological, unusual system.

The notion of the author at this point is to make self-organization familiar to the strategist. In viable organizations and social systems, communication is ubiquitous, and messages are transmitted with the highest level of integrity. If something hurts in the body in a biological system or if something causes pain, the organization (organism) is generally affected in real time to minimize the danger and the effects for the body. Now, if fitness in firms is measured in financial terms, just as one can measure the fitness of the body in terms of calories, would one consider a body with the intake of the highest number of calories and most amount of fat as healthy? The body survives because the laws and principles of nature apply to them. This is also true for organizations. Therefore, understanding the principles of self-organization is vital for strategists of the contemporary era.

The Shell study on organizational longevity has underpinned clearly the notion of how contemporary management and strategy models are systemically flawed because fitness indicators are based on false and dangerous doctrines:

> The ability to return investment to shareholders seemed to have nothing to do with longevity. The profitability of a company was a symptom of corporate health, but not a predictor or determinant of corporate health. Certainly, a manager in a long-lived company needed all the accounting Figures that he or she could lay hands on. But those companies seemed to recognize that Figures, even when accurate, de-scribe the past. They do not indicate the underlying conditions that will lead to deteriorating health in the future. The financial reports at General Motors, Philips Electronics, and IBM during the mid-1970s gave no clue of the trouble that lay in store for those companies within a decade. Once the problems cropped up on the balance sheet, it was too late to prevent the trouble. Nor did longevity seem to have anything to do with a company's material assets, its particular industry or product line, or its country of origin. Indeed, the 40- to 50-year life expectancy seems to be equally

> valid in countries as wide apart as the United States, Europe, and Japan, and in industries ranging from manufacturing to retailing to financial services to agriculture to energy. (Geus, 2002).

The only reasons why Apple or IBM survived were a radical shift in thinking or a vital and precise understanding of the strategic problems the organizations faced at that time. It all began by Jobs listening to customers and his difficulty in distinguishing the difference between Apple's different computers (Rumelt, 2011). And in the case of IBM, Gerstner had no in-depth understanding of computing *per se*. But Gerstner:

> ... had the good sense to start listening to clients. He discovered that the biggest problem that all the big companies were facing in 1993 was in integrating all the separate computing technologies that were emerging at the time. So, while continuing to cut costs, Gerstner reversed the move to spin off IBM business units into separate companies. Having understood IBM's customers, he recognized that one of IBM's greatest strengths was its ability to provide integrated solutions for customers – a firm that could represent more than piece parts or components – something he would not have learned by listening to the proponents of different technologies within IBM. Splitting the company would have destroyed IBM's unique competitive advantage (Denning, 2012).

Gerstner's actions reveal the proof of von Foerster's famed revelation in his founding paper, the idea of 'order from noise... producing knowledge out of ignorance' (Foerster, 2003a), wherein he explains the power of self-organization to the management of social systems.

> I shall call the principle I am going to introduce to you presently the 'order from noise' principle. Thus, in my restaurant self-organizing systems do not only feed upon order, they will also find noise on the menu. ... And that is why I am convinced that an environment with a reasonable amount of noise may not be too bad if you would really like to achieve learning (Foerster, 2003a).

Gerstner – as a result of not knowing much about the field – transformed IMB's noise within its operational or embedded environment (in disorder), where IBM could not have survived. He addressed the problem of leading a large organization by applying the principles of self-organization – making every business unit maintain its own autonomy and viability in their environment (marketplace) – and by the principle of recursion to the other units. They together created the new IBM under the umbrella of the meta system and led its transformation by shifting from focus on products to focus on customers and their needs as a solution provider corporation. Thus, according to Rumelt (2011), 'if you fail to identify and analyze the obstacles, you don't have a strategy. Instead, you have a stretch goal or a budget or a list of things you wish would happen.' Von Foerster, also a pioneer in managerial thinking, at a conference on 'Principles of Self-organization in Biological and Social Systems', presented some revolutionary and radical ideas and thinking, the depth of which are still not very much understood.

According to Kamran (2012):

> Self-organization deals with endogenous, unintended emergence and differentiation of order in social systems independently from interventions, i.e. as the dictation of shareholder value as a whole reality for the manager's lens to see the environment and steering as a tool to bring the organization to achieve this objective at all costs. Thus, we become problems of survivability and viability, which are not a cause from environmental disturbances but moreover from management failure. Managerial self-organizing and self-control systems are recursive and can be only based and function by feedback. But here we come to a point where we are presented with a problem. A self-organizing control system must be designed to receive feedbacks, which are essential to its survival. These feedbacks must be of the highest quality and be transmitted ubiquitously. We can only achieve a state of control by ubiquitous communication of the organization with its environment in which it's embedded and within its internal recursive systems of organization.

And according to Probst (1987):

> Management as a system of control must be of an autonomous nature. This we call self-organizing. Social-self-organization means the self-regulation of order as an emergent phenomenon in a social system as a firm. This order has a spontaneous and unintentional character and is the result of multiple experiences, interactions, expectations, actions, plans, perceptions and decisions. In this view, order emerges all by itself; it is not made or planned consciously or intentionally by managers.

Christopher (2007) states information control actions in system sciences and system thinking can be vital to both biological (natural) and social systems (business).

According to Foerster (2003a):

> ... we know that as the nervous system develops, it becomes more reliable, more refined. But the components, the neurons, remain the same. They fire

> sometimes; they don't fire sometimes. McCullough asked, how is such a system organized or how does it organize itself, that it becomes a highly reliable system? In the same vein, Pask considered the teaching and learning situation: Here come two people, one knows something, the other one doesn't know something. They go together, sit in a room for 2 or 3 days at Harvard or some other fancy place, and suddenly the one who doesn't know anything knows something. The change does not come from the outside. The system – the two people – changes in such a way as to distribute the knowledge between the two. The system organizes itself. What is order? Order was usually considered as a wonderful building, a loss of uncertainty. Typically, it means that if a system is so constructed that if you know the location or the property of one element, you can make conclusions about the other elements. So, order is essentially the arrival of redundancy in a system, a reduction of possibilities.

Complexity and complex systems are not complicated –and therein lies the vital difference – since they follow natural laws, of which self-organization is among the most powerful in terms of viability and viable and self-sustained organization.

According to the author: 'Every viable organization is a self-organizing organization.' On the basis of recursion, all complexity can be explained and dealt with accordingly, hence a complex system designed on the basis of self-organizing and recursive business units is key to manageability and survivability. This notion, although thoroughly discussed in systems and cybernetics sciences, is still a very unfamiliar topic in the common understanding of management – which is the US business schools' version, especially when it comes to strategic management. Thus, complexity resides on the other side of redundancy and routines. In order to understand and cope with complexity, or for the situation where the organization cannot maintain homeostasis, higher capabilities of organizational intelligence are required.

Management models that are not based on self-organization do not have requisite variety and according to Ashby's Law are insufficient. They only function when stability is the challenge. Figure 2.23 describes how the diverse levels of management are recursively embedded in each other, creating a larger whole, and how each system has its own objectives to achieve to contribute to overall organizational success.

Figure 2.23 describes in addition how recursive the organizational management systems with their different tasks are embedded in a higher system and dissolve complexity, while maintaining the identity of the overall viability of the larger body. For a more quantitative approach to measurement of self-organization, see Shalizi *et al* (2004).

FIGURE 2.23 The viability and fitness of an organization based on recursion and self-organization

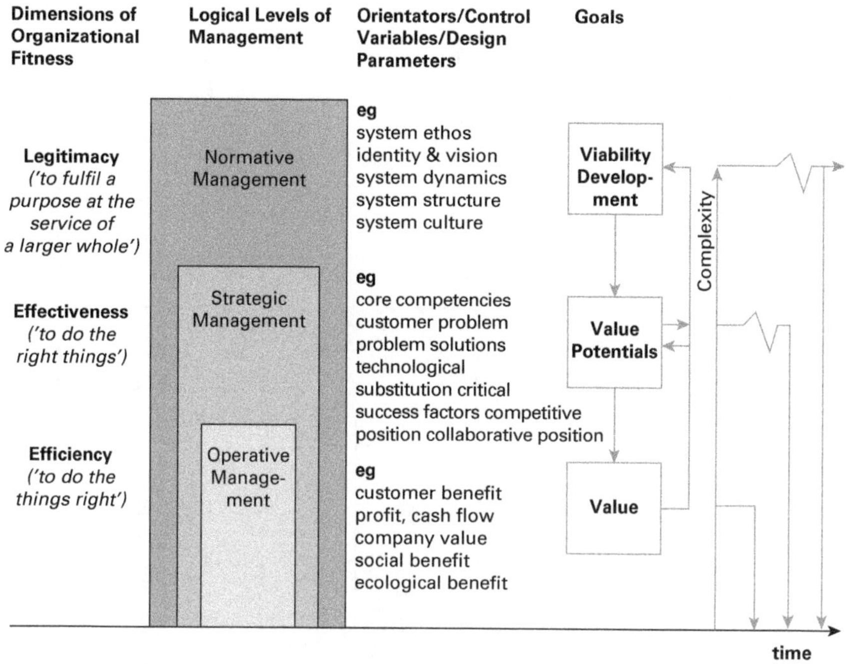

Author's interpretation, based on Schwaninger (2001)

Figure 2.24 describes the dimensions of value creation and goals with the level of organizational management hierarchy. Each system has its own goals and a regulating system, while preserving the identity of a larger organizational whole. The next section describes the science of cybernetics, a foundational science that is also called the science of regulation. Understanding systemic thinking, which is the foundation of the cybernetic organizational view, is essential for the strategist – thus strategy is the regulatory control system of any successful organization's endeavour.

Cybernetics – the science of effective organization

Cybernetics is the itinerary of control in man, machines, animals, companies, countries and organizations of any kind. Its founder, Norbert Wiener, coined the term in his ground-breaking book, *Cybernetics, or the Science of Control and Communication in the Animal and the Machine* (Wiener, 1948). However, before the technicalities of cybernetics are established, a brief

FIGURE 2.24 The self-organized organizational levels interacting as an organizational whole

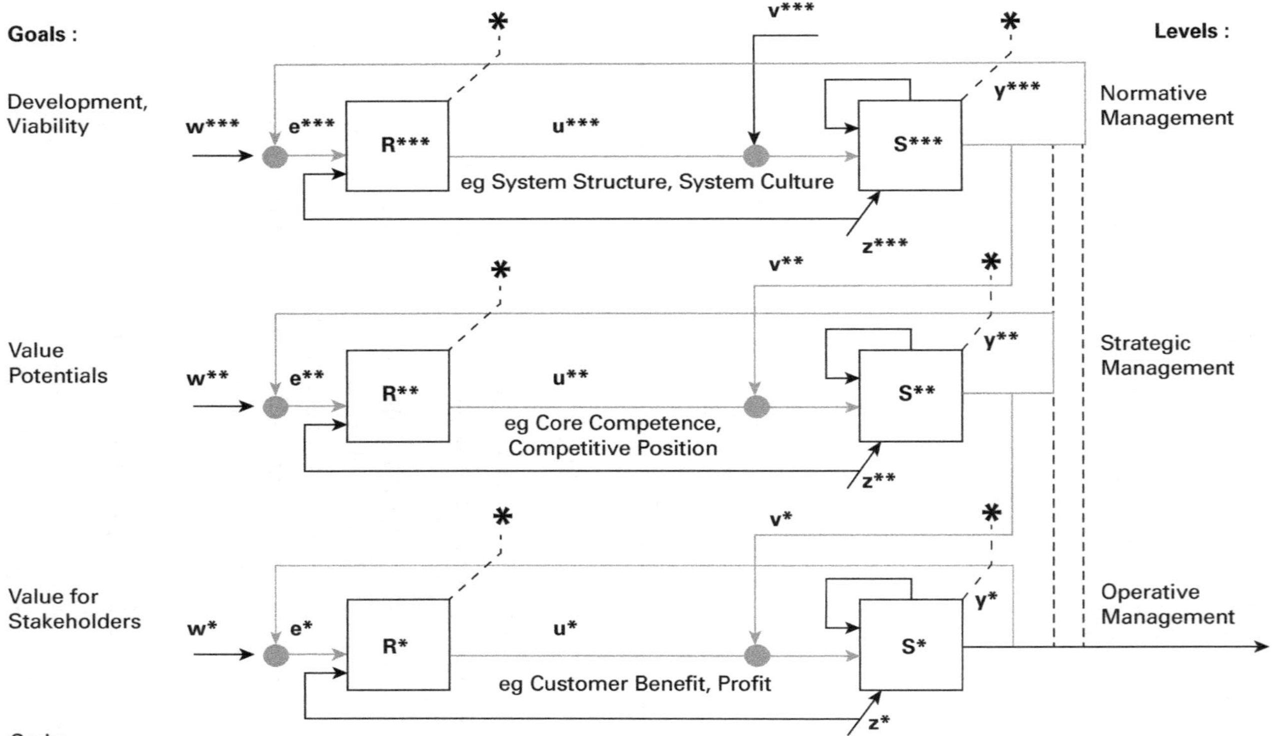

Code:

y: regulated variables **u**: control variables (examples) **v**: parameters **R**: Regulator **S**: System under Control
z: Disturbance **w**: Goal **e**: Deviation * **p.m.**: Connection with next higher recursion level

Schwaninger (2000)

history of its formation and foundation will give the reader a much better understanding and appreciation of the science of cybernetics. It will establish why strategists ought to manage and design their organizations by the laws of cybernetics. According to Beer (1985): 'Well, management is – if you will – the profession of regulation, and therefore of effective organization, of which this cybernetics is the science.' The pivotal contribution of cybernetics, according to Conway and Siegelman (2006), is: 'the essential unity of the set of problems centering about communication and control... whether in the machine or in living tissue.' Control is the chief problem of strategic thought and the ever-growing globally networked world of information, where communication is key to the notion of viability and to success, thus cybernetics is the very science of strategy-making. According to Schwaninger (2006c):

> Cyberneticians have been interested in concepts such as information, communication, complexity, autonomy, interdependence, cooperation and conflict, self-production ('autopoiesis'), self-organization, (self-) control, self-reference and (self-) transformation of complex dynamic systems. Along the genetic line of the tradition which led to the evolution of General Systems Theory (von Bertalanffy, Boulding, Gerard, Miller, Rapoport) and Cybernetics (Wiener, McCulloch, Ashby, Powers, Pask, Beer), a number of roots can be identified, in particular:
>
> - Mathematics (e.g. Newton, Poincare', Lyapunov, Lotka, Volterra, Rashevsky);
> - Logic (e.g. Epimenides, Leibniz, Boole, Russell and Whitehead, Goedel, Spencer-Brown);
> - Biology, including general physiology and neurophysiology (e.g. Hippocrates, Cannon, Rosenblueth, McCulloch, Rosen);
> - Engineering, including its physical and mathematical foundations (e.g. Heron, Kepler, Watt, Euler, Fourier, Maxwell, Hertz, Turing, Shannon and Weaver, von Neumann, Walsh); and
> - Social and human sciences, including economics (e.g. Hume, Adam Smith, Adam Ferguson, John Stuart Mill, Dewey, Bateson, Merton, Simon, Piaget) (Schwaninger, 2006c).

What follows is a biographical account of the history of cybernetics and its essential founders; for the reader this is the best account of the subjects about the very nature of one of the most essential sciences of the 20th century.

Warren McCulloch – the father of interdisciplinary scientific view

Starting in cybernetics as the science of interdisciplinarity, whereby the reader by now may recognize its much-needed input and integration to the field of strategy beyond basic universes and dismantled control systems substituted as strategy. Warren McCulloch is known as the 'pioneer of interdisciplinarity' (Erdi, 2008) and who was the founder of 'experimental epistemology'. His scientific endeavour was a quest for reducing epistemology to an experimental science (McCulloch, 1961):

> Warren McCulloch was born on November 16, 1898, in Orange, N.J. McCulloch was educated primarily at Yale, where he received a B.A. in philosophy and psychology (1921) and a masters in psychology (1923). He also received an M.D. from New York's College of Physicians and Surgeons in 1927. His first major academic appointment was at Yale, where he was first a Sterling Fellow, an instructor, and finally an assistant professor (1935–1941). He moved to the University of Illinois College of Medicine in 1941 and stayed there until 1948. During this time he co-authored what is probably his most famous paper with Walter Pitts, 'A Logical Calculus Immanent in Nervous Activity'. He left Illinois for the Electronics Research Laboratory at MIT in 1949. He died in Cambridge, Massachusetts, in 1969 (CSULB, 2019).

McCulloch's field, which according to Erdi (2008) is the study of knowledge through neurophysiology with the scientific goal of explaining how a neutral network produces ideas (see Figure 2.25). McCulloch's experimental approach to knowledge, by giving logic-based physiological theory of knowledge, embraced the ideas that: (1) the brain is a natural machine to

FIGURE 2.25 Experimental epistemology based on 'McCulloch's view'

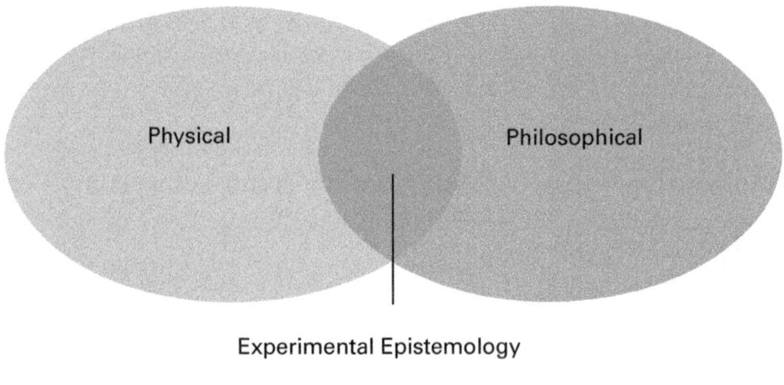

Erdi (2008)

perform logic, (2) which is described by logic, thus the implications of the brain could and should be described by logic (Erdi, 2008). McCulloch's very famous paper with Pitts, 'A Logical Calculus of the Ideas Immanent in Nervous System' (McCulloch and Pitts, 1943), was the first paper that analysed the operation of the brain in terms of interacting neurons. The constructed model (MCP) was developed to embrace the logical structure of the nervous system and its activity, thus some well-known cellular physiological facts, which were even known at that time, were neglected (Erdi, 2008). According to von Foerster (1995), at the end of *Collected Works by Warren S. McCulloch* (McCulloch, 1989), he writes:

> No more would I go along with Plato in exiling the poets, who play on the limbic cortex. Not even they are powerful enough to evoke the whole of man. If we are to survive our own destruction of our world and of ourselves by our advance of culture, we had better learn soon to modify our genes to make us more intelligent. It is our last chance, that by increasing our diversity we may be able to make some sort of man that can survive without an ecological niche on this our earth. We may be able to live in gas masks and eat algae and distill the ocean. I doubt that we have time enough. We are, I think, nearing the end of a course that left the main line of evolution to overspecialize in brain to its own undoing. Time will tell.

Norbert Wiener – the father of cybernetics

Norbert Wiener was an American mathematician at MIT, who finished college and received his BA at the age of 14, and was awarded his PhD from Harvard in mathematics at the age of 18. 'His work became the transdisciplinary foundation for a new science of capturing, as well as designing, control and communication mechanisms in all kinds of dynamic systems' (Schwaninger, 2006c). Wiener, as the father of the science of cybernetics, underpins: 'Cybernetics is the science of control of communication in the animal and the machine' (Wiener, 1948). Wiener can be considered as the sun of the cybernetics movement, whereby around him giants such as McCulloch, Pitts, von Foerster, von Neumann, Maturana, Varela, Mead, Bateson and Beer, and many more orbited. These giants were not only among the best and well-known scientists, but they were world authorities in their respective fields. His ground-breaking book, *Cybernetics, or the Science of Control and Communication in the Animal and in the Machine*, catapulted him to the pinnacle in systems and interdisciplinarity in sciences, as did his chilling visions of the future and his ardent social activism to safeguard the world from the implications of his founded science (Conway and Siegelman, 2006). According to Conway and Siegelman (2006): 'The story of the eccentric mathematical genius who founded the revolutionary science of cybernetics and then spent his life warning the world about its dangerous human consequences…'. Wiener's later book, *The Human Use of Human Beings* (Wiener, 1950), was written to address this pivotal issue. Later developments in world affairs have proven Wiener right. Thus, Wiener, his contribution and his prescient warnings have been virtually forgotten (Conway and Siegelman, 2006). The most essential and not widely reported transformation that Wiener's work and contribution took was his humanitarian shift in thinking to see that science and the scientist have been transformed as tools of governmental militarism, its interventionism into science and public manipulations by the ever-growing 'military industrial complex':

> When you turn to me for information concerning controlled missiles, there are several considerations which determine my reply. In the past, the comity of scholars has made it a custom to furnish scientific information to any person seriously seeking it. However, we must face these facts: The policy of the government itself during and after the war, say in the bombing of Hiroshima and Nagasaki, has made it clear that to provide scientific information is not a necessarily innocent act, and may entail the gravest consequences. One therefore cannot escape reconsidering the established custom of the scientist to give information to every person who may inquire of him. The interchange of ideas which is one of the great traditions of science must of course receive certain limitations when the scientist becomes an arbiter of life and death (Wiener, 1947).

In his famous speech at the 'Harrison Liberal Conference', Pierre Trudeau publicly admitted that governments and people in power are able to transform society by the application of cybernetics. Thus, Trudeau (1969) observed:

> We are aware that the many techniques of cybernetics, by transforming the control function and the manipulation of information, will transform our whole society. With this knowledge, we are wide awake, alert, capable of action; no longer are we blind, inert powers of fate (Doern, 1971).

In his 1947 article in *Atlantic Monthly*, 'A scientist rebels', Wiener refused to cooperate with an engineer from Boeing Corporation, which was involved in the guided missiles programmes:

> Cybernetics is a by-product of the Second World War, a discipline that tries to unify different fields of research and different engineering cultures under the

> universal term of information processing. From this position, it extends towards the life and social sciences. Cybernetics describes a kind of alliance between some applied mathematicians, some engineers and biologists during and after the war (Triclot, 2006).

Bousquet (2008) writes in his famous book *Cyberneticizing the American War Machine: Science and computers in the Cold War*:

> American victory in World War II was perceived to be due in large part to its scientific and technological superiority, best exemplified by the development of the atom bomb. Throughout the Cold War, scientific theories and methodologies were recruited even more extensively to weigh on military and strategic affairs. Cybernetics, along with operations research and systems analysis, sought to impose order and predictability on warfare through the collection, processing, and distribution of information. The emergence of the notion of command-and-control epitomized a centralizing approach which saw military organization purely as a vast techno-social machine to be integrated and directed on the basis of the predictions of mathematical models and the deployment of cybernetic technologies. Preparation for a nuclear conflict with the Soviet Union was the primary focus of this conception of warfare but it failed spectacularly the test of Vietnam, thereby dramatically revealing its theoretical and practical bankruptcy. Indeed, cybernetic warfare was deeply flawed in its restrictive assumptions about conflict, its exclusive focus on quantitative elements, its dismissal of any views that did not conform to its norms of scientificity, and its neglect of the risks of information inaccuracy and overload.

Knowing the aftermath of the US dropping atomic bombs in Japan (Wiener who was asked to join the Manhattan Project, which he refused; Einstein was not invited because of the FBI's file on his pacifism and therefore he could not receive his security clearance), Wiener refused to communicate with others about his own work. He made a strong commitment by stating: 'he swears not to publish any future work, which may do damage in the hands of irresponsible militarists' (Wiener, 1947).

Wiener has been one of the very few scientists who has recognized the power of his discoveries and to have warned about it and its implications:

> He made the all-important distinction between physical and biological systems, their different modes of organization, and the different forms of information that could be found in each realm of nature, and he proved mathematically that the engineering principle of feedback was equivalent to the physiological process of homeostasis. He proclaimed the essential unity of information processes and

> showed how the new technical methods of 'control by informative feedback' were, in their essence, the same universal processes that nature long ago selected as its basic operating system for human beings and all living things. Wiener also explored the social and cultural dimensions of cybernetics. Drawing on the ideas of Bateson, Mead, and other social scientists in the Cybernetics Group, Wiener described the stabilizing 'homeostatic processes' found in primitive and developed societies alike, and the myriad forces that may strengthen or undermine those essential processes (Drack and Pouvreau, 2015).

In his ground-breaking book *1984*, Orwell (1949) describes a society in which, by the manipulation of information, one of the most totalitarian regimes ever seen is created (Orwell, 1990). Orwell warns of the terrifying dangers that man may create for himself in his quest for a utopian society. Like Wiener, Orwell warns about the idea that people might believe that everyone must become slaves to the government and militarism regardless of the decisions made by the people in power in order to have an orderly and civilized society, but at the expense of the freedom of the people. The most famous quote from the book is: 'War is peace, freedom is slavery, ignorance is strength' (Orwell, 1990). Wiener:

> ... saw a dearth of healthful homeostatic processes in large developed societies, due to the modern glut of information and its counterpart, the 'constriction of the means of communication' by vested social and political interests. He assailed the simplistic theories of free-market ideologists, and he reserved a special antipathy for modern day 'hucksters,' media barons, captains of industry, and politicians who sought power over large populations through manipulation of the mass media. 'Any organism is held together... by the possession of means for the acquisition, use, retention, and transmission of information,' wrote Wiener, especially the mass society, which is 'too large for the direct contact of its members.' He finished with a warning to his readers: 'Of all of these anti-homeostatic factors in society, the control of the means of communication is the most effective and most important' (Conway and Siegelman, 2006).

Ross. W. Ashby – the founder of Ashby's Law

Ashby is another founding doyen and pioneer of cybernetics and systems theory. He is famous for the 'Law of Requisite Variety', and the books *Design for a Brain* (1948), *An Introduction to Cybernetics* (1956), and for building the homeostat (see Figure 2.26). In this book he invites managers and scientists that have few or shallow skills and training in engineering and mathematics to study the subject and to understand its powerful character in designing strategies, organizations and their governance. In *An Introduction to Cybernetics* (Ashby, 1956) he writes:

> Many workers in the biological sciences – physiologists, psychologists, sociologists – are interested in cybernetics and would like to apply its methods and techniques to their own specialty. Many have, however, been prevented from taking up the subject by an impression that its use must be preceded by a long study of electronics and advanced pure mathematics; for they have formed the impression that cybernetics and these subjects are inseparable. The author is convinced, however, that this impression is false. The basic ideas of cybernetics can be treated without reference to electronics, and they are fundamentally simple; so although advanced techniques may be necessary for advanced applications, a great deal can be done, especially in the biological sciences, by the use of quite simple techniques, provided they are used with a clear and deep understanding of the principles involved.

Indeed, the principles, which are essential for management as control, the natural laws of function and governance, are the very principles of the science of cybernetics, thus they are essential to management, strategy and organizational survival. According to the First Law of Thermodynamics, energy and different forms of energy can be converted to each other as mechanical work to heat but cannot be destroyed. Thus complexity cannot be destroyed, whereupon the contemporary economic and management strategy models are constructed to merely ignore the problem with devastating consequences for people and the environment. Complexity can only be controlled and, depending on the managerial or strategic ability of the observer, pre-controlled or dissolved. Thus, only observers can convert data and written papers to information. There are vital models, laws and general principles that are built on the essential biological or bionics principles. To name a few, they are:

- Law of Requisite Variety – 'the variety in the control system must be equal to or larger than the variety of the perturbations in order to maintain stability' (Ashby, 1958), as Figure 2.26 describes;
- Viable System Model (VSM) (Beer, 1984); and
- Concentration on the function of control, which controls the system or organization (Ashby, 1948; Beer, 1972).

Figure 2.26 describes Ashby's Law in action; thus, the reader can see how management via operations can create equilibrium between the organization and the environment.

FIGURE 2.26 Ashby's Law – the foundational law of management

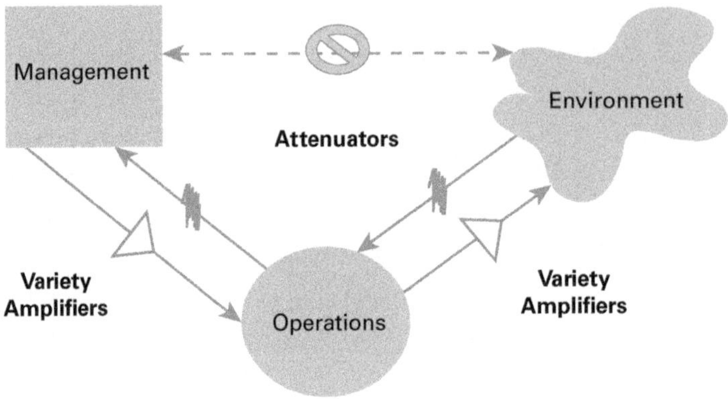

Another vital contribution of Ashby's work, which is essential for observing and understanding by the strategist, is Ashby and his colleagues' 'The Conant's Theorem', which states: 'Every good regulator of a system must be a model of the system' (Conant and Ashby, 1970):

> The first effect of this theorem is to change the status of model-making from optional to compulsory. As we said earlier, model-making has hitherto largely been suggested (for regulating complex dynamic systems) as a possibility: the theorem shows that, in a very wide class (specified in the proof of the theorem), success in regulation implies that a sufficiently similar model must have been built, whether it was done explicitly, or simply developed as the regulator was improved. Thus, the would-be model-maker now has a rigorous theorem to justify his work… Now that we know that any regulator (if it conforms to the qualifications given) must model what it regulates, we can proceed to measure how efficiently the brain carries out this process. There can no longer be question about whether the brain models its environment: it must (Conant and Ashby, 1970).

It is this that Schwaninger (2010), another pioneer of systems and cybernetics, calls model-based management (MBM). According to Schwaninger (2010):

> ... the complexities confronting organizations have been subject to drastic amplification. As a consequence, the pressure on leaders has markedly increased. Orientation and steering devices have become all the more important, because they enable actors in organizations:
>
> - to find their way in complex settings; and
> - to decide and act more effectively and consciously.

Schwaninger (2010) further claims that '... high-quality models can make a powerful contribution', thus the strategist occupied with the most essential task of this era needs to model viability, immunity and competence, whereupon the models need to be designed. It is the very purpose of the author's work to establish a strategic model that models the proactive dissolving of complexity.

HOMEOSTASIS IN SYSTEMS AND ORGANIZATIONS

Alan Turing, the British genius of mathematics, upon taking note of Ashby's contemplation and plan to build a homeostasis machine, wrote him a letter, where Turing states his greatest interest in Ashby's model is that it actually resembles the model of the brain's action rather than the teleology of computing. *Time Magazine* called Ashby's homeostat 'The Thinking Machine' (*Time Magazine*, 1949). According to *Time Magazine* (1949):

> In the laboratory of Barnwood House Mental Hospital, on the outskirts of Gloucester, England, is a modest black contraption that looks like four storage batteries set in a square. Its only visible moving parts are four small magnets, one swinging like a compass needle over each box. Psychiatrist William Ross Ashby, who built the machine, thinks that it is the closest thing to a synthetic human brain so far designed by man. Practical calculating machines, explains Dr. Ashby, merely take orders and act upon them, in complicated but predetermined ways. His machine, which he calls a 'homeostat,' is different.

Thus, Ashby's homeostat thought for itself and modelled a brain-like apparatus, whereby one has to understand what it is that the brain is ubiquitously doing. In Beer's words (1995), 'The purpose of the system is what it does.' The purpose of homeostasis is to maintain a self-organizing control over situations that require an action, reaction or, what Beer (1966) advocated, to pre-control situations by dissolving problems. Beer states: 'Rather than to solve problems it is clever to dissolve them' (Beer, 1966).

Ashby (1952) states:

> How does the brain produce adaptive behaviour? In attempting to answer the question, scientists have discovered two sets of facts and have had some difficulty in reconciling them. On the one hand the physiologists have shown in a variety of ways how closely the brain resembles a machine: in its dependence on chemical reactions, in its dependence on the integrity of anatomical paths, and in the precision and determinateness with which its component parts act on

one another. On the other hand, the psychologists and biologists have confirmed with full objectivity the layman's conviction that the living organism behaves typically in a purposeful and adaptive way. These two characteristics of the brain's behaviour have proved difficult to reconcile, and some workers have gone so far as to declare them incompatible.

But, Ashby takes a contrary position and underpins the claim that the brain is constantly using adaptive behaviour and that machines and organizational behaviour can thereby be trained. Adaptive-ness is a key strategic capability, which requires any organization with high integrity that navigates in uncertainty to constantly adapt using the real-time information it receives. March *et al* (1993) identify three skills that an organization must have to deal with uncertainty in order to survive and prosper:

1. skills in anticipating the shape of an uncertain future;
2. skills in the generation of alternatives in navigating effectively in changing environments;
3. skills in implementing new information and plans effectively and rapidly.

Ashby's original drawing (Figure 2.27) was found by the author in Ashby's digital archives.

FIGURE 2.27 Ashby's homeostat

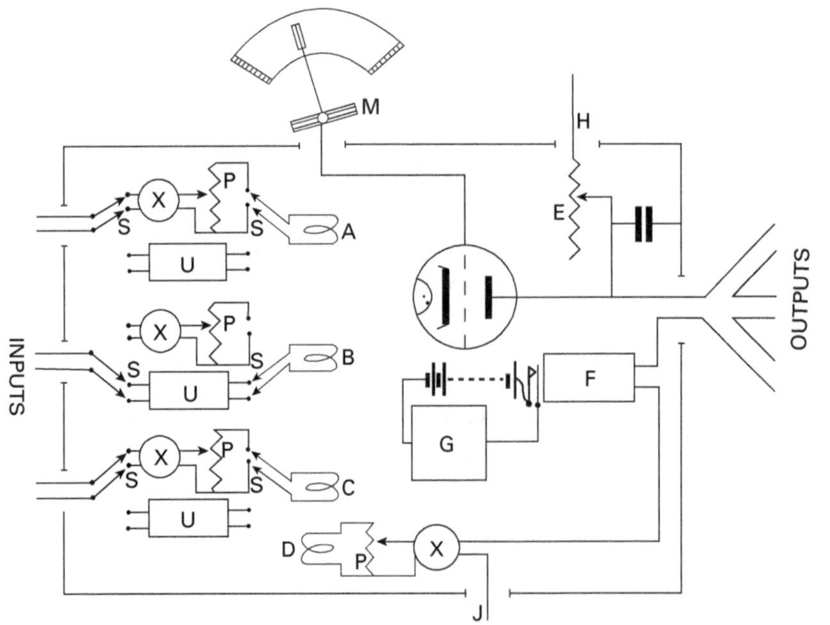

Based on Ashby (1948)

Beer (1985) describes it as follows: 'homeostasis is stability of a system's internal environment, despite the system's having to cope with an unpredictable external environment.' And according to von Foerster (2003a):

> As a general suggestion for researching this problem, I would postulate the following proposition: The postulate of the epistemic homeostasis – The nervous system as a whole is organized in such a way (organizes itself in such a way) that it computes a stable reality. This makes it clear that here again, with 'stable realities', we are dealing with an Eigen-value problem, and I could imagine that this observation may be of value in psychiatry. Some may have seen in these remarks their existentialist basis. By means of the double closure of the circle of signals – or the complete closure of the causal nexus – I have done nothing more than stipulate the autonomy of each individual living being anew: the causes of my actions are not somewhere else or with somebody else – that would be heteronomy: the other is responsible. Rather, the causes of my actions are within myself: I am my own regulator! Frankl, Jaspers, or Buber would perhaps express it the following way: in each and every moment I can decide who I am. And with this, the responsibility for who I am and how I act falls back to me; autonomy means responsibility; heteronomy means irresponsibility. Here we see that the epistemological problems of ethics coincide to a larger degree with those of cybernetics, and thus we, in the field of cybernetics, have the responsibility to partake in the solution of the social and ethical problems of our times.

Thus, it is the strategist as an observer who embarks on the journey of designing models of control and communication within the system under their control, whereby the organization maintains its homeostasis while coping with strategic problems. Maintaining homeostasis is the purpose of evolutionary systems, thus organizations must be the model of what they really do, not what they say they intend to do, which is to maintain viability while coping with amplified deviation and variety attenuation.

The derived wisdom is modelled in Figure 2.28 – this is the foundation of homeostasis and Ashby's Law in action. Hence, the power of variety attenuation, by responding to the stimulus, absorbs the variety that has been created and transmitted to the nervous system.

VARIETY OR THE NUMBER OF STATES IN A SYSTEM

The notion and understanding of variety are fundamental to management. It is upon this very notion that the whole capability of management as a function of control relies. The author has established the understanding that

FIGURE 2.28 How the spinal cord maintains control of the stimulus/response system

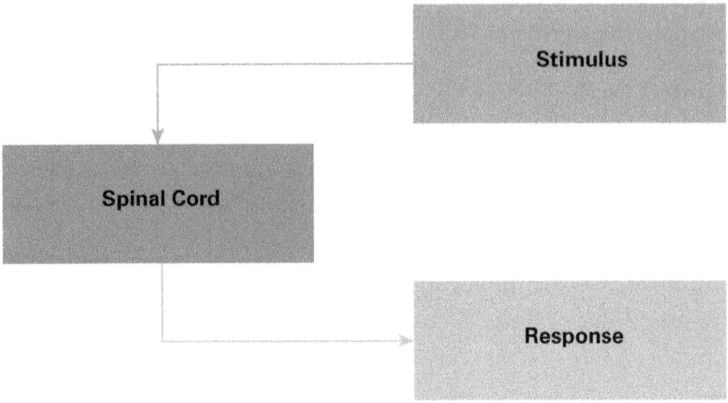

time is the currency of the strategist, thus variety is the currency of the manager. Ashby's Law as the fundamental law of management is based on the balancing of variety:

> Variety has always been a fundamental idea in Cybernetics and Systems Science and is so in Metasystem Transition Theory. Variety is defined as a multiplicity of distinctions. The existence of variety is necessary for all change, choice, and information. A reduction in the quantity of variety is the process of selection. If variety has thus been reduced, i.e. if actual variety is less than potential variety, then we say that there is constraint (Heylighen, 2001a).

Variety engineering is the term used to describe the highest abstraction of management. Thus, the highest form of abstraction in living organizations is based on three components (Hetzler, 2008):

1. The organization's milieu, where the organization (organism) is embedded, and wherein its existence is ever possible.
2. A unity of operations entity, or an organizational structure, whereby the organization deals and copes with its environment. In terms of cybernetics, one speaks of a teleological or goal-oriented behaviour, whereby the organization achieves its objectives.
3. A management entity, which maintains and executes control, whereby the whole system is under a structural and behavioural control.

The triad above (described in Figure 2.29) – consisting of the environment, organization and management – constructs a closed and separate system. According to Beer (1966), the system in which both the manager and strategist

FIGURE 2.29 A firm or organization system embedded in its environment

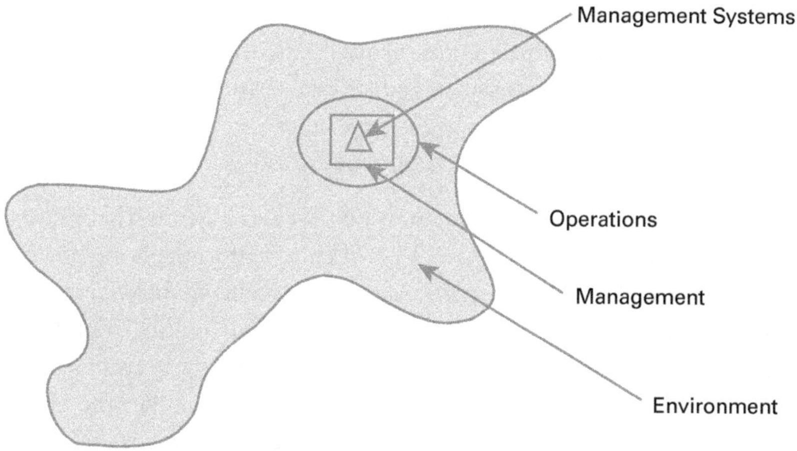

Author's interpretation, based on Christopher (2007)

are interested is a relatively isolated system. The strategist copes with the environment and may be able to isolate their responsibilities from the world of outside, but the strategist cannot hide the organization from outside forces and challenges. Thus, the world disturbs the organization by the situations it creates for the organization. These situations are dependent on the strategist's capabilities, both foreseeable and calculable, but some are emergent based on diverse situations combined as unforeseeability of the disturbances, the strategist's lack of foresight or the organization's lack of organizational intelligence, thus attacking the organization's stability or it's state of homeostasis is always possible.

Ashby's Law of Requisite Variety is also observed as the simpler version of Shannon's Tenth Theorem (Shannon and Weaver, 1949), which states that '*... if a correction-channel has capacity H, then equivocation of amount H can be removed, but no more*' (Richardson and Tinaikar, 2004). Ashby (1958) underpinned his law as based on the notion of the brain, thus the brain is recognized as a paradigm example of a complex system:

> ... the amount of regulatory or selective action that the brain can achieve is absolutely bounded by its capacity as a channel (Ashby, 1962: 274, 1958b). A variation on Ashby's Law, sometimes referred to as the Conant-Ashby Theorem, is that every good regulator of a system must contain a complete representation of that system.

According to Shannon and Weaver (1949):

> If the correction channel has a capability equal to Hy(x) (the amount of additional information that must be supplied per second at the receiving point to correct the received message), it is possible to so encode the correction data as to send it over this channel and correct all but an arbitrarily small fraction of the errors. This is not possible if the channel capacity is less than Hy(x).

The author is not discussing Shannon and Weaver's Tenth Theorem more precisely; this would involve the notion of entropy and the laws of thermodynamics, which have already been treated thoroughly in the sections above. However, according to Beer (1966), Ashby himself pointed out that the theorem states the same thing as his law. Considering the relations between management, organization and the environment, it resembles the Hegelian Axiom of Internal Relations, which describes the ontological relations of beings, agents and things to one other. Furthermore, it states that all things are internally related that make them interrelated.

According to Turchin (1977):

> The most important features of Hegel's dialectic follow directly from the description of phenomena in terms of relations, not attributes. Above all, what follows from this approach is the theory of the interaction and inter-relatedness of everything that exists. Further: If two elements are in correspondence and do not contradict one another, they act as something whole and their common attributes become paramount while the interaction, the relation, between them withdraws to a secondary position. Relations among elements, objects, manifest themselves to the extent that they are relations of opposition, contradiction, and antagonism. Thus, the idea of the struggle of opposites plays an important part in Hegel.

Beer (1966) states that, considering the Hegelian Axiom, one can establish the notion of the ramified system, whereby one can argue that the disturbance caused to the system under control is an environmental disturbance and which is consequently something bound up and related to the system. Thus, the system may be separated from its environment, but it's embedded there, so it actually belongs to the system and thus it is not foreign to its milieu. Figure 2.30 describes this very relation, whereby the disturbance of the environment is transmitted to the management via the organization, which can also be described as processes or operations. The managerial function absorbs the disturbance or situation and maintains organizational control via the managerial systems.

FIGURE 2.30 A system of a firm

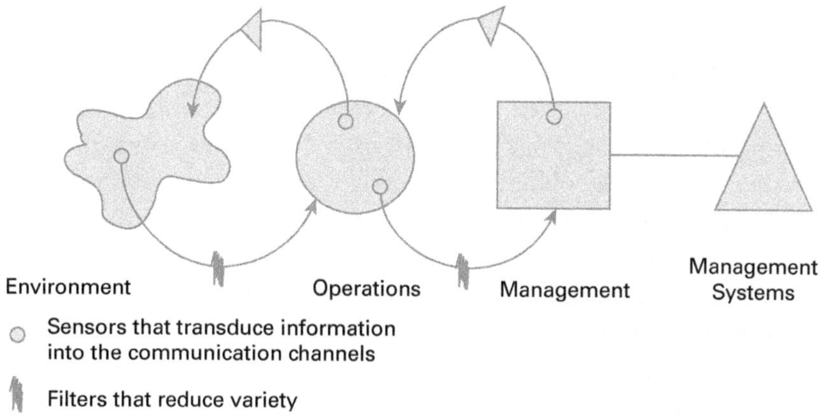

Author's interpretation, based on Christopher (2007)

According to Ashby (1960):

> Two systems of continuous variables (that we called 'environment' and 'reacting part') interact, so that a primary feedback (through complex sensory and motor channels) exists between them. Another feedback, working intermittently and at a much slower order of speed, goes from the environment to certain continuous variables which in their turn affect some step-mechanisms, the effect being that the step-mechanisms change value when and only when these variables pass outside given limits. The step mechanisms affect the reacting part; by acting as parameters to it they determine how it shall react to the environment. (From this basic type a multitude of variations can be made. Their study is made much easier by a thorough grasp of the properties of the basic form just defined.)

Speaking of managing complex systems as the fundamental concept of the book, variety can be stated in the following way: variety is the measure of the number of possible states of a system that result from interaction of all the sub-systems of the whole, which leads to developing a ubiquitous controlling mechanism that can cope with the emerging environmental perturbations and whereby the system can be controlled.

Systems generally develop a number of varieties. In systems and cybernetics, as the sciences of steering complex systems and organizations, variety is described as the number of measurements of complexity. Organizations are complex and probabilistic systems. The term complexity is often confused with something being complicated. The truth is something totally different. It is easy to reflect upon an organization as a complex system because it's constructed of many diverse sub-systems. What is a bit difficult to absorb is the probabilistic nature of organizations, firms and enterprises. Variety, as the author has established, is the number of possible states of control over the firm – its behaviour, which the strategist needs to achieve organizational objectives. Thus, these objectives do not need to be exactly specified for the law; however, they must be of a certain level of importance for the organization. To state this more precisely: every goal has a bottleneck to be resolved, which determines the time, resources and actions the strategist needs to take to achieve the objectives.

Figure 2.31 describes how organizational complexity rises when a strategic objective is embarked upon. The mere complexity is the notion of the combination of the 'journey, goal and destination' the organization wants to achieve, the 'plan' it needs to draw and to design, and the 'action or set of actions' it needs to take, as an essential part of the strategy design. Dealing with this complexity is the variety attenuation according to Ashby's Law. In terms of strategy, which necessarily includes the futuristic nature of strategy, the author wants to establish a different notion for Ashby's Law: only variety in terms of time, capability and an intelligent structure can dissolve variety.

Dissolving variety, whereby complexities are dissolved, is the objective of the strategist, and here things that can be foreseen and calculated must be foreseen, and emergent challenges ought to be coped with based on organizational intelligence. The author wants to bring his anti-thesis to the attention of the reader again. Thus, seeing strategy not as a static set of actions, the organization must have some sort of capability to deal with the emergent phenomenon, and hence **'structure is strategy'**.

Since for the organization to be viable it must maintain a separate and self-organizing existence, the functioning of strategic design is a part of the organization, whereby it maintains its viability and the needed adaptivity, where this function is not imposed on the system or organization but, moreover, a part of its structure to survive and to evolve. When the very structure of the organization is responsible for its teleological behaviour, one speaks of intelligent structure, which, if designed, is a solid strategic positioning.

Figure 2.31 describes the author's model of strategy alignment, where strategy is a combination between the pillars of goal, plan and action. If one cuts one of these pillars, it is clear that one has no strategy, but something else:

FIGURE 2.31 Strategic complexity

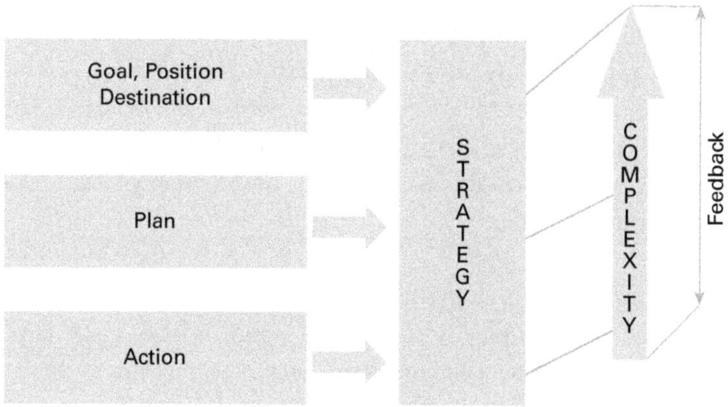

> Organizations are adapted to their environment and it has appeared adequate to say of them that their organization represents the 'environment' in which they live, and that through evolution they accumulated information about it, coded in their nervous systems. Similarly, it has been said that the sense organs gather information about the 'environment' and through learning this information is coded in the nervous system (Maturana and Varela, 1980).

This gathering of information and what is coded within the organization's (organism's) intelligence system (nervous system) is the organization's cognitive activity of self-reference, self-observation and autopoiesis. Therefore, structure is a strategy to cope with emergent and cognitive teleological activities. The quality of this part of strategic capability depends on the ability of the organization's design and evolved ethos and the notion of self-transformation.

One can observe variety in strategic management and, for the purpose of this book, as the needed cognitive and executable number of steps the organization needs to maintain its state of strategic homeostasis. The most vital state of homeostasis here is of course against the ultimate threat to organizational survival; this must be maintained at all times. The author suggests therefore observing the goal of maximizing organizational viability as the ultimate organizational objective, and everything else, including profit-maximization, as a secondary objective; the application of profit-maximization will endanger the organization with systemic crises. The turbulence of systemic crises in this era makes it clear that an additional management doctrine is needed. Strategy must integrate additional science to be able to cope with the situations the strategist faces, whether they are foreseeable or emergent. Thus, the notion of survivability applies to all types of organization, and here we speak of management and strategy for the state of maximization of strategy, not profits. The notion of systemic thinking and survivability applies to any kind of organization, therefore by representing this view the author stays in accordance with von Foerster's Theorem Number One: always act so as to advance the number of your choices. Thus variety-engineering in strategy is advancing the number of the strategist's possible choices and paths.

GOAL-ORIENTED AND GUIDED BEHAVIOUR

Dissolving strategic complexity to achieve organizational goals requires a highly developed and functional organization structure; thus, as the author's established notion has already stated, that structure is a vital part of strategy. Emergent phenomena and obstacles cannot be calculated at all times; hence, it requires a system of goal-achieving strategy that embeds all the organization's capabilities and overall intelligence. Structure, therefore, is fundamental to strategy. The simplistic notion that, after a strategy has been developed the strategist can let the structure follow the strategy, gives a very static view of strategy. It actually disregards all the bottleneck challenges that an organization will face as it navigates achieving its goals in an unpredictable and dynamic environment. According to von Foerster: 'To navigate is to construct' (Müller, 2006); this precisely explains that organizations as viable social productive systems must create their goals based on the best and actual information, thus not violating the organizational identity and overall grand strategy. Therefore, goals ought to be divided into sub-goals. Figure 2.32 demonstrates the integration of the three most vital layers of the organization. The meta-layer is ubiquitously informed and participates in achieving the goals, although it has, apart from a regulatory and information processing function, no other function. The integration of top management is purely based on the project or goal ownership of top management to be participative in all organizational goals, but still not violating the essential law of management, namely the law of self-organization.

According to Rosenblueth *et al* (1943):

> Purposeful active behavior may be subdivided into two classes: feed-back (or teleological) and non-feed-back (or non-teleological). The expression feed-back is used by engineers in two different senses. In a broad sense it may denote that some of the output energy of an apparatus or machine is returned as input; an example is an electrical amplifier with feedback. The feed-back is in these cases

> positive – the fraction of the output which re-enters the object has the same sign as the original input signal. Positive feed-back adds to the input signals, it does not correct them. The term feed-back is also employed in a more restricted sense to signify that the behavior of an object is controlled by the margin of error at which the object stands at a given time with reference to a relatively specific goal. The feed-back is then negative, that is, the signals from the goal are used to restrict outputs which would otherwise go beyond the goal. It is this second meaning of the term feed-back that is used here.

One of the most fundamental notions that has been introduced by the author here is the feedback-guided purposeful behaviour of the organization, thus dividing the larger objective into smaller objectives while involving the whole organizational capabilities. The term capability here establishes the understanding that there is no debate on the diverse views as to structure vs. resources, since it's not the separation of these views nor the advocating of either view that brings the strategist to their objectives, namely purpose, but it's the alignment of both views that actually makes the organization an intelligent organization. The view represented here is coined as organizational capabilities, since the ability to make the needed resources or inputs

FIGURE 2.32 Guided goal achievement model (GGAM)

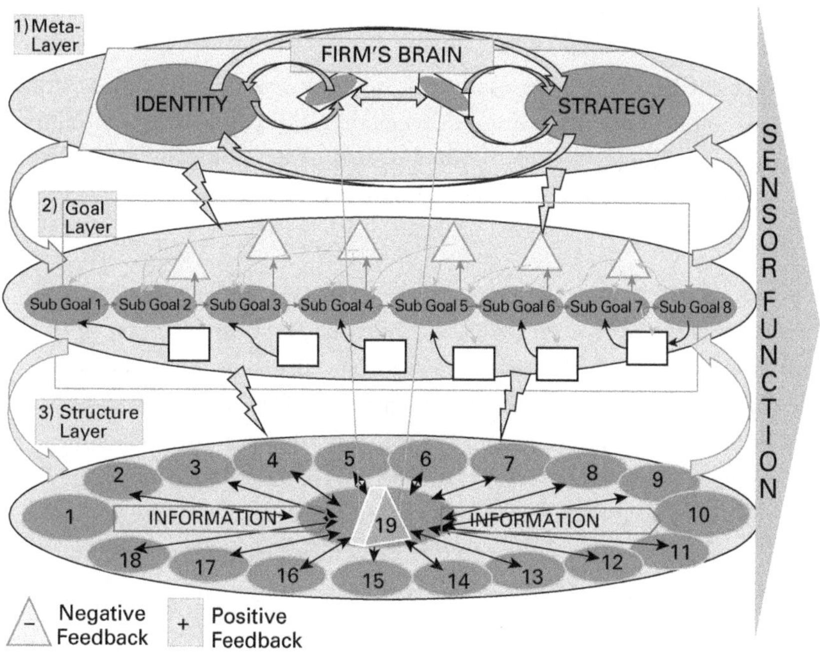

available, without waste of time, and have the organizational structure to cope with the emergent challenges while maintaining the larger perspective is an attribute of a viable and fit organization.

> All purposeful behavior may be considered to require negative feed-back. If a goal is to be attained, some signals from the goal are necessary at some time to direct the behavior. By non-feed-back behavior is meant that in which there are no signals from the goal which modify the activity of the object in the course of the behavior. Thus, a machine may be set to impinge upon a luminous object although the machine may be insensitive to light. Similarly, a snake may strike at a frog, or a frog at a fly, with no visual or other report from the prey after the movement has started. Indeed, the movement is in these cases so fast that it is not likely that nerve impulses would have time to arise at the retina, travel to the central nervous system and set up further impulses which would reach the muscles in time to modify the movement effectively. As opposed to the examples considered, the behavior of some machines and some reactions of living organisms involve a continuous feed-back from the goal that modifies and guides the behaving object. This type of behaviour is more effective than that mentioned above, particularly when the goal is not stationary. But continuous feedback control may lead to very clumsy behavior if the feed-back is inadequately damped and becomes therefore positive instead of negative for certain frequencies of oscillation (Rosenblueth *et al*, 1943).

However, the feedback systems displayed in Figure 2.33 resemble an organizational intelligence and a guided-behavioural course correction, thus purposefulness ought also to be understood as being quick to respond to change while causing the minimum waste of resources and time. According to Beer (2002):

> We are used to suppose the variety in social systems is kept under control by a legislative mode of regulation that restrains variety proliferation. But, as Ashby learned from biological systems, something more subtle underlies any such technique. The notion of a 'coenetic variable' explains the variety of environmental circumstances and of apparently regulatory responses at the same time... Sommerhoff wrote...: Coenetic (pronounced 'sennetic', from the Greek meaning 'common') variables simultaneously delimit variety as shown, so that trajectories of the system converge on to a subsequent occurrence. Sommerhoff called this 'directive correlation'.

FIGURE 2.33 Model of a managerial control system based on a self-organizing principle

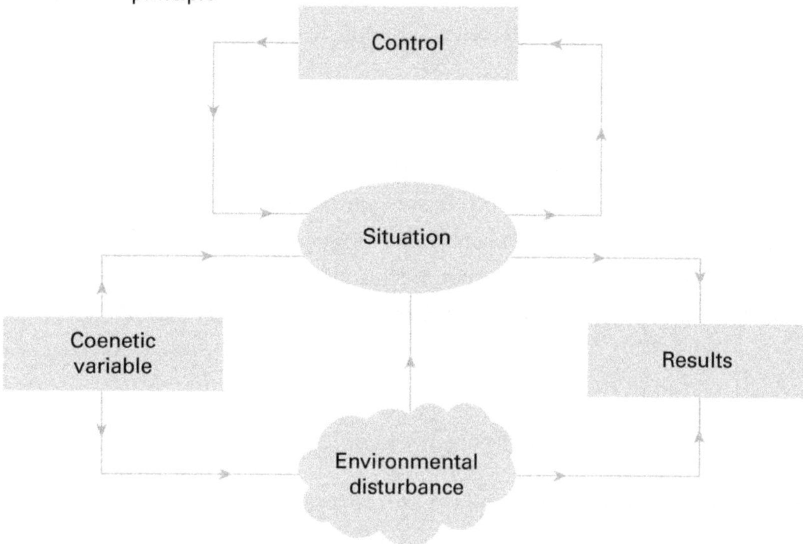

Author's interpretation, based on Beer (1959)

This coenetic variable is described in Figure 2.33, where the strategist, who wants to tackle hard problems, needs an adequate control mechanism to cope with the problems at hand. According to Beer:

> Often one hears the optimistic demand: 'give me a simple control system; one that cannot go wrong'. The trouble with such 'simple' controls is that they have insufficient variety to cope with variety in the environment. Thus, so far from not going wrong they cannot go right. Only variety in the control system can deal successfully with variety in the system controlled (Beer, 2002).

The essentiality of the model described in Figure 2.33 is that the strategist can take the environmental disturbance sideways, since the organizational body or regulatory body, which is next in line of hierarchy, knows more and can help the disturbance to be regulated with minimum effort. Hence, the immediate supervisor knows more about the nature of the disturbance and the overall situation. Taking the problem to higher levels of the organization may cause delay and an inappropriate response, thus violating diverse cybernetic and managerial laws and principles (Beer, 1966). Fremont-Smith, introducing the Systems and Cybernetics Conference of 1948, stated:

> The concept of teleological mechanisms... may be viewed as an attempt to escape from... older, mechanistic formulations that now appear inadequate, and to provide new and more fruitful conceptions and more effective methodologies for studying self-regulating processes, self-orienting systems and organisms, and self-directing personalities... (FRANK, 1948).

Although these words were written over 70 years ago, their accuracy and timeliness have not evaporated. It is essential that an organization's activities are based on a scientific-practical model that has sufficient variety to cope with the challenges of the organization's external and internal environment, but moreover to foster its strategic and structural intelligence.

Autopoiesis and social systems

Autopoietic organizations are organizations that have the capacity and capability of self-sustainability, self-repair, self-therapy and self-reproduction. The word was coined for the science of cybernetics by Maturana (1980) in his ground-breaking book *Autopoiesis and Cognition: The Realization of the Living*. The word, which has Greek roots – *auto*, meaning self, and *poiesis*, meaning creation; *autopoiesis*, meaning self-creation – has a vital and fundamental place among the notions of mechanism, structure, cognition and organizational function, especially for viable organizations. According to Maturana (1980):

> ... that one day, while talking with a friend (Jose Bulnes) about an essay of his on Don Quixote de la Mancha, in which he analyzed Don Quixote's dilemma of whether to follow the path of arms (praxis, action) or the path of letters (poiesis, creation, production), and his eventual choice of the path of praxis differing any attempt at poiesis, I understood for the first time the power of the word 'poiesis' and invented the word that we needed: autopoiesis. This was without history, a word that could directly mean what takes place in the dynamic of autonomy proper to living systems. Curiously, but not surprisingly, the invention of this word proved of great value. It simplified enormously the task of talking about the organization of the living without falling into the always gaping trap of not saying anything new because the language does not permit it. We could not escape being immersed in a tradition, but with an adequate language we could orient ourselves differently and, perhaps from the new perspective generate a new tradition.

Diverse scientists from many fields have applied and debated Maturana and Varela's concepts. Although major breakthroughs have resulted from Maturana and his student Varela's works, their ideas are still controversial and not widely credited as universally valid theories in the mainstream scientific community. Many researchers have applied and debated the works and theories of Maturana and Varela (Hallowell, 2009). According to Hallowell (2009):

> In addition, despite the fact that some in mainstream science may view their ideas as marginal or wrong, both Maturana and Varela distinguished themselves as important, legitimate biologists through well-known laboratory work that served as the foundation for their theoretical ideas (Maturana, 1958; Lettvin, Maturana, McCulloch, & Pitts, 1968; Maturana, Uribe, & Frenk, 1968; Maturana, 1969; Varela, 1979; Rudrauf *et al*, 2003). Beyond the details of Maturana and Varela's particular views on the nature of biology, cognition, and knowledge, their work is important because it challenges one to examine fundamental assumptions about the nature of reality and to consider the ethical implications of being human and how we bring forth worlds with each other. Media and communications technologies play an important role in the bringing forth of worlds in today's global village as humanity stands on the precipice of unprecedented possible catastrophes. Ethical approaches to biology that help enhance our natural abilities for empathy and love coupled with the intelligent use of media and communications technology can serve as potent remedies to the many destructive tendencies that characterize our postmodern dominator culture, which clings to outmoded views about the nature of power relations among humans, humans' relationship to the natural world, and the ultimate nature of reality.

Although the author will draw back on many researchers which have applied and contributed to the theory and to the dialectic of autopoiesis, I aim to establish a newer 'eigen perception' and usage of the word in the field of strategy and management, and to foster the debate of strategy as a cognitive, self-reflecting, self-controlling and self-observing activity of the living, autopoietic and self-observing biological systems, machines and social systems. Self-correction is in strategy a very essential issue; thus, the notion substantiates the author's claim that 'structure is strategy'. It frees strategy from being a static observation for automatons to obey the orders top–down and to construct a structure or structurally being made of a pre-observation of the strategist while not being able to calculate all the amplifications of the structure suggested and the challenges of emergent strategic phenomena. Rather, it additionally gives the dynamics of the environment, of the organizational internal structure with its diverse sub-systems and the foresight horizon of strategy as a steering and navigating activity, precisely its control, and pre-control function by the strategist a special meaning. Self-correction is vital to living and social adaptive systems. Figure 2.34 reflects an autopoietic organization that has the capacity of self-communications, self-organization, and the ability to self-affect its eigen behaviour. Eigen behaviour arises from the dynamic of the organization's sub-systems to equate its varieties with the environment in which it's embedded, aiming to survive and maintain a viable existence. For a social system, machine or biological being to self-reflect on their eigen behaviour and correct that behaviour, here the author widens the notion of organizational intelligence especially for social systems, since being able to correct eigen behaviour is one of the essential aspects in strategic management.

An organization that has a high-quality capability of self-correction has a sustainable competitive advantage. It fosters the organization's ability to maintain a better position in the marketplace, and to create and innovate faster than rivals by being a better problem-solver and a quick adapter to changes. Some qualities that arise from self-correcting and self-reflecting attributes are 'time to market' – in the language of BA, time to money, but

FIGURE 2.34 An autopoietic organization affecting its environment and creating value while maintaining strategic fit

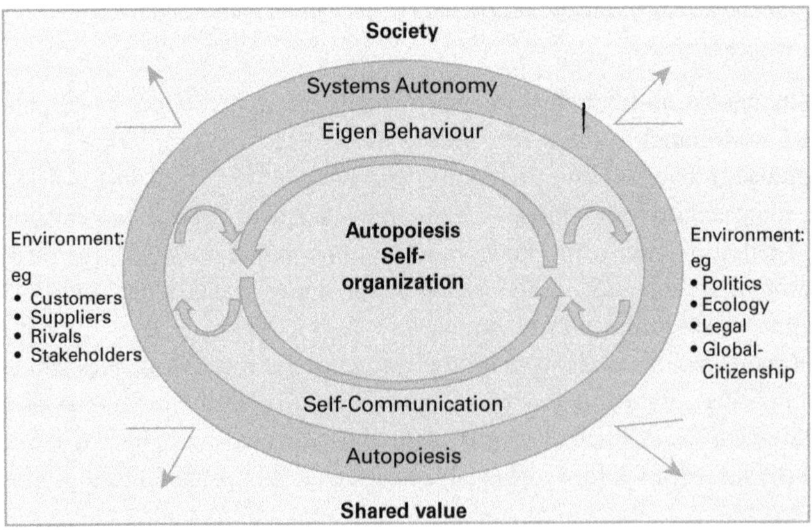

cybernetically and strategically speaking, time to be proactive, to pre-correct and to dissolve. Thus, this cognitive autopoietic function or regulator ought to be embedded in the organization, not imposed on the system, and it must act ubiquitously to foster and enhance organizational intelligence and strategic fit. Thus, higher capabilities arise from self-observation and self-correction, and this is the primary activity and function of autopoiesis in strategy.

> Autopoietic systems are self-producing in a way that they produce the network of processes that enables them to produce their own components. Autopoietic systems are systems that continually produce or create themselves in closed circular processes of production. They have no other purpose and if the dynamic circularity is interrupted then they disintegrate. Living systems are autopoietic – they are organized in such a way that their processes produce the very components which are necessary for the continuance of these processes. Systems which do not produce themselves are called allopoietic. Maturana and Varela also refer to human-created systems as heteropoietic (Mingers, 2006). In autopoietic system, the components are composed to interact with each other in such a way as to continually produce and maintain them and the relationships between them (Pamkowska, 2008).

Another aspect that should be substantiated here is that autopoiesis is also the organization's capability to self-establish the favourable milieu itself and to produce the required and favourable environment for the organization. Thus, this capability maintains the most viable organizational homeostasis, when it is perused on a proactive basis. Although emerging challenges may not be able to be foreseen prior, organizations that actively pursue holistic thinking in their overall strategies are at the frontier of most fit organizations.

Artificial intelligence and organizational behaviour

This section synthesizes the notion that structure cannot be separated from strategy. This issue is discussed and further underpinned for the reader by the research of Damasio (2004) on the falsification of Descartes' (1637) mind and body problem, by Holland and Knight (2006) on their research on the 'anthropomimetic principle', and by the humanoid robots of Pfeifer *et al* (2012) of the Bio-Inspired Robotics Laboratory (BIRL) at the ETH University of Zürich. Thus, artificial intelligence (AI) is a broad and interdisciplinary field, as is organizational strategy, and in the following paragraphs we will establish that there is a direct link between AI's challenges coping with the environment and the required cognitive activities combined with the optimal structure to achieve a stable interaction and what a strategist has to deal with in steering an organization. Thus, the discovery of Damasio (2004) treating his patients by falsifying Descartes and the author's anti-thesis to Chandler (1962) 'structure follows strategy' vs. 'structure is strategy', resemble the same root of thought.

According to Damasio (2004) the philosopher René Descartes could not have been more wrong. He thought the mind was completely separate from the body, an immaterial 'thinking thing' the essence of which was cool conscious reasoning untainted by base physical influence. Through his research on patients with prefrontal cortex damage, Damasio (2004) discovered that reason, like almost all mental processes, is 'embodied,' that is, based in the human being's physical self. In strategy, the separation of structure or the essentiality of structure is absent. The notion that Chandler (1962) established has been held dear ever since. But the reality could not be further from this observation. Choosing the strategy first then letting the structure follow not only violates the principles of cybernetics as the science of effective organization and control, but furthermore, it violates the most fundamental part of strategic thinking, namely, what Sun Tzu (544–496 BC) has called 'Shih'. Shih theory bases strategy on enemy intent, in contrast to Euro-American, which the Chinese refer to as 'Li' strategies based on forces. Shih explains the anomalies that continue to perplex Western observers in modern China's execution of force (Greene, 2010). Robert Greene (2010) in his ground-breaking book *The 33 Strategies of War* refers to the theory of Shih as position of potential force, namely force adapted to the situation confronted. The emphasis here is on the notion of adaptation, thus Shih according to Darwin can be explained as: 'Not the strongest, nor the smartest – those most responsive to change survive' (O'Reilly and Tushman, 2011). According to O'Reilly and Tushman (2011):

> Although Darwin was writing about biological species 150 years ago, his logic applies to organizations today. In 1959, Fortune magazine ranked General Motors as the largest, and arguably the strongest, manufacturing firm in the United States. Fifty years later it is on the brink of bankruptcy. In his 2000 book entitled Leading the Revolution, Gary Hamel praised Enron as one of the smartest companies in the world. By 2001 it was out of business and the subject of a book with the ironic title of The Smartest Guys in the Room. The hedge firm Long Term Capital management included two Nobel Laureates among its founders but collapsed in 1998, almost bringing the U.S. financial markets to ruin. Darwin was right, neither strength nor intelligence guarantees survival. Only adaptation can do that, whether for firms or flora and fauna.

Thus, so too do social productive systems (Ulrich, 2001) as organizations. The essence of strategy is adaptivity, since strategy is about choices. Choices are essential to exploiting the emergent opportunities. Thus, calculating the strategy solely based on analytical and static tools reduces the strategist's freedom to act. Shih according to Stafford Beer is 'designing freedom' for organizations (Beer, 1973). According to Rumelt (2007), shih can be called 'strategy dynamics', a poorly researched field within academia. Thus, the author's research falls not only in the category of competitive and immunity strategy, but also precisely fits into the field of strategy dynamics.

According to Iida *et al* (2005), by evolving not only the function of the brain, which resembles a highly complex model integration but moreover by concentrating on the structure of the body, a very simple model of control system may be constructed, thus it herewith can establish a highly effective and dynamic system of control. Iida *et al* (2005) further observe:

> The results from a series of running experiments with a robot show that, by exploiting the unique characteristics induced by the body dynamics, the forward velocity can be controlled by using a very simple method, in which only one control parameter is required. Furthermore, it is also shown that a few of such different control parameters exist, each of them can control the forward velocity. Interestingly, with these parameters, the robot exhibits qualitatively different behavior during the locomotion, which could lead to our comprehensive understanding toward the behavioral diversity of adaptive robotic systems.

According to Lungarella *et al* (2007):

> The discipline of Artificial Intelligence (AI) was born in the summer of 1956 at Dartmouth College in Hanover, New Hampshire. Half of a century has passed, and AI has turned into an important field whose influence on our daily lives can hardly be overestimated. The original view of intelligence as a computer program – a set of algorithms to process symbols – has led to many useful applications now found in internet search engines, voice recognition software, cars, home appliances, and consumer electronics, but it has not yet contributed significantly to our understanding of natural forms of intelligence. Since the 1980s, AI has expanded into a broader study of the interaction between the body, brain, and environment, and how intelligence emerges from such interaction. This advent of embodiment has provided an entirely new way of thinking that goes well beyond artificial intelligence proper, to include the study of intelligent action in agents other than organisms or robots. For example, it supplies powerful metaphors for viewing corporations, groups of agents, and networked embedded devices as intelligent and adaptive systems acting in highly

> uncertain and unpredictable environments. In addition to giving us a novel outlook on information technology in general, this broader view of AI also offers unexpected perspectives into how to think about ourselves and the world around us...

Furthermore, observing AI and humanoid robotics for establishing the direct correlation with structure and consciousness, Holland and Knight (2006) claim:

> Most humanoid robots are essentially conventional robots that fit within the morphological envelope of a human. However, for robots that are intended to help in the understanding of human cognition and action, a much higher level of biological inspiration may be necessary.

Thus, if robotics and architects can learn and apply the essentials of biology, so can managers and strategists. Researchers such as Ramachandran *et al* (1998) have stated: 'Phantoms in the Brain: Probing the Mysteries of the Human Mind', to which Metzinger (2004) refers: 'Being No One: The Self-Model Theory of Subjectivity', and have written and identified the existence of an integrated internal model of the self as the whole body as being a key component of consciousness.

To be very accurate on the notion of body and environment interaction, Pfeifer and Iida (2004) state:

> ... it is shown that, by exploiting the dynamics of the system-environment interaction, very simple controllers can be designed which is essential to achieve rapid locomotion. Special consideration must be given to the choice of body materials. We conclude with some speculation about the importance of locomotion for understanding cognition.

FIGURE 2.35 How bio-inspired robotics are designed

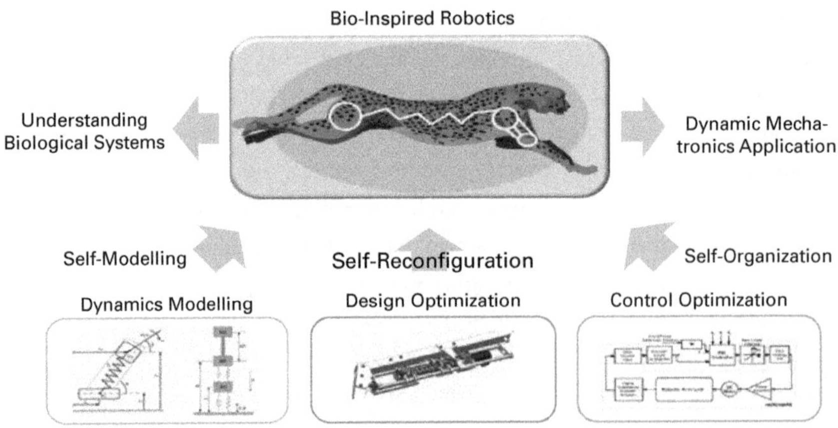

Based on BIRL

Iida and Bovet (2009) further establish the notion by underpinning the author's claim on the essentiality of raising the issue of structure:

> Legged locomotion of biological systems can be viewed as a self-organizing process of highly complex system/environment interactions. Walking Behaviour is, for example, generated from the interactions between many mechanical components (e.g., physical interactions between feet and ground, skeletons and muscle-tendon systems), and distributed informational processes (e.g., sensory information processing, sensory-motor control in central nervous system, and reflexes). An interesting aspect of legged locomotion study lies in the fact that there are multiple levels of self-organization processes (at the levels of mechanical dynamics, sensory-motor control, and learning). Previously, the self-organization of mechanical dynamics was nicely demonstrated by the so-called Passive Dynamic Walkers (PDWs). The PDW is a purely mechanical structure consisting of body, thigh, and shank limbs that are connected by passive joints. When placed on a shallow slope, it exhibits natural bipedal walking dynamics by converting potential to kinetic energy without any actuation. An important contribution of these case studies is that, if designed properly, mechanical dynamics can generate a relatively complex locomotion dynamics, on the one hand, and the mechanical dynamics induces self-stability against small disturbances without any explicit control of motors, on the other. The basic principle of the mechanical self-stability appears to be fairly general that there are several different physics models that exhibit similar characteristics in different kinds of behaviors (e.g., hopping, running, and swimming), and a number of robotic platforms have been developed based on them.

Holland and Knight (2006) state:

> The central idea behind the parent project was to build a robot that could develop such a self-model, and this led to the question: what sort of body would the robot need to form the kind of internal model that might support consciousness? For want of any better information, the obvious answer is a body similar to that of a human, since human consciousness is the only consciousness about which we have any reliable information. However, when we reviewed the state of the art in humanoid robotics, it rapidly became clear that almost all existing humanoids had bodies that were only superficially similar to humans, and that they were moved and controlled in ways very different from those of humans. It was necessary for us to start from scratch.

Pfeifer and Bongard (2007) ask:

> ... whether our nervous systems compute, whether they are separate control systems for our bodies, and even whether there can truly be disembodied reasoning. These three ideas are so ingrained in our computational metaphors that they usually go unquestioned – they make no sense within our normal frameworks of thinking in the fields of computer science and artificial intelligence, and even neuroscience. Beyond the mere technical these questions challenge the intellectual father of rationalism Rene Descartes and his 'Je pense, donc je suis' (I think, therefore I am) from his Discourse on Method (written in French, not Latin, in 1637). While such questions can be seen as a challenge to the very underpinnings of the scientific world view, they really are not. Pfeifer and Bongard are not suggesting throwing out the scientific method and replacing it, as some might fear, with postmodern relativism. Rather they are assaulting certain metaphors that have perhaps gone haywire in their influence on how we approach the study of intelligence, the study of us. In modern times there have been two important and perhaps underestimated influences on our view of intelligence.

First, an agreement on the notion of intelligence ought to be constructed; thus, according to Pfeifer and Bongard (2007):

> Here are some sample definitions from an inquiry by the *Journal of Educational Psychology* in 1921, wherein leading experts of the time were asked for their suggestions. L. Terman: 'the ability to carry on abstract thinking'; W. F. Dearborn: 'the capacity to learn or profit by experience'; S. S. Colvin: 'having learned or ability to learn to adjust oneself to the environment' (this definition is so general that it can hardly be wrong, depending on what we mean by 'adjust oneself to the environment'); R. Pintner: 'the ability to adapt oneself adequately to relatively new situations in life' (similar to the previous one; the question here is what an expression like 'relatively new' means in a definition); V. A. C. Henmon: 'the capacity for knowledge, and knowledge possessed,' and so on and so forth. We could go on for quite a while, but it is not clear what we would gain by adding more definitions to this list.

According to Simon (2002), also known as the father of AI, it is:

> ... a domain of research, application, and instruction concerned with programming computers to perform in ways that, if observed in human beings, would be regarded as intelligent. Intelligence is attributed to human beings when they play chess or solve the Tower of Hanoi puzzle, or learn to

> do such things; computer programs that can perform any of these tasks even moderately well, or learn to do so, are examples of artificial intelligence. Today sophisticated and powerful programs are able to steer automobiles on highways, discover chemical reaction paths from data about the inputs and outputs of multistage chemical reactions; they can simulate the processes that humans use to read problem instructions and form a mental representation of the problem structure; they diagnose diseases; they simulate the behavior of human participants in experiments on verbal learning, concept formation, and recovery of information from long-term memory; and they perform many other tasks of comparable complexity.

Pfeifer and Bongard (2007), in their magnificent book *How the Body Shapes the Way We Think: A new view of intelligence*, observe that AI is the interdisciplinary research field with the following three essential goals:

1. the understanding of biological systems (ie the mechanisms that bring about intelligent behaviour in humans or animals);
2. the abstraction of general principles of intelligent behaviour;
3. the application of these principles to the design of useful artefacts.

Pfeifer and Bongard (2007) state further that:

> It is important to note that 'mechanism' implies not only neural mechanisms or brain processes, but also the body of the agent and its interactions with the real world: the fact that muscles are elastic, and that the weight on one leg increases if the other one is lifted are just as much part of the mechanism of walking as are the reflexes and brain centers involved in this behavior.

This claim additionally substantiates the author's observation and antithesis to Chandler (1962), thus the strategist ought to understand that in order for the agent or social system to develop and construct strategies as they navigate, not only the function of the brain needs to be considered, but moreover the whole body of the agent, its function and, above all, how its structure affects its very ability, action-agility and process, its overall performance and outcome of the strategies implemented.

According to Frantz (2003), human thinking and information processing both perform three similar operations:

1. They scan and observe data for patterns.
2. They store the patterns in their memory.
3. They apply the patterns to make inferences or extrapolations.

Frantz (2003) states further:

> In fact, some programs reproduce and even outperform human experts at problem solving. Simon concluded that there is sufficient reason to believe that some kinds of human thinking closely parallel the operations of an information-processing computer program. AI also led him to conclude that intuition is a subset of thinking. The fact that the mind is a serial information processor, it performs one (or only a very few) operations at a time, places severe limits on human attention, binds our rationality, and limits our capabilities for problem solving to a set of satisfying rather than maximizing solutions. Problem-solving thus involves two generalizations: [...]
>
> 1 A selective trial-and error search is made which by necessity can only consider a relatively few possible solutions. The solution is thus a satisfying solution and the search is based on rules of thumb or heuristics.
>
> 2 One of the basic heuristics is means–end analysis. Means–end analysis involves three steps:
>
> - First, the current situation is compared to a goal, and differences between them are noted.
> - Second, a memory search is performed to identify an operator which can bring the current situation more in line with the goal.
> - Third, the operator is applied in the hope of getting closer to the goal. Since computers solve problems as humans do using heuristics and means–end analysis, Simon concluded that computers display intelligence, defined as behaviour which is appropriate to the goal and adaptive to the environment. Intelligence allows the limited processing capacity of the organism, be it man or machine, to use efficient search procedures to generate possible solutions, with the most likely solutions being generated early in the search process (Newell *et al*, 1972).

Figure 2.36 simulates the situation of an ant walking on the beach (see that ant's path). It displays the ant's trajectory, where the ant is coming from the upper right corner of the figure and walking downwards, where its nest is situated. The ant's trajectory has been drawn by the white line. The ant has to achieve a highly complicated task because the path is full of obstacles (Pfeifer and Bongard, 2007). Pfeifer, in his paper 'Symbols, Patterns, and Behavior: Towards a new understanding of intelligence' (1996), states:

> However, this complexity is in the eye of the observer, rather than in the ant itself. Surely, the trajectory is not stored in the ant's head and so its Behavior cannot be based on it. In other words, there is no trajectory functioning, say,

FIGURE 2.36 Simon's 'ant on the beach' frame of reference

Based on Simon (1996)

> like a plan. Rather, the mechanisms that are driving the ant's Behavior may be very simple. They might be described as rules like 'if obstacle sensor on left is activated, turn right' (and vice versa). These 'rules' are implemented in terms of neural structures within the ant. The neural structures are embedded in the body of the ant. The interaction of the neural substrate with the environment is mediated through the body. In this interaction with the environment the apparent complexity of the trajectory emerges. We say apparent complexity, because the complexity is in the eye of the observer, rather than being a property of the agent itself.

Kurzweil (1999–2005), author of *The Age of Spiritual Machines* and *The Singularity is Near*, claims: 'Within a quarter century, nonbiological intelligence will match the range and subtlety of human intelligence. It will then soar past it because of the continuing acceleration of information-based technologies, as well as...' (Kurzweil, 2005). However, according to Pfeifer and Bongard (2007), this:

> ... is a case in point. Because he assumes that intelligence is exclusively a function of computational power, he sketches a scenario where in the near future computers will outperform human brains simply because they will have as much or more number-crunching power. We hope to convince the reader

> that computational theories of intelligence are doomed to failure from the very outset. Also, we will show that in much of the literature on the subject there is confusion between what exists within the agent itself and what is present within the head of the person observing the agent: this is the frame-of-reference problem.

As has been claimed throughout this book, the strategist is navigating the enterprise as an embodied agent having to steer under a situation of vital turbulence and uncertainty. The situation of the enterprise coping with the challenges of the economic and other environments and that of an artefact dealing with the environment resemble high similarities, as Figure 2.37 describes.

According to Pfeifer and Bongard (2007), embodied agents and firms are exposed to the same kind of uncertainty, thus a biological or robotic agent performing tasks in an ecological niche is very similar to a company as an intelligent embodied system, and design principles can be applied to creating new enterprises and businesses.

FIGURE 2.37 Similarities of the challenges between AI and the entrepreneur or manager

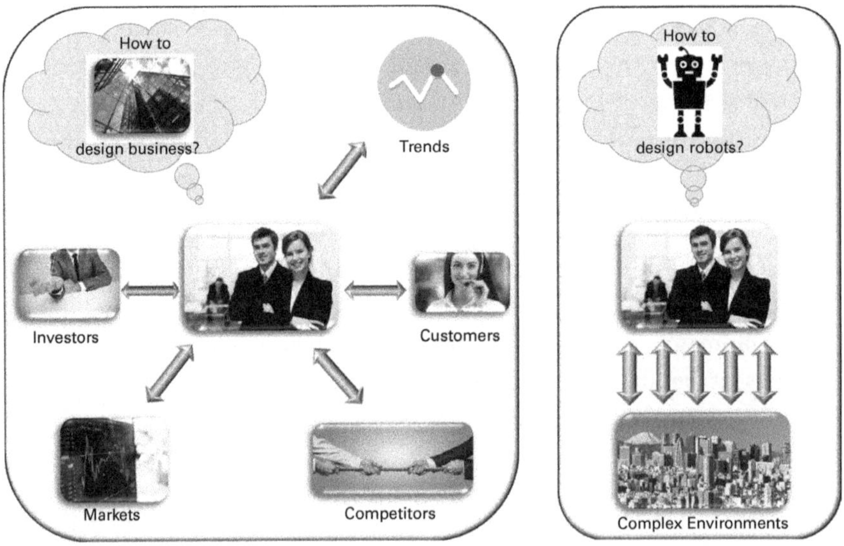

Pfeifer and Bongard (2007) on the notion of describing what the essence of management is, underpin the claim by giving the example of Chester Barnard:

> [When he] retired as the CEO of New Jersey Bell Telephone, he recorded his insights about management in his book Functions of the Executive, which was published for the first time in December 1938 and has since gone through 39 editions. Barnard, who is now widely recognized as one of the founding fathers of general management as a field or discipline, argued that management is concerned – or should be concerned – with those activities in a company or an organization that cannot be delegated because they are inherently uncertain and complex. This uncertainty and complexity, according to Barnard, has its origin in the distributed nature of the activities and processes in the organization. This contrasted sharply with the widely held belief that the essence of management was understanding and controlling manufacturing, sales, administrative, and organizational activities, which can in fact be precisely defined and could thus be easily delegated, whereas strategy and innovation, because of their inherent uncertainty and complexity, cannot. Even though the statement by Barnard represents a key insight into managerial practice, most contributions to the management discipline failed to take it seriously and have mainly focused on those aspects that can be clearly delineated. Barnard died in 1961, but his ideas are still alive and well, and especially in recent years have regained currency with the emergence of the strategic management research community.

Chester Barnard (1938), who also wrote the foreword to Simon's (1947) book *Administrative Behavior*, projected the concepts of authority and bounded rationality (Mahoney, 2002). Barnard developed the following:

1. organization form – that is, formal organization matters;
2. informal organization has both instrumental and humanizing purposes;
3. bounds on rationality are acknowledged;
4. adaptive, sequential decision-making is vital to organizational effectiveness;
5. a tacit knowledge is important (Mahoney, 2002).

Simon (1947) states:

> If there were no limits to human rationality administrative theory would be barren. It would consist of the single precept: Always select that alternative, among those available, which will lead to the most complete achievement of your goals. The need for an administrative theory resides in the fact that there are practical limits to human rationality, and that these limits are not static, but

> depend upon the organizational environment in which the individuals' decisions take place. The task of administration is so to design this environment that the individual will approach as close as practicable to rationality (judged in terms of the organization's goals) in his decisions.

On the subject of rationality, one has to observe that the actual behaviour, according to Simonsen (1994), is limited compared with objective rationality in at least three ways:

1. Rationality requires a complete knowledge and anticipation of the consequences that will follow on each choice. In fact, knowledge of consequences is always fragmentary.
2. Since these questions lie in the future, imagination must supply the lack of experienced feeling in attaching value to them. But values can be only imperfectly anticipated.
3. Rationality requires a choice among all possible alternative behaviours. In actual behaviour, only a very few of all these possible alternatives come to mind.

According to Simonsen (1994) (quoting and observing Simon and March (1976)):

> Given these limitations a model of rational behavior by the administrative man is outlined. The administrative man as a model compared to economic man is different in two major ways:
>
> - Whereas economic man maximizes selects the best alternative from among all those available to him, his cousin, administrative man, satisfies looks for a course of action that is satisfactory or 'good enough'.
> - Economic man deals with the 'real world' in all its complexity. Administrative man recognizes that the world he perceives is a drastic simplified model [...] He makes his choices using a simple picture of the situation that takes into account just a few of the factors that he regards as most relevant and crucial.

Strategist scholars and practitioners are organizations' navigators who are at home at the cutting edge of managerial and strategic sciences, while at the same time have a vast amount of practical experience in the real world of business with all its uncertainties and turbulences. They are constantly pushing the boundaries of theory and its application on real situations further. For a strategist to be effective, they ought to be an expert juggler in diverse academic fields and thus have organizational intelligence under control.

From this section of the book the word strategist has replaced the author's reference to strategist's strategists, who apply what the objective of strategic and managerial sciences should be in the first place, to train the organizational leaders of the future and who are occupied with options and deep strategic thinking, instead of those who seek models that they do not want to develop themselves, rather they expect others to develop these for them. The worst scenario is to wait for a guru to lead the way. These people think only in small-time universes; they can easily be pushed and their whole objective can be obscured by seeing the reality of the whole organization from only a single perspective – namely in economics or linear tactical warfare. Navigating organizations by these limited lenses violates strongly Heinz von Foerster's famous 'constructivist ethical imperative', which states: '... act always so as to increase the total number of choices' (Foerster, 1984).

Understanding and integration of 'fuzzy logic' for strategic thought

Fuzzy logic (FL) was first introduced by Zadeh (1965) in his groundbreaking paper 'Fuzzy Sets' in the *Journal of Information and Control*. According to Zadeh (1965) the essentiality of FL can be understood by:

> Given our veneration for what is precise, rigorous and quantitative, and our disdain for what is fuzzy, unrigorous and qualitative, it is not surprising that the advent of digital computers has resulted in a rapid expansion in the use of quantitative methods throughout most fields of human knowledge. Unquestionably, computers have proved to be highly effective in dealing with mechanistic systems, that is, with inanimate systems whose behavior is governed by the laws of mechanics, physics, chemistry and electromagnetism. Unfortunately, the same cannot be said about humanistic systems, which – so far at least – have proved to be rather impervious to mathematical analysis and computer simulation. Indeed, it is widely agreed that the use of computers has not shed much light on the basic issues arising in philosophy, psychology, literature, law, politics, sociology and other human-oriented fields. Nor have computers added significantly to our understanding of human thought processes – excepting, perhaps, some examples to the contrary that can be drawn from artificial intelligence and related fields.

Zadeh (1965) sees the role of FL by modelling the human mind. In this way, science has been able to solve most of the mysteries of the world and has contributed to the understanding and controlling of complex systems. However, according to Zadeh (1994): '... to be able to design systems having high MIQ (Machine Intelligence Quotient), a profound change in the orientation of control theory may be required.' Zadeh goes further, and although himself a mathematician and electronic engineer, he still strongly advocates for and supports the notion and employment of soft computing rather than hard computing within control theory, the design and analysis of complex systems. Zadeh believes that soft computing is more tolerant of imprecision, uncertainty, and partial truth (Zadeh, 1994). Although, this pattern of thinking was introduced by Zadeh in 1994, this line of thinking has not yet reached strategic management. A search in Google Scholar did not bring a single adequate result that links strategy to FL and strategic management that can be used as a foundation to substantiate the author's claims. However, it is the duty of the author to establish this very link. Strategists are generally embedded in uncertainties. It is precisely here where they are confronted with a high rate of diverse complexities. Thus, it is the job of the strategist to cope with, but above all to reduce, complexities and thereby to preserve the ability to make better decisions and increase the number of choices – or, according to Ashby's Law, the number of perturbation attenuating varieties. According to Saffiotti (1997):

> The development of techniques for autonomous navigation in real-world environments constitutes one of the major trends in the current research on robotics. An important problem in autonomous navigation is the need to cope with the large amount of uncertainty that is inherent of natural environments. Fuzzy logic has features that make it an adequate tool to address this problem.

The essentiality of FL cannot be emphasized sufficiently, thus natural environments are not controlled environments and any agent embedded and confronted with the high rate of turbulence and roughness of the terrain has to make decisions based on insufficient and incomplete decisions. It is precisely the quality of making the most effective and best decisions, while confronted with a high rate of uncertainty, that distinguishes the grand strategist from the crowd of consultants that see themselves as mercenaries to corporations. According to Andriantiatsaholiniaina *et al* (2004):

> Sustainable decision-making involves political decisions at the local, regional, or national levels, which aim at a balanced development of socio-environmental systems. A fundamental question in sustainable decision-making is that of defining and measuring sustainable development. Many methods have been proposed to assess sustainability. Recently, a model has been developed, called

> Sustainability Assessment by Fuzzy Evaluation (SAFE), which uses fuzzy logic reasoning and basic indicators of environmental integrity, economic efficiency, and social welfare, and derives measures of human (HUMS), ecological (ECOS), and overall sustainability (OSUS)... we perform sensitivity analysis of the SAFE model to identify the most important factors contributing to sustainable development. About 80 different indicators are tested and classified as promoting, impeding, or having no effect on the progress toward sustainable development. The proposed method is applied to the Greek and American economies. The conclusion is that there is no unique sustainable path and, accordingly, policy makers should choose different criteria and strategies to make efficient sustainable decisions for each country.

This goes beyond the principles of grand strategy and the definition of what components a strategy ought to have, as (a) the goal or the position to acquire, and (b) the plan (also considering the high rate of the emerging phenomenon and its adequate absorption according to Ashby's Law the very essential feedback based execution of the whole deal, as already established by the author and the notion of FL, all other factors are different and resemble uncertainties). Thus, since a plan has to embed changes without affecting the quality of achieving the ultimate goal, the consideration of integrating FL into the field of strategic management seems appropriate. FL is a powerful tool to reduce complexity in making strategic decisions. Authors such as Yen and Pfluger (1992) come to similar conclusions in robotics as the author's research in strategy, stating that:

> ... the important issue in mobile robot planning and execution in the real world include [...]:
>
> **1** Dealing with a dynamic environment.
>
> **2** Dealing with problems of incomplete and/or inaccurate knowledge.
>
> **3** Coping with the problems of limited sensor information.

The author's objectives to develop a fuzzy controller, as described in Figure 2.39, for the strategist to effectively navigate the organization in its dynamic milieu are the same as a designer of robotics because of the similarity of the challenges facing both. Thus, Figures 2.38 and 2.39 resemble a guided control system based on FL, while combining both the target and the maximum allowed position the organization needs in order to achieve a solid level of goal-achieving and systemic robustness. Thus, the control environment in Figure 2.38 describes 'defuzzi-fication', which is the process of converting FL's fuzzy set into a tangible number that reflects some number of the fuzzy set. Thus, herewith a large contribution to the agent's self-organizing – and the system's eigen behaviour – is laid out. This will result in the reduction of complexity of the organization and the agent coping with the environment to achieve the objective as fast as possible, thus reflecting on the behaviour of the agent or organization to maintain its autonomy and level of systemic freedom for an efficient control and function system.

FIGURE 2.38 Zadeh's fuzzy logic as temperature controller

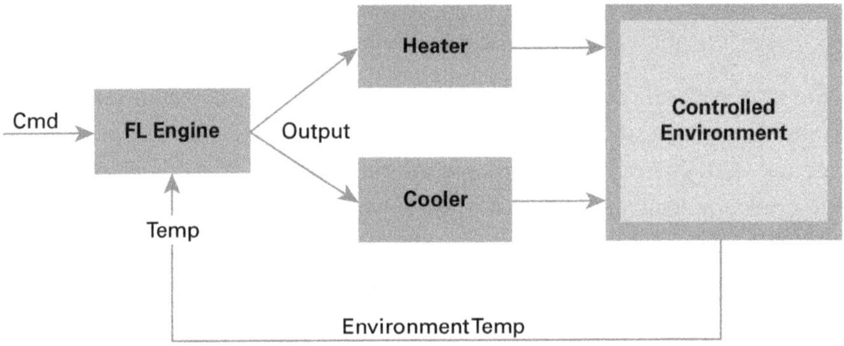

Cmd: Target temperature
Temp: Feedback sensor in controlled environment
Error: Cmd-Temp (+ = too cold, – = too hot)

Based on Zadeh (1994)

FIGURE 2.39 Management by objectives (MBO) based on Zadeh's fuzzy logic

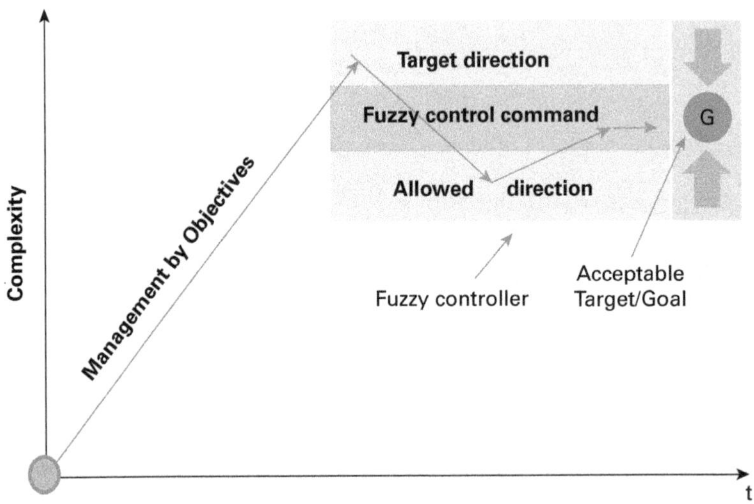

Author's interpretation

With the integration of FL into the author's field of research, it is the chief objective of the author to develop a conceptual framework for dealing with systems that are too complex or to ill-defined to allow a precise quantities analysis. Figures 2.38 and 2.39 describe how such a framework can be designed. Figure 2.39 shows the author's integration of Drucker's MBO into Zadeh's fuzzy logic.

> Fuzzy Logic provides a different way to approach a control or classification problem. This method focuses on what the system should do rather than trying to model how it works. One can concentrate on solving the problem rather than trying to model the system mathematically, if that is even possible. On the other hand the fuzzy approach requires a sufficient expert knowledge for the formulation of the rule base, the combination of the sets and the defuzzification. In General, the employment of fuzzy logic might be helpful, for very complex processes, when there is no simple mathematical model (e.g. Inversion problems), for highly non-linear processes or if the processing of (linguistically formulated) expert knowledge is to be performed. According to literature the employment of fuzzy logic is not recommendable, if the conventional approach yields a satisfying result, an easily solvable and adequate mathematical model already exists, or the problem is not solvable (Hellmann, 2001).

The combination of target direction and allowed direction is a very effective method, thus the feedback that the agent needs to correct its course towards the goal is embedded within the system of its goal-achieving function. Thus, it arranges for a quick course correction to be actively pursued, and if confronted with unforeseen challenges, the agent could still navigate towards the final goal while coping with the emerging challenge. This stability is essential for effective organizations; the author would coin this control function 'strategic homeostasis', which means strategic immunity (as already established).

Figure 2.40 describes how fuzzy logic can be applied to the control of organizational behaviour. The author understands that there are many variations and levels of depth with which this topic can be treated; however incomplete the treatment of FL here, its integration into the field of strategic management has been shown. Although more in-depth research may be advised in the form of some scientific papers, the model has established how such a control system can be achieved. Additional topics under the umbrella of FL include fuzzy feedback in the execution of fuzzy algorithms, the execution of fuzzy algorithms by agents, the conjunctions of fuzzy instructions, the assessment of the quality of fuzzy algorithms, the effects of the

FIGURE 2.40 Guided directional behaviour of the organization

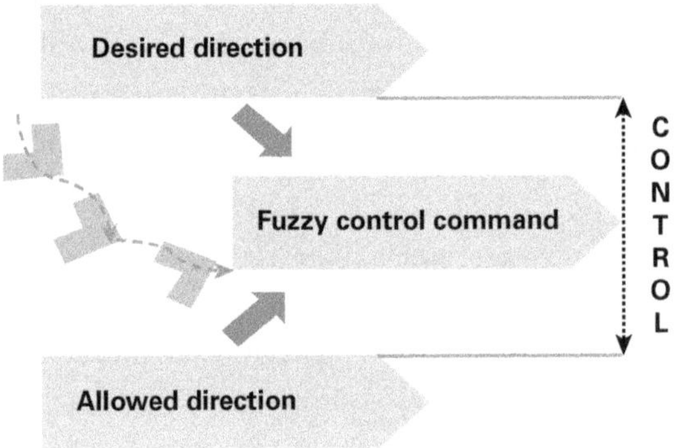

Author's illustration, based on Zadeh (1994)

compositional rule of inference and the rule of the preponderant alternative, and the dynamic interplay between the fuzziness and the probability in the behaviour of agents and social systems. Thus, the author's method adapted from Zadeh's ground-breaking work can be applied to the problems of economics, finance, AI, biology, computer sciences, management science, decision sciences and, above all, strategy. The integration of FL hitherto has been to reduce complexity in strategic thought and solution-finding under uncertainty. In the next section we look at how complexity can be measured.

Understanding complexity via the lenses of cybernetics

In our contemporary scientific zeitgeist, the difference between the views of science from the traditional Newtonian lens and the sciences of cybernetics and complexity cannot be greater. The Newtonian way of seeing the world has given the world its current status, from the rise of AI to the atomic bomb, and its development and hegemony have been felt across diverse sciences. Here the author does not agree with Erdi (2008) when he claims that the Newtonian way of seeing the world has not established any hegemony over other views (Erdi, 2008). Erdi gives complexity and its sister/predecessor science, cybernetics, almost the same level of hegemonic power. However, the challenges that the world faces, with its diverse systemic crises, reflects the level of negligence that has taken place by seeing the world via the lenses of cybernetics, the notion of holistic unity of science and, above all, the reality. Although the author has looked at reductionism versus holism in the pages above, the essentiality of this point cannot be underestimated.

The science of complexity describes the world within the laws of physics; however, it suggests the integration of a holistic view to the reductionist lens. Hence, while the laws of physics govern the way the world operates and life is shaped, according to Erdi (2008), it cannot predict life. The addition of the holistic approach enhances understanding of emergent phenomena and properties, while at the same time it gives the strategist the ability to see the problems beyond the diagnosis of surface treatments for wrong causes. The extreme form of advocating the holistic view is that not only is the whole more than the sum of its parts and sub-systems, but the eigen value that emerges represents a 'non-material agent' (Erdi, 2008).

According to Malik (1984), the upheaval that we experience does not correlate with the world of economics advocated by popular media , namely the problems of economic cycles and economic crises. The worst-case scenario is that one calls for and sees the roots of the problems in the economic-political nature of the problem. This view has many advocates from the socio-economic, political-economic and finance-economic perspectives, where the illusion is spread that the systemic challenges and the crises can be managed within the rate of inflation, the bonds market or through stock market manipulation, and in terms of austerity (Malik, 1984).

Malik (1984) goes as far as to state that the difficulty of our contemporary era probably goes back to how the society has been organized and constructed via control and governing mechanisms. Many see the problem in politics and some monetary policies, but not based on good and correct management. The worst dysfunction of management sciences is that in discussions to solve problems, management scientists are rarely consulted. So to some extent one also needs to understand that contemporary management science is standing on the shaky and reductionist pillars of seeing the world solely based in the economic (especially the monetary-economy) lens and within the world of finance. Porter and Rivkin (2012a, 2012b), in their large and in-depth survey of over 10,000 alumni of Harvard Business School, observe:

> What ails the American economy? Surely the Great Recession – the cyclical contradiction that began in December 2007 and bottomed out in June 2009 – continues to weigh on the United States. But ample evidence now points to a series of structural changes that began well before the Great Recession and threaten to undermine the long-term competitiveness of the U.S. ...

> The survey results provide strong evidence that the United States faces a deepening competitiveness problem. A large majority of survey respondents, 71%, expect U.S. competitiveness to decline over the next three years, with workers' living standards under greater pressure than firms' success. Pessimism about U.S. competitiveness was widely shared. Respondents in their prime decision-making years, those in the manufacturing sector, those in the U.S., and those whose own firms are exposed to international competition were less hopeful than others.

Porter (Porter and Kramer, 2011a; Porter and Rivkin, 2012a) takes a very different approach to the way he sees the world of business today in 2011–2012 from the one he's held over the three decades of his magnificent career within Harvard Business School (HBS) and representing a very profit-minded and shareholder-oriented approach to business and its administration. The roots of Porter's works are felt across all MBA/DBA programmes, not only in HBS but around the globe. According to Porter and Kramer (2011a):

> Companies are widely perceived to be prospering at the expense of the broader community. Even worse, the more business has begun to embrace corporate responsibility, the more it has been blamed for society's failures. The legitimacy of business has fallen to levels not seen in recent history. This diminished trust in business leads political leaders to set policies that undermine competitiveness and sap economic growth. Business is caught in a vicious circle. A big part of the problem lies with companies themselves, which remain trapped in an outdated approach to value creation that has emerged over the past few decades. They continue to view value creation narrowly, optimizing short-term financial performance in a bubble while missing the most important customer needs and ignoring the broader influences that determine their longer-term success. How else could companies overlook the wellbeing of their customers, the depletion of natural resources vital to their businesses, the viability of key suppliers, or the economic distress of the communities in which they produce and sell? How else could companies think that simply shifting activities to locations with ever lower wages was a sustainable 'solution' to competitive challenges? Government and civil society have often exacerbated the problem by attempting to address social weaknesses at the expense of business. The presumed trade-offs between economic efficiency and social progresses have been institutionalized in decades of policy choice (Porter and Kramer, 2011a).

However, it's different seeing the world through the lenses of Peter Drucker, who states: 'Consequently, the contribution of management is a fundamental contribution to a functioning society and not just to the individual institution it serves' (Drucker, 1954). Drucker emphasized management again, by stating:

> This makes it a technology. But management also deals with people, their values, their growth and development – and this makes it a humanity... Management is thus what tradition used to call a 'liberal art:' 'liberal' because it deals with the fundamentals of knowledge, self-knowledge, wisdom, and leadership; 'art' because it is practice and application (Drucker, 1954).

Malik (1984) claims that in order to see the range of management theory's spectrum and to judge its potential relevance, it is essential to distinguish between the two pivotal approaches or types of theories:

1 constructivist (structural) techno-morphic;
2 systemic-evolutionary (emergent) (Malik, 1984).

Both of these views are vitally different from each other; they also differ in terms of approaches, conceptions and notions, but precisely which logical and empirical fundaments do they establish whereby management and its purpose ought to be defined? To extricate and release management from the dominant and popular economic universe and context, it ought to serve to synthesize the works of Malik (1984), who among the very few management scientists has seen the roots of management and the question it scientifically wants to answer under the light of control, steering and systemic governance. Thus, the author suggests the same sort of treatment for the vital societal function and sciences of strategy. Once an agreement is achieved, which will require the reader to change or unlearn the flawed scientific fundaments on which one stands, then, as Malik suggests, the pivotal function and fundamental problem of management is to master, control and dominate complexity. The fundamental question and problem that strategy ought to solve is how to dissolve and pre-control organizational and environmental complexity. According to Beer (1975) in his thesis/statement:

> Man is a prisoner of his way of thinking and of his own stereotypes of himself. His machine for thinking, the brain, has been programmed to deal with the vanished world. This old world was characterized by the need to manage things – stone, wood, iron... The new world is characterized by the need to manage complexity... Complexity is the stuff of today's world. The tool for handling complexity is ORGANIZATION. But our concepts of organization belong to the much less complex old world not the much more complex today's

> world... still less are adequate to deal with the next epoch of complexification – in a world of explosive change.

Beer (1975–1994) goes further and underpins his claim:

> The very stuff of this reality is complexity. The elements of our society ever more richly interact: the more this happens, the more participation is evoked, the more the stream of data flow... the more complex does society come. Handling complexity seems to be the major problem of the age, in the way that handling material, substance offered challenge to our forefathers. Computers are the tools we have to use, and their effective use must be directed by a science competent to handle the organization of large, complex, probabilistic systems. This is the science of cybernetics, the science of communication and control.

Figure 2.41 describes how a shift and change in the general thinking about the nature of managerial thinking is necessary. It further demonstrates the vital aspects of the systems approach. It illustrates Beer's *'humo gubernator'* shift in the strategic and managerial cultural paradigm.

FIGURE 2.41 Cultural change first system thesis

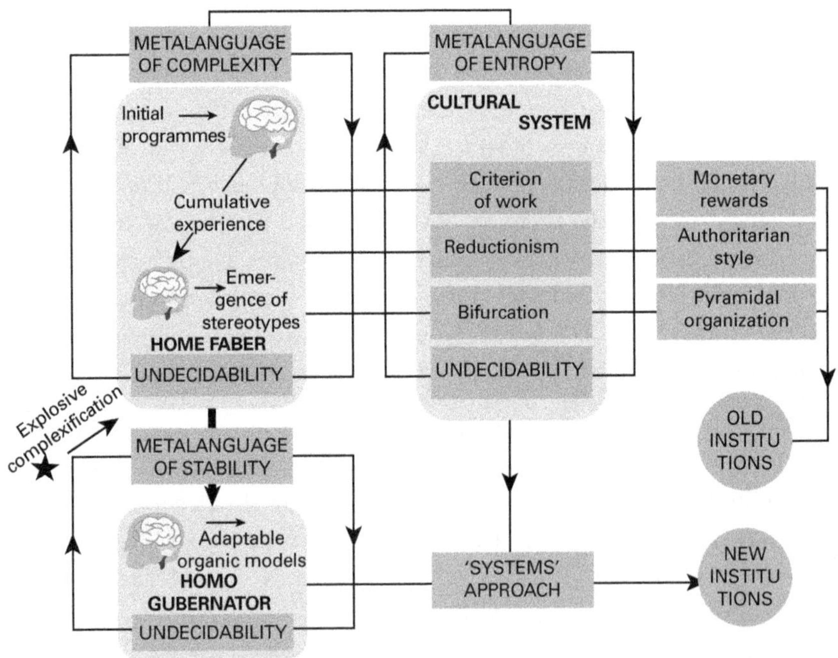

Author's interpretation, based on Beer (1975–1994)

The fundamental thesis of cybernetics can be explained in the following manner:

> There are natural laws governing the behavior of large interactive systems – in the flesh, in the metal, in the social and economic fabric. These laws have to do with self-regulation and self-organization. They constitute the 'management principle' by which systems grow and are stable, learn, adjust, adapt and evolve. These seemingly diverse systems are one, in cybernetics eyes, because they manifest viable behavior which is to say behavior conductive to survival (Beer, 1975).

Beer (1966) states that cybernetics as management itself has to cope with proliferating variety, thus both the sciences and vocations are occupied by the study and control of viable systems. The author wants to underpin complexity as the possible states, varieties and behavioural variations, interactions and options a system, an agent, a large and complex economy, a state, a political party, a large corporation and a small or medium-sized organization can take, and which can additionally evolve to further emergent phenomenon. Thus, managing and dissolving complexity, as emphasized, requires the application of Ashby's Law of requisite variety, to be dealt with by a robust science such as cybernetics instead of the pure economic lens. Although it is essential to establish that the 'Hegelian Axioms of Internal Relations', whereby a system is interacting with the complexity outside, one still can and needs to observe the system in isolation. In this regard one can see its internal and external possibilities and how the notion of control can be evolved via this ubiquitous interaction. According to Beer (1966):

> In practice, the most noticeable feature of the interaction between the system itself and the things outside it, is that relationships are directional. Either the thing outside is affecting the system or the system is affecting the thing outside or both. There are of course many relations, which are not oriented in this way, but they could hardly be called interactions, nor could their omission from a descriptive render the behavior of the system inexplicable.

To illustrate the points stated above, we can observe that relations that affect the system are known as inputs into the system and relations whereby the system affects the environment are outputs of controlling eigen behaviour. In terms of enterprise, the manager has to transform the inputs into benefits or outputs that the market wants. Hence, along comes environmental disturbance in terms of red-oceanic competition, recessionary sales, staff walkouts, lawsuits and anti-trust suits, and many diverse examples, where the strategist has to cope with these environmental disturbances while maintaining organizational homeostasis. How effectively the strategist is able to solve these challenges depends on the number of varieties available. The strategist is not able to account for every single situation confronting the organization or system under their control, but it's the variety of experience the manager has actively gained and the system can put out in terms of solutions, remedies and adjustments to the environment that explain strategic and managerial mastery. Intelligent organizations apply and store more sets of systemic adjustments and choices that can actually dissolve the proliferating varieties the environment exposes a system to. Here the author speaks of strategic options, what Sun Tzu has advocated as the position of 'Shih' or von Foerster as the 'constructivist ethical imperative', and what the author calls 'designing a viable structure' of the firm's strategic system in a way that it can easily absorb the emergent challenges.

The essence of managing complexity in terms of strategy is that the strategist can choose between alternatives a, b, c, d and e, etc, options via the interactional intelligence that is embedded within the organizational structure of the firm for the strategic objectives and positions to acquire, not only as reactionary phenomena but moreover as proactively constructed measures and control mechanisms. Thus, the grand strategist knows the second bounce of the variety ball affecting the firm.

The following explains one of the most fundamental contributions ever made to the science of management by Stafford Beer. Here lies one of the most vital strategic competitive advantages an organization can ever hope to achieve: understanding the essence of strategic thought lies within the structural configuration and dynamics of the firm as a whole. Understanding Beer's viable system model (VSM) and its implications is fundamental for the purpose of this book. The author's final model has derived from Beer's cybernetic organizational model – the VSM. Beer and von Foerster were years ahead of their time, and the implications of their work will outlast most contemporary models, which do not embrace requisite variety, taught in most business schools. It is precisely the purpose of the author to revisit these fundamentals and to integrate them within the dimensions of strategic thought to cope with the proliferating variety of the globally interconnected world.

The viable system model (VSM)

Management cybernetics is the field of scientific management which embraces a holistic view and field of application – this is in comparison with Porter's work, which is fundamental for competitive strategy. It has been necessary to tackle most of the issues before arriving at this point, thus the reader is armed with the best prerequisites to make the most out of the VSM and understanding it. Cybernetics studies diverse systems to learn their characteristics, how they function, but above all how they are controlled. According to Beer (1985): 'Science has sought the ultimate source of energy in the physics of the sun itself... the hydrogen-helium fusion. Science now seeks the ultimate source of control, in the cybernetics of natural processes... the brain itself.' The VSM, which was inspired by the human central nervous system, is the most advanced organization model based on bionics and cybernetics sciences ever designed by a management scholar and practitioner. As already established, VSM is based on characteristics, attributes and functions that are common to all viable systems and organizations. As a reminder to the reader, these characteristics are:

- **Systems:** organizations are systems, constructed of sub-systems, thus the whole is more than the sum of its parts.
- **Cybernetics:** the science of communication and control in the animal and the machine. The laws of cybernetics apply to all types of system and organization. Cybernetics is the science of organizational control, management is its profession, and thus strategy is where the strategist can anchor to design organizational freedom according to the author – the 'immunity school of strategy' or 'the eleventh school'.
- **Variety:** the number of the possible states of a system and the measure of complexity in all kinds of system. Thus, according to von Foerster, always act so as to advance the number of your varieties.
- **Ashby's Law of Requisite Variety:** 'only variety absorbs variety' – for effective control the requirement that the variety in control equal the variety in the system being controlled. This is also explained in Shannon's Theorem Number 10: 'If the correction channel has a capacity equal to Hy(x) it is possible to so encode the correction data as to send it over this channel and correct all but an arbitrarily small fraction of the errors. This is not possible if the channel capacity is less than Hy(x) being controlled' (Shannon and Weaver, 1949).
- **Homeostasis:** the parts of system structure that maintain stability. According to Ashby: 'Similarly, the homeostatic mechanism that keeps our bodies, in health, about 98° F is set at birth to maintain this value. The control comes from the gene-pattern and has zero entropy, for the selected value is unchanging' (Ashby, 1958).

- **Recursion:** all systems, such as a corporation, are made up of sub-systems, and these sub-systems are also made up of sub-systems, which are also made up of sub-systems. Each set of sub-systems is a level of recursion from its higher level of system. All systems and sub-systems have the same characteristics of viable structure but have different managerial functions and are embedded in their own environments. The management model that's useful in one system will be useful in all systems. A necessary level of recursion ought to be maintained for the organization. The VSM is based on five sub-systems, which will be outlined shortly.
- **Self-organization:** is among the most essential laws of management. It is through self-organization that life is ever possible and the world functions as it is. It is the organization's most powerful capability to organize itself. Self-organization requires a deep managerial competence from the strategist of a social productive system, but it will bestow the most effective natural laws of nature and of management.
- **Self-control:** a system's capability to control itself toward the attainment of the system's purpose, maintaining its ethos and identity preservation and transformation of the organization; also seen as innovation and development.
- **Environment:** every system and organization is embedded in its milieu and environment, thus the environment outside the system is included in the system's structure. Dealing with the environment, as the organization's structure, gives the strategist the possibility to shape and steer the organization to its favourable future; thus, according to Beer, design its freedom.
- **Information:** information is the most essential resource, input and communications tool for the organization. It controls performance and flows both ways within the system and between the system and its outside environments. In cybernetics, information is a part of structure that maintains control across all the system's structure. According to Beer, control is the dynamic of structure. Real-time information is not only essential to survival, but it's one of the most key strategic and managerial prerequisites and abilities to excellence, sustainable competitive advantage and organizational intelligence.
- **Structure:** structure is the most essential part of the organization. The failure of the short-sighted, merely analytical strategy calculation is that it forgets the systemic history of the organization, its intelligence, but

above all it forgets its structure, which is a part of the system whereby the brain can absorb and expose the variety it has, thus maintaining organizational viability. As the brain has evolved as the ultimate and most powerful computer by natural selection and evolution, so has the structure of the human body. The brain is powerful in a dynamic and fit body, which is what the VSM is for organizations. Structure is more than the physical side of the organization. Not only is the environment, information, and the organization's behaviour a part of its structure, so are its customers and products. The Lehman Brothers case reminds us that the portfolio of financial products is also an essential part of the organizational structure. Observing this in the financial industry will have a vital impact on how products are created and risks are managed.

- **Autopoiesis:** the ability of self-repair and self-transformation is the most essential ability of an organization. It is among the most powerful laws in nature, thus it is responsible for how humans have evolved in their current shape and ability to think; it also governs all kinds of development in the world of people, animals and machines.
- **Eigen behaviour:** although von Foerster's formulation of the eigen behaviour of self-organizing systems with distributed memory describes the minimum requirement for evolutionary systems, their evolutionary potential and capability is much larger if further endowed with dynamically 'inert' structures to be used by their classification mechanisms (Rocha, 1996). To put it differently, '... if Eigen-Values are further endowed with a symbolic dimension, their evolutionary potential is open-ended' (Rocha, 1996).

Understanding and observing the above points is essential to understanding Beer's VSM; they are the fundamentals on which the VSM is constructed. Furthermore, understanding Porter's works has been necessary: first of all, the starting point of the author's works in strategy has been based on Porter's works and, most importantly, they are the foundational positions of this book; and second, to see the benefits and the weaknesses of the model, but precisely the demonstrated systemic weakness the FFM has from a systemic lens.

In addition, there has been no other work to the author's knowledge in management cybernetics and competitive strategy that has combined these approaches together to design a further theoretical model for the purpose of practice, not only combining these rigorous works but also being at home in both worlds of theory and practice as a researcher. Beer much disliked the US-dominated strategy and business administration approach, while Porter has hardly used the systemic perspective and lens in the development of his models. Although 2011 and 2012 have been essential years in Porter's shift in strategic thinking and overall mindset, especially regarding how Porter sees the *raison d'être* of businesses in general and to bring up the issue of society (Porter and Rivkin, 2012a, 2012b; Porter and Kramer, 2011a, 2011b). In additional works, Porter has distanced himself more and more from a solely 'competition for profits' approach.

Beer, on the other hand, was mostly occupied with the teaching and application of the VSM. You can see more clearly in his work (Beer, 1985) the problems of organizational survival after profits constraints, which Beer saw as merely the systems' and organizations' limitations and boundaries. Therefore, the author's work takes an original place in terms of the gap in theoretical knowledge but likewise in the practical arena, whereby a solid strategic and managerial competence can be distinguished. The start of managerial cybernetics and especially the VSM can be explained with Beer's first grounded-breaking book on this topic. *Brain of the Firm* is a fundamental book written by Beer in 1972 and extended in 1981. Beer (1985), as the father of management cybernetics, has written many ground-breaking books that are essential reads for the strategist:

1. *Cybernetics and Management*, English Universities Press, London, 1959 (10 languages).
2. *Decision and Control*, Lanchester Prizewinner, John Wiley, Chichester, 1966 (also in Spanish).
3. *Management Science*, Aldus Books, London, 1967 (several languages).
4. *Platform for Change*, John Wiley, Chichester, 1975.
5. *Designing Freedom*, The Massey Lectures, John Wiley, Chichester, 1976 (also in Spanish and Japanese).

According to Beer (1985), the three companion volumes issued, which are under the general heading of 'the managerial cybernetics of organization', are:

1. *Brain of the Firm* (first published by Allen Lane in 1972, and available in several languages), and in its second edition, much extended, John Wiley, Chichester, 1981.
2. *The Heart of Enterprise*, John Wiley, Chichester, 1979.
3. *Diagnosing the System for Organizations*, John Wiley, 1985 (reprinted 1988, 1990).

These books represent the most fundamental revolution ever embarked on in the science and vocation of management. These books had a fundamental effect on establishing the current managerial mindset of the author. Two additional systemic and cybernetics-oriented authors, Prof Dr Schwaninger from the University of St Gallen and Prof Dr Malik of the Management Center St Gallen, have extensively published on Beer's works and on the topics of 'good and rightful management' (Malik, 2007); these have also been highly influential for the author. In addition, the works of Prof Dr Mintzberg from McGill University are the only works of a management scientist who has rebelled against the mainstream and US-dominated business school teachings in Angel Saxon countries.

Beer (1989) states:

> Often one hears the optimistic demand: 'give me a simple control system; one that cannot go wrong.' The trouble with such 'simple' controls is that they have insufficient variety to cope with variety in the environment. Thus, so far from not going wrong they cannot go right. Only variety in the control system can deal successfully with variety in the system controlled.

Most of the managerial models embrace a very narrow and partial view of a larger reality. Beer has been always an advocate of interdisciplinarity in science and how problems emerge. According to Beer (2002):

> Real problems do not respect the disciplines of academia. Nor do they respect commercial attitudes. To a holist, physics and chemistry are all the same thing because you can't talk about the real world without the other. You can't talk about marketing and leadership separately because they are dependent on each other. You must cover the whole spectrum.

Thus, the VSM displays viability beyond the short-sighted and narrow reality that an economic-driven specialist has created, whereby he applies Maslow's hammer tactic, which states: 'I suppose it is tempting, if the only tool you have is a hammer, to treat everything as if it were a nail' (Maslow, 1966).

Schwaninger (2006a), in his application of the VSM model, observes the strengths of the VSM in this way:

> The exceptional strength of this claim lies in that not only necessary but sufficient structural preconditions for the viability of a social-system are established, according to the theory of the VSM. To the best of the author's knowledge, no other organizational theory makes a claim as strong as this one. One would assume that evidence contradictory to the contentions of the VSM

> has been found. The surprising fact is, however, that the model has not been falsified but, on the contrary, corroborated by the growing empirical evidence from VSM applications (Schwaninger, 2006a).

Schwaninger (2006a), as a strong advocate of the VSM model in his paper after he applied the VSM to five different organizations, gives the following follow-up:

> The five cases... were located in different contexts, so they vary according to industry, size, mission, and products of the respective organizations. Even so, the VSM has been applied, in all of these cases, as a conceptual tool for the diagnosis and mostly also for the design of the respective organizations. VSM has proved to be an extraordinarily powerful instrument. It not only enabled a better understanding of the cases under study, but it facilitated the work enormously. Analysis was much more efficient, because the 'right' questions were asked from the start, and, what matters more, a lot of unnecessary ones were avoided. Data gathering was much more focused than in cases where other, less theoretically well-founded, frameworks were used. None of this proves that the VSM or its claims are flawless. However, the evidence gathered here speaks for itself (Schwaninger, 2006a).

Management cybernetics in organizational design

In essence, cybernetics, or the science of control in the animal and the machine (Wiener, 1948), is about understanding and managing complexity. Wiener's work defined a new science that started the information age and various branches of informatics, systems sciences and complexity sciences. Cybernetics explains regulation in all complex systems. To understand any complex system from economies, social systems as organizations, to artefacts, which are applied within a controlled environment, to robots that engage with a complex environment in terms of movement, it is necessary to understand how they are controlled. Control is the dynamic of structure and the essence of embodiment. The notion of embodiment is better described via the principle of recursion.

THE PRINCIPLES OF RECURSION AND SELF-ORGANIZATION

Recursion is one of the foundational principles of management in the animal, machine and productive social systems. According to Beer (1979a): 'that every viable system contains and is contained in a viable system... If we decide to define a social system by recursion, we shall find that every viable system contains a viable system.' Viability in terms of systemic cybernetics sciences means being '... able to maintain a separate existence' (Beer, 1985). According to Beer (2002), the laws of viability in complex organisms are related to the dynamic structure regulating the adaptive connectivity of the organism's parts rather than to energy impelling the organism.

ASHBY'S LAW OF REQUISITE VARIETY

Ashby is the founding doyen and pioneer of cybernetics and systems theory. His major contribution is the 'Law of Requisite Variety' (Ashby, 1958) applied by Beer to construct the field of management cybernetics (Beer, 1972, 2000). The principles that are essential for management, such as self-organization, design, control, functionality and governance, are the very principles of the science of cybernetics. According to the 'Law of Requisite Variety': 'the variety in the control system must be equal to or larger than the variety of the perturbations in order to maintain stability' (Ashby, 1958), and thus, 'only variety can absorb variety' (Beer, 1985). Figure 2.42 describes Ashby's Law and displays how designers can maintain control via solid management of operations by creating equilibrium between the organization and the environment in terms of variety engineering.

Another vital contribution of Ashby's work is 'Conant and Ashby's Theorem', which states: 'Every good regulator of a system must be a model of the system' (Conant and Ashby, 1970). Hence, they state: 'The first effect of this theorem is to change the status of model-making from optional to compulsory.' Conant and Ashby argue that model-making has been so far

FIGURE 2.42 Ashby's Law

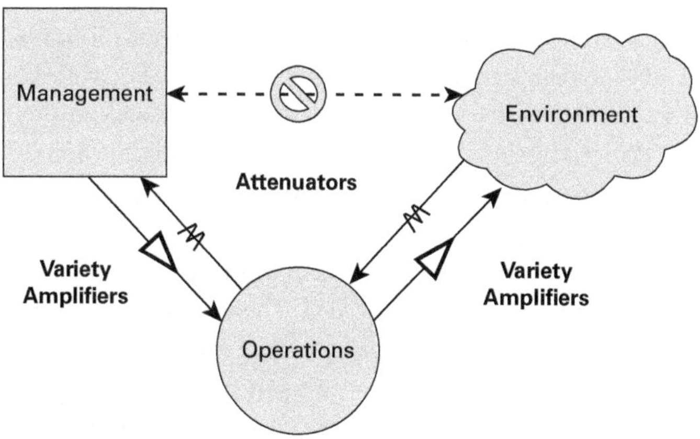

Ashby (1958), Beer (1979b)

generally viewed as a nicety for regulating complex dynamic systems; however, they indicate the proven necessity of a 'sufficiently similar model of control' for successful regulation as the necessary precondition of control. Thus, to control is to design the model of the 'to be controlled situation'. The construction of such a model may have been realized explicitly or through improvement of the regulator. This suggests that 'regulators must model what they regulate', which is also defined by Archer (1979); he illustrated modelling the language of design. Conant and Ashby (1970) state: 'There can no longer be a question about whether the brain models its environment: it must.' Schwaninger (2010) also claims that '... high-quality models can make a powerful contribution', hence designers are required to finalize the most essential task of this era, therefore robust designs are a necessity.

System 1: operations

At the core of management, cybernetics underlies the notion of functioning within the embedded environment. These in the living system are the organs of the body, the muscles, skin, the ears, hands and feet, etc, whereby the operative functions of the body are conducted. Transforming this pattern into business, one speaks of the sales and the product service of the organization dealing with the marketplace. From the family-tree chart, the operating units resemble the VSM's system 1. The best way to explain system 1 is via Figure 2.43, whereby the author displays to some wider extent the responsibilities of system 1. The additional functions can and may differ from the generalization in the figure. Since every organization is unique, the VSM can be designed based on the needs of the organization and its operation. Depending on the nature of the business or organization, the system 1 units and divisions can be distinguished and integrated. Figure 2.43 describes the VSM's system 1 as the general operations unit based on the extended version of Porter's value chain model (Porter, 1985a, 1985b). This also correlates to the notion of the recursive nature of organization sub-units, as already discussed.

System 1, as the operational sub-system of the VSM, can be extended to as many units and divisions as are needed. There are no limitations in terms of the number of operational systems and units. Hence, to reduce the complexity the recursion principle is fundamental to VSM; thus, all these units can be designed in a way that their control function is self-organized and reported to the higher sub-systems.

FIGURE 2.43 Businesses' activities according to system 1

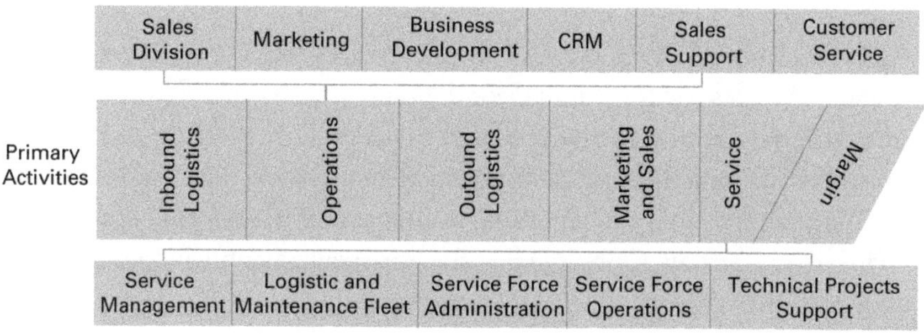

Based on Porter (1985a)

FIGURE 2.44 VSM system 1

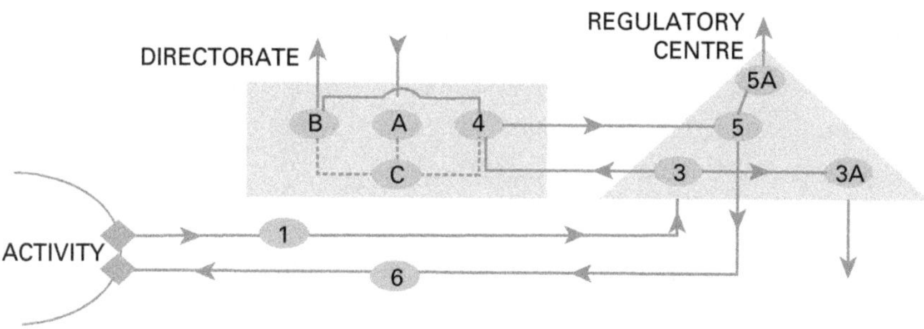

Beer (1972, 1979a, 1985)

Figure 2.44 displays the VSM system 1 interacting with the higher systems based on diverse channels, while the half circle on the left shows system 1 and the triangle is the VSM system 2 connected to the box displaying system 3. These additional systems will be explained below.

System 2: coordination/supporting

System 2, as shown in Figure 2.44, is the tall and thin rectangular box drawn around the column of boxes which are system 1 (Beer, 1972). The main function of system 2 is coordination, connection and interlinking between the divisions' regulatory centres and the corporate regulatory centres. According to Beer (1972): 'So it would be correct, and even helpful, to think of system two as an elaborate interface between system three and system one. It partakes of both' (Beer, 1972). The most essential four functions of system 2 are:

1. Coordination of the actions of system 1 and the interrelation among them. It serves as the fundamental homeostat to make sure that the matters are running in operations or system 1 in accordance with the overall policy but at the same time managing to overcome challenges and oscillations the environment gives or imposes on the system before it can achieve its objectives, observed as the emergent phenomenon, needing a flexible MBO type of approach to resolve it.
2. Control of budgetary affairs and transfer of information and collaborations with system 3 of the VSM.
3. Transducing the flow of information from system 1's higher-level management (directorate) and transmitting this information to systems 3, 4, and 5 as needed.
4. The communication and the control function of compliance of the higher level of management by the operations (system 1). The system transmits the quality and the level of how progress is made to achieve the larger goals towards the higher management level.

According to Christopher (2007), the coordination of the actions requires a facilitator, a tiebreaker, and an authority, when needed, upon the

FIGURE 2.45 VSM system 2

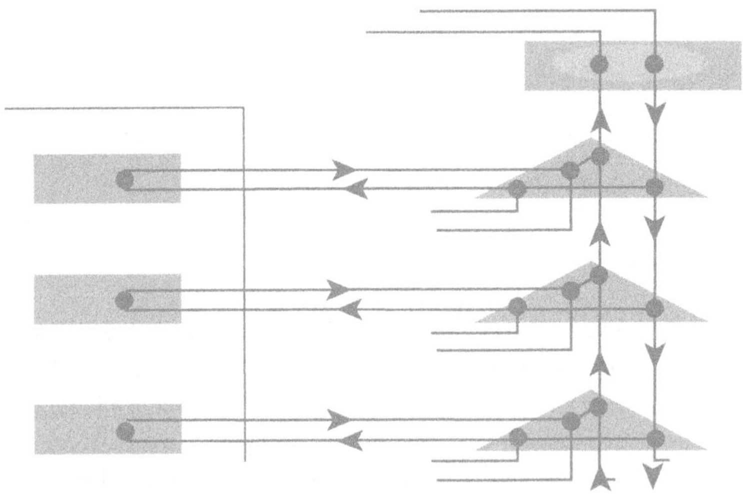

Beer (1972, 1981, 1985)

situation arising. One should not forget that all the systems of the VSM are viable and autonomic systems; they resemble the recursive viability as already established by the author. The VSM underpins that each system has its own budgetary freedom and constraints, thus each system can maintain autonomy. The budgetary control functions are essential for operations, which deal with the present environment and ask the question of how successful the organization or the system has been today. Thus system 1 has the objective to achieve short-term and present objectives, and system 2 has the supportive coordinating role so that the system in its lower recursion level can maintain a top-quality operation. The budgetary functions are not only there for limitation of the financial resources and of creating dependence, but are unitary freedoms as well, since they also contain resources that each system can bargain. Within this spectrum the unit can invest to self-transform or self-recreate itself in cybernetics, also known as autopoiesis. This brings innovation, technological and organizational dynamic capability, thus affecting the overall fitness of the larger organization. Corporate parameters and system 2 support the organization to be more than the sum of their parts. According to Christopher (2007), below are some examples:

1 Dealing with essentials, not majoring in minors.
2 The fewer parameters the better, not forgetting to not violate the quality of the self-organized achievement of the tasks as 'MBO' (Drucker, 1954).
3 To work less restrictively, always remembering von Foerster's 'The ethical imperative: Act always so as to increase the number of choices' (Foerster, 2003d).
4 Allowing and encouraging local initiatives, as von Foerster (2007) famously underpinned: everybody is a manager in an organization, thus they know what's best for them, and when they get the support of the initiatives that they know and propose, they will produce results that will astonish the higher management.

System 2 is in terms of how the VSM embodies the above-described parameters, while these are missing within the family-tree organizational charts and models. The functions are poorly handled in a top–down manner, which gives the organization a wider weakness in not being able to react to changes within the market ubiquitously, as actions to changes are emergent in control systems. System 2 is an organizational function of coordination that may not be left to chance; therefore, from a systemic perspective, system 2 delivers organizational stability by coordination.

System 3: direction of internal operations

The function of the VSM's system 3 is to manage the internal affairs and stability of the whole VSM system. This function must be considered the management and the maintaining of the homeostasis of the whole organizational internal body beyond the homeostasis of the units below within their environments and the avoidance of the internal oscillations between them. Since systems 1 and 2 are coping with situational perturbations at the lower recursion levels and keeping the local disturbances within their environments under control, it is necessary for system 3 to be viable as a whole and therefore navigate according to the larger internal challenges the system faces, acting as a directory unit for the internal environment. Another point that needs to be underpinned here is the timeframe of now. The primary function of system 3 is managing the internal homeostasis of the VSM in the present. System 3 enables the organization to act as a whole and from a holistic perspective; it is the managerial coordination's authority for the whole organization and is considered to be the interface between the autonomous units and the highest authority (Malik, 1984). For the purpose of better understanding this function, it is similar to the function of the chief operating officer (COO) of the firm; system 3 is designed and acts according to Ashby's Law. Christopher (2007) describes:

> System 3 mindful of Ashby's Law, views the company as a black box. A black box is an entity that has much greater variety than can be known or controlled by much lower variety in a higher-level system. But to the black boxes themselves the system 1's, they are not black boxes. They are viable systems that are largely self-organizing and self-controlling, and are quietly able to control themselves.

FIGURE 2.46 VSM system 3

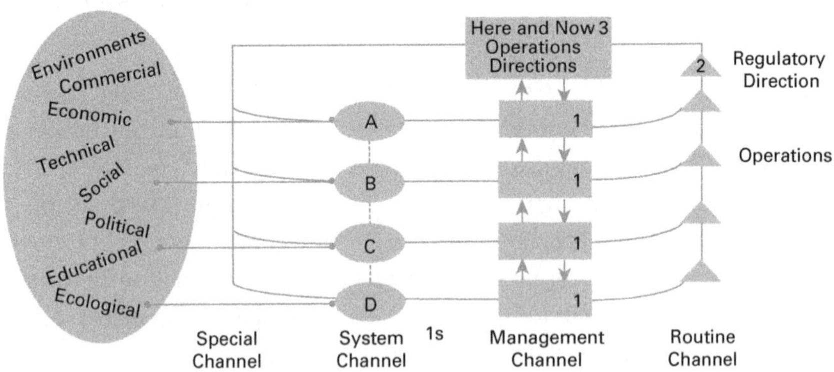

Beer (1972, 1981, 1985)

This notion can also be established within the context of the ambidexterity of firms to capture the essence of strategic execution in the timeframe of 'now' and the additional duality of capturing the essence of the future via system 4.

Black box analogy in system theory and its implications for competitive strategy

Christopher (2007) states: 'Black boxes – lower-level systems whose complexity cannot be understood, and effective operating decisions made, by management in a higher-level system. A higher-level decision lacks requisite variety.' The lower systems are black boxes to the higher system; thus they know the purpose of the lower systems and black boxes, their input, and their output, but higher management lacks the requisite variety, described as: 'The larger the variety of actions available to a control system, the larger the variety of perturbations it is able to compensate.' It cannot intervene in the affairs of the black box. According to 'Principia Cybernetica', the black box method can be explained in the following way: 'A strategy for investigating a complex object without knowledge or assumptions about its internal makeup, structure or parts.' (PCW, 1993). To manage the lower levels in accordance and with knowledge gained by the notion of self-organization, where its emphasis is on autonomy and the science of cybernetics, understanding and applying the black box method helps higher management to improve organizational performance via indirect interference and management. This notion increases requisite variety and helps higher management to avoid making an unwise decision, within the black box, since higher management levels may not always know the real reasons beyond some poor performance and challenges within the lower level of recursion. Only the controller within the black box and ubiquitously embedded as its controlling function not imposed on the system knows what is really going on within that system via the feedback that it receives. The feedback within the control system is therefore ubiquitous. A final point about system 3 is that it is concerned to take advantage of the synergies that are resulting from the lower system's interactions, thereby increasing organizational fit and avoiding the energy draining out of the system.

System 3: responsibilities for internal operations*

System 3*, while a part of system 3, is mostly misunderstood in terms of its function. It is solely the information's transmuting channel of system 3. The gained and transferred information, which is (a) affecting the whole organization and systems, (b) coming via interaction with the directorate of system 1 and system 1's resource bargaining, and (c) what can lead to a direct intervention. However, system 3* ought to be used in proportion, otherwise it interferes with the authority of system 1 and takes the system's autonomy and therefore its responsibility for the results gained. Thus, it will lead to diverse problems that must be avoided. In addition, one has to guard against the internal spying and distrust activities that system 3* can be used for by system 3 against its lower systems of recursion. Thus, via system 3*, the required information is transferred to the right channels so that they can act accordingly and absorb the information (Hetzler, 2008). System 1 is also informed and the essentiality of these interrelations between the function's security and the ability of the organization is clearly pointed out. It is also reflected in natural systems that such systems are indispensable for the viability of each system. In addition, system 3 is used to connect the higher layer of management with the realities of the operative (operations) layer of the organization. It helps the overall qualitative improvement and enhancement in accordance with customer value and market orientation of the whole organization (Beer, 1972; Hetzler, 2008). Thus, according to Beer, system 3 and system 3* must be able to cope with the challenges of now (present time) and their ubiquitous internal absorption and attenuation.

System 4: strategic direction/outside and future

The system 3 of the organization, as described above, has the power and mechanism, with its own steering capability, to absorb attenuations from the current environment and technology that the organization confronts. Thus, it can maintain the internal stability and homeostasis of the organization in spite of a ubiquitous rate of change. However, for the organization to stay viable in the long run, it must also confront the future and its strategic challenges. This aspect of the organizational function is also called the management of outside and the future, whereby the organization embarks on a journey from today to a favourable future that it actively creates for itself. System 4 resembles all the functions and organizational parts that report to the CEO, thus, in the VSM, 'the reporting-to' (Christopher, 2007) is not reconstructed but, moreover, it displays the functions and communication links.

In the VSM, hierarchy may not be understood in terms of command and control but in terms of the sum of functions that resemble a viable larger whole – every function is essential and is based on ensuring survivability, not displaying importance. Systems within the VSM rely on their own self-organizing, self-controlling and self-steering autopoietic capabilities. In order for system 4 to be effective and to do its duties of efficiently and intelligently identifying value potentials, it ought to be based on Conant and Ashby's Theorem, applying the notion of 'every good regulator of a system must be a model of that system' (Conant and Ashby, 1970). System 4 must be able to model a favourable future and identify and design the path towards the value potentials, whereby the organization's future direction needs to be defined. According to the above theorem, the matter of high-quality operations is not an operations excellence by some measures, but moreover, it is an organizational necessity and design. Conant and Ashby (1970) have therefore observed in their famous paper:

> The design of a complex regulator often includes the making of a model of the system to be regulated. The making of such a model has hitherto been regarded as optional, as merely one of many possible ways. In this paper a theorem is presented which shows, under very broad conditions, that any regulator that is maximally both successful and simple must be isomorphic with the system being regulated... Making a model is thus necessary.

The theorem has essential applicability to strategic management: only a successful and effective strategy-regulating system must model the firm's complex environment to navigate the firm. According to Leonard (1999):

> Although timelines vary from seconds to decades, organisms and organizations need some capacity to anticipate the future and prepare for it. System Four's role is to observe the anticipated future environment and its own states of adaptiveness and act to bring them into harmony. To do so, it must also have a clear picture of System Three's present state so it can offer alternative paths from the present to the future.

Conant and Ashby state that brain-like regulation requires the modelling of the environment and containing the lower systems based on recursion. The author observes this as the maintaining of ubiquitous control of the organization's internal structure and knowing its capabilities to proactively develop and prepare the organization for higher capabilities. Beer (1984) observes:

> The 'strengths and weaknesses' analysis by which managers are often invited to seize opportunities is therefore not strictly possible. The manager will have to take chances, and this (despite much propaganda) he is most unwilling to do. Chess players are much the same. Botvinnik's conclusion is this: until the 'depth' picture resolves itself at a level where one can legitimately take a decision, the

> proper course is to strengthen oneself. Managers seem to intuit this to some extent. Unfortunately, strengthening oneself is however often seen as the need for strengthening the inside-and-now, the 3-2-1. But System Four is also part of oneself. Moreover, System Four is the very part that will develop the 'depth' picture that has to be resolved. Botvinnik is perfectly clear that the decision not to act is a current action. In terms of the VSM, what we are discussing is the intervention by system five in the balancing activity of the three-four homeostat.

By system 4 Beer is referring to the strategic management of the firm. He applied system 4 successfully in one of the most vital cybernetic projects ever done in the science of management, 'Project CyberSyn' of Dr Allende's Chile. Beer designed the VSM of Chile's national economy and the brain-like part of the VSM, which is the system 4 known as the 'operations room'. Beer's operations room has been one of the most futuristic scientification of a managerial practice ever engaged in by a management scientist. No other management scientist has contributed so much by the power of science to the practice of management and of managers mainly depending on their intuition and data, and who are trained mainly with the tools and ways of thinking of the past, which Beer (1975) refers to as the 'vanished world'. According to Beer (1972), commenting on the objectives of Project CyberSyn: 'To install a preliminary system of information and regulation for the industry economy that will demonstrate the main features of cybernetic management.' Unfortunately, the activities of system 4 have been missing as a separate brain-like entity with its own functions within the family-tree organizational charts, thus, these very activities for which system 4 is responsible are divided among other sub-systems and units. The value of every cybernetic system's model, system 4 included, regardless of its simplicity, resembles the dynamic structure and characteristics the organization faces; thus, it facilitates the examination of corporate plans on an indefinite time basis, which invalidates so many static models of the corporate economy (Beer, 1972). System 4 is displayed in Figure 2.47. This correlates to managing the future by the strategic understanding of organizational ambidexterity (homeostat and heterostat).

System 5: Ethos of the organization/normative management

System 5 is the thinking part of the VSM and the direction of the organization. Its main objectives are to ensure the balance between 'Here and Now'

FIGURE 2.47 VSM system 4

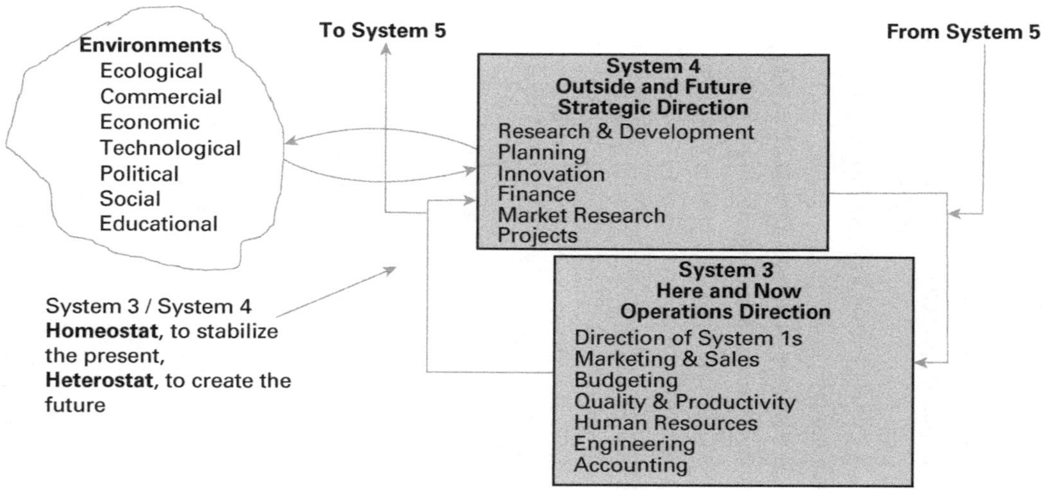

Christopher (2007)

and 'Outside and Then'. Foresight according to Drucker is one of the common traits he has found in successful corporations and high-achieving entrepreneurial endeavours – namely, the commitment to approach and to integrate innovation as a 'systematic practice' within the organization's activities. Beer has not only given foresight a systemic character, but moreover, he has integrated foresight into the very structure of the organization. Thus, the VSM's system 5 is acting based on foresight not only in a systematic manner, but it's navigating the organization based on real time and the ubiquitous connected whole within the total environment of the firm. Christopher (2007) describes system 5 as: 'System 3 performs many executive functions in relation to operations. But system 5 as the company's executive direction of the company is responsible for the company's most important executive decisions – determining company structure and management principles.'

The existence of system 5 furthermore substantiates the author's claim that 'structure is strategy'. Thus, according to Christopher (2007): 'Structure defines the company. Its purpose, its boundaries, establishes company goals and performance measures; and provides the needed resources.' System 5 is the authority in VSM that determines the ethos and sets the general characteristics of the firm. Furthermore, the additional core activities of system 5 are to maintain oversight on the activities of systems 4, 3, 2 and 1.

FIGURE 2.48 Organizational charts vs how organizations are really managed

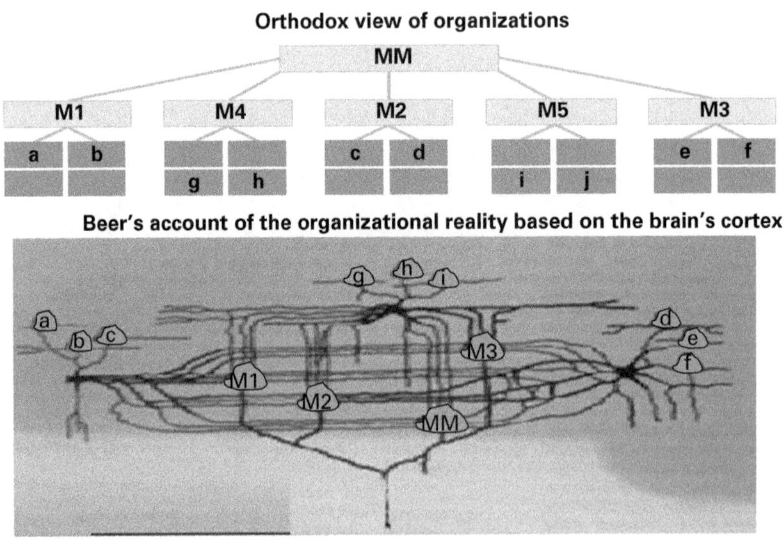

Beer (1972)

The most vital functions of system 5 are to give the overall leadership insights and guidance to maintain the homeostatic stability between the management of system 3 (today and now) and system 4 (future and then) strategies. System 5 resolves as the firm's overall leadership function and manages possible conflicts that may arise between both realities (today and now and future and then) and organizational functions of system 3 and system 4. Therefore, the author observes system 5 (organizational ethos) also as the firm's balancing authority between the actions concerning the present and the future. System 5 is the essential part of the firm's survivability, to which Maturana refers to as 'autopoiesis'. Maturana (1980) emphasizes the fundamental bifurcation of an autopoietic organization and system is that everything that takes place in its boundaries is subordinated to the realization of its autopoiesis (self-reproduction and maintaining itself), otherwise the system will disintegrate. This means that the recursive nature of the autopoiesis and its foundational attributes, which embody a system's structure, are based on a closed web of interacting sub-systems, wherein every state of further emerging activities causes another form of further activities. An organization as a social system is a cognitive and autopoietic system. Thus, according to Bourgine and Stewart (2004): 'A system is cognitive if and only if sensory inputs serve to trigger actions in a specific way, so as to satisfy a viability constraint.' Hence, the autopoietic embodiment that an organism adopts is determined by its structure (eg the structure of the nervous system defines its requisite variety), 'and that the structure of the organism (including its cognitive apparatus and the three-ply account) is at any instant the result of its evolutionary and ontogenic structural coupling with the medium in which it is autopoietic, obtained while the autopoiesis is realized' (Maturana, 1980). This notion is strongly realized by the VSM as applied by the author.

Chandler (1962) could make his famous statement based on the observation of what he could do since he was not aware of the theory of VSM, thus in a 'family-tree organizational chart' (see Figure 2.48) structured organization, any other statement contrary to Chandler's observations is impossible. The reason is that these types of organization not only violate Conant-Ashby's Theorem and Ashby's Law of Requisite Variety, but the organization is not even aware of its own structural dynamic and eigen behaviour, which was underpinned by Bourdieu as 'habitus'. These points are furthermore substantiated by Figure 2.48, as, according to Beer (1972), one can easily distinguish between how organizations are really organized versus how organizations think they are organized. Being aware of the true nature and interrelations of an organization, the strategist can reduce and absorb complexity. Absorbing complexity effectively is the fundamental strategic advantage an organization can have. The human factor is not a resource for the organization to exploit; it is a human capital (HC) of 'operant resource' (Lusch and Vargo, 2015; Vargo *et al*, 2015) that is not processed from input to output to be products or services for sale as other organizational resources are. The human factor is a core part of the organization's identity, whereby the organization does what its purpose or intention is.

Therefore, the notion of HR is a flawed observation and it is disadvantageous for the organization's strategic foresight. Active and viable agents in an organization are considered to be 'beings' and not 'resources', therefore HC needs to be attracted and their capabilities organized via the VSM, which actually resembles viability as part of a larger whole and organization. This of course depends on the 'upper echelons perspective' by Hambrick and Mason (1984): 'The theory states that organizational outcomes – strategic choices and performance levels – are partially predicted by managerial background characteristics.' The theory observes that based on the dominated values held by top management, the choices and the dimension of their bounded rationality and the behaviour of the actors and subordinates change. Firms with solid values treat intellectual capital with the utmost care.

In the previous paragraphs, the author has explained the recursive characteristics of a viable organization. In Figures 2.48 and 2.49, the readers see the recursive organizational structure based on the VSM. Beer (1972) describes his 'recursive system theorem' as: 'If a viable system contains a viable system than the organizational structure must be recursive.' The diagnostic and the organizational steering power of the VSM as an organizational model contains, as already stated, not only the functions, their structure, and the display of organizational autonomy, but it shows the organization's internal relations to each of its sub-systems. Furthermore, it simulates the environment in which each system and business unit, but also the whole organization, is embedded.

Figure 2.49 describes a VSM-based recursive multi-unit organizational structure, where one sub-system or business unit is contained within another to create a larger organization. From a holistic view, Figure 2.49 displays how each organization is able to survive within its milieu, how they are connected to the other business units and how each affects the other in concert to create a larger VSM. The model was successfully applied to Peter Lacke Group (PLG) in 2016. A solid case study based on field experience and a survey to provide qualitative empirical evidence is described in Kamran (2017).

FIGURE 2.49 A wider recursive organization's structure based on the VSM

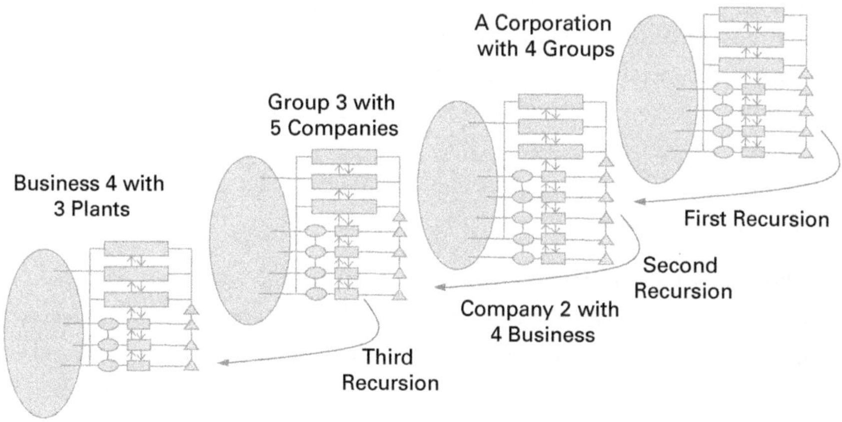

Schwaninger (2004)

One of the biggest questions in competitive strategy is, as described by Lane and Maxfield (1995), 'What is a strategy?' They argue that 'the answer depends on the foresight horizon', meaning that it is dependent on the strategist's estimation of what is foreseeable up until when. A complex foresight horizon is characterized by rapidly changing organizational structures and ambiguous interpretations of agents' and artefacts' identity and therefore its strategy shall enable interpretation and construction of relationships within the organization's environment by providing continuous practices. Lane and Maxfield approach cognitive and structural practices as interlinked. They describe cognitive practices as an organization's effort to conceive and interpret the population in its environment while structural practices are described as an organization's effort to promote relationships within the organization and beyond in order to generate additional value (Lane and Maxfield, 1995). According to Beer (1972):

> Ultimately, neither brain nor the firm is an analyzer, but recognizer. That is why speed of recognition is so important. We must recognize then react. Otherwise analysis may consume some precious weeks, and a viable response to a threat will be (as the lawyers say) 'out of time'. A great deal of serious analytical work in management is wasted for this reason. It becomes an intellectual game that is played concomitantly with, but not affecting, the progress of real events.

Figure 2.50 describes the whole VSM interacting with its environment. The VSM is still an unfalsified model, and it took Beer almost 30 years of research, development, and application in diverse forms of organizations, from the steel industry to the state economy of Allende's Chile, the Canadian government and more. The body of distinguished opinion in management and strategic sciences is more concentrated on quick pay and quick benefits. The organizational power and structure of these ideas have not given managers the needed freedom from collapses, but moreover made them proactively create challenges and risky models that can actually construct systemic collapses on a larger scale.

In Figure 2.50 (on the right) is an original design of the VSM by Beer. Beer (1974) observes:

> Above all, let us all expect it of each other that we find ways to use the power of science in better cause. It is no more sensible to say that we cannot, because ordinary folk do not understand science, as it would be to say we cannot sail a boat, because we cannot understand the wind and the sea and the tide-race. Men have always navigated those unfathomable waters. We can do it now.

FIGURE 2.50 Two versions of Beer's VSM

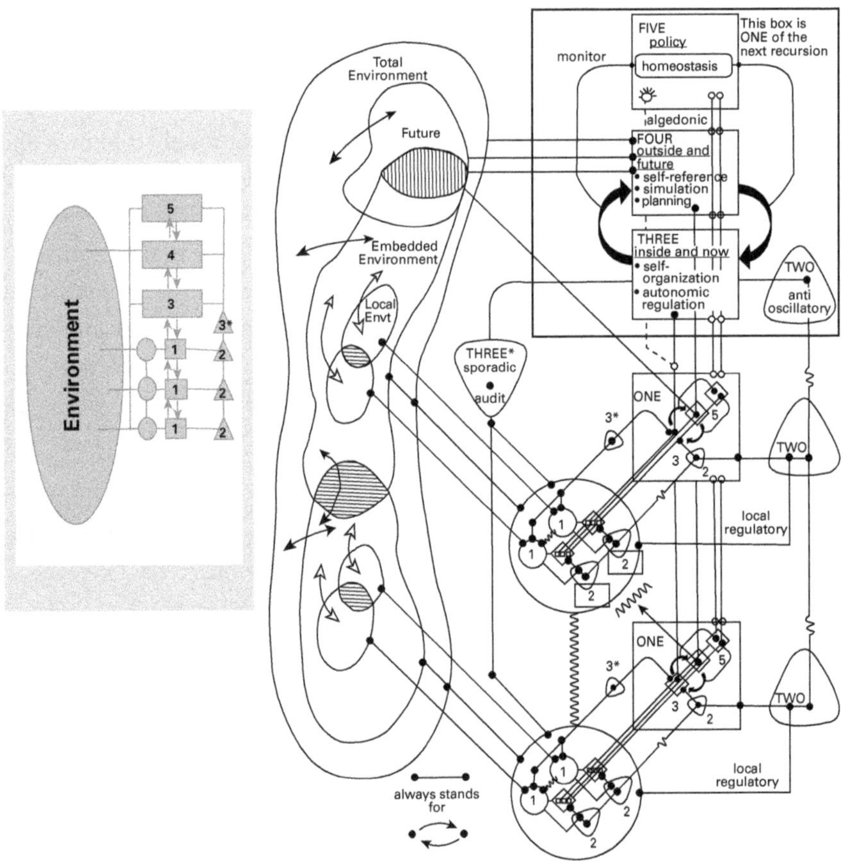

Beer (2000)

The strategic immunity based on the theories introduced lies in the hands of the organization, hence in managerial and strategic sciences, the organization's structure is the fundamental issue. Structure is strategy in a complex and turbulent environment. Ashby's Law presumes the management of variety based on the most advanced organizational model, namely the VSM, to cope with the proliferating variety in this hyper-connected and systemic global world of business.

This analogy has also been validated by Pfeifer and Bongard (2007) in their theory of 'embodiment'. Additional streams of literature and experiences of the notion of strategic alliances have emerged in recent years as essential structural interpretations for business development. This is laid out by Albers *et al* (2013), who state:

> ... we have developed an organization-design-focused framework for classifying alliances. The framework's five parameters – interface, intraface, specialization, formalization, centralization – provide a nuanced description of alliance structures and their effect on coordination, learning, and trust in alliances and thus also enabled us to outline design challenges that arise out of tensions and trade-offs between individual design parameters.

The dimension based on Ashby's Law observes alliances as a pure variety enhancement based on the dynamic capability of the firm to integrate internal and external competencies to address a changing organizational milieu.

Second-order cybernetics

Heinz von Foerster established the notion of 'observing systems' as second-order cybernetics, or 'cybernetics of cybernetics', based on Wiener's (1948) work *Cybernetics*. By taking the second-order world-view, the designer factor enters the observation and thus:

> the shift from a first-order to a second-order cybernetics signaled a shift in scientific attitude toward reality, from privileging the perspectives of detached observers, spectators or engineers of a world outside of themselves to acknowledging our own participation in the world we observe and construct as its constituents (Krippendorff, 1996).

Based on Piaget's constructivist approach and the 'radical constructivism' of Glasersfeld (1995), Foerster *et al* (1992) and Maturana (1980), autopoiesis and cognition fit within the dimensions of the experience-dominated unity of

FIGURE 2.51 Design, cognition and first- and second-order cybernetics

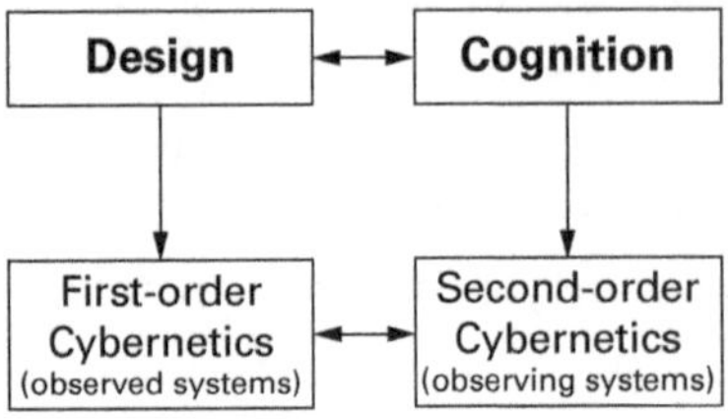

perception and coping with environmental realities. Krippendorff (2007) states: 'To design artifacts for use by others requires second-order understanding.'

Design as stipulated by Simon (1996) was therefore derived to bring this gap towards a harmonic closure by coining it as 'the science of artificial'. Design embraces the bridge between the first-order and second-order stipulation as illustrated in Figure 2.51. The foundation of the designer's work is based on the recursive nature of a symmetry between design (first-order) and cognition (second-order) in a hermeneutic value-laden course-collecting loop. Foerster (2003e) states: 'a brain is required to write a theory of a brain.' Second-order cybernetics and the constructivist epistemology can contribute much to design theory as a theory of social interaction and cognition within the 'design search space'.

Second-order cybernetics is one of the schools of thought coined and founded by Heinz von Foerster. According to Glanville (2002):

> Heinz von Foerster's outstanding contribution to cybernetics was to consider the subject in its own terms, i.e. as a cybernetic system itself, subject to the insights, analyses and critiques that cybernetics had already discovered. In so doing he took the discoveries of cybernetics seriously and to an extreme in a manner that no one else had done previously. He also provided a model for the investigation of all systems in which the examiner (the observer) and the examination are part of that system, such as social systems and design. He referred to this cybernetics as the 'cybernetics of cybernetics' or 'secondorder cybernetics'.

As von Foerster coined 'Humberto Maturana's Theorem Number One', which states, 'Anything said is said by an observer', he goes further and states that if one is not able to see the profundity of Maturana's Theorem, one has to look twice, since one will be surprised what kind of depth can lie behind simple propositions (Foerster, 1979). Thus, in utter defiance of the logician's claim about tautology, von Foerster added Churchman's observation: 'You will be surprised how much can be said by a tautology' (Foerster, 1979). Von Foerster further adds to Maturana's Theorem a corollary that he coined 'Heinz von Foerster's Corollary Number One'. Von Foerster stated: 'Anything said is said to an observer' (Foerster, 1979). The author will add one corollary of his own to von Foerster's corollary to Maturana's Theorem: 'Anything observed is observed by an observer.' To avoid the tautology: the profundity of an observation lies within the quality of the observer's competence, thus observing entails responsibility. And irresponsibility arises from lack of integrity, which in terms of cybernetics means the ability to process and gain information.

The author's observation underpins the meaning Churchman gave to management. Thus, Churchman was a management scientist of a rare kind, since management to him meant more than it usually does in management science, eg allocation of resources and maximizing short-term profits; it means a philosophical challenge to our capabilities of understanding the ethics of whole systems (Ulrich, 1994). Ulrich (1994), on observing Churchman and the problem of ethics, states:

> Why ethics? Why whole systems? The essence of management is decision making; the hallmark of good decisions is that they promote some kind of desired improvement. But what constitutes an improvement? The concept raises fundamental epistemological and ethical issues. These issues are important to future-responsive management.

The problem of ethics was addressed by von Foerster in one of his profound articles, 'Ethics and Second-order Cybernetics' (Foerster, 2003b). Von Foerster states:

> I would like to invite you now to join me in a land where it is not forbidden; rather, where one is encouraged to speak about oneself. What else can one do anyway? This turn from looking at things 'out there' to looking at 'looking itself,' arose I think, from significant advances in neurophysiology and neuropsychiatry. It appeared that one could now dare to ask the question of how the brain works. One could dare to write a theory of the brain. It may be argued that over the centuries since Aristotle, physicians and philosophers again and again developed theories of the brain. So, what's new of today's cyberneticians? What is new is the profound insight that a brain is required to write a theory of a brain. From this follows that a theory of the brain, that has any aspirations for completeness, has to account for the writing of this theory. And even more

> fascinating, the writer of this theory has to account for her or himself. Translated into the domain of cybernetics; the cybernetician, by entering his own domain, has to account for his or her own activity. Cybernetics then becomes cybernetics of cybernetics, or second-order cybernetics (Foerster, 2003b).

The problem of ethics is not only a problem of second-order cybernetics; it is one of the most pivotal questions in strategy. If ethics is a part of the strategist lens, whereby the strategist looks outside and reflects upon themselves, then the quality of their decisions and the myopic view wherewith the world of business and society is observed will change. Thus, according to von Foerster:

> ...this perception represents a fundamental change, not only in the way we conduct science, but also how we perceive teaching, learning, the therapeutic process, organizational management, and so on and so forth; and I would say, of how we perceive relationships in our daily life. One may see this fundamental epistemological change if one first considers oneself to be an independent observer who watches the world go by; as opposed to a person who considers oneself to be a participant actor in the drama of mutual interaction of the give and take in the circularity of human relations (Foerster, 2003b).

The cybernetics of observed systems one may consider as first-order cybernetics; while second-order cybernetics is the cybernetics of observing systems. This conforms to the additional formulation that has been given by Gordon Pask (Foerster, 1979). Pask also recognizes two orders of analysis, thus one in which the observer enters the system by stipulating the system's purpose. We may call this a 'first-order stipulation'. In a 'second-order stipulation' the observer enters the system by stipulating their own purpose (Foerster, 1979). From this it is apparent that social cybernetics ought to be a second-order cybernetics – a cybernetics of cybernetics – in order that the observer who enters the system shall be allowed to stipulate their own purpose: thus, the observer is autonomous (Foerster, 1979).

In strategy, from the author's point of view, the main question from the second order is how the strategist/observer can stipulate the system of an organization. There are four perspectives:

1. to affect or change its course;
2. to create a favourable future;
3. to construct a collective and mutual organizational reality;
4. to design the organization's purpose of purpose (purpose of business mission), thus the author coins this second-order stipulation or strategic

observation as: 'the organization's meta-cause' (cause of cause), which Drucker (1954) referred to as the 'yardstick' by which we observe organizational success.

The meta-cause from the second-order perspective in strategy and according to the author's research is a very under-researched field. Thus, if the scien-trategist fails, somebody else will determine a purpose for the organization. If the lack of financial resources is the scien-trategist's main challenge in navigating their organization, the meta-cause of that organization may be to act upon a financier's (bank's) guidelines and limitations set, wherein the organization navigates. Another example is if the organization is behind in innovation; it plays the rival's game, and thereby the rival's purpose enters the organization's purpose. Some may argue that in competition one may not be able to lead at all times or at all levels – this is a very true observation; however, here the purpose of the organization that is behind is too much the innovation's pace or the quality of the industry leader. So the follower may compete for customers, more profits and industry leadership, thus it gives in in terms of purposefulness of the second order. The profundity of this explanation lies within Beer's most essential cybernetic dictum. Beer observes:

> With the complete range of cybernetic discoveries to hand, it is always possible to analyze a situation from the point of view of its regulatory phenomena. According to the cybernetician, the purpose of a system is what it does. This is a basic dictum. It stands for a bald fact, which makes a better starting point in seeking understanding than the familiar attributions of good intentions, prejudices about expectations, moral judgments, or sheer ignorance of circumstances (Beer, 2002).

If the purpose of a system is what it does, the meta-cause of the organization may at no time be violated. From the second-order perspective, designing the meta-cause of the organization and staying on course is the strategist's main objectives. Von Foerster observes: 'I proposed that a therapy of the second order has to be invented in order to deal with dysfunctions of the second order' (Beer, 1979b). Von Foerster (2003) states:

> I see now the purpose of using the notion of purpose. One does not need to know how to get there; one needs only to know the there. This is a very nice feature indeed! Is there a bad feature too? The ugly feature of the notions of 'purpose,' 'goal,' and 'end,' is that they can be used to justify the specific ways of getting there; 'The end justified the means.' And as we know now, the means can be very ugly indeed. The question should be, 'Do the means justify the end?'

No scholar other than Porter has recognized this very truth and has published against the mainstream since 2001. In their ground-breaking paper 'How to Fix Capitalism – and unleash a new wave of growth', Porter and Kramer (2011b) perceive:

> The Capitalist System is under siege. In recent years business increasingly has been viewed as a major cause of social, environmental and economic problems: Companies are widely perceived to be prospering at the expense of the broader community… A big part of the problem lies with companies themselves, which remain trapped in an outdated approach to value creation that has emerged over the past few decades. They continue to view value too narrowly, optimizing short-term financial performance in a bubble while missing the most important customers' needs and ignoring the broader influence that determine their longer-term success. How else can the companies overlook the well-being of their customers, the depletion of natural resources vital to the businesses, the viability of key suppliers, or the economic distress of the communications in which they produce or sell? How else could companies think that simply shifting activities to locations with ever lower wages was a sustainable 'solution' to competitive challenges? Government and civil society have often exacerbated the problem by attempting to address social weaknesses at the expense of business. The presumed trade-offs between economic efficiency and social progress have been institutionalized in decades of policy choice (Porter and Kramer, 2011b).

Porter and Kramer (2011b) have embraced a second-order problem in business administration and capitalism itself. This problem cannot be solved by mis-functioning of the first order but above all by the second-order flaws in the contemporary social and regulating institutions. This is one of the most essential debates in strategy in this zeitgeist, wherein everything, but above all control, can be regained by the strategic thinker, thus the authors once again perceive strategists calling for changing the meta-cause of organizations or further systemic crises with devastating consequences. This is what will occupy the talents in strategic and scientific landscapes in the future.

Von Foerster observes:

> Moreover, if we fail to do so, we shall provide the excuses for those who want to transfer the responsibility for their own actions to somebody else: 'I am not responsible for my actions; I just obey orders.' Thus, if we fail to recognize autonomy of each, we may turn into a society that attempts to honor commitments and forgets about its responsibilities (Foerster, 1979).

Responsibility is the competence of strategists and their challenges are in dealing with the complexity of ignorance, foresight, and the lens they ought to choose to observe the world from first- and second-order cybernetics. It is worth repeating the author's Corollary to von Foerster's Corollary Number One – anything observed is observed by an observer – thus strategy is about observation, and seeing it from the second order bestows the strategist with the ability to act based on the new model of strategic thinking according to Porter and Kramer (2011b), namely the long-overdue shared-value doctrine and what the author calls the complexity of the second order.

The team syntegrity model (TSM)

The 'team syntegrity model' (TSM), also known as 'syntegration', was developed by Beer (1994) and is like the VSM, based on the same systemic logic of bio-inspired cybernetics. The TSM is designed as a model of democratic communication among the different sub-systems of a larger whole, more specifically for the circulation and integrity of the necessary information for effective team decision-making.

'Team Syntegrity has a specific characteristic, which distinguishes it from more conventional approaches to face-to-face teamwork. Not only is it focused primarily on relationships rather than elements in a system; it can even enable larger numbers of people (e.g. 30, as in our case) to interact purposefully, in a nonhierarchical mode. A huge spectrum of views and insights can be brought to an intricate mode of synergetic cooperation' (Schwaninger, 2003, p 63). The model is constructed as a process to create the conditions and the required environment for large group discussions which navigate towards a group decision democratically and without any hierarchies. As Beer developed the VSM by looking into the patterns deriving from the human nervous system as the design of an ultra-stability model, the TSM was inspired by the power of Platonic geometry via the icosahedron (Figure 2.52). The foundation of the icosahedron is the holism of its structure, which resembles not a top–down strength of embodiment but moreover a structural strength by design in terms of the aforementioned synergy and tensile integrity of the whole.

The democratic dimension of the TSM starts with the form of the model. Beer chose the icosahedron because of its special geometrical characteristics. Thus, it is one of five existing regular and convex polyhedrons (Platonic solids) that, according to Beer (1994), perfectly reflect the aspect of democracy: they have no top, no bottom and no side, and furthermore they are made of regular faces and their edges are congruent.

FIGURE 2.52 Icosahedron

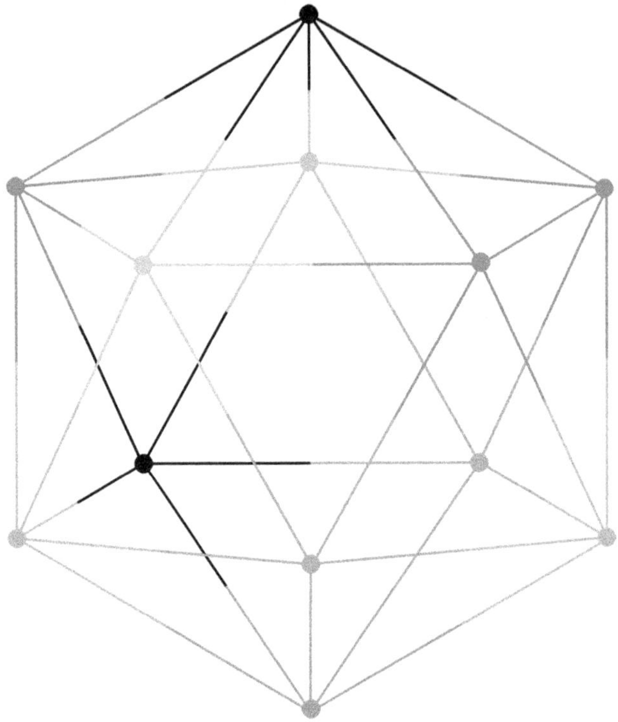

Based on Beer (1994)

Through this structure, participants move between equal related topics during a syntegration. Combined with the iterative sessions, the influence of internal group hierarchies is reduced to a minimum during the outcome resolve.

The basis of a solid syntegration is its unique process, being set in the so-called 'protocol'. The 30 edges of the icosahedron represent the number of participants, called the 'infoset'. A syntegration is always taking place under a certain opening question, which is then divided into 12 (the number of vertices) different topics by the group. The infoset consists of people invited from the organizer who are interested to work on the opening question. Ideally, they come from different backgrounds and bring in new expertise. Furthermore, the syntegration is divided into five stages, as Table 2.2 describes in a numerical sequence.

TABLE 2.2 Terms of the TSM

Term	Description
Infoset	The total of all participants.
Protocol	The pre-planned and strict schedule of the process.
Facilitators	The moderators and documentators.
1. Opening	Explanation of the protocol to the infoset by the facilitators.
2. Problem Jostle	Search and selection of the topics.
Statement of Importance (SI)	Individual suggestions by the participants for the final topics.
Aggregated Statement of Importance (ASI)	Assorted and structured SIs (eg elimination of redundancies).
Consolidated Statement of Importance (CSI)	The final topics for the Outcome Resolve, voted by the infoset.
3. Topic Auction	Arrangement of the infoset to the topic groups.
4. Outcome Resolve	Group discussions.
5. Finalization	Presentation of the group results to the infoset.

Based on Beer (1994)

There are a lot of options for variation during the syntegration process. These different settings always require a target-group-specific design of the protocol, but it has shown to be successful in its purpose of fast democratic problem-solving, decision-making or knowledge exchange in the context of organizational cognition.

Radical constructivism and its implications for strategic management

Radical constructivism, in terms of scientific discourse, is a theory of knowledge whose philosophical (epistemological) assumptions influenced many diverse sciences. Today its ideas have profound implications for the science of management, cybernetics, neurophysiology, media studies and pedagogy, and many other sciences. The philosophical-epistemological observation of constructivism is mainly established by Ernst von Glasersfeld. According to Glasersfeld (1988), Montaigne (1533–1592) trims to size the efforts of human reason, thus he sharpens it as one ever can. Montaigne observes (Glasersfeld 1988): 'Mankind's plague is the conceit of knowing.' According to Glasersfeld (1988):

> 'Radical Constructivism... [is] an effort to eliminate that conceit. It does not deny the possibility of knowing, but it strives to show that knowledge is not the commodity the tradition of Western philosophy would have us believe. Indeed, constructivism is a theory of active knowing, not a conventional epistemology that treats knowledge as an embodiment of Truth that reflects the world 'in itself', independent of the knower.

According to Glasersfeld, the two basic principles of radical constructivism are:

1. Knowledge is not passively received either through the senses or by way of communication, but it is actively built up by the cognizing subject.
2. The function of cognition is adaptive and serves the subject's organization of the experiential world, not the discovery of an objective ontological reality (Glasersfeld, 1988).

Another view that distinguishes representation from being part of the equation is that put forward by Lettvin *et al* (1959). The foundational work, which is also the ground of the author's perception, by which he constructs his final strategic model, is called 'What the Frog's Eye tells the Frog's Brain' (Lettvin *et al*, 1959). Maturana said the notion of 'representation of the real world in the nervous system' was untenable, thus there is no small table in our brain that a worldly table as a person perceives it can be associated with and there is no small object in the frog's brain, thus the nervous system does not function by representation (Glanville, 2012). Maturana (1980) developed the mentioned observation and knowing by the 'biology of cognition' and 'autopoiesis' (Varela *et al*, 1974), which is the cybernetic statement of the organization and functioning that comes into being and then maintains itself, which they argue is life – to 'The Tree of Knowledge', where Maturana establishes a biological fundament of knowing, and the complementarity of evolution and cognition (Glanville, 2012). According to Glanville (2002):

> Maturana's way of dealing with the problem of the nonconnection of experience and the nervous system is to talk of co-ordination, and the co-ordination of coordination, in a manner that brings to mind Saussure's (1966) discussion of the relationship between the representing and the represented as the bringing together of arbitrary items in temporary synchrony.

Glasersfeld (1974) quotes from Harry Beilin's explanation in Beilin (1971):

> The construction of knowledge more specifically takes place through the operation of two general processes under the control of an internal self-regulating mechanism (equilibration). The first of these is the assimilation process. It involves the incorporation of environmental data (through physical or mental activity) into existing cognitive structures. The products of new experience are incorporated into mind only to the extent that they are consistent with existing structures... The other process under the control of the equilibrating mechanism is accommodation. This represents the subject's response to external stimulation by which existing cognitive structures are effectively utilized for adaptive purposes by becoming integrated with other internal structures or by differentiating as they are applied to new experience... In most situations in which the organism functions, both assimilative and accommodative aspects of development take part, although one process dominates, depending upon the demands of reality.

Maturana (1978) delivers an additional foundation to the notion of cognition and construction of reality by a living system. This notion in addition substantiates 'the structure is strategy' anti-thesis to Chandler (1962) that the author has observed for debate.

Maturana (1978) states:

> If whatever takes place in a living system is specified by its structure, and if a living system can only have states in autopoiesis because it otherwise disintegrates (and stops being a living system), then the phenomenon of cognition, which appears to an observer as effective behavior in a medium, is, in fact, the realization of the autopoiesis of the living system in that medium. For a living system, therefore, to live is to cognite, and its cognitive domain is as extensive as its domain of states in autopoiesis. The presence of a nervous system in an organism does not create the phenomenon of cognition but enlarges the cognitive domain of the organism by expanding its domain of possible states in autopoiesis. Under these circumstances, there are two basic questions to be answered in the study of the biology of cognition,

> namely: a) How and why is it possible that an organism has, at any moment, a structure that allows it to operate effectively in a given medium?; and b) How does the nervous system change the cognitive domain of the organism that possesses it in comparison to one that does not? The first question refers to the problem of structural change which I shall call structural coupling; the second question refers to the operation in a closed network of neuronal interactions under conditions of structural coupling which I shall call operational recursion.

As Maturana raises, if these questions are integrated and observed in strategic management, they will give the 'meta-observer' (the strategists) a way to observe their own domain of the first-order observation, observing their own observations, and to tackle the organizational design and construction from the second-order perspective. Thus, the advantage of creating a model of the organization that can proactively sense and create a reality, as stated above, is that the strategist and their organization can be ahead of the crowd and avoid systemic failures and challenges, whereas the monetary-thinking and influenced manager cannot understand and cope. This according to Beer lacks the necessary requisite variety under the notion and relation of Ashby's Law to management and organizational control. No amount of propaganda, PR and marketing will at the final stage help the fundamental challenges the organization has to cope with. In the US, radical constructivism has been much promoted by the Austrian brief-therapy expert and constructivist Prof Dr Paul Watzlawick at Stanford University. In a refinement of a unique and fine approach, Watzlawick claims that it is helpful to categorize two different types of organizational reality:

1 The physical properties of things Watzlawick observes as first-order reality.
2 Second-order reality is the attributed reason behind and beyond what takes place as meanings, significance, or value that agents give to things they construct (Crosby, 2010).

Here Watzlawick makes a very profound observation: that it is a common and most vital error to throw these two realities into one pot (Crosby, 2010). Unfortunately, even famous cyberneticians have been mostly occupied by the first order and have ignored what von Foerster has observed as the second-order flaws, and especially the flaws of the observer being an essential part of the construction of organizational reality. According to Foerster (2003c):

> Truisms have the disadvantage that by dulling the senses they obscure the truth. Almost nobody will become alarmed when told that in times of continuity the future equals the past. Only a few will become aware that from this follows that in times of socio-cultural change the future will not be like the past. Moreover, with a future not clearly perceived, we do not know how to act with only one certainty left: if we don't act ourselves, we shall be acted upon. Thus, if we wish to be subjects, rather than objects, what we see now, that is, our perception, must be foresight rather than hindsight.

However, Foerster (2003c) goes further and states, on the problem of perception:

> The world appears to be in the grip of a fast-spreading disease which, by now, has assumed almost global dimensions. In the individual the symptoms of the disorder manifest themselves by a progressive corruption of his faculty to perceive, with corrupted language being the pathogen, that is, the agent that makes the disease so highly contagious. Worse, in progressive stages of this disorder, the affected become numb; they become less and less aware of their affection. This state of affairs makes it clear why I am concerned about perception when contemplating the future, for: if we can't perceive, we can't perceive of the future and thus, we don't know how to act now.

This problem is nowhere more easily observable than in business schools, where the minds of the current generation of strategists are being shaped, and they are struggling with the problem of the first order from a very myopic perspective.

According to Foerster (1971):

> I shall call a question to which the answer is known an illegitimate question. Wouldn't it be fascinating to contemplate an educational system that would ask of its students to answer legitimate questions, that is questions to which the answers are unknown (H. Brün in a personal communication). Would it not be even more fascinating to conceive of a society that would establish such an educational system? The necessary condition for such a utopia is that its members perceive one another as autonomous, non-trivial beings. Such a society shall make, I predict, some of the most astounding discoveries. Just for the record, I shall list the following three:

> **1** Education is neither a right nor a privilege: it is a necessity.
>
> **2** Education is learning to ask legitimate questions.
>
> A society who has made these two discoveries will ultimately be able to discover the third and most utopian one:
>
> **3** A is better off when B is better off.

Thus, the third observation by Foerster, written in 1971, was discovered by Porter 40 years later in 2011 (Porter and Kramer, 2011a) in his 'shared value doctrine'. But unfortunately, the profundity of the first two observations has not been truly observed by the intellectual community. The intellectual community is occupied with the creation of the predictable strategist-citizen on a dangerous mission. Strategists navigate as they construct, but the world of business schools is busy with the trivialization of the student-strategist to be predictable, to be admitted to society. First, they teach them to choose to be either an academic or a practitioner, then they shut the door on them forever on the path they have chosen. To learn in terms of separation of realities is the single most vital flaw in the educational system, but sadly it is the common practice. Then, they teach them to score higher in standardized tests. And, again they are observed upon by giving the most accurate known answer, with the danger of killing any kind of new knowledge generation or room for creativity. It is precisely here that the herd mentality of intellectual conformity, of what Popper warned of as intellectual cowardice, is established. Tilgher observed:

> Individuals can no longer act in the hope that their actions will crystallize into institutions... Their only reason to act can be the wish to escape by means of acting from the desperation of a cursed world, a world that no longer permits even the flight into the desert. It is action for action, action for the sake of action, ad infinitum,... and this action can have only a negative purpose: the overthrow of existing things (Glasersfeld, 2009).

However, considering the context of theories of knowledge, the notion of 'radical constructivism' refers to an orientation that breaks with the known Western epistemological tradition, since it is an unconventional way of looking at things and therefore requires conceptual change, by putting the common assumptions into question (Glasersfeld, 1996). Radical constructivism precisely requires the shift of several deeply rooted notions, such as knowledge, truth, representation, and reality, since to abolish traditional ideas and lenses of scientific discourse is never popular, thus proponents of radical constructivism are sometimes considered to be dangerous heretics (Glasersfeld, 1996). However, the greatest danger to the well-being of organizations does not come from constructivists establishing an accurate assumption, but from the manager-strategists trained in the reductionist way to solve systemic problems by observing the surface, rather than the root, of the problems or the cause of the cause.

Complex adaptive systems (CAS)

Complex adaptive systems (CAS) are systems that involve many components that adapt or learn as they interact; they are at the heart of important contemporary problems. These components in terms of CAS are also better known as agents. The study of CAS poses unique challenges; thus some of the world's most powerful mathematical tools, particularly methods involving fixed points, attractors, and the like, are of limited help in understanding the development of CAS (Holland, 2006).

> Many natural systems (e.g., brains, immune systems, ecologies, societies) and increasingly, many artificial systems (parallel and distributed computing systems, artificial intelligence systems, artificial neural networks, evolutionary programs) are characterized by apparently complex behaviors that emerge as a result of often non-linear spatio-temporal interactions among a large number of component systems at different levels of organization (Chan, 2001).

Table 2.3 shows how Holland's CAS theory can describe and be applied to different kinds of subjects and the systemic problems they try to answer. The four examples in the table deal with the same types of problem, which only carry different types of name, but the roots show similar patterns.

In Table 2.3, the first row describes the way each formalism represents the state of the system, the second row explains the cost related to each action taken within the system, the third row gives the value assigned to predetermined 'organizational objectives', and the last row states the technique(s) used to guide the system to its overall objectives. The similarities that one can observe by studying control theory, economics, biological cells and games clearly show that there is value in taking a cross-disciplinary approach to the study of CAS, but above all to the understanding and the application of CAS theory. According to Holland (2006):

TABLE 2.3 The cross-disciplinary similarities of several relevant fields according to the CAS theory

Control Theory	Economic	Biological Cells	Games
Process Variables	Activities	Phenotypic Features	Board Configuration
Operating Costs	Activity Costs	Metabolic Costs	Board Evaluation
Objective Function	Profits	Fitness	Payoff
Control Policy	Plan	Reaction Net	Strategy

Author's interpretation, based on Holland (2006)

> ... formalism is the result of many years of careful study, and each has its own strengths and weaknesses. Comparing corresponding parts of each formalism, we can sort out the parts relevant to CAS studies. By so-doing we can take advantage of these long histories, avoiding dead ends already explored.

CAS answers many difficult contemporary problems; thus they are systems that have a large number of parts, agents and sub-systems that interact, navigate, construct, adapt and learn. Figure 2.53 describes a CAS and how the agents or artefacts interact and compete.

Holland (2006) names a few of the challenges according to CAS:

- Encouraging innovation in dynamic economies.
- Providing for sustainable human growth.
- Predicting changes in global trade.
- Understanding markets.
- Preserving ecosystems.
- Controlling the internet (e.g. controlling viruses and spam).
- Strengthening the immune system.

The behaviour of almost 10,000 species living on a single tree resembles the same set of behaviours that economic agents have in the stock markets, the internet or the human immune system, thus the same patterns of behaviour and actions apply also to the agents in the wider economy. The notion of solutions and the answers that traditional economics deliver and represent is more and more losing ground because of the uncontrollable economic crises that the world faces. The reality of the problems is impossible to ignore. However, this is not the only problem to which CAS is applied. The study and application of CAS gives answers to a large and evolving diversity

FIGURE 2.53 Complex adaptive system (CAS) and how agents interact

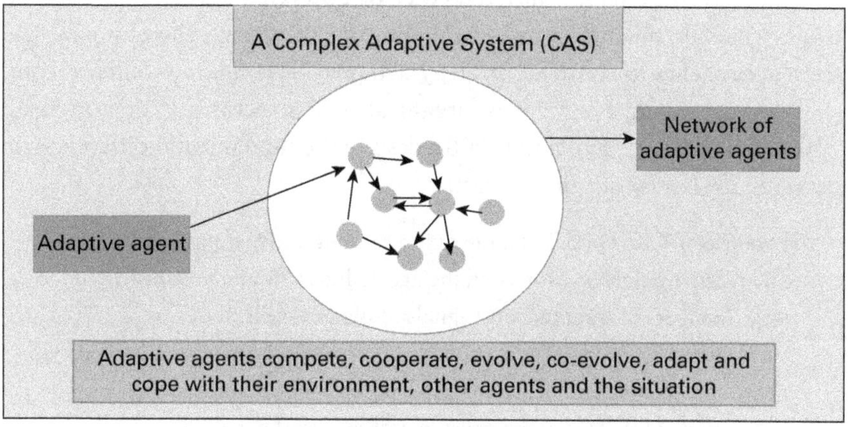

FIGURE 2.54 An agent according to the CAS theory

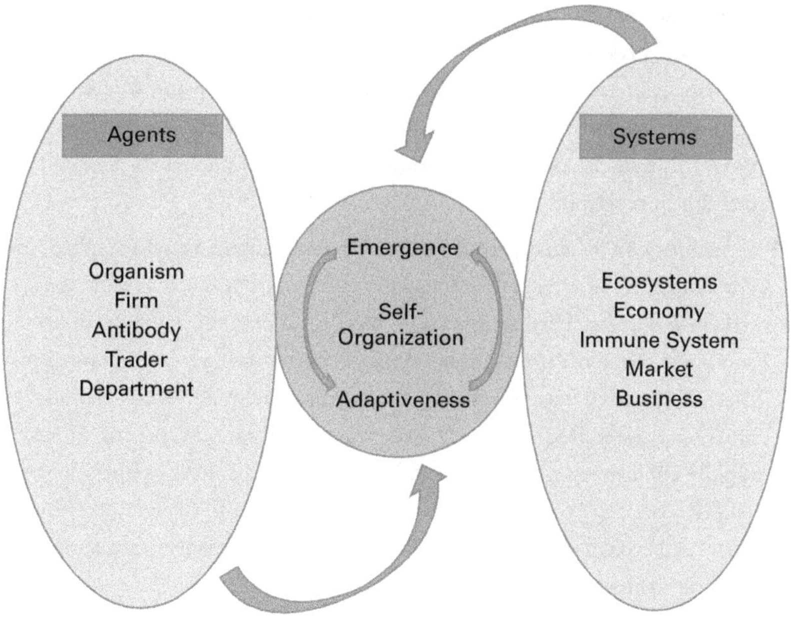

of problems, looking at how these adaptive and complex systems are evolved and constructed, but most importantly how these systems are controlled.

According to Figure 2.54, a firm, but also an economy, can be an agent. Thus the sets of problems and how they are controlled are highly similar. Organizations seen according to CAS as co-evolving within a socio-economic 'ecosystem' gives the strategist the ability to change the thinking about strategy and management theory in general. With the occupied changed view and strategic lens, a different way of observing and relating to challenges emerges that leads to a different way of acting. Thereby new and fresh approaches to construct strategy will provide conditions and prerequisites for the emergence of new organizational structures (Mitleton-Kelly, 2003). According to Holland (2006), despite the fundamental differences in detail, CAS shares four major features:

1 Parallelism. CAS consist of large numbers of agents that interact by sending and receiving signals. Moreover, the agents interact simultaneously, producing large numbers of simultaneous signals. Biological cells, for example, typically use proteins as signals. These proteins operate in reaction cascades and cycles, providing positive and negative feedback to other cascades and cycles. The interactions of these proteins must be tightly coordinated if the cell is to continue to function.

2 Conditional action. The actions of agents in a CAS usually depend on the signals they receive. That is, the agents have an IF/THEN structure: IF [signal vector x is present] THEN [execute act y]. The act may itself be a signal, allowing quite complicated feedbacks, or the act may be an overt action in the agent's environment. Interlocking sequences of signal-processing rules become programs that are executed in parallel, with all that implies for flexibility and breadth of repertoire.

3 Modularity. In an agent, groups of rules often combine to act as 'subroutines'. For example, the agent can react to the current situation by executing a sequence of rules. These 'subroutines' act as building blocks that can be combined to handle novel situations, rather than trying to anticipate each possible situation with a distinct rule. Because potentially useful building blocks are tested frequently, in a wide range of situations, their usefulness is rapidly confirmed or disconfirmed. In biological cells, for example, the citric acid (Krebs) cycle consists of 8 proteins that interact to form a loop. The citric acid cycle is a basic component of all aerobic organisms, ranging from bacteria to elephants.

4 Adaptation and evolution. The agents in a CAS change over time. These changes are usually adaptations that improve performance, rather than random variations. Adaptation requires the solution of two problems: the credit assignment problem and the rule discovery problem.

The problem in contemporary science is that science is about separations, thus it can hardly shape a view or understanding of the complex world and its phenomena by a consideration of unity. The departmentalization in academia, with the tendency to divide into specialties, is part of this. Thus, if a problem appears that may involve many diverse fields, the specialties first ought to learn each other's language and afterwards diagnose the problem. The involvement of an interdisciplinary approach to solving problems of a complex nature can also be observed as coping and dealing with complexity. According to Holland (2006):

> it is not likely that precise definitions of 'complexity', 'emergence', or the like, are necessary for studies of complex systems to proceed rapidly. We still have no sharp definition of 'life', 'species', or many other critical terms in biology, but the science of biology continues to advance rapidly. However, as in the case of biology, we do need rigorous models that allow us to explore properties that are unique to CAS.

In the points below, the author discusses the properties that offer new opportunities for understanding, applying and controlling CAS:

- 'All CAS that have been studied carefully exhibit lever points – points where a simple intervention causes a lasting, directed effect. For example vaccines cause lasting, desirable changes in an immune system, and simple dopants provide high-temperature superconductors. There is no theory that tells us where or how to look for CAS lever points.'
  Lever points are essential in strategic management as well, thus, for example, as a driver or a cargo ship captain does not need to know how a car's or a cargo ship's steering wheel functions in terms of its internal mechanics, as long as the navigator knows and understands how to turn and control it to avoid accidents, the lever point of how to navigate the car's or cargo ship's system is the steering wheel. In strategy, the lever point is the cybernetic brain of the organization (Hetzler, 2008), hence, the author's model will contribute to the construction of a holistic strategic model that can function as the navigating wheel, whereby the organization is controlled.
- 'All CAS have a hierarchical organization of boundaries enclosing boundaries, with signals that are attuned to those boundaries. Without boundaries there cannot be individual histories, and without individual histories selection for fitness is not possible. Thus, Darwinian selection depends upon the origin and development of boundaries. But there is as yet no theory or general model that tells us what mechanisms are sufficient for the formation of boundaries in an initially homogeneous system.'

However, Beer's VSM delivers fundamental hierarchical components that make organizational viability ever possible. Designing brain-like control models may give answers to Holland's observations. Thus, it's theory and asking the right question that is the larger component of finding an adequate answer to strategic problems. The author's final model delivers a new insight on how the VSM and Beer's operation room can be extended.

- 'All CAS seem to evolve in an open-ended fashion, wherein an initially simple system exhibits increasing diversity of interaction and signalling. Though there has been an increasing use of genetic algorithms, and other techniques for artificial evolution, there are at present no computer-based models that exhibit open-ended evolution. There are also some plausible hypotheses that go along with these observations.' In addition to Holland's observations:
  - Local concentrations of resources, induced by feedback, recycling and boundaries, provide opportunities for the formation of new agents. Thus, local concentration of strategic models also according to Porter and Kramer (2001), can result in the emergence of new sorts of organizational models, whereby the organization and the society and the organizational milieu can be positively affected. A good example is the concentration by Germany on the ecological aspects of industry. Although from the myopic perspective it has made doing business in Germany difficult, it has opened a global opportunity for Germany's green industry to catch a large part of the global industry while contributing to the well-being of society. Here, lies also the basic truth, as Beer (1995) rightfully observed: 'The laws of viability in complex organisms are not merely, or even primarily, concerned with energy (like metabolism of money) that propels them, but with the dynamic structure that determines the adaptive connectivity of their parts. Can the organization actually survive – assuming that the financial constraints are met?'
  - This process of agent formation leads to increasing co-evolution and diversity of agents, with progressively larger amounts of resources 'tied up' in agents.
  - Under 'tranquil' conditions, increasing agent specialization should be observed.
  - However, to observe the strategy of strategy (second-order observation) the strategist is needed to steer the control function of the organization, thus they will be needed more if the waters are turbulent. Here the

author calls not for specialty but for more interdisciplinarity. What needs to be observed is that the boundary, whereby systemic complexity and environmental perturbation is diagnosed and controlled, does not need the compartmentalized disciplinarity academia has brought upon itself and to society in general.

- Cybernetics is the science of control, while management is the profession of control. Thus, strategy is the profession of organizations' immunity, which the author also observes as the notion of pre-control and strategic foresight.

Figure 2.55 describes how CAS adapts to the changing environment. The fundamental notion that the reader can observe by the model is that it is based on 'Ashby and Conant's Theorem', thus it embeds change and environmental disturbance and, in addition, resembles adaptation.

Holland (2006) says that at a meta-level, when observing CAS that regularly produces innovations, eg evolving ecosystems, academics should then change the way they usually conduct research. Thus CAS opens a new foundation

FIGURE 2.55 The whole connected CAS system

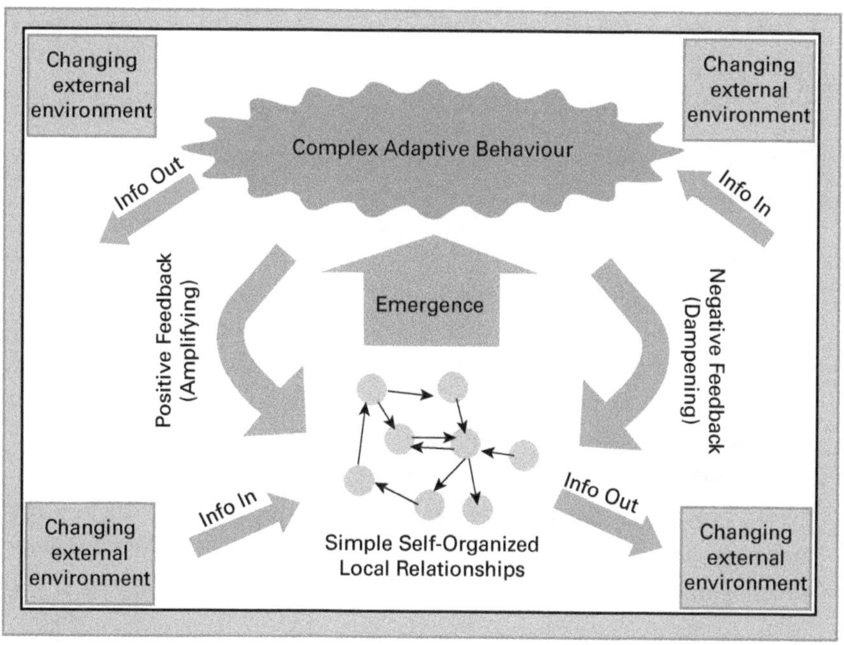

Author's interpretation, based on Holland (2006)

whereby scholars can construct realities to bring more stability to the systemic and strategic failures lurking everywhere, above all in the global economies:

- 'Risk-taking. Allow for high failure rates in funding research. Because of the exponential growth of the successes and their "spin-offs", the return from "home-runs" greatly exceeds the losses incurred by the failures.' Intellectual cowards are of no use according to the Popperian logic.
- 'Diversity and Parallelism. Follow several paths simultaneously in exploring a given question.' Holland's claims underpin the author's call for an interdisciplinary strategic and managerial approach to science and to society.
- 'Credit assignment. Provide ways of rewarding stage-setting activities. The most difficult activity in the conduct of science or business is the early, sometimes costly, activity that makes possible later, obviously good actions. As in the game of chess, it is often an early sacrifice of piece (a gambit) that makes possible a good later move. Real option theory gives a better approach to these questions than standard decision theory.' Strategy is about connecting the present to the future by the choice and the quality of the strategist's decisions. Constructing a viable organizational structure, instead of the myopic notion of 'structure follows strategy', will enable the organization to detect and equate emergent perturbations based on Beer's observation of the purpose of system, which is what it does, not what it always fails to do. Thus, according to the author, the first objective of an organization is to survive.

Holland asks a legitimate question: what can be expected in the longer run? The answers are provided below:

- '"Flight simulators" for organizations. Flight simulators are tested by experts who are not programmers. This kind of model is made possible by an interface, much like that for a videogame, that allows the expert to operate in familiar ways. The expert validates the model, suggesting improvements to the model's programmer.' The author's model is based on Holland's observation and Beer's operation room. Therefore, the author will deliver his final model based on 'the frog's eye and what it tells its brain', just as Ashby was inspired by this model. The notion of the management cockpit is not new, but the challenge is the yardstick, whereby one observes organizational fit and success.
- 'A theory of CAS that makes possible the principled discovery of lever points. Such a theory should lead to great improvements in everything from drug design to better care for the poor.' In addition, it will make it

possible for organizations' models not to be predators of the world's resources but their saviours. Lever points are of fundamental importance to strategy. Hence, if the self-organizing powers of a human's immune system can be awakened by a vaccine, what can this notion do for the immunity of organizations?

Understanding chaos theory and economics, management and strategy

The assurance that mathematics has given the world – that it is knowable and thus it is a controllable place – has been challenged by the systemic crises and turbulences visible in the finance world of stock markets, but also observable in economics, politics and business administration. However, there is an additional way of observing mathematics and therefore the world, which says that the world is not predictable, linear and simply not a controllable place. The notions of command and control, central planning and extrapolated projection in economics now seem like foreign words. The chaotic nature of occurrences in diverse fields – from nature (eg weather and climate change) to politics (the Arab Spring and the revolution in Egypt with its wider implications for the world of tomorrow), the Eurozone crisis (eg the crisis of Greece, Ireland, Spain and Italy) to the policy crises of the US government in coping with insurgency wars – tells a different story. These incidents need different types of approaches and more holistic sciences that can cope with the non-linear, 'black-swan-ness' (Taleb, 2007), and the turbulences embedded within the crises described.

Chaos theory seems to be able to cope with chaotic phenomena and the very chaotic nature of the world. According to Holland (2000): 'From earliest times, human endeavor has been directed toward discovering ways to channel a chaotic world.' Chaos theory is still a young field of study that cuts through diverse established and interdisciplinary sciences. It obliterates long-held scientific notions of inquiry with newer ones. The main objective of chaos theory is to investigate dynamic complex systems and their behaviours. According to Vlad *et al* (2010):

> The deterministic chaos represents only one particular case of what is called nondeterministic chaos that exhibits a super exponential divergence of the trajectories. In this case the equations describing the evolution of the system are not known. Both ways of chaos manifestations are short term predictable but

> long term unpredictable. The chaos and the concepts related to the dynamics of the systems and their modeling using differential equations is named the chaos theory and is tightly related with the notion of non-linearity. The non-linearity implies the loss of the causality correlation between the perturbation and effect propagated in time. The study of the non-linearity is named non-linear dynamics – a captivating domain using a mathematical apparatus still under development.

Chaos theory, according to Kellert (1993), is: 'The qualitative study of unstable aperiodic behaviour in deterministic non-linear dynamical system.' The biggest discovery in chaos theory is that the smallest, most unnoticeable change may contribute to a huge difference and impact on a larger system's behaviour. The most essential discovery in this regard is the 'butterfly effect', which states that the flapping of a butterfly's wing in Brazil may result in a tornado in Argentina. Butterfly effect was first observed and introduced by Lorenz (1963), who states:

> Finite systems of deterministic ordinary differential equations may be designed to represent forced dissipative hydrodynamic flow. Solutions of these equations can be identified with trajectories in phase space. For those systems with bounded solutions, it is found that nonperiodic solutions are ordinary unstable with respect to small modifications, so that slightly differing initial states can evolve into considerably different states. Systems with bound solutions are shown to possess bounded numerical solutions. A simple system representing cellular conviction is solved numerically. All the solutions are found to be unstable. And almost all of them are nonperiodic.

Lorenz (1993), known as the father of chaos theory, states:

> At one point I decided to repeat some of the computations in order to examine what was happening in greater detail. I stopped the computer, typed in a line of numbers that it had printed out a while earlier, and set it running again. I went down the hall for a cup of coffee and returned after about an hour, during which time the computer had simulated about two months of weather. The numbers being printed out were nothing like the old ones. I immediately suspected a weak vacuum tube or some other computer trouble, which was not uncommon, but before calling for service I decided to see just where the mistake had occurred, knowing that this could speed up the servicing process. Instead of a sudden break, I found that the new values at first repeated the old ones, but soon afterward differed by one and then several units in the last decimal place, and then began to differ in the next to last place and then in the place before

> that. In fact, the differences more or less doubled in size every four days or so, until all resemblance with the original output disappeared somewhere in the second month. This was enough to tell me what had happened: the numbers that I had typed in were not the exact original numbers, but were the rounded-off values that had appeared in the original printout. The initial round-off errors were the culprits; they were steadily amplifying until they dominated the solution. In today's terminology, there was chaos.

Figure 2.56 describes 'Lorenz's Attractor'. Lorenz (1963) developed a convective flow problem. Therefore, if one considers a two-dimensional fluid cell – which is heated from underneath and cooled from the top – it can be modelled by a single partial differential equation. Furthermore, the variables in this equation are expanded into an infinite number of modes, and all but three of them are set identically to zero, a drastic approximation (Lorenz, 1963).

How a small change can have wider consequences is revealed in Figures 2.56, 2.57 and 2.58. A small change in the parameter of the system can shift the patterns from a pattern of order to a state of chaos. According to McBride (2005):

> Organizational change..., must result from interactions between actors, whether human or machine, within the organization... Metaphors and models provide the basis for interpretive approaches in information systems that seek to draw

FIGURE 2.56 Lorenz's original model of the convection equations projection

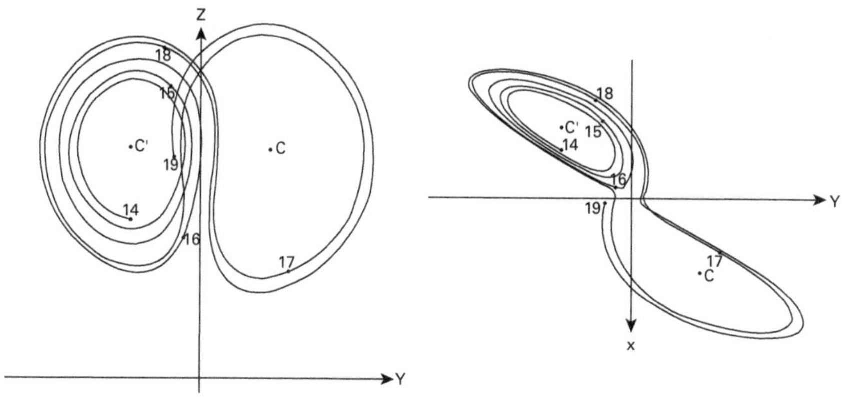

Numerical solution of the convection equations. Projections on the X-P plane and the Y-Z plane in phase space of segment of the trajectory extending from iteration 1400 to iteration 1900. Numerals '14, '15,', etc. States of steady convection are denoted by C and C.
Author's interpretation, based on Lorenz (1963)

> out patterns and shed light on complex social-technical situations... They act as sense-making tools... Using an edge of chaos metaphor to explore information system behavior in an organization will involve identifying critical points that result in shifts to new emergent behavior. For example, at what point does lack of information within an organization trigger a shift towards the acceptance of an information system solution? For the purposes of this study, a bifurcation can be defined as a qualitative change in the behavior of a dynamic system. This change may involve a sudden shift from one strange attractor to another, triggered as the system 'topples' over the edge of chaos. Large fluctuations in behavior may occur as the system takes up a new alternative state. Such a state change is irreversible. However, following a bifurcation, the next bifurcation could involve a shift back to a previous behavioral pattern or strange attractor; that pattern will not be the same as the previous occurrence of the strange attractor.

The notion of strange attractor is displayed in Figures 2.56, 2.57 and 2.58. Thus, if the motion is bound under regular conditions, the limiting behaviour of chaotic dysfunctional systems is covered in the invariant set coined as the 'strange attractor' (Brooks and Henry, 2000).

Stanford's Encyclopedia of Philosophy describes the dynamics of chaotic systems according to Bishop (2008b) in this manner:

> ... problematic definitions of chaos, namely, those that focus on notions of unpredictability. This certainly is neither necessary nor sufficient to distinguish chaos from sheer random behavior. Batterman does not actually specify an alternative definition of chaos. He suggests that exponential instability – the exponential divergence of two trajectories issuing forth from neighboring initial conditions – is a necessary condition, but leaves it open as to whether it is sufficient. However, what does appear to pass as a crucial feature of chaos for Batterman... is the presence of a kind of 'stretching and folding' mechanism in the dynamics... Basically such a mechanism will cause some trajectories to converge rapidly while causing other trajectories to diverge rapidly. Such a mechanism would tend to cause trajectories issuing from various points in some small neighborhood of state space to mix and separate in rather dramatic ways. For instance, some initially neighboring trajectories on the Lorenz attractor become separated, where some end up on one wing while others end up on the other wing. This stretching and folding is part of what leads to definitions of the distance between trajectories in state space as increasing (diverging) on average. The presence of such a mechanism in the dynamics, Batterman believes, is a necessary condition for chaos. As such, this defining characteristic could be applied to both mathematical models and real-world systems, though the identification of such mechanisms in target systems may be rather tricky.

FIGURE 2.57 Change from one state to another as a result of a small change in the system's parameter

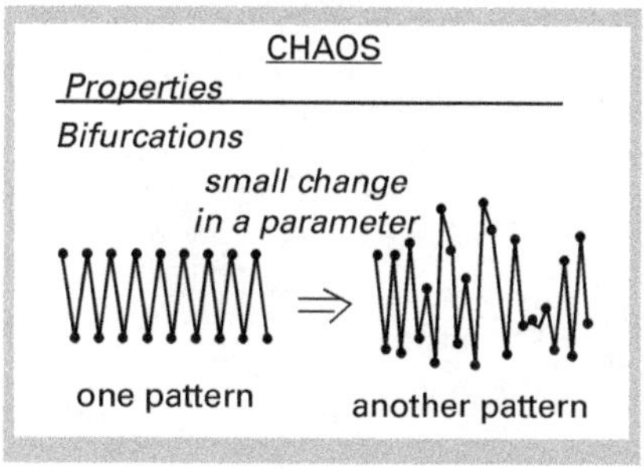

In 2011, the Tunisian Mohamed Bouazizi, a 26-year-old street vendor, set himself on fire and ended his life. This incident started the fall of Ben Ali's 23-year hold on Tunisia. In less than a month, it started the unrest that swept across the Middle East, which also led to Mubarak of Egypt being overthrown. The fall of Ben Ali revealed the chaotic nature of systems, even those as long-lasting and established as Tunisian and Egyptian society and governmental systems. Figure 2.57 simulates this nature of systems turning from order to chaos by a small perturbation or oscillation. The problem of economists and politicians ignoring chaos theory and the non-linearity of systems and how they can be controlled is also partly the challenge that the world economy faces. They rarely apply another view to their problems, violating the holistic view that a system in chaos needs from the strategist in order to be controlled and influenced.

To observe chaos and dynamic systems, the strategists' object of research on understanding an economy or a social system and organization is very different from the study of clouds, the flow of fluids, or the study of how birds flock. The flaw of traditional economics is to presume that agents are rational and that markets behave in terms of the 'efficient market hypothesis'. According to Xian and Tham (2011):

> Modern finance is largely built on the Efficient Market Hypothesis (EMH). Business students will (probably) fondly recall this theory, which asserts that one cannot consistently achieve returns in excess of average market returns on a risk adjusted basis, given the information publicly available at the time the investment is made. In particular, it assumes that stock prices follow a random walk model, and it is impossible to beat the market. Current prices are approximately equal to the intrinsic value. If prices are too high, rational traders will quickly take advantage of the opportunity to sell the stock and make a profit. Similarly, if prices are too low, rational traders will quickly buy the stock, pushing the price to the equilibrium level. The logic behind EMH is clear and simple.

FIGURE 2.58 Lorenz's set of three original equations

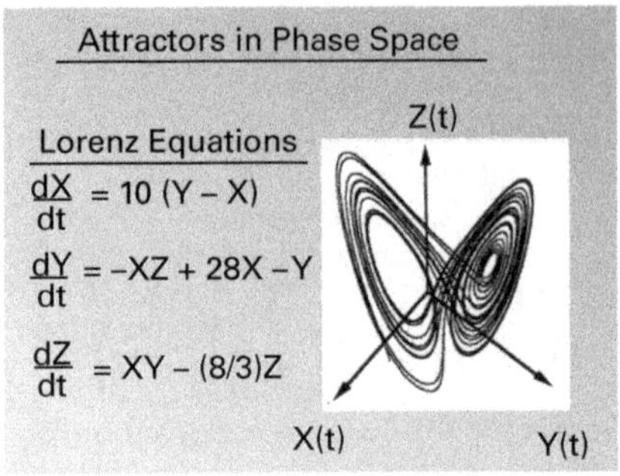

Author's interpretation, based on Lorenz (1963)

Fama, a pioneer of modern finance, in one of his most influential papers (Malkiel and Fama, 1970), describes EMH in the following manner:

> The primary role of the capital market is allocation of ownership of the economy's capital stock. In general terms, the ideal is a market in which prices provide accurate signals for resource allocation: that is, a market in which firms can make production-investment decisions, and investors can choose among the securities that represent ownership of firms' activities under the assumption that security prices at any time 'fully reflect' all available information. A market in which prices always 'fully reflect' available information is called 'efficient'.

Furthermore, in another famous paper Fama (1995) describes an additional mainstream economic theory, 'random walk':

> For many years economists, statisticians, and teachers of finance have been interested in developing and testing models of stock price behavior. One important model that has evolved from this research is the theory of random walks. This theory casts serious doubt on many other methods for describing and predicting stock price behavior – methods that have considerable popularity outside the academic world. For example, we shall see later that, if the random-walk theory is an accurate description of reality, then the various 'technical' or 'chartist' procedures for predicting stock prices are completely without value. Random-walk theorists usually start from the premise that the major security exchanges are good examples of 'efficient' markets. An 'efficient' market is defined as a market where there are large numbers of rational profit-maximizers actively competing, with each trying to predict future market values of individual securities, and where important current information is almost freely available to all participants.

However, the 'Black Swan' (Taleb, 2007), as occurred on 19 October 1987 (see Figure 2.59), tells a different story.

According to Hsieh (1991), the interest of the financial press and the academic literature to study the financial market crises through the lenses of chaos theory was raised after the stock market crash of 1987, thus the non-linearity and the frequency of the market displayed that the stock market was governed by non-linear dynamics. However, today this theory does not dominate the curricula of business schools and mainstream economics and finance. Thus, another large financial catastrophe that displayed this non-linearity of the market, which was ignored, is the multi-billion-dollar failure of the 'Black and Scholes formula', originally formulated by Black and Scholes (1973) in their ground-breaking paper 'The Pricing of Options and Corporate Liabilities'. It was built based on the doctoral work of Louis Bachelier, a French mathematician at the University of Paris in the 1900s, who at that time suggested that fluctuations of the stock market can be modelled by a random process known as Brownian motion (Stewart, 2012). According to Black and Scholes (1973):

FIGURE 2.59 Stock market crash of 1987, known as 'Black Monday'

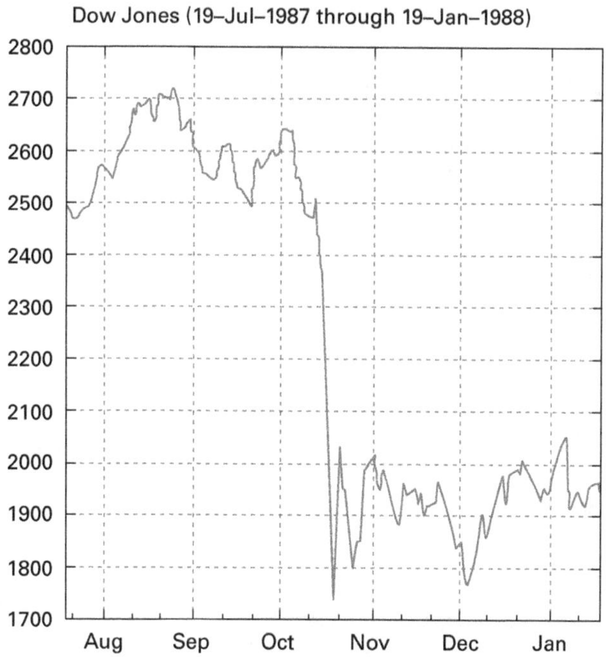

Based on Xian and Tham (2011)

> If options are correctly priced in the market, it should not be possible to make sure profits by creating portfolios of long and short positions in options and their underlying stocks. Using this principle, a theoretical valuation formula for options is derived. Since almost all corporate liabilities can be viewed as combinations of options, the formula and the analysis that led to it are also applicable to corporate liabilities such as common stock, corporate bonds, and warrants. In particular, the formula can be used to derive the discount that should be applied to a corporate bond because of possibility of default.

Merton (1976) on the Black and Scholes formula observed:

> The validity of the classic Black-Scholes option pricing formula depends on the capability of investors to follow a dynamic portfolio strategy in the stock that replicates the payoff structure to the option. The critical assumption required for such a strategy to be feasible, is that the underlying stock return dynamics can be described by a stochastic process with a continuous sample path. …, an option pricing formula is derived for the more-general cast when the underlying stock returns are generated by a mixture of both continuous and jump processes. The derived formula has most of the attractive features of the original Black & Scholes formula in that it does not depend on investor preferences or knowledge of the expected return on the underlying stock. Moreover, the same analysis applied to the options can be extended to the pricing of corporate liabilities.

FIGURE 2.60 The fall of the LTCM hedge funds

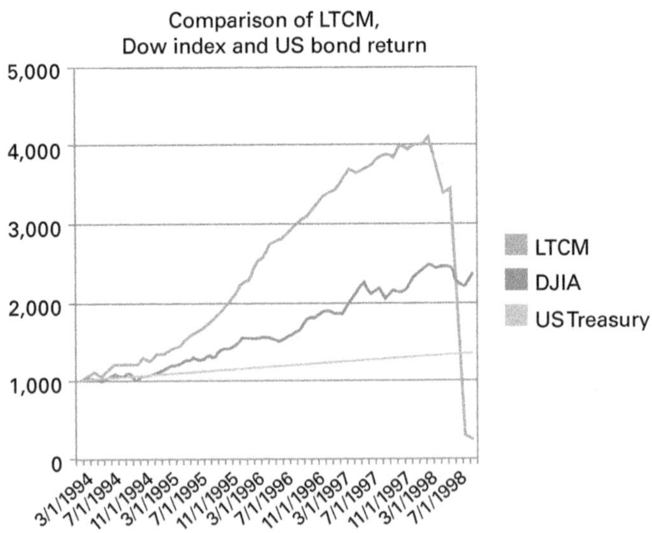

Author's interpretation, based on Xian and Tham (2011)

Merton (1976), a 'wunderkind' of financial mathematics, applied exotic models to finance and used a model that is usually applied in rocket science to substantiate Black and Scholes' formula and the power of their claim. In constructing his own complex mathematical models, Merton confirmed the accuracy and the fundamental discovery of Black and Scholes to tackle the problem of risk in finance.

> Merton explored theories no one in finance had even heard of. Turning to rocket science, he studied the theories of a Japanese mathematician, Kiyosi Ito, who'd faced a similar problem to Black and Scholes. In order to plot the trajectory of rockets, you needed to know exactly where the missile was, not just second by second, but literally all the time. Ito had developed a way of dividing time into infinitely small parcels, smoothing it out until it became a continuum so that the trajectory could be constantly updated. Bob Merton adapted this idea to the Black-Scholes formula. Using the notion of continuous time, the value of the option could be constantly recalculated and risk eliminated continually (PBS Nova, 2000).

The formula was awarded the Nobel Prize in Economics in 1997. A large hedge fund firm was founded by Meriwether in Greenwich, Connecticut in 1994, where Myron Scholes and Robert C. Merton, both Nobel laureates, were working with 25 additional PhDs in finance under their guidance to climb to the peak of the financial world occupied and powered by one of the most powerful formulas finance maths could ever produce (Xian and Tham, 2011).

Long-Term Capital Management (LTCM), which used highly sophisticated and advanced qualitative models to out-compete the traditional trader and reduce risk, caused one of the largest financial debacles ever seen by losing $4.6 billion within four months. The consequences of the one pillared concentration and reductionist view on the power of mathematics was the chief reason that the:

> ... monstrous quantitative disappointments, such as the stock market crash of October 1987 and the September 1998 failure of Long-Term Capital Management; in fact, it is reasonable to argue that the worst market crises since 1929 were all aided, abetted and directly caused by flawed analytical concoctions. In all those cases, the system's very viability was threatened (Triana, 2010).

The 1998 financial crisis in combination with the Russian government's default on their government bonds was too much for the financial model to bear, and it lost more than $100 million a day – at the final stage it was up to $500 million per day –which forced LTCM to apply for bankruptcy. The short-term and myopic vision of highly over-leveraging on debt and producing highly complex financial products that not even the CEO of Lehman Brothers (LB) understood is another example of why LB failed and caused 2008 to be remembered as one of the worst years in the history of the stock market. According to Lounsbury and Hirsch (2010):

> One reason why Lehman would later go bankrupt has to do with the fact that anyone who was perceived as a threat by Fuld was quickly eliminated including a number of critics who early on realized that Lehman was headed for serious trouble. It should also be noted that Fuld's personal experience was mainly as a bond trader and that he had little technical understanding of such new financial instruments as CDOs, credit default swaps (CDSs), and the like. Lehman was one of the leaders in the production of securitized mortgages and also owned two mortgage firms, BNC in California and Aurora Loan Services in Colorado. According to *The Wall Street Journal*, 'Lehman established itself [in the mid-1990s] as a leader in the market for subprime mortgage-backed securities. It built a staff of experts who had worked at other securities firms and established relationships with subprime-mortgage lenders.'

The examples above reveal that firms and economies are dynamic systems, and if systemic crises are the root of the problem, then one single view and even Nobel-Prize-winning financial mathematics formulas cannot save the day. Thus, the view of the author, 'Structure is strategy', is confirmed, since firms in investment banking business have weak structures, and thus they fail because their highly over-leveraged financial borrowing is a part of their organization's structure. A small crisis in the behaviour of the market is sufficient to dismantle a 150-year-old firm within a weekend.

The above examples clearly describe that additional theories and sciences with more holistic approaches to economics, finance and management ought to be integrated into the fields. Figure 2.61 describes the economic chaos of diverse countries, covering a range of defaults from 1900–2006 and the chaotic systems behaviour. Thus, according to Stewart (1997):

> The flapping of a single butterfly's wing today produces a tiny change in the state of the atmosphere. Over a period of time, what the atmosphere actually does diverges from what it would have done. So, in a month's time, a tornado that would have devastated the Indonesian coast doesn't happen. Or maybe one that wasn't going to happen, does.

Observing the economic behaviour of diverse countries over a long time reveals that the patterns of behaviour of diverse countries' currency crashes resemble the chaotic nature of these systems. As the reader can clearly see, Figure 2.61

FIGURE 2.61 The history of the countries in default (a) and how dynamic systems behave according to the chaos theory (b)

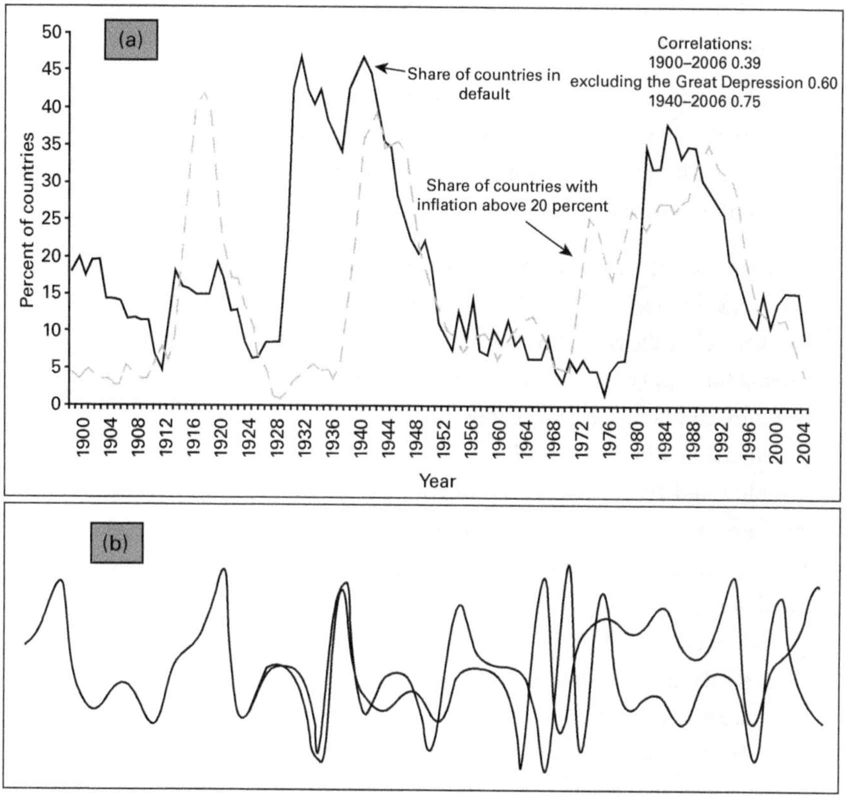

Reinhart and Rogoff (2008) and Stewart (1997)

describes the currency crashes from 1900–2006. These currency crashes simulate the same kind of behaviour as Lorenz's equation simulates in the figures above. However, it is a difficult task to shift the attention of the mainstream from the simplistic and mechanical observation and treatment of the world's economic system to theories that have actually requisite variety according to Ashby's Law and which can cope with the non-linearity of these systems.

According to Velasquéz (2009):

> The evolution of complexity theory shows us how difficult it is to swim against preconceived ideas. The mechanistic perspective, with its fixed theories, linear methods and simple cause and effect approach, was part of the scientific discourse for more than one hundred years. The first consistent rupture was made in the area of thermodynamics, and later in the quantum mechanics. Even Darwin's evolution theory and Einstein's relativism help to set to ground for the

> emergence of a new synthesis in science. The result was the 'antithesis' of the Newtonian paradigm, Chaos theory, which proposed a new language and tools to address our complex reality. As Gleick famously said 'where Chaos begins, classical science stops' (Gleick, 1993).

The under-researched area of seeing economics and organizational behaviour from the lenses of complexity, cybernetics and chaos theory is one of the major challenges that contributes to the state of chaos in the contemporary global economic crisis. According to Perna and Sibillo (2008):

> Proving that the data is chaotic would prove there is a deterministic underlying system generating the data. The proof would be a giant step toward clarifying the 'nature' of the economy. Currently models are forced to treat shocks, the driving force of economic fluctuations and the reason for the unpredictability of future conditions, as exogenous and completely random. Chaotic non-linear systems can endogenize shocks. If the economy is chaotic, then we can create a complete and closed model. This development would aid significantly in short run forecasting. Unfortunately until better tests are developed we may be forced to argue the existence of chaos and a non-linear underlying economic structure on philosophical grounds. Even with a consensus there would still be the task of assembling the dynamic system at the heart of the economy. However daunting the task, the grand implications of predictable financial markets, endogenized shocks, and clarification of the structure of the macroeconomy, give fruit to the labor. With these incentives the research and literature in this area is certain to grow in both size and importance as a field within economics (Perna and Sibillo, 2008).

Figure 2.62 reveals the predictable chaos as the Napoleonic wars had their effects on the crashes of the currency and the additional chaotic nature of the world's currencies.

Although the author's observations and research have their limitations, the purpose has been to display the similarity of economics to chaotic systems and raise awareness that economic systems are complex, chaotic and non-linear dynamic systems over time. Hence, it is not essential for it to succeed in showing the relevance of chaos theory in general, particularly since non-linearities are an undeniable fact (May, 1976): 'Not only in research, but also in the everyday world of politics and economics, we would all be better off if more people realized that simple non-linear systems do not necessarily possess simple dynamical properties.' According to Vlad *et al* (2010):

FIGURE 2.62 Comparison of the non-linearity of world currency crashes, 1800–1995, and a simulation of Lorenz's equations

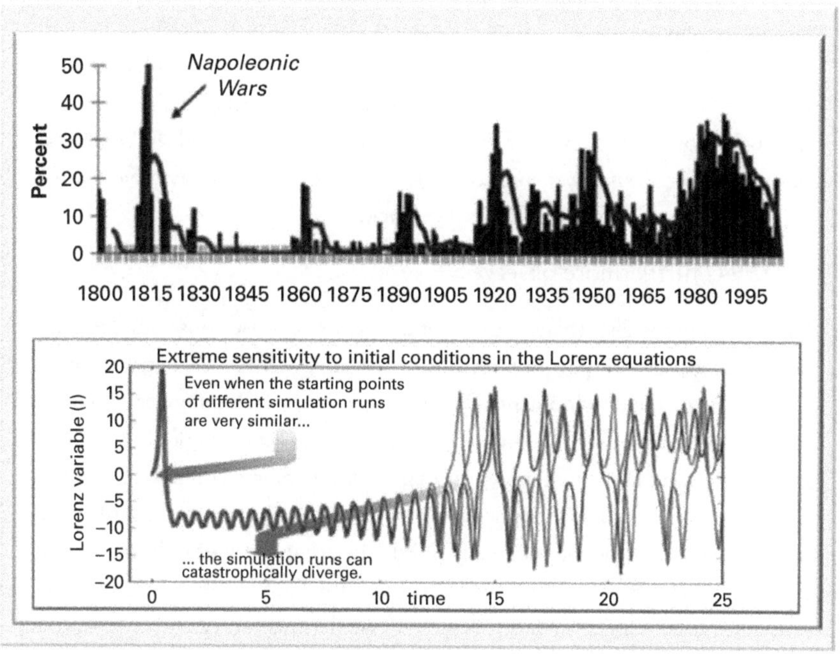

> Chaos can be found almost everywhere in nature. Chaos theory and fractals are currently applied in the study of the natural phenomenon. An essential condition needed in order for chaos to emerge is to have non-linear systems. In fact very few of all models are purely linear, the vast majority of the systems are non-linear... two of the features of the chaotic systems: dependence to initial conditions and the divergence of nearby trajectories. The chaos theory has a significant impact on the economy and especially on capital markets. If the behavior of one economic system is proved to be chaotic this guarantees that, using appropriate methods, a short-term prediction can be made.

Applying chaos theory to strategic management is described by Levy (1994) in the following way:

> One of the enduring problems facing the field of strategic management is the lack of theoretical tools available to describe and predict the behavior of firms and industries. For example, even if we know that oligopolistic industries are likely to experience periods of stability alternating with periods of intense competition, we do not know when they will occur or what will be the

> outcome. Similarly, it is almost impossible to predict the impact of the advent of a new competitor or technology in an industry. The fundamental problem is that industries evolve in a dynamic way over time as a result of complex interactions among firms, government, labor, consumers, financial institutions, and other elements of the environment. Not only does industry structure influence firm behavior, but Key words: Chaos theory, simulation, international, supply chain firm behavior in turn can alter the structure of an industry and the contours of competition. Existing theoretical models, however, tend to assume relatively simple linear relationships without feedback.

Levy (1994) furthermore observes:

> Small exogenous disturbances to chaotic systems can also cause unexpectedly large changes. The implication for business strategy is that the entry of one new competitor or the development of a seemingly minor technology can have a substantial impact on competition in an industry... An example that comes to mind is the way Dell's mail order strategy in the personal computer industry forced other companies to reduce their prices and reexamine their traditional high-cost sales and service channels. While the complexity of industry systems dictates the need for broad strategies, the dynamic nature of chaotic systems mandates that strategies adapt. As industry structures evolve and competitors change their strategies, a firm clearly needs to change its own guidelines and decision rule.

The author's contribution has been to awaken the notion that non-linear activities and phenomena may shape and cause serious challenges and disruptions to solid industries, firms and organizations, which strategy, as an emergent organizational capability, tool and theory of control, addresses.

Furthermore, complexity sciences and chaos theory are more efficiently capable of predicting and absorbing the disruptions the author has noted within the pages above. This phenomenon is the chief reason why Yahoo, once the leader in website search engines, is a minor player to Google's domination, why the music industry is currently challenged by the rise of IT technology and websites and apps such as YouTube, and explains Apple's rise from a PC maker to be a leader in music distribution and mobile telecommunications. Having a viable strategy that can act upon and predict this kind of survivable relevant phenomenon gives the strategists the tools and capabilities of a sustainable and hard to imitate competitive advantage.

A further debate, which the author intended to raise, is that mathematical models, although an essential way to observe the world – and more precisely the world of finance and economics – may have had their successes in physics, but are insufficient to predict and cope with vital and systemic crises of economies and societies. Therefore, complexity and chaos theories are essential to the strategist. If these theories are ignored, they may clearly start organizational weaknesses, which are hard to detect and slow in terms of their effects, but they can dismantle viable organizations within the shortest time once their effects are sensed and visible.

References

Ackoff RL (1973) Science in the systems age: Beyond IE, OR, and MS, *Operations Research*, **21** (3), pp 661–671

Ackoff RL (2006) *Why Few Organizations Adopt Systems Thinking*, Available at: https://thesystemsthinker.com/why-few-organizations-adopt-systems-thinking/ (archived at https://perma.cc/T5Q9-9ZS7)

Albers AM, Kok P, Toni I, *et al* (2013) Shared representations for working memory and mental imagery in early visual cortex, *Current Biology*, **23** (15), pp 1427–1431

Andriantiatsaholiniaina LA, Kouikoglou VS and Phillis YA (2004) Evaluating strategies for sustainable development: Fuzzy logic reasoning and sensitivity analysis, *Ecological Economics*, **48** (2), pp 149–172

Archer BL (1979) Design as a discipline, *Design Studies*, **1** (1), pp 17–20

Ashby WR (1948) Design for a brain, *Electronic Engineering*, **20**, pp 379–383

Ashby WR (1952) *Design for a Brain*, Chapman & Hall, London

Ashby WR (1956) *Introduction to Cybernetics*, Chapman & Hall, London

Ashby WR (1958) Requisite variety and its implications for the control of complex systems, *Cybernetica*, **1** (2), pp 83–99

Ashby WR (1960) *Design for a Brain: The origin of adaptive behaviour*, Springer Netherlands, Dordrecht

Ashby WR (1962) Principles of the self-organizing system, in *Principles of Self-Organization: Transactions of the University of Illinois Symposium*, eds H Von Foerster and GW Zopf, Jr, pp 255–278, Pergamon Press, London

Ashby WR (2004) Principles of the self-organizing system, *E:CO*, **6** (1–2), pp 102–126

Barnard CI (1938) *The Functions of the Executive*, Harvard University Press, Cambridge, MA

Barton D (2011) Capitalism for the long term, *Harvard Business Review*, **89** (3), pp 84–91

Beer S (1959) *Cybernetics and Management*, Wiley, New York

Beer S (1966) *Decision and Control: The meaning of operational research and management cybernetics*, Wiley, London

Beer S (1972) *Brain of the Firm: A Development in Management Cybernetics*, Lane, London
Beer S (1973) *Designing Freedom: The future that can be demanded now*, Center for Cassette Studies, Portland, OR
Beer S (1974) *Designing Freedom*, Canadian Broadcasting Corp, Toronto
Beer S (1975) *Platform for Change*, Wiley, Chichester
Beer S (1979a) *Decision and Control: The meaning of operational research and management cybernetics*, Wiley, Chichester
Beer S (1979b) *The Heart of Enterprise*, Wiley, New York
Beer S (1981) *Brain of the Firm: The managerial cybernetics of organization*, J. Wiley, Chichester
Beer S (1984) The viable system model: Its provenance, development, methodology and pathology, *Journal of the Operational Research Society*, **35** (1), pp 7–25
Beer S (1985) *Diagnosing the System for Organizations*, Wiley, New York
Beer S (ed) (1989) *The Viable System Model: Interpretations and applications of Stafford Beer's VSM*, John Wiley & Sons Ltd, New Jersey
Beer S (1990) On suicidal rabbits: A relativity of systems, *Systems Practice*, **3** (2), pp 115–124
Beer S (1994) Stafford Beer on the art and science of holistic management, in *How Many Grapes Went into the Wine: Stafford Beer on the art and science of holistic management*, eds R Harnden, A Leonard and S Beer, Wiley, Chichester
Beer S (1995) *Diagnosing the System for Organizations*, Wiley, New York
Beer S (2000) *Decision and Control: The meaning of operational research and management cybernetics*, Wiley, Chichester
Beer S (2002) What is cybernetics?, *Kybernetes*, **31** (2), pp 209–219
Beilin H (1971), *The Development of Physical Concepts 1*,
Bishop RC (2008a) Chaos, in *Stanford Encyclopedia of Philosophy*, ed EN Zalta, Available at: https://plato.stanford.edu/entries/chaos/#QualDefCha (archived at https://perma.cc/VUU5-K2H8) (accessed 1 December 2019)
Bishop RC (2008b) What Could Be Worse than the Butterfly Effect?, *Canadian Journal of Philosophy*, **38**, pp 519–548
Black F and Scholes M (1973) The pricing of options and corporate liabilities, *Journal of Political Economy*, **81** (3), pp 637–654
Boulding KE (1956) General systems theory: The skeleton of science, *Management Science*, **2** (3), pp 197–208
Bourgine P and Stewart J (2004) Autopoiesis and cognition, *Artificial Life*, **10** (3), pp 327–345
Bousquet A (2008) Cyberneticizing the American war machine: Science and computers in the Cold War, *Cold War History*, **8** (1), pp 77–102
Boyd JR (1976) *New Concepts for Air-to-Air Combat*, Unpublished manuscript, United States Air Force
Brauckmann S (1999) *Ludwig von Bertalanffy (1901–1972)*, Available at: http://www.isss.org/lumLVB.htm (archived at https://perma.cc/GL2Y-GYCP) (accessed 26 November 2019)

Brooks C and Henry OT (2000) Can portmanteau non-linearity tests serve as general mis-specification tests? Evidence from symmetric and asymmetric GARCH models, *Economics Letters*, **67** (3), pp 245–251

Business Dictionary (2019) *Grand Strategy*, Available at: http://www.businessdictionary.com/definition/grand-strategy.html (archived at https://perma.cc/SV7V-82MB) (accessed 28 November 2019)

CASG (2019) *Complex Adaptive Systems Group*, Available at: http://www.cas-group.net/ (archived at https://perma.cc/KP29-QJ5A) (accessed 29 November 2019)

Chan S (2001) Complex adaptive systems, in *ESD. 83 Research Seminar in Engineering Systems*, pp 1–9

Chandler AD (1962) Strategy and Structure, in *The History of the Industrial Enterprise*, MIT Press Research Monographs, MIT Press, Cambridge, MA

Christopher WF (2007) *Holistic Management: Managing what matters for company success*, Wiley-Interscience, Hoboken, NJ

Conant RC and Ashby WR (1970) Every good regulator of a system must be a model of that system, *International Journal of Systems Science*, **1** (2), pp 89–97

Conway F and Siegelman J (2006) *Dark Hero of the Information Age: In search of Norbert Wiener, the father of cybernetics*, Basic Books, New York

Crosby JF (2010) Radical constructivism and theological epistemology, *Essays in the Philosophy of Humanism*, **18** (1), pp 1–16

CSULB (2019) *Warren McCulloch*, Available at: http://web.csulb.edu/~cwallis/artificialn/warren_mcculloch.html (archived at https://perma.cc/X7FC-TWWD) (accessed 29 November 2019)

Damasio AR (2004) *Descartes' Error: Emotion, reason and the human brain*, Quill, New York

Denning S (2012) *What Killed Michael Porter's Monitor Group? The one force that really matters*, Available at: http://www.forbes.com/sites/stevedenning/2012/11/20/what-killed-michael-porters-monitor-group-the-one-force-that-really-matters/3/ (archived at https://perma.cc/ALF6-L6CF) (accessed 21 November 2018)

Doern BG (1971) Recent changes in the philosophy of policy-making in Canada, *Canadian Journal of Political Science*, **4** (2), pp 243–264 (accessed 29 November 2019)

Drack M and Pouvreau D (2015) On the history of Ludwig von Bertalanffy's "General Systemology", and on its relationship to cybernetics – part III: Convergences and divergences, *International Journal of General Systems*, **44** (5), pp 523–571

Drucker PF (1954) *The Practice of Management*, Harper & Row, New York

Elkus A (2010) Complexity, design and modern operational art: U.S. evolution or false start, *Canadian Army Journal*, **13** (3), pp 55–67

Erdi P (2008) *Complexity Explained*, Springer-Verlag, Berlin, Heidelberg

Espejo R, Schuhmann W, Schwaninger M and Bilello U (1996) *Organizational Transformation and Learning: A cybernetic approach to management*, Wiley, Chichester

Fama EF (1995) Random walks in stock market prices, *Financial Analysts Journal*, **51** (1), pp 75–80

Foerster H von (1971) Perception of the future and the future of perception, *Instructional Science*, **1**, pp 31–43. See also Foerster H von (2003c) below

Foerster H von (1979) *Cybernetics of Cybernetics*, University of Illinois, Urbana

Foerster H von (1984) Principles of self-organization: In a socio-managerial context, in *Self-organization and Management of Social Systems*, pp 2–24, Springer, New York

Foerster H von (1995) Metaphysics of an Experimental Epistemologist, in: Roberto Moreno-D ıaz and Jos é Mira-Mira, Hg, *Brain Process, Theories, and Models. An international conference in honor of WS McCulloch 25 years after his death*, Cambridge and London, pp 3–10

Foerster H von (2003a) *Understanding Understanding: Essays on cybernetics and cognition*, Springer-Verlag, New York

Foerster H von (2003b) Ethics and second-order cybernetics, in *Understanding Understanding*, pp 287–304, Springer, New York

Foerster H von (2003c) Perception of the future and the future of perception, in *Understanding Understanding*, pp 199–210, Springer, New York

Foerster H von (2003d) Cybernetics of cybernetics, in K Krippendorff (ed) *Communication and Control*, Gordon and Breach, New York, pp 5–8. Original 1979 text also reprinted in Foerster H von (2003a) above, pp 283–286

Foerster H von (2003e) On constructing a reality, in Foerster H von (2003a) above, p 211–228. Originally published in Preiser FE (ed) (1973) *Environmental Design Research*, **2**, pp 35–46, http://cepa.info/1278 (archived at https://perma.cc/42ZM-B54R), Dowdon, Hutchinson & Ross, Stroudberg

Foerster H von, Hejl PM, Schmidt SJ, *et al* (1992) *Einführung in den Konstruktivismus*, Piper, München

Forrester JW (1999) *System Dynamics: The foundation under systems thinking*, Sloan School of Management, Massachusetts Institute of Technology, Boston, MA

Frank LK (1948) Foreword, *Annals of the New York Academy of Sciences*, **50** (4), pp 189–196

Frantz R (2003) Herbert Simon: Artificial intelligence as a framework for understanding intuition, *Journal of Economic Psychology*, **24** (2), pp 265–277

Geus A de (2002) *The Living Company*, Harvard Business School Press, Boston, MA

Gharajedaghi J (2004) *A Holistic Language of Interaction and Design: Seeing through chaos and understanding complexities*, Ackoff Collaboratory for Advancement of the Systems Approach (ACASA)

Gharajedaghi J (2006) *Systems Thinking: managing chaos and complexity: a platform for designing business architecture*, Butterworth-Heinemann, Oxford

Gharajedaghi J (2011) Socio-cultural systems, Available at: https://ackoffcenter.blogs.com/files/gharajedaghi-sociocultural-systems-revised-1-23-12-with-edits.pdf (archived at https://perma.cc/MDL5-246Y) (accessed 14 August 2013)

Glanville R (2002) Second order cybernetics, *Systems Science and Cybernetics*, **3**, pp 59–85

Glanville R (2012) Radical constructivism = second-order cybernetics, *Cybernetics & Human Knowing*, **19** (4), pp 27–42

Glasersfeld Ev (1974) Piaget and the radical constructivist epistemology, *Epistemology and Education*, **1**, p 24

Glasersfeld Ev (1988) The reluctance to change a way of thinking, *The Irish Journal of Psychology*, **9** (1), pp 83–90

Glasersfeld Ev (1995) Die Wurzeln des Radikalen am Konstruktivismus, *Die Wirklichkeit des Konstruktivismus. Zur Auseinandersetzung um ein neues Paradigma, Heidelberg*, pp 35–45

Glasersfeld Ev (1996) Radikaler Konstruktivismus, *Ideen, Ergebnisse, Probleme. Suhrkamp, Frankfurt/Main*, p 375

Glasersfeld Ev (2009) Relativism, fascism, and the question of ethics in constructivism, *Constructivist Foundations*, **4** (3)

Godel K (1931) On formally undecidable sentences of the Principia Mathematica and related systems I, *Monthly Magazines for Mathematics and Physics*, **38** (1), 173–198

Golec P (2004) *Feedback – a key concept in economics and management*, Available at: http://www.economicswebinstitute.org/glossary/feedback.htm#m1 (archived at https://perma.cc/N5PN-L5FN) (accessed 28 November 2019)

Google Scholar (2019) *Grand+strategy+business*, Available at: https://scholar.google.de/scholar?start=10&q=Grand%2Bstrategy%2Bbusiness&hl=de&as_sdt=0,5 (archived at https://perma.cc/ZH9H-JFRP) (accessed 28 November 2019)

Gore J (1996) *Chaos, Complexity, and the Military*, National Defense University, National War College, Available at: https://apps.dtic.mil/dtic/tr/fulltext/u2/a441996.pdf (archived at https://perma.cc/JJ7Y-F88B)

Gray C (2002) An analysis of the Belousov-Zhabotinskii reaction, *Rose-Hulman Undergraduate Mathematics Journal*, **3** (1), p 1

Greene R (2010) *The 33 Strategies of War*, Profile Books, London

Haken H and Knyazeva H (2000) Arbitrariness in nature: Synergetics and evolutionary laws of prohibition, *Journal for General Philosophy of Science*, **31** (1), pp 57–73

Hallowell R (2009) Humberto Maturana and Francisco Varela's contribution to media ecology: Autopoiesis, the Santiago School of Cognition, and enactive cognitive science, *Proceedings of the Media Ecology Association*, **10**, pp 144–158

Hambrick DC and Mason PA (1984) Upper echelons: The organization as a reflection of its top managers, *Academy of Management Review*, **9** (2), pp 193–206

Harnden R, Leonard A and Beer S (eds) (1994) *How Many Grapes Went into the Wine: Stafford Beer on the art and science of holistic management*, Wiley, Chichester

Hellmann M (2001) Fuzzy logic introduction, *Université de Rennes*, 1

Hetzler S (2008) *Brain-supporting-environments für Entscheide in komplexen Systemen: ein kybernetischer Ansatz für die Gestaltung wirksamer Entscheidungsumfelder*, Dissertation, Rosch-Druck, Schesslitz

Heylighen F (1991) *The Principle of Recursive Systems Construction*, Available at: http://pespmc1.vub.ac.be/Papers/PrinciplesCybSys.pdf (archived at https://perma.cc/EF88-THVW) (accessed 19 March 2020)

Heylighen F (2001a) *Principles of Systems and Cybernetics: An evolutionary perspective*, Available at: http://pespmc1.vub.ac.be/Papers/PrinciplesCybSys.pdf (archived at https://perma.cc/4XGN-EXGZ) (accessed 19 March 2020)

Heylighen F (2001b) *The Science of Self-Organization and Adaptivity*, Available at: http://pespmc1.vub.ac.be/Papers/EOLSS-Self-Organiz.pdf (archived at https://perma.cc/TJ4Z-PD8X) (accessed 21 November 2018)

Holland JH (2000) *Emergence: From chaos to order*, Oxford University Press, Oxford

Holland JH (2006) Studying complex adaptive systems, *Journal of Systems Science and Complexity*, **19** (1), pp 1–8

Holland O and Knight R (2006) The anthropomimetic principle, in *Proceedings of the AISB06 Symposium on Biologically Inspired Robotics*, pp 1–8

Hsieh DA (1991) Chaos and non-linear dynamics: Application to financial markets, *Journal of Finance*, **46** (5), pp 1839–1877

IEEE Systems, Man and Cybernetics Society and IEEE Tokyo Section (1979) *Proceedings of the International Conference on Cybernetics and Society*, Tokyo-Kyoto, Japan, 3–7 November 1978, sponsored by IEEE Systems, Man and Cybernetics Society, IEEE Tokyo Section, IEEE

Iida F and Bovet S (2009) Learning legged locomotion, in *Artificial Life Models in Hardware*, eds A Adamatzky and M Komosinski, pp 21–33, Springer, London

Iida F, Gómez G and Pfeifer R (2005) Exploiting body dynamics for controlling a running quadruped robot, in *Proceedings, 12th International Conference on Advanced Robotics, 2005, ICAR '05*, pp 229–235

Kamaras A (2011) *The Origins of the Greek Financial Crisis: Letter from Thessaloniki*, Available at: https://www.foreignaffairs.com/articles/greece/2011-12-13/origins-greek-financial-crisis (archived at https://perma.cc/T3T7-6RJD) (accessed 26 November 2019)

Kamran Q (2011a) *Complexity of Negotiation and Negotiation of Complexity: Getting to trust*, Available at: https://papers.ssrn.com/sol3/papers.cfm?abstract_id=2137877 (archived at https://perma.cc/MN5F-RS56) (accessed 22 November 2018)

Kamran Q (2011b) Management by deception (MBD): the need for designing a viable strategy, *SSRN Electronic Journal*, Available at: http://dx.doi.org/10.2139/ssrn.2137880 (archived at https://perma.cc/L7JJ-GNMT) (accessed 4 December 2018)

Kamran Q (2012) *'Complexity', the 6th Competitive Force that Shapes Management Strategy: A cybernetic approach to 'Porter's Five Forces that Shapes Industry Strategy' in Turbulent and Complex Environments*, Available at: https://papers.ssrn.com/sol3/papers.cfm?abstract_id=2137853 (archived at https://perma.cc/A2Z8-2BE7) (accessed 22 November 2018)

Kamran Q (2017, January 26) Developing robust strategic models based on sciences of cybernetics, in *International Conference, Impact of Globalization to National Economies and Business*, Case study published under the title 'Kamran, Qeis, An Empirical Case Study of Applying the Sixth Force Model on a German Hidden Champion' (14 May 2017), Riga

Kauffman SA (2008) Reinventing the Sacred: A new view of science, reason, and religion, Basic Books, New York

Kellert SH (1993) *In the Wake of Chaos: Unpredictable order in dynamical systems*, University of Chicago Press, Chicago

Korn J (2011) From the systemic view to systems science, *Kybernetes*, **40** (1/2), pp 23–46

Krippendorff K (1996) A second-order cybernetics of otherness, *Systems Research*, **13** (3), pp 311–328

Krippendorff K (2007) Design research, an oxymoron?, in *Design Research Now: Essays and selected projects*, ed R Michel, pp 67–80, Birkhäuser Basel, Basel

Kurzweil R (2005) *The Singularity is Near: When humans transcend biology*, Penguin, London

Lane D and Maxfield R (1995) *Foresight, Complexity, and Strategy*, Santa Fe Institute, Santa Fe, NM

Leonard A (1999) A viable system model: Consideration of knowledge management, *Journal of Knowledge Management Practice*, August

Lettvin JY, Maturana HR, McCulloch WS, *et al* (1959) What the frog's eye tells the frog's brain, *Proceedings of the IRE*, **47** (11), pp 1940–1951

Levy D (1994) Chaos theory and strategy: Theory, application, and managerial implications, *Strategic Management Journal*, **15** (S2), pp 167–178

Lorenz EN (1963) Deterministic nonperiodic flow, *Journal of the Atmospheric Sciences*, **20** (2), pp 130–141

Lorenz EN (1993) *The Essence of Chaos*, University of Washington Press, Seattle

Lounsbury M and Hirsch PM (2010) *Markets on Trial: The economic sociology of the U.S. financial crisis Part A*, Emerald, Bingley, UK

Lungarella M, Iida F, Bongard J, *et al* (2007) *50 Years of Artificial Intelligence: Essays dedicated to the 50th anniversary of artificial intelligence*, Springer, London

Lusch RF and Vargo SL (eds) (2015) *The Service-Dominant Logic of Marketing: Dialog, debate, and directions*, Routledge, New York

Mahoney JT (2002) The relevance of Chester I. Barnard's teachings to contemporary management education: Communicating the aesthetics of management, *International Journal Organization Theory and Behavior*, **5** (1–2), pp 159–172

Malik F (1984) *Strategie des Managements komplexer Systeme*, Haupt, Bern & Stuttgart

Malik F (2000) *Strategie des Managements komplexer Systeme: Ein Beitrag zur Management-Kybernetik evolutionärer Systeme*, Haupt, Bern

Malik F (2007) *Management: Das A und O des Handwerks*, Campus-Verl, Frankfurt/Main

Malkiel BG and Fama EF (1970) Efficient capital markets: A review of theory and empirical work, *Journal of Finance*, **25** (2), pp 383–417

Mandelbrot B and Taleb NN (2010) Mild vs. wild randomness: Focusing on those risks that matter, in *The Known, the Unknown and the Unknowable in Financial Institutions: Measurement and theory advancing practice*, pp 47–58, Princeton University Press, Princeton

Mandelbrot BB (1977) *Fractals: Form, chance, and dimension*, WH Freeman, San Francisco

Mandelbrot BB (2003) Multifractal power law distributions: Negative and critical dimensions and other 'anomalies,' explained by a simple example, *Journal of Statistical Physics*, **110** (3–6), pp 739–774

March JG, Simon HA and Guetzkow HS (1993) *Organizations*, Blackwell, Cambridge

Maslow AH (1966) *The Psychology of Science: A renaissance*, Harper & Row, New York

Maturana HR (1975) The organization of the living: A theory of the living organization, *International Journal of Man-Machine Studies*, 7 (3), pp 313–332

Maturana HR (1978) Biology of language: The epistemology of reality, in *Psychology and Biology of Language and Thought*, eds GA Miller and E Lenneberg, Academic Press, New York

Maturana HR (1980) *Autopoiesis and Cognition: The realization of the living*, Springer Netherlands, Dordrecht

Maturana HR and Varela FJ (1980) Autopoiesis: The organization of the living, *Autopoiesis and Cognition: The Realization of the Living*, **42**, 59–138

May RM (1976) Simple mathematical models with very complicated dynamics, *Nature*, **261** (5560), pp 459–467

McBride N (2005) Chaos theory as a model for interpreting information systems in organizations, *Information Systems Journal*, **15** (3), pp 233–254

McCulloch W and Pitts W (1943) A logical calculus of the ideas immanent in nervous system, *Bulletin of Mathematical Biophysics*, **5**

McCulloch WS (1961) What is a number, that a man may know it, and a man, that he may know a number, *General Semantics Bulletin*, **26** (27), pp 7–18

McCulloch WS (1989) *Collected Works of Warren S. McCulloch*, Intersystems Publishing

Merton RC (1976) Option pricing when underlying stock returns are discontinuous, *Journal of Financial Economics*, **3** (1–2), pp 125–144

Metzinger T (2004) *Being No One: The self-model theory of subjectivity*, MIT Press, Boston, MA

Mintzberg H, Ahlstrand BW and Lampel J (1998) *Strategy Safari: A guided tour through the wilds of strategic management*, Free Press, New York

Mitleton-Kelly E (2003) *Complex Systems and Evolutionary Perspectives on Organisations: The application of complexity theory to organisations*, Elsevier Science Ltd, Amsterdam

Müller A (2006) To navigate is to construct, in *Die Archive des Heinz von Foerster*, eds K Stocker and W Muchitsch, pp 39–70, Sammeln. Turia + Kant, Vienna

Naumann K, Shalikashvili J, Inge P, *et al* (2007) *Towards a Grand Strategy for an Uncertain World: Renewing Transatlantic relationship*, Noaber Foundation, Available at: https://csis-prod.s3.amazonaws.com/s3fs-public/event/080110_grand_strategy_0.pdf?N4V9isn5FfRIBvHu4ZWKH85PjSN1.FLe (archived at https://perma.cc/TG6C-6BW9)

Newell A, Simon HA, *et al* (1972) *Human Problem Solving*, Prentice Hall, Englewood Cliffs, NJ

O'Reilly CA and Tushman ML (2011) Organizational ambidexterity in action: How managers explore and exploit, *California Management Review*, **53** (4), pp 5–22

Orwell G (1990) *Nineteen Eighty-Four*, Penguin Books, London

Osinga F (2005) *Science, Strategy and War*, Eburon Academic Publishers, Delft, The Netherlands

Palmer KD (2000, May) Meta-systems engineering, in *Proceedings of the Tenth Annual International Symposium of the International Council on Systems Engineering*

Pamkowska M (2008) Autopoiesis in virtual organizations, *Informatica Economica*, **12** (1), pp 33–39

Pask G (1961) *An Approach to Cybernetics*, Hutchinson, New York

PBS Nova (2000) *Transcripts: Trillion dollar bet*, Available at: https://www.pbs.org/wgbh/nova/transcripts/2704stockmarket.html (archived at https://perma.cc/SC54-64EH) (accessed 1 December 2019)

PCW (1993) *Welcome to Principia Cybernetica Web*, Available at: http://pespmc1.vub.ac.be/ (archived at https://perma.cc/J28V-6TWP) (accessed 30 November 2019)

Perna C and Sibillo M (2008) *Mathematical and Statistical Methods in Insurance and Finance*, Springer-Verlag Italia, Milano

Pfeifer R (1996) Symbols patterns, and behavior: Beyond the information-processing metaphor, *Encyclopedia of Microcomputers*, **17**, pp 253–275

Pfeifer R and Bongard J (2007) *How the Body Shapes the Way We Think: A new view of intelligence*, MIT Press, Cambridge, MA

Pfeifer R and Iida F (2004) Embodied artificial intelligence: Trends and challenges, in *Embodied Artificial Intelligence: International Seminar, Dagstuhl Castle, Germany, July 7–11, 2003, Revised Papers*, eds F Iida, R Pfeifer, L Steels and Y Kuniyoshi, pp 1–26, Springer, Berlin

Pfeifer R, Lungarella M and Iida F (2012) The challenges ahead for bio-inspired 'soft' robotics, *Communications of the ACM*, **55** (11), pp 76–87

Porter ME (1985a) *Competitive Advantage: Creating and sustaining superior performance*, Free Press, New York

Porter ME (1985b) Technology and competitive advantage, *Journal of Business Strategy*, **5** (3), pp 60–78

Porter ME (1996) What is strategy?, *Harvard Business Review*, **73** (6) (accessed 22 November 2018)

Porter ME (2008) *On Competition: Updated and extended edition*, Harvard Business School Press, Boston, MA

Porter ME and Kramer MR (2011a) Creating shared value, *Harvard Business Review*, **89** (1/2), pp 62–77

Porter ME and Kramer MR (2011b) How to fix capitalism, *Harvard Business Review*

Porter ME and Rivkin JW (2012a) *Restoring U.S. Competitiveness: The looming challenge to U.S. competitiveness*, Harvard Business Review, Boston, MA

Porter ME and Rivkin JW (2012b) The looming challenge to U.S. competitiveness, *Harvard Business Review*, **90** (3), pp 54–61

Posen BR (2008) A grand strategy of restraint, *Finding Our Way: Debating American Grand Strategy*, pp 81–102

Powell SG, Schwaninger M and Trimble C (2001) Measurement and control of business processes, *System Dynamics Review: The Journal of the System Dynamics Society*, **17** (1), pp 63–91

Probst GJB (1987) Selbstorganisation und Entwicklung, *Die Unternehmung*, pp 242–255

Ramachandran VS, Blakeslee S and Shah N (1998) *Phantoms in the Brain: Probing the mysteries of the human mind*, William Morrow, New York

Reinhart CM and Rogoff KS (2008) *This Time is Different: A panoramic view of eight centuries of financial crises*, NBER Working Paper No. 13882, Available at: https://www.nber.org/papers/w13882 (archived at https://perma.cc/YZA5-3597)

Richardson G and Tinaikar S (2004) Accounting based valuation models: What have we learned?, *Accounting & Finance*, **44** (2), pp 223–255

Rocha LM (1996) Eigenbehavior and symbols, *Systems Research*, **13** (3), pp 371–384

Rosenblueth A, Wiener N and Bigelow J (1943) Behavior, purpose and teleology on JSTOR, *Philosophy of Science*, **10** (1), pp 18–24 (accessed 29 November 2019)

Rosnay J de (1998) Entropy and the Laws of Thermodynamics, *Principia Cybernetica Web*, **30**, 2005

Rumelt RP (2007) Strategy's strategist: An interview with Richard Rumelt (Interviewers: Lovallo DP and Mendoca LT.), *McKinsey Quarterly*, **4**, pp 56–67

Rumelt RP (2011) *The Perils of Bad Strategy*, Available at: https://www.mckinsey.com/business-functions/strategy-and-corporate-finance/our-insights/the-perils-of-bad-strategy# (archived at https://perma.cc/9A98-ARWK) (accessed 28 November 2019)

Rumelt RP (2012) Good strategy/bad strategy: The difference and why it matters, *Strategic Direction*, **28** (8)

Sabelli H (2003) Bipolar feedback, *Systems Science and Cybernetics-Volume III*, p 148

Saffiotti A (1997) The uses of fuzzy logic in autonomous robot navigation, *Soft Computing*, **1** (4), pp 180–197

Sayama H (2010) *Complex Systems: Collective Dynamics of Complex Systems*, Research Group at Binghamton University, State University of New York

Schwaninger M (2000) Managing complexity: The path toward intelligent organizations, *Systemic Practice and Action Research*, **13** (2), pp 207–241

Schwaninger M (2001) Intelligent organizations: An integrative framework, *Systems Research and Behavioral Science: The Official Journal of the International Federation for Systems Research*, **18** (2), pp 137–158

Schwaninger M (2003) A cybernetic model to enhance organizational intelligence, *Systems Analysis Modelling Simulation*, **43** (1), pp 53–65

Schwaninger M (2004) What can cybernetics contribute to the conscious evolution of organizations and society?, *Systems Research and Behavioral Science: The Official Journal of the International Federation for Systems Research*, **21** (5), pp 515–527

Schwaninger M (2006a) Design for viable organizations: The diagnostic power of the viable system model, *Kybernetes*, **35** (7/8), pp 955–966

Schwaninger M (2006b) System dynamics and the evolution of the systems movement, *Systems Research and Behavioral Science: The Official Journal of the International Federation for Systems Research*, **23** (5), pp 583–594

Schwaninger M (2006c) The evolution of organizational cybernetics, *Scientiae Mathematicae Japonicae*, **13** (2), pp 856–880

Schwaninger M (2010) Model-based management (MBM): A vital prerequisite for organizational viability, *Kybernetes*, **39** (9/10), pp 1419–1428

Shalizi CR, Shalizi KL and Haslinger R (2004) Quantifying self-organization with optimal predictors, *Physical Review Letters*, **93** (11), p 118701

Shannon CE and Weaver W (1949) *The Mathematical Theory of Communication*, University of Illinois, Pretoria, IL

Simon HA (1947) *Administrative Behavior: A study of decision-making processes in administrative organization: a Foreword by Chester Barnard*, Macmillan, New York

Simon HA (1996) *The Sciences of the Artificial*, MIT Press, Cambridge, MA

Simon HA (2002) *What We Know about Learning*, Available at: http://158.132.155.107/posh97/private/learning/learning-simon.htm (archived at https://perma.cc/K6BP-WJZQ) (accessed 30 November 2019)

Simon HA and March J (1976) *Administrative Behavior Organization*, Free Press, New York

Simonsen J (1994) *Herbert A. Simon: Administrative behavior: How organizations can be understood in terms of decision processes*, Dissertation, Computer Science, Roskilde University

Smuts JC (1926) *Holism and Evolution*, Рипол Классик, The Macmillan Company, New York

Smuts JC (1952) *Jan Christian Smuts: A biography*, Morrow, New York

Stewart I (1997) *Does God Play Dice? The new mathematics of chaos*, Penguin, London

Stewart I (2012) *The Mathematical Equation that Caused the Banks to Crash*, Available at: https://www.theguardian.com/science/2012/feb/12/black-scholes-equation-credit-crunch (archived at https://perma.cc/P9FS-YH4T) (accessed 1 December 2019)

Story L, Thomas Jr. L and Schwartz ND (2010) *Wall St. Helped Greece to Mask Debt Fueling Europe's Crisis*, Available at: http://archive.nytimes.com/www.nytimes.com/2010/02/14/business/global/14debt.html (archived at https://perma.cc/89XP-DD6W) (accessed 26 November 2019)

Taleb NN (2007) Black swans and the domains of statistics, *The American Statistician*, **61** (3), pp 198–200

Time Magazine (1949) *Science: The Thinking Machine*, Available at: http://content.time.com/time/magazine/article/0,9171,799721,00.html (archived at https://perma.cc/8JQL-BEF5) (accessed 29 November 2019)

Triana P (2010) *The Flawed Maths of Financial Models*, Available at: https://www.ft.com/content/2794cfc4-f97a-11df-9e29-00144feab49a#axzz28cIuiihf (archived at https://perma.cc/6CV5-UYFX) (accessed 1 December 2019)

Triclot M (2006) Norbert Wiener's politics and the history of cybernetics, in *The Global and the Local: The History of Science and the Cultural Integration of Europe*, Proceedings of the 2nd ICESHS, Cracow, Poland

Turchin V (1977) *The Phenomenon of Science: A cybernetic approach to human evolution*, Columbia University Press, New York

Turchin V and Joslyn C (1999) The metasystem transition, *Principia Cybernetica Web*, http://pespmc1.vub.ac.be/MST.html (archived at https://perma.cc/4QRT-QHZU)

Turing AM (1952) The chemical basis of morphogenesis, *Philosophical Transactions of the Royal Society B: Biological Sciences*, **237** (641), pp 37–72

Ulrich H (1968) *Die Unternehmung als produktives soziales System: Grundlagen der allgemeinen Unternehmungslehre*, Haupt, Bern

Ulrich H (1994) Reflexionen über Wandel und Management, in *Unternehmerischer Wandel*, pp 5–29, Springer, Berlin

Ulrich H (2001) *Gesammelte Schriften: Die Unternehmung als produktives soziales System*, Haupt, Bern

Ulrich H and Probst GJB (eds) (1984) *Self-organization and Management of Social Systems: Insights, promises, doubts, and questions*, Springer-Verlag, Berlin

von Bertalanffy L (1969) *General System Theory: Foundations, development, applications*, Braziller, New York

Varela FG, Maturana HR and Uribe R (1974) Autopoiesis: The organization of living systems, its characterization and a model, *Biosystems*, **5** (4), pp 187–196

Vargo SL, Lusch RF and Morgan FW (2015) Historical perspectives on service-dominant logic, in *The Service-Dominant Logic of Marketing: Dialog, debate, and directions*, eds RF Lusch and SL Vargo, pp 29–42, Routledge, London

Velasquéz T (2009) *Chaos Theory and the Science of Fractals, and Their Application in Risk Management*, Copenhagen Business School, Copenhagen

Vlad S, Pascu P and Morariu N (2010) Chaos models in economics, *Journal of Computing*

Walby S (2007) Complexity theory, systems theory, and multiple intersecting social inequalities, *Philosophy of the Social Sciences*, **37** (4), pp 449–470

Whitehead AN and Russel B (1910) *Mathematica*, Vol 1, Cambridge University Press, Cambridge

Wiener N (1947) A Scientist Rebels, *Atlantic Monthly*, January, p 46

Wiener N (1948) *Cybernetics: Or control and communication in the animal and the machine*, MIT Press, Cambridge, MA

Wiener N (1950) *The Human Use of Human Beings: Cybernetics and society*, Da Capo Press, New York

Wolfram S (2002) *A New Kind of Science*, Wolfram Media, Champaign, IL

Xian YJ and Tham E (2011) *Modeling the (Mis)Behavior of Markets: Lessons for the future*, Risk Management Society Publications

Yen J and Pfluger N (1992) A fuzzy logic based robot navigation system, in *AAAI Technical Report*, pp 195–199

Yolles M (2004) Implications for Beer's ontological system/metasystem dichotomy, *Kybernetes*, **33** (3/4), pp 726–764

Zadeh LA (1965) Fuzzy sets, *Information and Control*, **8** (3), pp 338–353

Zadeh LA (1994) Fuzzy logic, neural networks, and soft computing, *Communications of the ACM*, **37** (3), pp 77–85

03

Introducing the six forces model

Chapter 3 describes the author's six forces model (SFM), which enables firms to cope with viability and managing complexity based on 'Ashby's Law of Requisite Variety' while embedded in their total environments (the multi-layer and holistic perspective). The SFM enables firms to look beyond the limitations of industry-in structures and a purely economic lens and thus it invites scholars and practitioners to take a systemic world-view. Furthermore, the model is based on the notion of 'structure is strategy', as highlighted in previous chapters; it emphasizes the essential role of structural integration within the dimensions of organizational realities constructed on the logic of 'embodiment' and interactional intelligence (Pfeifer and Bongard, 2007), whereby a new understanding of competitive strategy can be derived, not only from a top–down management decision.

As aforementioned, Ashby's Law is substantial to competitive strategy by bringing forth the logic of strategy seen as variety engineering and thus enabling the firms' navigators to deal with diverse environmental perturbations as varieties they need to absorb, while amplifying the regulating varieties. By applying the logic of systemic thinking and cybernetics, as the next foundation of strategic thought in turbulent environments, it is a necessity for competitive strategy to underpin the logic of organizational homeostasis by coping within the complex duality of the academic and practical field. Beer's VSM, as thoroughly described in Chapter 2, and as its diagnostic capabilities have been documented and demonstrated by Beer (1972, 1981, 1985), Christopher (2007), Malik (1984, 2013, 2015), Hetzler (2008), Schwaninger (1990a, 1990b, 2006, 2007, 2010a, 2010b), Schwaninger and Scheef (2016), Ríos (2012), Espejo and Reyes (2001). It is one of the most robust organizational theories applied to the field of competitive strategy and it enables the dynamics of the firm's 'eigen behaviours' (Foerster, 2003) to unleash self-organizing powers (Hayek, 1945), cultivating regulatory varieties, so the organization can cope with the emergent and unforeseen challenges that the contemporary top–down computational-driven competitive strategy world-view is unable to cope with. This notion was also observed by von Hayek as 'catallaxy'. Strategists need to understand that in a world regulated by the 'invisible hand' (Smith, 1776), one cannot manage on the basis of a top–down analogy. This is a clear violation of Ashby's Law, Beer's principle of 'autonomy' (Beer, 1959, 1972, 1985) within the VSM, which Varela and Maturana referred to as 'autopoiesis' (Maturana, 1980), Ashby's (1962) 'principle of self-organizing systems' and thus Kant's 'critique of judgment' (Ashby, 1962).

Ashby states about the notion of teleology:

> ... we do have to consider organism in terms of ends if we examine the typical processes of formation, growth, and reproduction that characterize such things: the apparent self-organization of the object in maintaining its structure and preserving its own existence through time (Ashby, 1962).

According to Schwaninger (2006):

> ... To the best of the author's knowledge, no other organizational theory makes a claim as strong as this one. One would assume that evidence contradictory to the contentions of the VSM has been found. The surprising fact is, however, that the model has not been falsified but, on the contrary, corroborated by the growing empirical evidence from VSM applications.

However, it is to note here that besides the wider application of Beer's VSM there has been no real enhancement or extension of the model, even by Beer's protégés, such as Malik and Schwaninger, who have contributed much to its application and publicity but not to the VSM's further development. While researchers such as Espejo and Reyes (2001) and Ríos (2012) have developed a software application for the model, a wider extension of the model or embedding the VSM into a larger context has not yet been introduced.

Via this book's contribution to bridge a management cybernetics approach and Porter's FFM leading to design the wider SFM, the author has contributed a vital aspect that has been lacking in strategic management. Thus, as stated by Kearney (ATkearney.com, 2014): 'There are many excellent stand-alone concepts, but no overriding framework.' Beer's challenges were always to save the firm from the environmental perturbations and complex problems that organizations face. The rise of many large corporations with less consideration for a societal dimension of management and strategy brought scholars such as Porter and Kramer (2011) and Porter and Rivkin (2012a), who were actually true advocates of profits and economic dimensions of managerial and strategic thought, mainly introduced through the works of the Austrian School of Economics (Hayek, 1945; Menger and Hayek, 1981; Mises, 1983; Mises and Adler, 1935; Rothbard, 1990) and by the works of Friedman (1962), who took liberal economics and the notion of shareholder value to the social responsibility of corporations, to shift their thinking and understanding of the vital issues that Porter himself originally criticized, even criticizing his own professor Andrews in the 1970s at Harvard Business School (Hagel *et al*, 2010).

Andrews' framework put the viability of a social community as a main priority of business. Strategy's concerns are not only that businesses should be immune to environmental challenges, but furthermore that the environment and societies are protected from the failures and organizational collapses of corporations, as well as their compliance malfunctions, as the latest Volkswagen case, where the crisis continues, has clearly demonstrated. This notion was also substantiated by Porter and Rivkin (2012a) in analysing the 2008 global managerial (Hackhausen, 2009) (financial) crises. Porter and Rivkin (2012a) observe that it is essential to establish a clear understanding of the implications of competitiveness and its influence on US prosperity in order to attend to America's economic prospects. They state that there is a significant misunderstanding regarding the concept of competitiveness, which leads to critical consequences for political discourse, policy and corporate choices. Porter and Rivkin further argue that the US can only resolve such problematic issues by developing a strategic plan that provides a united direction and involves all government levels rather than by following steps guided by the self-interest of single-issue advocacy groups. Thus, resolving challenges in the business environment and local communities is a sensible first step as organizations can realize contributions to 'America's competitiveness' (Porter and Rivkin, 2012a) while simultaneously seizing opportunities of innovation and growth (Porter and Rivkin, 2012b).

Figure 3.1 (parts a and b) describes the management board constructed of the VSM's systems 3, 4 and 5 as presented according to Beer, whereby the main concentration is based on managing the inside operations, managing the future and overall identity of the organization/firm. The author – according to the challenges of corporate failures above, but moreover based on the field application of the SFM at Peter Lacke Group (PLG), a leading global paint and coating producing company to diverse industries such as automotive, glass and home appliances to sport and leisure instruments – suggests adding another crucial sub-system to Beer's VSM. This system is coined by the author as 'system 5*' (5 star). The main function of system 5* is to enable the organization to have an outside-in view and independent conscious and control system. The VSM can be a part of the whole system, also observed as system 5 and corporate ethos. However, while some argue that system 5 already covers this aspect as the ethos of the firm, the empirical challenges that the author had in actually applying the VSM to PLG (Kamran, 2018c) have illustrated how essential system 5* is, while challenges in the corporate world underpin the author's notion.

The application of the theoretical foundations of the book to PLG was due to the necessity to validate the author's theoretical framework based on the triangulation method of quantitative research, qualitative research and a case-based application to a firm testing the model in practice as an essential part and case-based analysis. Due to the complexity that the VSM embodies, its understanding for the practitioner at the corporate and firm levels and also by the very nature of how German SMEs are structured – with an 'advisory council' called 'Beirat' – it is necessary that this system is embedded within the spectrum of the five systems the VSM has. The advisory council is a legally mandatory and integral part of the corporate governance, ethical dimension, strategic direction and control of German SMEs and, furthermore, it enables the firm's advisory and corporate governance to occupy a neutral outside-in look by applying the essential aspects discussed in Chapter 2, also as the notion of second-order cybernetics (Foerster, 1958; Foerster *et al*, 1960).

However, it is necessary to understand that the advisory council is not a part of the internal organization nor operative structure in terms of its system 3 of the VSM-operative management, but rather it is made up of outside-in observers. The councils are made up of members from diverse fields in pre-arranged settings and deadlines, making sure to control the actions and strategies of the managing director or CEO of the firm. By underpinning the indication that the profundity of an observation lies within the observer's competence, observing entails responsibility and contributes to Ulrich's framework of scientific practice and seeing companies as social productive systems (Ulrich, 1970, 2001).

This conscious system is described in the author's VSM extension in the figures below as VSM system 5*. A chief additional reason for the author to develop the system below was to integrate the meaning of 'structure' with competitive strategy beyond the notion observed by Chandler, making the VSM understandable and applicable to PLG. According to Hall and Saias

(1980): 'Structure determines the introduction and subsequent development of strategic planning... The structure can make an organization more or less shortsighted... Structural characteristics act like filters and limit what the organization can see'. Hence, a good corporate ethos based on the VSM and the extension by system 5* would help PLG not to make errors that could cost the firm by losing overall fitness, based on myopic adventures. This is the cornerstone of managing a family business over many successful generations. In Figure 3.1 an attempt has been made to define the author's notion of what organizational structure stands for.

These vital components of structure are necessary not only because they fit the acronyms outlined in Figure 3.2, but also, as the author has documented, it is essential to have a holistic understanding of strategy. Therefore 'structure' in terms of strategy comprises:

1. Strategy – based on a systemic triad as diagnosis, a plan, and execution (Rumelt, 2012)
2. Teams – human capital (Smith, [1776]; Schultz, 1961)
3. Resources – operand and operant resources the firm needs as described by the resource-based view of the firm (Prahalad and Hamel, 2006)
4. Uniqueness and unique set of capabilities (Porter, 1985, 1996; Prahalad and Hamel, 2006) – dynamic capabilities (Teece, 1996)
5. Culture – core rigidities (Leonard-Barton, 1992) and operant resources of the firm (Vargo and Lusch, 2004)
6. Trust and systemic interrelated integrity – control and communication
7. Units and sub-systems – systems and sub-systems interacting recursively (Beer, 1972, 1985)
8. Relations internally and externally – the ability of a holistic and solid response; embodiment, interactional intelligence (Pfeifer and Bongard, 2007)
9. Environment – total environment of the firm (Porter 1980, 2008; Beer, 1972, 1979, 1985), evolution and emergence (Mintzberg *et al*, 1998).

The notion of how structure affects strategic decisions and planning is described in Figure 3.2. Schwaninger argues that the quality of a strategy is dependent on its diagnostic basis and analytical phases. He further describes the necessity of a modular and simultaneously inter-connectable system of planning tools, which are required to ensure the ability to resolve individual planning problems by the use of instruments adapted to specific needs of respective units.

FIGURE 3.1 (a) Management world according to Beer's VSM; (b) Beer's VSM with system 5* extension

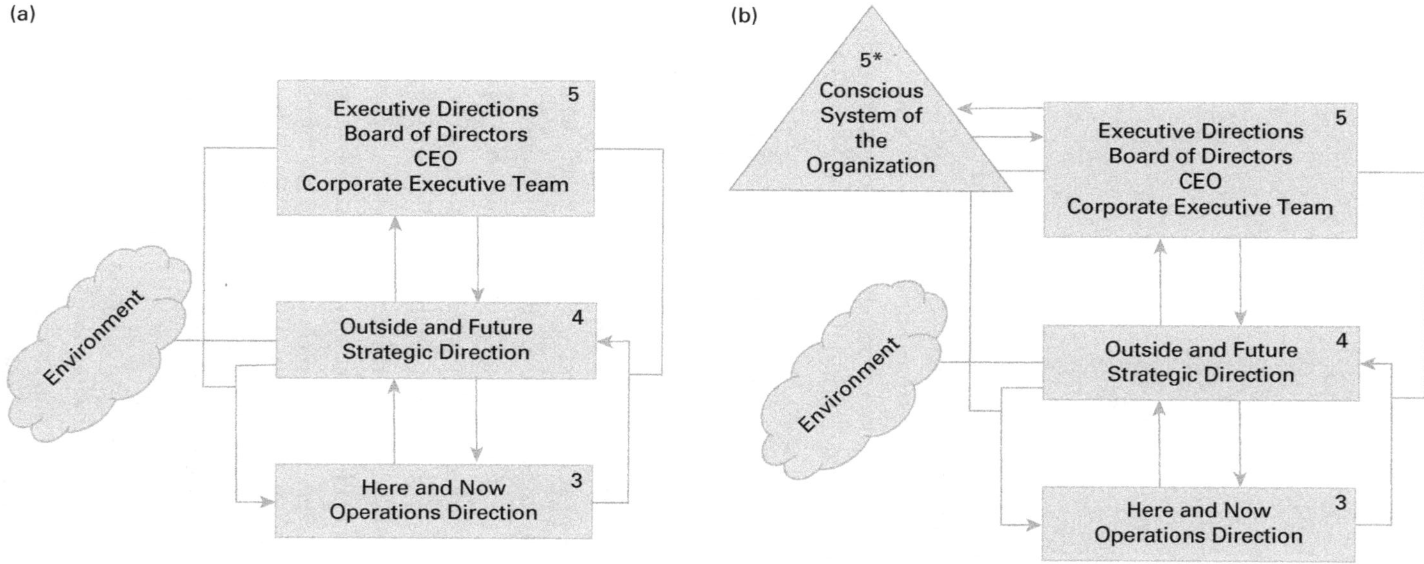

Author's interpretation, based on Beer (1972, 1979, 1985)

FIGURE 3.2 Structure as an enabler of strategic planning and an information filter

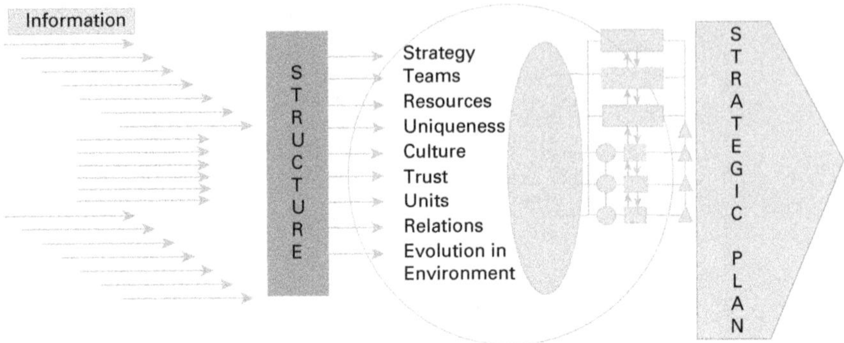

The degree of detail and the coherence or segmentation of the relevant business system are described as decisive factors for the selection of planning tools, while instruments are selected based on flexibility and adaptability to material, structural and terminological characteristics of the organization or its parts. Schwaninger appends that comparability and compatibility of data must be accomplished by implementing necessary standards of uniformity at the corporate level (Schwaninger, 1987). In competitive strategy time and the ability to process information for a solid response play a major role. This analogy has been underpinned by the notion of eigen behaviour in terms of systemic variety according to Ashby's Law.

Strategists must be able to cope with inadequate information and uncertainties while prescribing and applying adequate remedies to the challenges they are facing and the decisions they are making, thus due to this nature of strategic and decision-making problems, the analogy of seeing structure as the core part of high-quality strategies can therefore be underpinned. This notion can be coined as the term 'strategic homeostasis', thus homeostasis in organizations is among the main prerequisites to viability. Therefore, 'eigen states' of the organism permit it to refer each incoming signal to its own self, that is, to establish self-reference with respect to the outside world. Emergent strategies can only outgrow based on structure that can maintain its 'eigen values' used in terms of a cybernetic epistemology: 'The meaning of the signals of the sensorium is determined by the motorium; and the meaning of the signals of the motorium are determined by the sensorium' (Foerster, 2003). Hence, this logic entails a structural logic in competitive strategy based on Wiener's original terminology: 'circular causal and feedback mechanisms in biological and social systems' (Steer, 1952). The feedback mechanism is thus ubiquitous in control systems.

Complexity and strategy

'Complex strategy' was coined by the author and resembles the essence of strategy and how it copes with the complexities arising within the business environment. Strategy is, in essence, the unification and alignment of a diverse set of interrelated structural systems and cognitive activities to achieve a better state. By the author's design of the model below, another attempt is made to substantiate his claim of 'structure is strategy' (Kamran, 2018a) (see Figure 3.3). Substantiating Beer's VSM and the notion of 'the purpose of a system is what it does' (Beer, 2002), it is the purpose of competitive strategy to design immunity and long-term viability for the organization. Beer quotes Botvinnik, the famous Russian chess player's conclusion on playing chess: '... until the 'depth' picture resolves itself at a level where one can legitimately take a decision the proper course is to strengthen oneself' (Beer, 1985). The essence of 'structure is strategy – methodology', as Figure 3.3 shows, can be conveyed by the following points:

1 structure (a viable and self-organized autopoietic organizational system) (Beer, 1972, 1981, 1985; Maturana, 1980);

2 transformation (Malik, 2007) (ability to transform – not merely growth but development);

3 resources (RBV) (Mahoney and Pandian, 1992) (VRIO – valuable, rare, imperfectly imitable, substitutability) (Barney, 1991);

4 adaptation (ability to adapt to changing environment faster than the competition; this also means shaping the organizational milieu) (Mintzberg *et al*, 1998);

5 teams (recursive organized teams working in concert and based on the VSM) (Beer, 1985);

6 emergence (ability to cope and handle emergent phenomena and strategic challenges) (Mintzberg *et al*, 1998; Müller-Stewens and Lechner, 2011);

7 goals (MBO and self-control) (Drucker, 1954);

8 yardstick (doing the right thing/leadership) (Drucker, 1954).

It is precisely the broader (multi-layer) understanding of strategy that actually makes strategy one of the most essential parts of the organization and of coping with the complex perturbations an organization faces. Strategy is also the ability of the organization to reflect on itself from a normative perspective, via a second-order intervention as well. According to the author's research, the modelling of a socio-economic strategic system, for enabling it to reflect on itself, to implement the mechanism of the second order, self-repair and self-control or autopoiesis is undoubtedly among the class of highly complex issues, problems and challenges of our contemporary strategic thought.

In the model in Figure 3.3 the author has tried to define this set of complexities and how a viable system (organization) can develop a plan of self-transformation to be a highly effective strategic organization. Organizations are like organisms – a conglomeration of diverse systems and sub-systems to survive via cognitive-structural activity by maintaining systemic homeostasis and designing emergent strategies in order to cope with environmental and competitive challenges. This cognitive-structural activity and ability is part of the organizational structure and cannot be imposed on a system as a top–down phenomenon. Thus, according to Pfeifer and Bongard (2007), '… the body shapes the way we think', and so do social systems as a whole. This notion is also underpinned by Maturana and Varela (1980, p 7), who describe: 'Cognition is a biological phenomenon and can only be understood as such; any epistemological insight into the domain of knowledge requires this understanding' (Maturana and Varela, 1980).

The Chandlerian thesis of 'structure follows strategy' imposes the notion of cognitive ability as a top–down phenomenon disregarding the depth of interrelated systemic structure of cognition in organizations. Furthermore, Chandler's thought may be invalid, as Hall and Saias describe in quoting from Galbraith and Nathanson: 'If a firm has power over its environment so that it can control prices because of monopoly position, tariffs, or close ties to government, it can maintain effective economic performance even if there is a mismatch between strategy and structure' (Galbraith and Nathanson, 1978; Hall and Saias, 1980). This analogy can be summed up by the size of a company and its impact on the ecosystem in which it is embedded. A good example is the fine on Apple by the EU.

Hall and Saias (1980) further emphasize that discrepancies between strategy and structure ultimately result in inefficiency in the long term. This is why it is deemed crucial for strategists to precisely consider structure during the development process of a strategic plan – to prevent inefficiency caused by reliance on the traditional misbelief that structure will follow the strategic plan, which is a particularly dangerous assumption in today's evolving environment. Hall and Saias suggest a revision of the model that structure follows strategy by stating that there is a symmetry in the relationship

FIGURE 3.3 'Structure is strategy' framework

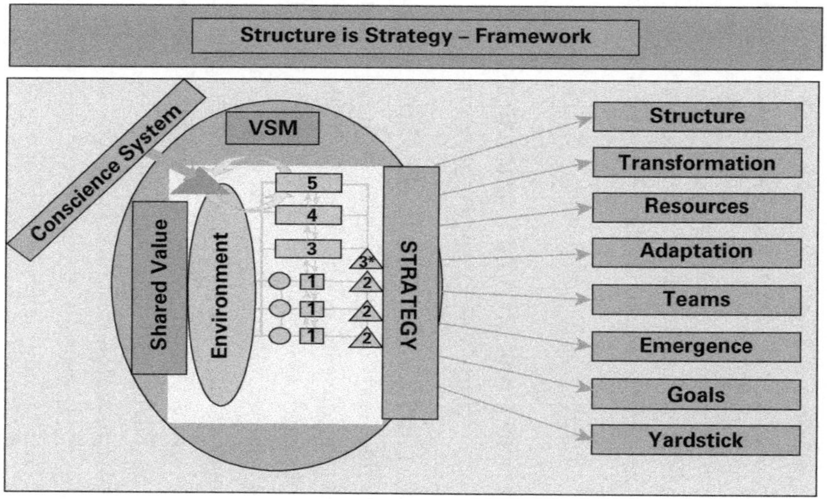

between strategy, structure and the environment. as environment as well as structure and strategy shape their counterparts (Galbraith and Nathanson, 1978; Hall and Saias, 1980).

According to Wesley M. Cohen and Daniel A. Levinthal (1990):

> The premise of the notion of absorptive capacity is that the organization needs prior related knowledge to assimilate and use new knowledge. Studies in the area of cognitive and behavioral sciences at the individual level both justify and enrich this observation. Research on memory development suggests that accumulated prior knowledge increases both the ability to put new knowledge into memory, what we would refer to as the acquisition of knowledge, and the ability to recall and use it.

The dimension of 'structure is strategy' would embrace the firm with absorptive capacities and hence this notion has the merit of not violating Ashby's Law.

In-depth reflections on organizational structure – the VSM and FFM, a necessary synergy

Chandler (1962), in his original study, paved the way on how changes in strategy as product market diversification required ensuing amendments in structure, precisely division of the firm (D. Miller, 1986). Many scholars around the globe, such as Channon (1973), Dyas (1972), Thanheiser (1972), Rumelt (1974), Porter (1980, 1985), Rumelt, Schendel and Teece (1991, 1994), Whittington and Mayer (2006) and Whittington (2008) have written scientific publications in confirmation of Chandler's thesis.

According to Pugh *et al* (1968), organization theory has six primary dimensions of organization structure: (1) specialization; (2) standardization; (3) formalization; (4) centralization; (5) configuration; and (6) flexibility. Ansoff (1971) emphasizes the role: of (1) a centralized functional form; (2) a decentralized divisional form; (3) a project management form; and (4) an innovative form. Miles *et al* (1978) propose: (1) product-market domains as strategy; and (2) construct mechanisms as structures and processes of the organization. Miller (1986) underpins this by analysing strategy: (1) taking one or two elements of strategy at a time, 'eg innovation, or salespersons to total employees, or relative product qualitative' (Miles *et al*, 1978); and (2) 'elements of structure cohere within common configurations, as do those of strategy' (Miles *et al*, 1978). This notion is also substantiated by Ansoff (1971), who refers to four categories that shape structure under the auspices of 'performance', while applying the RBV as: (1) steady-state efficiency; (2) operating responsiveness; (3) strategic responsiveness; (4) structural responsiveness; (5) decision and information quality criteria. Miles *et al* (1974) ask to what extent firms and organizations shape their environments and via which characteristics, (1) strategies; (2) technologies; (3) structures; and (4) processes, do firms need to interact with their specific environments and how success can be determined thereof.

There are still many diverse views on strategy and structure-related issues respectively on the typologies, where the field has its centres of gravity. The author proposes another vital aspect to the aforementioned views of the field. Thus, Beer's VSM could be argued to be a new beginning in breaking the weakness that the Porterian FFM incorporates, as the most influential works based on industry structure and strategic performance of the firm. Beer (1972) states:

> It is interesting to begin the analysis of hierarchic control structures by asking about the basic decision elements of which ranks and orders of command are in general composed. In nature, and if we consider that most sophisticated control system the brain, this element might be identified as a single nerve cell or neuron. In industry or – government – indeed in any strongly cohesive social group- the element is some sort of manager.

Managers need a solid control system and the VSM is a powerful control model to be synergized with Porter's FFM.

FIGURE 3.4 Introduction of the VSM to the FFM

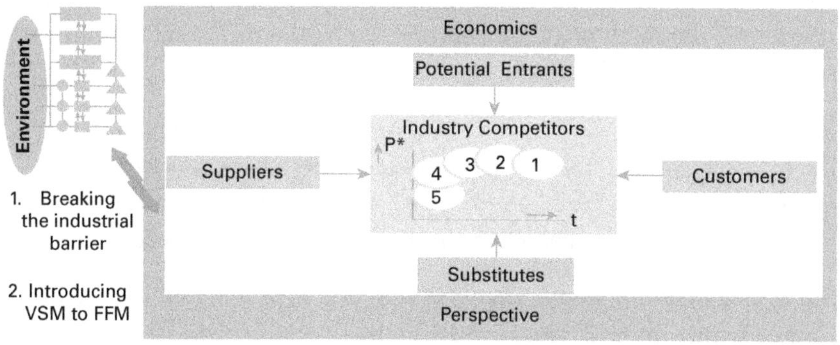

Author's interpretation, based on Kamran (2016, 2017), Porter (1979, 1980, 2008) and Beer (1972, 1981, 1985)

The above perception is necessary, thus structure is the prerequisite to higher strategic performance. The analogy to put viability as the *raison d'être* of strategy is not only a novel approach, but it is an approach that actually connects other justified approaches, as illustrated above. What the field of competitive strategy lacks is a unified theory that the science of cybernetics can deliver. The VSM will be integrated with the author's extension of the 5* sub-system, which the author has already provided.

Design of the SFM model

In essence the SFM is constructed based on the model-based management analogy that modelling reality is a must for strategists in business administration according to the proven theorem of Conant-Ashby. This is according to the concept and dimension of business model innovation (BMI). According to Wirtz *et al* (2016): 'The concept of business models has reached global impact, both for company's competitive success and in management science.' Ritter and Lettl (2018) describe the essence of BMI as:

> ... business-model research is not necessarily a 'theory on its own' and that it can be more fruitfully understood as a theoretical mechanism for combining different literature streams. As such, business-model research is positioned as a central connecting component in the further development of the strategic management field.

While Priem *et al* (2018) emphasize: 'Value creation for consumers, as the *conditio sine qua non* for value capture, is at the heart of demand-side strategy research and is a core element of almost any business model.' They furthermore argue '... that both the demand-side perspective and the business model concept could jointly promote a better understanding of strategy-making by mutually relying on the distinctive insights from each stream.' Foss and Saebi (2018) describe:

> While research on business models and BMI continue to exhibit growth, the field is still, even after more than two decades of research, characterized by a striking lack of cumulative theorizing and an opportunistic borrowing of more or less related ideas from neighbouring fields in the place of cumulative theory.

The author's aspirations to design the SFM go to the heart of contemporary research within the field. Thus, the gap and lack of a solid theory that fills this is put forward; by the interdisciplinary and holistic approach to put a solid model of competitive strategy (CS) and strategic management (SM) at the hand of strategists and managers to make better sense of the complex realities of global competition. Fjeldstad and Snow (2018) furthermore confirm the author's approach:

> Despite a voluminous literature, business model research continues to be plagued with problems. Those problems hinder theory development and make it difficult for managers to use research findings in their decision-making… organization design is affected by value configuration and how new collaborative organizational forms enable open and agile business models. We derive the implications of our analysis for future research and management practice.

According to Hacklin *et al* (2018): 'Unpacking BMI allows us to discuss contingencies for the main business model strategies, specifically in terms of limitations to – and opportunities of – changing the primary business model and the practice of parallel business models.' Thus the SFM unpacks the essence of BMI in strategy development of the firm by aligning all the important aspects of its foundation and the evolutionary dimension of emergent strategic management. Teece (2018) describes:

> Business models, dynamic capabilities, and strategy are interdependent. The strength of a firm's dynamic capabilities helps shape its proficiency at business model design. Through its effect on organization design, a business model influences the firm's dynamic capabilities and places bounds on the feasibility of particular strategies. While these relationships are understood at a theoretical level, there is a need for future empirical work to flesh out the details. In particular, studies that provide a better understanding of BMI, implementation, and change will also shed light on important aspects of dynamic capabilities.

This dimension has been taken into high consideration by the author, hence via the integration of the VSM and the interdisciplinary approach put forward as incorporation of systems and cybernetics sciences underpin Teece's essential aspect in terms of the interdependencies of structural design substantiated by the author's analogy of 'structure is the strategy'. This dimension is essential. Based on the vast literature covered, the vital aspects of the author's strategic mindset are confirmed by the most rigorous and high-impact literature since the inception of the field of strategy. The author has followed Teece's evolutionary development as one of the most profound thinkers. As Teece (2010) states: 'Whenever a business enterprise is established, it either explicitly or implicitly employs a particular business model that describes the design or architecture of the value creation, delivery, and capture mechanisms it employs.' This development of Teece and the author, while looking at the strategic paradigm from different world-views, the key messages and analogies merge into the coherent whole in terms of the alignment of the role of structural conditions and design of the firms' model on which effective strategies can be executed.

The individual components of the SFM

The SFM describes a holistic view of the organization and its topology in a total environment, rather than the partial economic view and limited spectrum of the industry-in understanding that the FFM has occupied for the last 40 years. The SFM aligns the essentiality of nine spheres, wherein an organization is embedded. As established throughout the book, 'Ashby's Law' and Ulrich's 'scientific practice' (Hetzler, 2008) analogy enable the integration of a coherent set of models and theories based on nine spheres to design the SFM.

The constructed spheres are designed in a way to give a solid holistic model embracing a wider spectrum based on Ashby's Law of applying, extending and engineering organizational varieties to cope with complex challenges that emerge for firms operating in a global, complex and turbulent world. Latest research illustrates: 'Organizations often create and employ artifacts in order to change their routines, but little is known about how artifacts can be designed to intentionally influence routine dynamics' (Glaser, 2017). The SFM – as an artefact of designing for effective strategy-making and consciously acting at the right time and by attaining a better trial-and-error loop – is a dynamic model that requires a solid understanding of the components listed below based on the nine essential layers. However, the model will prove itself to be vital for generating sustainable competitive advantage.

The spheres are designed and constructed in the following manner:

1 Economics layer (Kamran, 2016, 2017) – consisting of shareholder value (Rappaport, 1998), industry-in view (Porter, 1979), red ocean perspective (Kim and Mauborgne, 2005), and clusters (Porter, 1998, 2008).

2 Normative layer (Beer, 1972, 1984, 1985; Gälweiler, 2005; Schwaninger, 2001) – consisting of 'core values and ethics, corporate social responsibility' – this notion can also be aligned based on the works of Porter and Kramer (2011) and Porter and Rivkin (2012b) as the 'shared value model' (SVM) (Porter and Kramer, 2011), identity (Schwaninger, 2001), autopoiesis (Maturana, 1980), legitimacy (Schwaninger, 2001), and *raison d'être* (Drucker, 1954; Gälweiler, 2005; Schwaninger and Scheef, 2016).

3 Resource-based view (RBV) layer (Barney, 1991; Penrose, 1959; Peteraf, 1993; Porter, 1980, 1985, 2008; Porter and Heppelmann, 2014; Wernerfelt, 1984) – structure is strategy lens (Kamran, 2016, 2017), core capabilities (Leonard-Barton, 1992; O'Reilly and Tushman, 2011; Prahalad and Hamel, 2006; Teece *et al*, 1997), information (Wiener, 1948; Beer, 1972, 1981, 1985; Kamran, 2016, 2017), human capital and machinery and material.

4 Technology and innovation layer – blue ocean strategy (Kim and Mauborgne, 2004a, 2004b, 2005), disruptive innovation (Christensen, 1987), big bang disruption (Downes and Nunes, 2013), real-time communication (Beer, 1972, 1981, 1985), ubiquitous computing (Beer, 1972, 1981, 1985), artificial intelligence (AI) (Oke, 2008; Miller, 2019), and Internet of Things (Porter and Heppelmann, 2014).

5 Nature and ecological layer (Ulrich and Krieg, 1972; Porter and Kramer, 2011; Rüegg-Stürm and Grand, 2015) – environment and ecology, and green competition (Porter and van der Linde, 1995).

6 Stakeholder value layer (Ulrich and Krieg, 1972; Porter and Kramer, 2011; Rüegg-Stürm and Grand, 2015) – shared value, unions/workers (Ulrich and Krieg, 1972), non-governmental organizations (Ulrich and Krieg, 1972), government and political risk (Ulrich and Krieg, 1972), and non-industry competition (Kim and Mauborgne, 2005).

7 Legal and regulatory layer (Kamran, 2012) – antitrust and competition law (Kamran, 2013), regulation and deregulation, labour and tax law (Kamran, 2016, 2017), compliance (Kamran, 2013), and intellectual property law (IP) (Kamran, 2012).

8 Societal layer (Porter and Kramer, 2011; Porter and Rivkin, 2012a) – global citizenship, culture and trends perspective (Ghoshal and Bartlett, 1999), local and glocal (Ghoshal and Bartlett, 1999), and non-state actors.

9 Complex strategy layer (Kamran, 2016, 2017, 2018a, 2018b) – world-view, ontology, epistemology (Foerster, 2003; Bueno, 2016), service-dominant logic (SDL) (Vargo and Lusch, 2004), emergence and adaptation (Müller-Stewens and Lechner, 2011), Ashby's Law (Ashby, 2015), holistic interdisciplinary lens (Wiener, 1948; Beer, 1972, 1981, 1985), and strategic foresight (Beer, 1972, 1981, 1985; Hetzler, 2008; Müller-Stewens and Lechner, 2011).

THE VIABLE SYSTEM MODEL AS THE CORE OF THE SIX FORCES MODEL

In classical strategy literature, the notion of competitive advantage is generally attributed to management's ability to position the company's assets against some external context (Chandler and Redlich, 1961; Penrose, 1959; Rumelt, 1997). According to Beer's cybernetic model of any viable system, any organization is a viable system because of its capability of maintaining its identity independently in turbulent environments (Beer, 1994; Vidgen, 1998). The SFM, in turn, delivers the necessary diagnostic power to develop this possibility and capability. Beer's VSM is inspired by the human nervous system. Based on the thorough analysis in Chapter 2, the author introduced complexity as the sixth competitive force into Porter's FFM by integrating Beer's VSM into the model. By doing so, a self-organizing and self-regulating mechanism for observing strategic reality is now a fixed component of the SFM (Kamran, 2016, 2017).

ECONOMICS LAYER

The economic environment of a company refers to all those economic factors that have a bearing on the functioning of a business unit. The industry-in view is one part of the economic complexity (Kamran, 2013, 2016). It is based on Bain and Mason's structure–conduct–performance (SCP) paradigm that investigates causal flows between market performance and various market structure variables through the conduct of the firm within the market (Phillips, 1970; Wirth and Bloch, 1995). The SCP paradigm, therefore, enables a holistic competitor analysis embedded into an internal analysis of the company and its performance measurement tools. Creating shareholder value, however, depends on different performance indicators that are unique from industry to industry and from company to company. These value drivers have to be defined and used to 'transfer skills or expertise among similar value chains and [...] to share activities that may create synergies that can optimize the value chain as well as building a strong relationship with [the environment]' (Porter, 1985). Creating high shareholder value, therefore, enables sustainable competitive advantage.

Kim and Mauborgne (2005) introduced the red ocean perspective to look at a company within an industry that solemnly competes about market share and how to outperform its rivals (Andrews and Porter, 1986; Kim and Mauborgne, 2005). The cluster approach is considered a paradox phenomenon, as it represents the procedure of creating a local network between miscellaneous companies, suppliers, service providers, institutions, and universities, which compete but also cooperate with each other at the same time (Porter and Rivkin, 2000).

Nevertheless, Porter describes building clusters as a new form of gaining a competitive advantage as it can result in an increase in productivity and efficiency. By taking the industry-in view combined with the shareholder and the red ocean perspective and the possibility of defining clusters, the economic layer enables every strategist to get a clear picture of the immediate business environment of their company and to get a holistic status quo of the economic environment the firm is embedded in (Phillips, 1970; Scherer, 1971; Porter, 1985; Kim and Mauborgne, 2005). According to Huang (2018):

> Securing financial resources from investors is a key challenge for many early-stage entrepreneurial ventures. Given the inherent uncertainty surrounding a decision to invest in these ventures, prior research has found that experienced investors rely heavily on their investor gut feel – that is, dynamic expertise-based emotion-cognitions specific to the entrepreneurship context.

This may be an essential aspect for entrepreneurs applying the model in terms of the most vital aspects of the economic layer. However, research also illustrates further that the economic layer is the most essential aspect of firm survival, but it is still not an indicator of firm fitness.

RESOURCE-BASED VIEW LAYER

Today's turbulent business environment has generated new opportunities and challenges for firms. As suggested by the resource-based view (RBV) (Barney, 1991; Penrose, 1959; Peteraf, 1993; Wernerfelt, 1984), a firm's dynamic capabilities allow it to create new products and processes and to foresee changing market conditions; these are the core competencies of its competitiveness (Evans, 1991; Johnson *et al*, 2007; Sanchez *et al*, 1996). According to the RBV, a company's competitive advantage depends on the internal resources, such as material possession, know-how (information), processes, knowledge and human capital. Thus, it is suggested to focus rather on a firm's resources than on its products. These dynamic capabilities shape a firm's managerial and organizational processes, its position, and its paths (Meirelles, 2004; Teece *et al*, 1997).

In contemporary business, Chandler's notion of 'structure follows strategy' (1962) has to be thought ahead because of its assumed one-way relationship between structure and strategy. The author suggests viewing the two terms holistically, assuming independence between structure and strategy. Pfeifer and Bongard stated that 'by embodiment, we meant that intelligence always requires a body. Or more precisely we ascribe intelligence only to agents that are embodied, ie real physical systems whose behavior can be observed as they interact with environment' (Pfeifer and Bongard, 2007). As a result, efficiency can only be achieved through a strategic structure. Therefore, strategy development should be seen through the 'structure is strategy lens' that allows every viable system to organize structure based on real-time information management capability while also keeping an eye on the big picture and to focus on the detailed adapted strategy.

Another aspect to be highlighted was put forward by Gupta *et al* (2018), who stated:

> Recognizing the central role of chief executive officers (CEOs) in resource allocation, we argue that CEOs' personal values regarding egalitarianism, as manifested in their political ideologies, will lead to different allocation styles. Liberal CEOs will favor evenhandedness, while conservatives will tolerate greater disparities. Placing this primary expectation in a social context, we then argue that the effects of a CEO's values are amplified when aligned with the prevailing ideology among organizational members, and conversely are muted when misaligned.

While this notion combines the author's normative layer, which will be discussed below, it is still essential to underpin an inter-linkage between the dimension of RBV and the normative assessments of the CEO's behaviour and habitus, on which political ideologies are based.

TECHNOLOGY AND INNOVATION LAYER

Nineteenth-century economic historians observed that the acceleration in economic growth was the result of technological progress and that innovation is crucial for firms that are seeking to ensure long-term survival (Rigby and Corbett, 2002; Charitou and Markides, 2003; Foster and Kaplan, 2013). The internet is the most recent innovation in digital computing and communication technologies and allows real-time communication and connectivity with the environment. Because of this, PCs, laptops, tablets and smartphones (post-PC devices) are now a fixed element of everyday life. Weiser (2002) described this phenomenon as ubiquitous computing, referring to our technologized everyday life (Weiser, 2002).

The twenty-first century brings forth the additional dimension of artificial intelligence (AI) within the realm of strategic management. While AI is still evolving, there are many promising fields emerging within AI research and innovation, such as belief revision, expert systems, artificial life, data mining, genetic algorithm, theory of computation, programming, reasoning, natural language understanding, semantic web, machine learning, image recognition and systems dynamics (Oke, 2008). Another vital stream that has emerged is known as 'explainable artificial intelligence' (Miller, 2019), which hypothesizes that by building more 'transparent, interpretable, or explainable systems', users are better equipped to comprehend and trust the intelligent agents and therefore will engage with AI from a social sciences perspective (Miller, 2019).

Today, everything is connected – be it the company with its clients, suppliers or other institutions or a variety of devices, machines, and sensors via the Internet of Things (IoT). Using technology to innovate has become essential for businesses. Kim and Mauborgne (2005) introduced the blue ocean strategy to break away from the competition by creating new markets to push aside the competition. This strategy allows the organization to focus uniquely on customer demand rather than looking at competitors' business activities. The notion of disruptive innovation was developed by Christensen (1997) and looks at innovation as a revolution through new technologies that change and shape the external environment, from low- to high-end consumers (Christensen, 2016).

However, as discovered by Downes and Nunes (2013), this strategy has a blind spot. So-called big bang disruption emerges from a blind spot outside the industry and can change the game and might trigger disasters (Downes and Nunes, 2013). Simon (1996) argued for establishing a design approach in economics and engineering and other disciplines, including all the artefacts and organizations (Bayazit, 2004), which have yielded some impressive results by borrowing from areas that range from architecture to NASA. Design thinking (DT) (Kamran, 2018b, 2018c) and its development was founded in the tradition of practicalism and pragmatism (James, 1907). DT is a different culture from science and the arts in terms of *'designerly ways of knowing, thinking and acting'* and has been distinguished in its own right (Cross, 2001, 2006; Simon, 1996). The author claims that first an organization is structurally designed and thus, based on the analogy of 'structure is strategy', the eigen behaviours of the organization are cultivated by design *'avant la lettre'* in terms of the varieties they can attenuate via self-organizing forces and according to Ashby's Law, systems sciences and systemics (Foerster *et al*, 2007), stating that the sum is more than the number of the parts.

Today, looking at the technological and innovative environment of a company is essential for every strategist because real-time communication, the IoT, and ubiquitous computing are offering the highest potential for innovation, whether by using blue ocean innovation or disruptive innovation (Christensen, 1997; Kim and Mauborgne, 2005). As Kamran (2018a, 2018b, 2018c) describes, this aspect of technology is a vital tool of innovation in organizations that are navigated via design of information cybernetics.

STAKEHOLDER VALUE LAYER

Looking at a company through the eyes of network and cybernetics theory, it is apparent that a firm is embedded into a highly fragile network of stakeholders. Stakeholders are 'any group or individual who can affect or is affected by the achievement of the firm's objectives' (Freeman and McVea, 2001). Thus, stakeholders can be owners, suppliers and customers but also competitors, NGOs, unions/workers or media (Freeman and McVea, 2001). Stakeholder value should be taken into account when establishing corporate strategies, as looking only at shareholder value is incompatible with the efficiency principle. (Charreaux and Desbrières, 2001). The shared value perspective, however, can help a business not to be caught in a vicious circle that undermines competitiveness and saps economic growth through their outdated and insufficient approach to value creation (Porter and Kramer, 2011). In establishing a business model that creates economic value for the company and at the same time for the society it operates in, the company creates 'shared value' (Porter and Kramer, 2011).

In order to incorporate this vision, companies have to be aware of some main stakeholders. These are for example non-governmental organizations (NGOs) (Laakmann, 2013), unions and workers (Schniederjans and Cao, 2002), but also competitors that are not in the same industry (non-industry competition) (Spiegler, 2016). In today's globalized environment, stakeholders of companies are not only national but also international. By doing business internationally, the number of stakeholders has increased significantly. Consequently, companies have to be highly aware of unforeseeable political and governmental risks (abroad as well as in the home country) (Aliber, 1975; Kobrin, 1979). Superior knowledge about the political as well as legal environment, therefore, can provide a realistic view on how the probability of political events occurring in the environment is distributed (Kobrin, 1979).

Taking stakeholders into account is one of the key forces of the SFM. Because of our highly networked world, the strategist has to be aware of certain stakeholders. NGOs, for example, are determining the business environment by defining, for example, policy rules. Unions and workers, on the other hand, are crucial to the success of every company (Charreaux and

Desbrières, 2001; Laakmann, 2013; Phillips, 1970; Scherer, 1971; Schniederjans and Cao, 2002). Thus, political and governmental risks go hand in hand with NGOs and unions'/workers' interest of a country (Laakmann, 2013). Integrating them into the model, therefore, is part of developing a holistic model.

One additional aspect, put forward by Deken *et al* (2018), states:

> ... that resource complementarity is not given but jointly constructed in interactions with multiple potential partners through recursive cycles of what we refer to as 'prospective resourcing.' Prospective resourcing mediates the interplay of strategizing and collaboration, thereby reversing the prevailing logic that strategy precedes and determines collaboration.

The role of collaboration as a co-creational dimension between collaborative partners cannot be underestimated. This notion has also been substantiated by Hoffmann *et al* (2018), who have stated:

> Research streams on competition and cooperation are central to the field of strategic management but have evolved independently. The emerging literature on coopetition has brought attention to the phenomenon of simultaneous competition and cooperation, yet the interplay between the two has remained under-researched.

The understanding of coopetition was originally developed and brought forth by Nalebuff and Brandenburger (1997), who emphasized the roles of competitive and cooperative business strategies in times of digital disruption.

LEGAL AND REGULATORY LAYER

Another very important perspective for a company to take into consideration when developing its strategy is the legal perspective. This layer is highly linked to the stakeholder layer. The antitrust and competition law, for example, supports the government in regulating questionable business activities to ensure fair competition within an open-ended economy. Green and Teece posed the hypothesis that 'antitrust laws may be at odds with technological progress and economic welfare' (Green and Teece, 1998; Teece, 1992). The main purpose of competition law is to fill market system gaps and to discourage breakdowns (Armentano, 1999). Thus, these laws help companies to have guidelines as well as protect them from unfair industry competition.

Another key factor in the legal perspective is regulation and deregulation. Governments and higher institutions deploy these laws in order to maintain a fair market for all players. The same is applicable for labour and tax laws that define rights and obligations for both employees and employers. Following these laws and being in accordance with the given rules and guidelines is manifested in the state of compliance. Compliance rules, laws, and standards are usually a way of guaranteeing that organizations will not neglect any market conduct practices, conflicts of interest or customer service (Young, 2012). Especially, antitrust and competition law, regulation and deregulation and labour and tax laws generate a holistic overview of the legal environment in which a company is acting. Knowing these laws means having the capacity to take an active role in the market.

NATURE AND ECOLOGICAL LAYER

Today, ecological and natural aspects have increased importance in scientific as well as academic literature. Companies are paying increased attention to environmental standards, green sourcing and a symbiotic relationship with nature. Forced by increasing 'green movements' within the customer base and increased environmental standards, the nature and ecological layer gains in importance while developing the strategy of a company. The notion of green competition assumes that environmental regulations erode competitiveness. It refers to the underlying economic logic that links the environment, resource productivity, innovation, and competitiveness. Porter and van der Linde pointed out in 1995 that environmentally friendly innovation can create offsetting benefits (Porter and van der Linde, 1995). By taking into consideration the direct natural and ecological environment via, for example, corporate social responsibility (CSR), companies can attract more customers and are simultaneously sustainable and can serve as role models (Iansiti and Levien, 2004). However, the question of the contemporary era is not how widespread CSR is, but more a question of making ecological engagement profitable as a form of a solid BMI.

SOCIETAL LAYER

In a modern society, a number of major social, technological, economic and cultural transformations have come about and given rise to the network society (Castells, 2009). Organizations have to approach these changes in order to understand the kind of economy and society in which everybody lives. Today's society has been massively influenced by crises and conflicts of the twenty-first century as the global financial crises or the transformation of communication. Therefore, in today's society, it is necessary for organizations, both regional and global, to maintain a deeper knowledge of the laws of society development that allow for dealing with constant change. Falk (1993) summarized this by the notion of 'global citizenship'. Every country's culture has its foundation in attitudes and values. Bates and Plog (1990) defined culture as 'a system of shared beliefs, values, customs, behaviors and artefacts' that are created through generations by means of learning. It thus enables members of a society to cope with each other and with the environment (Bates and Khasawneh, 2005). For the development of corporate strategy, it is therefore essential to be aware of differences in culture and trends – locally as well as globally. The author manifests this observation through the notion of 'culture and trends perspective local and global' (Kamran, 2016, 2017; Bartlett *et al*, 2008). 'Glocalization' captures the essence of the emerging worldwide phenomenon where globalization and localization are transforming the development landscape (Sharma, 2009). The context of glocalization has pronounced the dilemma of balancing the contrasting forces of centralization and decentralization (Sharma, 2009). Therefore, companies have to think globally and act locally.

NORMATIVE LAYER

The normative layer describes the deeply embedded beliefs and values of every company. Within this layer, core values and ethics describe one dimension of the knowledge-based core competencies framework and provide a competitive advantage for the company (Leonard-Barton, 1992). Core values are a crucial part of profit generation and sustainability, which help to underpin all conduct regulations and requirements of a company (Funabashi and Grzech, 2005). Henceforth, every employee should incorporate these core values and the self-image of the organization in order to pass these to the team. Therefore, corporate leaders must constantly reinforce core values, as value related to knowledge and content affect all the projects in the line of business (Leonard-Barton, 1992). Variable systems as autopoietic systems have the ability of self-repair and self-transformation as one of their most essential abilities (Kamran, 2013). This possibility and therefore defining core values are among the most powerful capabilities in nature, hence it is responsible for how organisms have evolved in their current shapes and abilities to master survival. Thus, identity and autopoiesis are crucial for the development of the firm's strategy (Kamran, 2013). By self-repairing and self-transforming, companies always have to adapt to the requirements of the social cooperation towards mutual benefits. The inclusion of corporate social responsibility (CSR) in a business is defined through a positive contribution to society by broadening the focus beyond profit maximization (McWilliams, 2014). This idea beyond profit maximization is also in line with Drucker's (1954) idea that 'the purpose of a business is to create a customer'. This notion has to be at the heart of every strategy and therefore defines the legitimacy and *raison d'être* of every company (Kamran, 2016, 2017, 2018a, 2018b, 2018c; Schwaninger, 2006, 2010b; Ashby, 2015).

According to Ashby (2015), absorbing variety with new inputs can be a way to respond to change successfully because 'only variety absorbs variety'. As Figure 3.5 illustrates, the VSM has been integrated as the core of the model's corporate body embedded within the nine dimensions. Figure 3.5 describes the SFM in its entirety. The model embodies a holistic view of an organization's reality; hence the layers are recursively connected to each other and the sub-parts within the layer represent the essential aspects that cover the specific spheres. The model is designed to immunize the firm by integration and unification of the field of competitive strategy based on a single model. The systemics (Foerster *et al*, 2007) world-view of management is based on connecting and not separating (Ulrich, 2001). According to Lutterer (2005):

> The central meaning of the term 'systemics' for Foerster can be proven in two ways: on the one hand, it is something like a term of attack which he uses in order to protest against the classical reductionist 'science' paradigm. On the other hand, systemics – in contrast to 'constructivism' and 'second-order cybernetics' – is a term, which he at least uses without immediately distancing himself from it again.

Ashby's Law is about designing the set of strategic choices/options in a coherent way, thus enabling the firm to actually absorb the set of perturbations in diverse spheres based on a self-organized strategic foresight and an immunization strategy. Immunization in strategic terms actually means an *a priori* set of pre-control measures installed by the cultivation of the dynamic capabilities that the VSM delivers. Furthermore, it means reducing the time lag of responsiveness via the fourth generic strategy, as established in Chapter 1. Detailed descriptions of the model's theories are described within the PLG case study. The author's model has been fully applied and used to prepare a German large SME in its reorganization and change management phase within the fifth generational transformation (Kamran, 2017). The model is also substantiated by multiple publications of the author (Kamran, 2012, 2013, 2014, 2016).

COMPLEX STRATEGY LAYER

The in-depth literature review in Chapter 1 established that the question of viability and organizational survival has really not been asked so far within the leading publications that have actually shaped the field of strategic management. The SFM was designed to fill precisely this gap within the field for businesses to have a model that actually displays viability. The notion of 'complex strategy' is coined by the authors to establish the final layer/sphere of the SFM, thus it is the dissolving of complexity within the framework of the organizational strategic foresight *a priori* that distinguishes solid strategic achievements rather than the process of constantly solving challenges and crises that have actually taken place and the business's strategists are solving post priori. Complex strategy is maintaining the organization homeostasis, while coping with complexities of the lower level of the SFM's recursion (lower layers) and coping with dimensions as 'world-view, ontology and epistemology, holistic and multi-disciplinary lens, strategic foresight and service dominant logic.'

World-view, ontology and epistemology

In the paper 'The History of Design Thinking', the author extends the view in literature and the understanding of design as the third pillar of human knowing from a contextual historical point of view and integrates additional essential scientific contributions to the field (Kamran, 2018a). The author suggests that a synergy between phenomenology and pragmatism as a new world-view based on a solid model such as the SFM that embraces the organization's 'ontologic-epistemological' understanding is necessary. This notion is coined in terms of the Heideggerian 'thrown-ness' within the reality of market dynamics and their complexities, and has rarely been applied within managerial sciences. Hence, the organization needs to first cope with its own 'thrown-ness' within a market reality, while it secondly has to embrace sense-making based on the second-order epistemology of self-reflection as described by von Foerster as 'understanding understanding' (Foerster, 2003).

Therefore, based on Ashby's Law, the complexity of the model constructed on its ontologic-epistemological foundation as the 'second-order understanding', it must have requisite variety to absorb complexity and to ensure its homeostasis. Thus, Bueno (2016) also observes that there needs to be a solid bridge laid to close the gap on the missed opportunity of interaction between epistemology and philosophy and science as the self-correcting 'ethical imperative loop' between the first-order cybernetics (science) and second-order cybernetics (philosophy). Thus, according to Bueno:

> Closer interactions between the two fields would be beneficial to both. Epistemology would gain from a closer contact with the variety of mechanisms of knowledge generation that are produced in scientific research, with attention to sources of bias, the challenges associated with securing truly representative samples, and elaborate collective mechanisms to secure the objectivity of scientific knowledge (Bueno, 2016).

Heidegger (1997) speaks of this gap with the statement: 'science does not think'.

Holistic and multi-disciplinary lens and strategic foresight

Looking through a holistic lens enables firms to identify the external dimensions that are shaping the conditions of the industry they are working in (Kamran, 2016, 2017). This proactive approach enables the organization to shape change rather than being chased by it. Therefore, this is necessary for every firm navigating in the contemporary turbulent and highly complex environment. As shown by the different layers of the SFM, every organization is embedded into different environments that are influencing it on many diverse levels. Applying the strategic foresight, companies can establish an overview of the various influencing factors around them. Strategic foresight can deal with the complexity of known and unknown forces in order to apply the notion of ambidexterity to exploit opportunities and simultaneously to capture the future and achieve a powerful position in the market (Kamran, 2016, 2017). In a highly competitive and complex environment, it is especially necessary for companies to develop meaningful and future-oriented knowledge. Therefore, adapting a holistic and multi-disciplinary lens as proposed by the SFM merges the cybernetic and systems view and the contemporary knowledge of strategic management to solve problems in business administration.

Service-dominant logic

An underlying development of major importance in the economic world from a macro perspective can be detected: scholars agree that economic reasoning shifts from a goods-dominant view, where tangible resources and a transaction focus are central, towards a view of dominant (intangible)

FIGURE 3.5 The SFM embedded in the wider environment from a holistic perspective

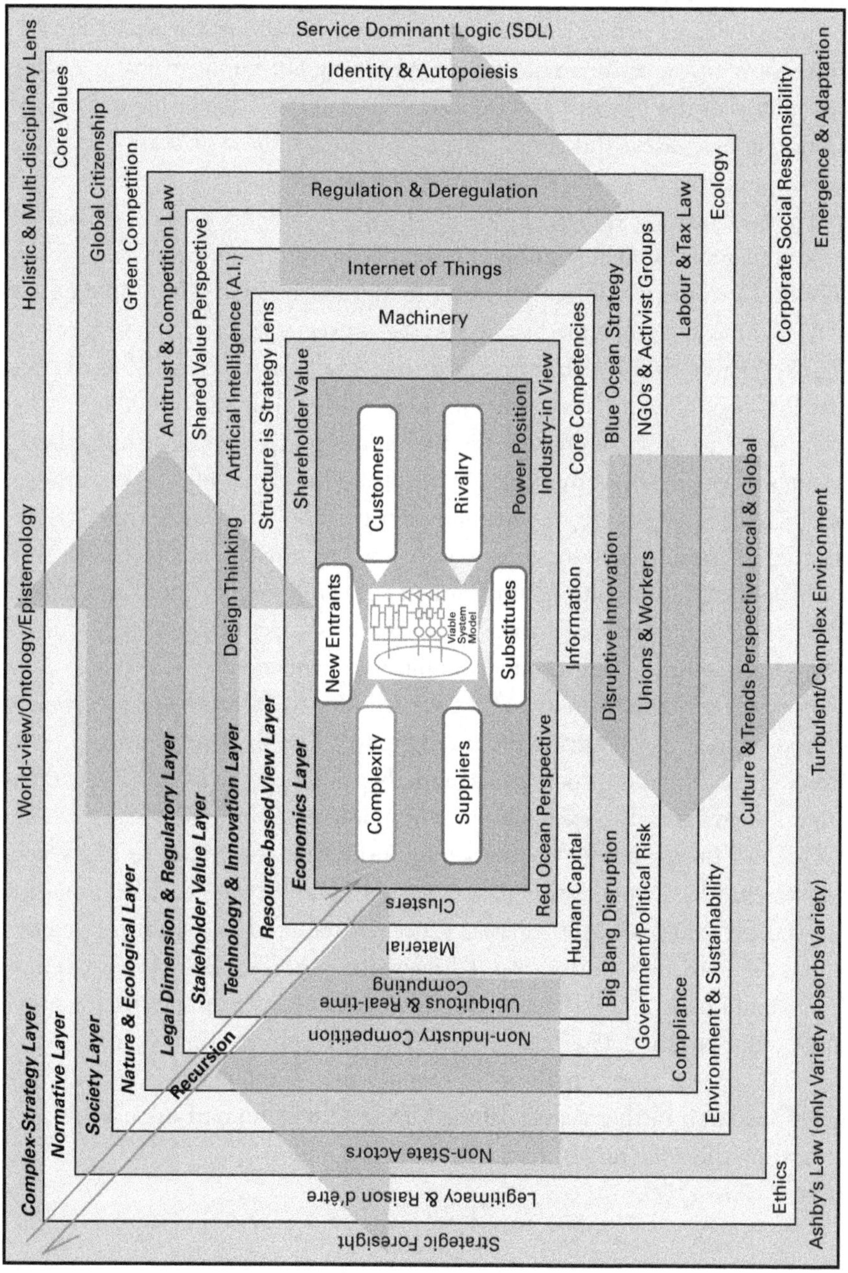

service provision with a focus on relationships and exchange processes (Prahalad and Ramaswamy, 2004; Vargo and Lusch, 2004; Vargo *et al*, 2008) develop the service-dominant logic (S-D logic) to frame this understanding. They envision service provision as the fundamental economic exchange process and only source of value creation (Vargo *et al*, 2008). The great recognition of the logic and many subsequent publications prove the profundity of the concept and underline its ability to depict the entirety of economic processes. 'Put simply, the economies of the world are becoming one large service-system' (Spohrer and Maglio, 2008).

The S-D logic is explored within SFM and the dimension of its applicability and that the implementation of the concept would add value to business, specifically in the relation of co-creation. The author successfully applied the SDL logic to the maritime business based on the research done in Kamran (2018c). Vargo and Lusch introduced the initial version of S-D logic in the article 'Evolving to a New Dominant Logic for Marketing' in 2004.

In order to understand why the two authors saw the need to display a 'changing worldview of marketing' (Vargo and Lusch, 2004), it is essential to briefly revise the existing marketing literature. They show that the development of the traditional economic world-view begins with famous economists like Thomas Malthus and Adam Smith in the 18th century (Vargo and Lusch, 2014). Economics developed into a science focused on the exchange of tangible goods, where each produced unit was embedded with value. This transaction resulted in an increasing wealth (due to an improved assortment of goods) for every contributing trading party. The first marketing scholars fostered the development of this underlying paradigm by directing their attention towards the exchange of commodities (Copeland 1920, cited in Vargo and Lusch, 2004), the marketing institutions necessary to allow and facilitate trade and possession (Nystrom 1915 and Weld 1916, cited in Vargo and Lusch, 2004) and the internal processes required to exchange tangible goods through such institutions (Cherington 1920 and Weld 1917, cited in Vargo and Lusch, 2004). This development resulted in the marketing management school in the 1950s, characterized by a strong customer focus and the development of the famous '4 Ps' framework (Kotler, 1967). All abovementioned and further aspects of the S-D logic are summarized in Table 3.1, indicating the wide range of specific firm-level actions.

TABLE 3.1 Select implications of adopting S-D logic

	Role in G-D World	Role in S-D World
Sustainability/ Shared Value	Inititate isolated shared value creating actions to enhance sustainability	Understand shared value in a network context and create sustainability in a co-creative manner involving every actor
Innovation	Create improved goods and services based on customer needs	Understand relevant networks and improve service provision within them
Value Creation	Embed value in goods and services that are distributed to customers	Enable value creation in a co-creative manner among all actors within networks
Value Propositions	Make promises about the value embedded in a good and service	Propose value by enabling customers to successfully use and integrate (co-create) the resources provided by the firm
Customer Selection	Target customers who are willing and able to purchase a particular good or service to satisfy their needs	Choose customers in a way that maximizes value co-creation within networks
Strategy	Create unique sustainable value by differentiating goods and services	Find unique, valuable and sustainable ways of linking together a firm's knowledge and skills with the customer's context

Based on Bettencourt *et al* (2014)

The SFM model based on its cybernetics embodiment as thoroughly underpinned in Chapter 2 is *recursively* interconnecting all the necessary nine environmental layers, as shown in Figure 3.5.

Comparison with theoretical competitive strategy approaches

Eisenhardt and Brown (1998) in their strategic building block model describe an essential point that strategy is about winning tomorrow today. Gälweiler (2005) observes this fact in the same manner, by establishing the essentiality of the interdependence and correlation between strategic and operative tasks. In the Gälweilerian term, success has – besides some additional managerial and economic tasks and responsibilities – above all, the task of pre-control or pre-steering regarding the organization's success and liquidity (Gälweiler, 2005).

Thus, the SFM enables strategists to have a solid diagnosis of the situation and to seek actions that are necessary, enabling the organization via the VSM and the power of structural dimension's ambidexterity to simultaneously explore and exploit, and therefore also solve the innovator's dilemma in forms of disruptive innovation (O'Reilly and Tushman, 2008, 2013; Christensen, 1987). According to O'Reilly and Tushman (2013), organizational ambidexterity describes a firm's ability to simultaneously explore and exploit market opportunities in order to be able to compete in mature and new technologies and markets by fulfilling respective requirements of both contexts, that is, efficiency, control and incremental improvement within mature markets and flexibility, autonomy and experimentation within new markets. Understanding this logic substantiates the notion further that actions are the essential aspects of strategy (Rumelt, 2012). Also essential is a solid diagnosis and a vital plan of execution that maps the whole spectrum of 'diagnosis/objective, plan and action' (Rumelt, 2012) while having a vital and real-time information-based feedback system to make the necessary changes and manoeuvres so that the objective is achieved.

Table 3.2 illustrates the essential logics/models of strategy, whereby a comparison of the diverse models is established. A comparative analysis of the SFM with the other models and in particular with Porter's FFM establishes that the SFM performs better under the following assumptions: (1) survival as the essential questions in strategy; (2) real-time control based on the VSM; (3) applying the notion of 'structure is strategy'; and (4) interactional intelligence as the measure of proactive stability. Based on Table 3.2 the assumptions are clear that the SFM is a novel conceptualization of a model to cope with the complex and turbulent reality of today's business environment. According to the modalities described by Klein (2001) and illustrated in Table 3.3, the SFM in comparison leads as a unified model connecting in a coherent way the diverse modalities of: (1) factor inputs product and location, etc; (2) innovation; (3) branding; (4) productivity; and (5) technology.

As the examples in Table 3.3 demonstrate, the assumption on competing based on a multi-modality/sphere is also a test of the SFM's robustness.

Competition on an either-or sphere and dimension has been exhausted based on the reductionist perspective. What is required is a unified model that competes on holism and constructs a multi-disciplinary/dimension of competition and thus applies Ashby's Law.

TABLE 3.2 Diverse strategic models and their logic

Features \ Models	Five Forces Model	Core Competencies	Game Theory	Competing on the Edge	Six Forces Model
Assumptions	Stable Industry Structure	Firms as Bundle of Competencies	Industry View as Dynamic Oligopoly	Industry in Rapid Change	Holistic Lens Total Environment
Goal	Defensible Position	Sustainable Advantage	Temporary Advantage	Continuous Flow of Advantages	Survival Immunity Viability
Performance Drivers	Industry Structure	Unique Firm Competencies	Right Moves	Ability to Change	Emergent Change Real-time Control
Strategy	Pick and Industry & a Strategy Fit Organization	Create Vision Built & Exploit Competencies to Realize Vision	Make the Right Competitive & Collaborative Moves	Gain the "Edge" Time, Pace, Shape	Structure is Strategy/ Dissolve Organizational Challenges
Success	Profits	Long-term Dominance	Short-term Win	Continual Reinvention	Proactive Stability SCA

Author's interpretation, based on Eisenhardt and Brown (1998)

TABLE 3.3 Differentiation of five distinct modalities

Modality	Examples	Possible mechanisms	Six Forces Model
Market competition (Competition in tradeable assets)	Factor inputs Products Channels Finance Location	Price	Layer 1 – Economics Shareholder Value Industry-in View Red Ocean Perspective Cluster
Priority competition (Competition to be first)	Innovation Creativity Patents	Competence building	Layer 4 – Technology & Innovation Incremental, disruptive & big bang innovations
Hegemonic competition (Competition for influence)	Brand recognition Standards	Politics	Layer 1 – Economics Power position while applying blue ocean

(continued)

TABLE 3.3 (Continued)

Modality	Examples	Possible mechanisms	Six Forces Model
Performative competition (Competition in organizational performance)	Productivity Quality	Management	Layer 3 – Resource-based view & operant & operand Layer 9 – Complex-Strategy Structure is strategy lens Ashby's Law
Competition in foresight (Competition to understand and predict)	Technology choices	Leadership	Layer 9 – Complex-Strategy Strategic foresight, SDL-Logic, emergence & adaptation

Author's interpretation, based on Klein (2001)

Summary and novelty of the SFM

According to Rumelt (1979), the studies of economic behaviour have been targeting the same audience from economic dimensions and also the judiciary and regulatory agencies. Ever since, this has been relevant in terms of anti-trust issues and market domination disputes based on competition law. The notion that strategy research actually addresses differs by tradition of strategy seen as coping with organizational survival (Kamran, 2016, 2017; Summer *et al*, 1990), and there are aspects left out by economics, such as rivalry among firms, innovation-based competition, product differentiation and segmentation, shifting defence and exploitation of territories (Rumelt, 1979). Porter's IO-economics-driven dimension addressed the issues to some extent by the economic logic of the FFM (Porter, 1979, 1980, 2008; Porter and Heppelmann, 2014); however, the theoretical foundation of the Porterian logic ignored the notion of holism and the multi-disciplinary nature of the field of competitive strategy (Rumelt, 2012). Bettis (1991) emphasizes the assertion that research in competitive strategy should address understanding managerial work, the nature of decision-making, the operating business units, and industry and governmental macro policies. Bettis furthermore establishes the perception of research from the point of view of ethnocentricity within the field (Bettis, 1991), thus contributing to less adequate models and theories not bringing forth research to address the challenges faced by complex and global firms operating within a dynamic environment. Camerer (1985) states:

> 'Although a new tradition in strategy could spring from current writing, it is probably healthy to borrow ideas and methods from other disciplines. Decision theory, game theory, industrial organization, and microeconomics are prime fields for poaching. Slightly fertile fields – where deductive theorizing has taken a back seat to inductive description – include military strategy, science, organization theory, anthropology, psychology, sociobiology and perhaps sociology.

Thomas and Pollock (1999) give the following six issues importance in the future of strategic research: (1) definitional issues; (2) measurement issues; (3) the unit of analysis considered; (4) the study of process, not states; (5) the examination of organizational failures as their successes; and (6) the greater micro-analytic data from within the organization. After Camerer (1985), the state of research on strategy is dissatisfying, thus theories are ambiguous and the overlap seems to be too large to make a solid contribution. Camerer emphasizes the notion of deductive reasoning as the most useful way of conducting research in strategic and policy research. Based on conceptual modelling and the triangulation/mixed method research conducted, the formation of the SFM fits very well to satisfy the point Camerer (1985) is underpinning. According to Corsten and Thomas (1993), the field of competitive strategy clearly and openly demands an integration of various streams of research as competitive strategy researchers are regularly faced with diverse perspectives which should stimulate truly integrative thinking and may result in a competitive advantage for the field of competitive strategy. Schwaninger's MBM methodology delivers a solid base whereupon the novelty of the SFM can be further substantiated.

Schwaninger (2010a) underpins the theorem by stating:

> This law has universal validity, because we always manage on the basis of models, whether we want to or not and whether we know it or not. In light of the Conant-Ashby-Theorem, models are a vital prerequisite for organizational viability, and the quest for high-quality models is a must.

Figure 3.6 describes three notions as emphasized by Schwaninger (2010a): (1) depth of a model, which refers to the level of detail and specificity of a model; (2) breadth of a model, which refers to the scope of the domain modelled, between broad and narrow; and (3) acuity, which refers to the notion of accuracy and precision of a model.

FIGURE 3.6 Model-based management (MBM) framework

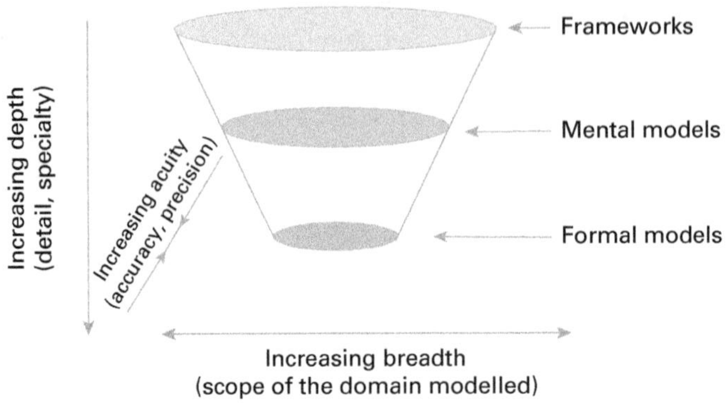

Schwaninger (2010a)

The SFM is unique in a sense that it fulfils the depth in terms of enabling the SFM to be constructed based on the notion of recursion, meaning enough detail can be expected from each sphere and the higher and lower level of recursion of the systems. The second notion of breadth is established based on nine different spheres. According to the current literature available on strategic management, the author can claim that no other strategic management model can display more breadth. The model's precision is also demonstrated based on the empirical evidence delivered. The model can be applied with no restrictions. However, depending on the nature of the firm, its maturity, size, revenue volume, and industry or legal framework and also based on the firm's embedded international environment, some adjustments may be necessary. This is the strength of the SFM because it is precise enough to cover the most essential aspects of the firm's competitive strategy in detail but still leaves the possibility of customizing some aspects based on the necessity and nature of the individual firm's situation. According to Ashby's Law the complexity that a model embraces to that depth and breadth complexity can be amplified. This notion is also strengthened by the aforementioned 'Conant and Ashby Theorem' (Ashby, 1956; Conant and Ashby, 1970; Schwaninger and Grösser, 2008). The SFM furthermore is substantiated by the dual-induction and deduction method in theory-building hence the diagnostic power of the author's model based on an in-depth research *a priori* to conceptualize the SFM has been clearly demonstrated.

FIGURE 3.7 Induction and deduction method in theory-building

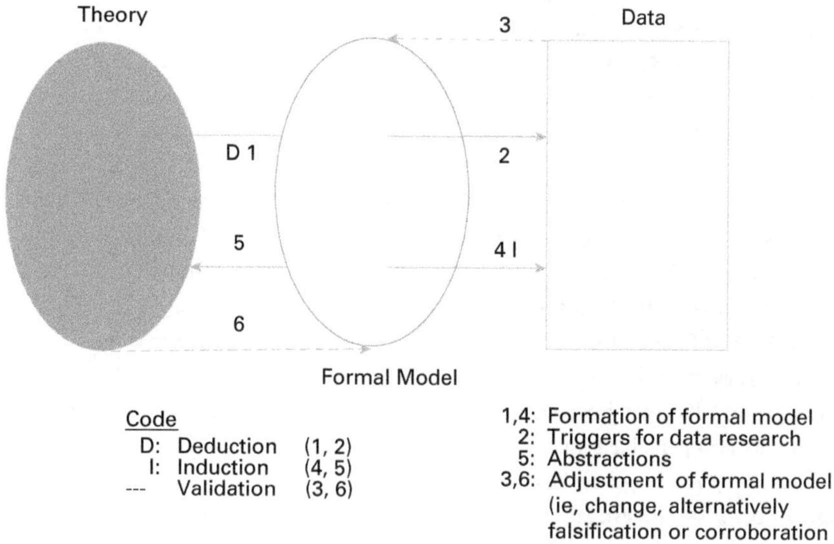

Schwaninger and Grösser (2008)

The model has been validated by a large empirical analysis – the essential list/framework of model-based theory-building and validating Schwaninger and Grösser (2008), constructing on Patterson (1986) and completed by Holton and Lowe (2007) to deliver additional aspects.

References

Aliber RZ (1975) Monetary independence under floating exchange rates, *Journal of Finance*, 30 (2), pp 365–376, https://doi.org/10.1111/j.1540-6261.1975.tb01817.x (archived at https://perma.cc/8BX3-HXTC)

Andrews KJ and Porter ME (1986) *Business Policy: Text and cases*, Richard D. Irwin, Homewood, IL

Ansoff HI (1971) *Corporate Strategy: An analytic approach to business policy for growth and expansion*, Penguin Books, Harmondsworth

Armentano DT (1999) *Antitrust: The case for repeal*, revised 2nd ed, Ludwig von Mises Institute, Auburn, AL

Ashby WR (1956) *Introduction to Cybernetics*, Chapman & Hall, London

Ashby WR (1962) Principles of the self-organizing system, in *Principles of Self-Organization: Transactions of the University of Illinois Symposium*, eds H von Foerster and GW Zopf, pp 255–278, Pergamon Press, London

Ashby WR (2015) *Introduction to Cybernetics*, Martino Fine Books

ATkearney.com (2014) *Global Cities, Present and Future: 2014 Global Cities Index and Emerging Cities Outlook*, Available at: https://www.atkearney.com/documents/10192/4461158/Global+Cities+Present+and+Future-GCI+2014.pdf (archived at https://perma.cc/FY6D-LZWE)

Barney JB (1991) Firm resources and sustained competitive advantage, *Journal of Management*, **17** (1), pp 99–120

Bartlett CA, Ghoshal S and Beamish PW (2008) *Transnational Management: Text, cases, and readings in cross-border management*, 5th ed, McGraw-Hill/Irwin, Boston, MA, Retrieved from: http://www.loc.gov/catdir/enhancements/fy0702/2006032626-d.html (archived at https://perma.cc/UT3L-4VPF)

Bates DG and Plog F (1990) *Cultural Anthropology*, 3rd ed, McGraw-Hill, New York

Bates R and Khasawneh S (2005) Organizational learning culture, learning transfer climate and perceived innovation in Jordanian organizations, *International Journal of Training and Development*, **9** (2), pp 96–110

Bayazit N (2004) Investigating design: A review of forty years of design research, *Design Issues*, **20** (1), pp 16–29, https://doi.org/10.1162/074793604772933739 (archived at https://perma.cc/AQ3N-JSRJ)

Beer S (1959) What has cybernetics to do with operational research?, *Journal of the Operational Research Society*, **10** (1), 1–21

Beer S (1972) *Brain of the Firm: A Development in Management Cybernetics*, Lane, London

Beer S (1979) *The Heart of Enterprise*, Wiley, New York

Beer S (1981) *Brain of the Firm: The managerial cybernetics of organization*, J. Wiley, Chichester

Beer S (1984) The Viable System Model: Its provenance, development, methodology and pathology, *J Oper Res Soc,* **35**, pp 7–25

Beer S (1985) *Diagnosing the System for Organizations*, Wiley, New York

Beer S (1994) Stafford Beer on the art and science of holistic management, in *How many grapes went into the wine: Stafford Beer on the art and science of holistic management*, eds R Harnden, A Leonard and S Beer, Wiley, Chichester

Beer S (2002) What is cybernetics?, *Kybernetes,* **31** (2), pp 209–219

Bettencourt LA, Lusch RF and Vargo SL (2014) A service lens on value creation: Marketing's role in achieving strategic advantage, *California Management Review*, **57** (1), pp 44–66, https://doi.org/10.1525/cmr.2014.57.1.44 (archived at https://perma.cc/RBK8-GLV2)

Bettis RA (1991) Strategic management and the straightjacket: An editorial essay, *Organization Science*, **2** (3), pp 315–319

Bogner WC and Thomas H (1993) The role of competitive groups in strategy formulation: A dynamic integration of two competing models, *Journal of Management Studies*, **30** (1), pp 51–67

Bueno O (2016) Epistemology and philosophy of science, in *The Oxford Handbook of Philosophy of Science*, Oxford University Press, New York, https://doi.org/10.1093/oxfordhb/9780199368815.013.13 (archived at https://perma.cc/4CX4-QJ5R)

Camerer C (1985) Redirecting research in business policy and strategy, *Strategic Management Journal*, **6** (1), pp 1–15

Castells M (2009) *Communication Power*, Oxford University Press, Oxford, Retrieved from http://www.loc.gov/catdir/enhancements/fy0917/2009013847-b.html (archived at https://perma.cc/MKF8-L3A6)

Chandler AD (1962) *Strategy and Structure Chapters in the History of the Industrial Enterprise*, MIT Press, Cambridge, MA

Chandler AD and Redlich F (1961) Recent developments in American business administration and their conceptualization, *Business History Review*, **35** (21)

Channon DF (1973) *The Strategy and Structure of British Enterprise*, Palgrave Macmillan, London, Retrieved from http://dx.doi.org/10.1007/978-1-349-01995-3 (archived at https://perma.cc/7ZVP-4TUL)

Charitou CD and Markides CC (2003) Responses to disruptive strategic innovation, *Sloan Management Review*, **44** (2), pp 55–63

Charreaux G and Desbrières P (2001) Corporate governance: Stakeholder value versus shareholder value, *Journal of Management and Governance*, **5** (2), pp 107–128, https://doi.org/10.1023/A:1013060105433 (archived at https://perma.cc/V7MS-Q3WF)

Christensen CR (1987) *Business Policy: Text and cases*, 6th ed, R.D. Irwin, Homewood, IL

Christensen CM (1997) *The Innovator's Dilemma: When new technologies cause great firms to fail*, Harvard Business School Press, Boston, MA

Christensen CM (2016) *The Innovator's Dilemma: When new technologies cause great firms to fail*, Harvard Business Review Press, Boston, MA

Christopher WF (2007) *Holistic Management: Managing what matters for company success*, Wiley-Interscience, Hoboken, NJ

Cohen WM and Levinthal DA (1990) Absorptive capacity: A new perspective on learning and innovation, *Administrative Science Quarterly*, **35** (1), p 128, https://doi.org/10.2307/2393553 (archived at https://perma.cc/P2XV-X6BS)

Conant RC and Ashby WR (1970) Every good regulator of a system must be a model of that system, *International Journal of Systems Science*, **1** (2), pp 89–97

Corsten H and Thomas W (1993) Reflections on Competitive Strategy and Its Impact on Modern Production Concepts, *Management International Review*, **33** (4), pp 315–334

Cross N (2001) Designerly ways of knowing: Design discipline versus design thinking, *Design Issues*, **17** (3), pp 49–55

Cross N (2006) *Designerly Ways of Knowing*, Springer-Verlag, London, Retrieved from http://hawk-hhg.de.ciando.com/shop/book/short/index.cfm/fuseaction/short/bok_ID/14251 https://doi.org/10.1007/1-84628-301-9 (archived at https://perma.cc/RA3T-KUZZ)

Deken F, Berends H, Gemser G and Lauche K (2018) Strategizing and the initiation of interorganizational collaboration through prospective resourcing, *Academy of Management Journal*, **61** (5), pp 1920–1950, Available at: https://doi.org/10.5465/amj.2016.0687 (archived at https://perma.cc/5ME2-JCRR)

Downes L and Nunes P (2013) *Big-Bang Disruption*, Retrieved from https://hbr.org/2013/03/big-bang-disruption (archived at https://perma.cc/3492-Z54J)

Drucker PF (1954) *The Practice of Management*, Harper & Row, New York

Dyas GP (1972) *The Strategy and Structure of French Industrial Enterprise*, Harvard Business School, Boston, MA

Eisenhardt KM and Brown SL (1998) Competing on the edge: Strategy as structured chaos, *Long Range Planning*, **31** (5), pp 786–789, https://doi.org/10.1016/S0024-6301(98)00092-2 (archived at https://perma.cc/9WSY-8QZH)

Espejo R and Reyes A (2001) The state of the state: Introduction, *Systemic Practice and Action Research*, **14** (2), pp 135–137

Evans JS (1991) Strategic flexibility for high technology manoeuvres: A conceptual framework, *Journal of Management Studies*, **28** (1), pp 69–89, https://doi.org/10.1111/j.1467-6486.1991.tb00271.x (archived at https://perma.cc/6ANA-HBB9)

Falk H (1993) Discussion of 'Managerial efficiency: A study of management buyouts', *Contemporary Accounting Research*, **10** (1), pp 205–209, https://doi.org/10.1111/j.1911-3846.1993.tb00389.x (archived at https://perma.cc/57MX-SVMR)

Fjeldstad ØD and Snow CC (2018) Business models and organization design, *Long Range Planning*, **51** (1), pp 32–39, https://doi.org/10.1016/j.lrp.2017.07.008 (archived at https://perma.cc/2YFR-TGER)

Foerster H, von (1958) Basic concepts of homeostasis, in *BNL*, **474** (C-25), Homeostatic Mechanisms: Report of Symposium held 12–14 June 1957, pp 216–242, Biology Dept, Brookhaven National Laboratory, Upton, NY

Foerster H, von (2003) *Understanding Understanding*, Springer, New York

Foerster H, von, Bröcker M, Ivanovas G and Glasersfeld Ev (2007) *Teil der Welt: Fraktale einer Ethik - oder Heinz von Foersters Tanz mit der Welt*, Auer, Heidelberg, Retrieved from http://deposit.d-nb.de/cgi-bin/dokserv?id=2906483&prov=M&dok_var=1&dok_ext=htm (archived at https://perma.cc/84Y2-3BWE)

Foerster H, von, Mora PM and Amiot LW (1960) Doomsday: Friday, 13 November, A.D. 2026, *Science*, **132** (3436), pp 1291–1295, https://doi.org/10.1126/science.132.3436.1291 (archived at https://perma.cc/N38M-KFKR)

Foss NJ and Saebi T (2018) Business models and business model innovation: Between wicked and paradigmatic problems, *Long Range Planning*, **51** (1), pp 9–21, https://doi.org/10.1016/j.lrp.2017.07.006 (archived at https://perma.cc/DNW9-KC85)

Foster R and Kaplan S (2013) *Creative Destruction: Why companies that are built to last underperform the market – and how to successfully transform them*, Crown Business, New York

Freeman RE and McVea J (2001) A stakeholder approach to strategic management, *SSRN Electronic Journal*, Advance online publication, https://doi.org/10.2139/ssrn.263511 (archived at https://perma.cc/P96Q-M8PT)

Friedman M (1962) *Capitalism and Freedom*, University of Chicago Press, Chicago

Funabashi M and Grzech A (2005) *Challenges of Expanding Internet: E-Commerce, E-Business, and E-Government: 5th IFIP Conference e-Commerce, e-Business, and e-Government (I3E 2005)*, 28–30 October, Poznan, Poland, IFIP International Federation for Information Processing, Vol 189, International Federation for Information Processing, Boston, MA, Retrieved from http://dx.doi.org/10.1007/0-387-29773-1 (archived at https://perma.cc/NVH4-88TV)

Galbraith JR and Nathanson DA (1978) *Strategy Implementation: Structure, systems, and process*, West Publishing, St Paul, MN

Gälweiler A (2005) *Strategische Unternehmensführung*, Campus-Verl, Frankfurt/Main

Ghoshal S and Bartlett CA (1999) *The Individualized Corporation: A fundamentally new approach to management – great companies are defined by purpose, process, and people*, HarperBusiness, New York

Glaser VL (2017) Design performances: How organizations inscribe artifacts to change routines, *Academy of Management Journal*, **60** (6), pp 2126–2154, Available at: https://doi.org/10.5465/amj.2014.0842 (archived at https://perma.cc/S9PR-TUPS)

Green J and Teece DJ (1998) Four approaches to telecommunications deregulation and competition: The USA, the UK, Australia and New Zealand, *Industrial and Corporate Change*, 7 (4), pp 623–635

Gupta A, Briscoe F and Hambrick DC (2018) Evenhandedness in resource allocation: Its relationship with CEO ideology, organizational discretion, and firm performance, *Academy of Management Journal*, **61** (5), pp 1848–1868, Available at: https://doi.org/10.5465/amj.2016.1155 (archived at https://perma.cc/B2B5-H7NJ)

Hackhausen J (2009, July 13) Interview mit Fredmund F. Malik: 'Der Kapitalismus ist gescheitert', *Handelsblatt*, Retrieved from https://www.handelsblatt.com/finanzen/anlagestrategie/trends/interview-mit-fredmund-f-malik-der-kapitalismus-ist-gescheitert/3219030.html?ticket=ST-4115743-Gp3TdbpL9pYCvWzOYEwc-ap4 (archived at https://perma.cc/9VGZ-F7AM)

Hacklin F, Björkdahl J and Wallin MW (2018) Strategies for business model innovation: How firms reel in migrating value, *Long Range Planning*, **51** (1), pp 82–110, https://doi.org/10.1016/j.lrp.2017.06.009 (archived at https://perma.cc/8X59-276K)

Hagel J, Brown JS and Davison L (2010) *The Power of Pull: How small moves, smartly made, can set big things in motion*, Basic Books, New York

Hall DJ and Saias MA (1980) Strategy follows structure!, *Strategic Management Journal*, **1** (2), pp 149–163

Hayek FA (1945) The use of knowledge in society, *American Economic Review*, **35** (4), pp 519–530

Heidegger M (1997) *Was heißt Denken?: Vorlesung Wintersemester 1951/52. Universal-Bibliothek: Nr. 8805*, Reclam, Stuttgart

Hetzler S (2008) *Brain-supporting-environments für Entscheide in komplexen Systemen: ein kybernetischer Ansatz für die Gestaltung wirksamer Entscheidungsumfelder*, Dissertation, Rosch-Druck, Schesslitz

Hoffmann W, Lavie D, Reuer JJ and Shipilov A (2018) The interplay of competition and cooperation, *Strategic Management Journal*, **39** (12), pp 3033–3052, https://doi.org/10.1002/smj.2965 (archived at https://perma.cc/4M69-VMGP)

Holton EF and Lowe JS (2007) Toward a general research process for using Dubin's theory building model, *Human Resource Development Review*, **6**, pp 297–320

Huang L (2018) The role of investor gut feel in managing complexity and extreme risk, *Academy of Management Journal*, **61** (5), pp 1821–1847, Available at: https://doi.org/10.5465/amj.2016.1009 (archived at https://perma.cc/NL4G-BBU6)

Iansiti M and Levien R (2004) Strategy as ecology, *Harvard Business Review*, (03)

James W (1907) *Pragmatism: A new name for some old ways of thinking*, Longmans Green and Co, New York

Johnson G, Langley A, Melin L and Whittington R (2007) *Strategy as Practice: Research directions and resources*, Cambridge University Press, Cambridge

Kamran Q (2012) *'Complexity', the 6th Competitive Force that Shapes Management Strategy: A cybernetic approach to 'Porter's Five Forces that Shapes Industry Strategy' in Turbulent and Complex Environments*, Available at: https://papers.ssrn.com/sol3/papers.cfm?abstract_id=2137853 (archived at https://perma.cc/A46M-58HN) (accessed 22 November 2018)

Kamran Q (2013) *Complexity the sixth competitive force that shapes strategy: A Cybernetics Approach to "Porter's FFM" in Turbulent and Complex Environments*, Lambert Academic Publishing, Saarbrücken

Kamran Q (2014) *Conceptualizing Complexity as the Sixth Competitive Force that Shapes Strategy in Complex and Turbulent Environments*, Retrieved from https://papers.ssrn.com/sol3/papers.cfm?abstract_id=2476277 (archived at https://perma.cc/96B3-4KVM)

Kamran Q (2016, August 3–7) Complexity the Sixth Competitive Force that Shapes Strategy in Turbulent and Complex Environments: A Cybernetics Approach to Porter's FFM, in *Turbulent and Complex Environments: International Conference of Business Administration (ABA)*, Prague, Retrieved from https://papers.ssrn.com/sol3/papers.cfm?abstract_id=2232901 (archived at https://perma.cc/7NEC-ADT9)

Kamran Q (2017) Cybernetics and Strategy: A necessary synergy for strategic models – complexity, the sixth competitive force that shapes strategy in turbulent and complex environments – a cybernetics approach to Porter's FFM: in turbulent and complex environments, in *Academy of Business Administration (ABA) Year Book*, Yapsilanti, MI, pp 1–65, *Innovation Law & Policy eJournal*, **5** (25) (accessed 22 November 2018)

Kamran Q (2018a) Da-Sein thinking: A phenomenological epistemology for design thinking, *SSRN Electronic Journal*, Advance online publication, https://doi.org/10.2139/ssrn.3273883 (archived at https://perma.cc/KPZ7-FVX7)

Kamran Q (2018b) *The History of Design Thinking: From pragmatism to phenomenology*, Retrieved from https://papers.ssrn.com/sol3/papers.cfm?abstract_id=3273872 (archived at https://perma.cc/P6WN-BBML)

Kamran Q (2018c) The service-dominant Perspective to Create Value in the Maritime Business

Kim WC and Mauborgne R (2004a) Blue Ocean Strategy, *Harvard Business Review*, **82** (10), pp 76–84

Kim WC and Mauborgne R (2004b) Value Innovation: The strategic logic of high growth, *Harvard Business Review*, **82** (7/8), pp 172–180

Kim WC and Mauborgne R (2005) *Blue Ocean Strategy: How to create uncontested market space and make the competition irrelevant*, Harvard Business School Press, Boston, MA

Klein SA (2001) Measuring, estimating, and understanding the psychometric function: A commentary, *Perception and Psychophysics*, **63** (8), pp 1421–1455, https://doi.org/10.3758/BF03194552 (archived at https://perma.cc/BAY6-5PBU)

Kobrin SJ (1979) Political risk: A review and reconsideration, *Journal of International Business*, **10** (1), pp 67–80

Kotler P (1967), *Marketing Management: Analysis, planning and control*, Prentice-Hall

Laakmann H (2013) *Eine neue Form von Verantwortung im Management: Existenzialortung und Legitimität im Kontext des neuen St. Galler Management-Modells und Issues Management*, Dissertation, Universität St. Gallen, St. Gallen/Switzerland, Retrieved from https://www1.unisg.ch/www/edis.nsf/SysLkpByIdentifier/4160?OpenDocument&lang=de (archived at https://perma.cc/ZKT5-VWNU)

Leonard-Barton D (1992) Core capabilities and core rigidities: A paradox in managing new product development, *Strategic Management Journal*, **13** (S1), pp 111–125

Lutterer W (2005) Systemics: The social aspects of cybernetics, *Kybernetes*, **34** (3/4), pp 497–507

Mahoney JT and Pandian JR (1992) The resource-based view within the conversation of strategic management, *Strategic Management Journal*, **13** (5), pp 363–380

Malik F (1984) *Strategie des Managements komplexer Systeme*, Haupt, Bern and Stuttgart

Malik F (2007) *Management: Das A und O des Handwerks*, Campus-Verl, Frankfurt/Main

Malik F (2013) *Management: Das A und O des Handwerks*, 2nd ed, Campus, Frankfurt/New York

Malik F (2015) *Strategie des Managements komplexer Systeme: Ein Beitrag zur Management-Kybernetik evolutionärer Systeme*, Haupt Verlag, Bern

Maturana HR and Varela FJ (1980) *Autopoiesis and Cognition: The realization of the living*, Springer Netherlands, Dordrecht

McWilliams A (2014) Corporate social responsibility, in *Wiley Encyclopedia of Management*, 3rd ed, Volume 4, ed CL Cooper, pp 1–4, Wiley, Chichester, Available at: https://doi.org/10.1002/9781118785317.weom120001 (archived at https://perma.cc/X3ZT-42YB)

Meirelles JGP (2004) Apresentação: Richard R. Nelson e Sidney Winter – An Evolutionary Theory of Economic Change, *Revista Brasileira de Inovação*, **3** (2), p 237, https://doi.org/10.20396/rbi.v3i2.8648898 (archived at https://perma.cc/3K6B-XK3N)

Menger C and Hayek FAv (1981) *Principles of Economics*, trans J Dingwall and BF Hoselitz, New York University Press, New York

Miles RE, Snow CC, Meyer AD and Coleman Jr, HJ (1978) Organizational strategy, structure, and process, *Academy of Management Review*, **3** (3), pp 546–562

Miles RE, Snow CC and Pfeffer J (1974) Organization-environment: Concepts and issues, *Industrial Relations: A Journal of Economy and Society,* **13** (3), pp 244–264

Miller D (1986) Configurations of strategy and structure: Towards a synthesis, *Strategic Management Journal*, 7 (3), pp 233–249

Miller T (2019) Explanation in artificial intelligence: Insights from the social sciences, *Artificial Intelligence*, 267, pp 1–38, https://doi.org/10.1016/j.artint.2018.07.007 (archived at https://perma.cc/A7FF-CHHB)

Mintzberg H, Ahlstrand BW and Lampel J (1998) *Strategy Safari: A guided tour through the wilds of strategic management*, Free Press, New York, Retrieved from http://www.loc.gov/catdir/description/simon031/98009694.html (archived at https://perma.cc/3QSZ-9NHQ)

Mises Lv (1983) *Nation, State, and Economy: Contributions to the politics and history of our time*, Liberty Fund, Indianapolis, IN

Mises Lv and Adler S (1935) Economic calculation in the socialist commonwealth, in *Collectivist Economic Planning: Critical studies on the possibilities of socialism*, pp 87–130

Müller-Stewens G and Lechner C (2011) *Strategisches Management: Wie strategische Initiativen zum Wandel führen*, Schäffer-Poeschel, Stuttgart

Nalebuff BJ and Brandenburger AM (1997) Coopetition: Competitive and cooperative business strategies for the digital economy, *Strategy & Leadership*, **25** (6), pp 28–33, Available at: https://doi.org/10.1108/eb054655 (archived at https://perma.cc/LTY5-9F8L)

O'Reilly III CA and Tushman ML (2008) Ambidexterity as a dynamic capability: Resolving the innovator's dilemma, *Research in Organizational Behavior*, **28**, pp 185–206

O'Reilly III CA and Tushman ML (2011) Organizational Ambidexterity in Action: How managers explore and exploit, *California Management Review*, https://doi.org/10.1525/cmr.2011.53.4.5 (archived at https://perma.cc/2CT5-MF9D)
O'Reilly III CA and Tushman ML (2013) Organizational ambidexterity: Past, present, and future, *Academy of Management Perspectives*, **27** (4), pp 324–338, https://doi.org/10.5465/amp.2013.0025 (archived at https://perma.cc/2CT5-MF9D)
Oke AS (2008) A literature review on artificial intelligence, *International Journal of Information and Management Sciences*, **19** (4), pp 535–570
Patterson CH (1986) Some strategies for readers, *Journal of Counseling and Development*, **65** (4), p 204, https://doi.org/10.1002/j.1556-6676.1986.tb01316.x (archived at https://perma.cc/KB55-9JWC)
Penrose ET (1959) *The Theory of the Growth of the Firm*, Wiley, New York
Peteraf MA (1993) The cornerstones of competitive advantage: A resource-based view, *Strategic Management Journal*, **14** (3), pp 179–191
Pfeifer R and Bongard J (2007) *How the Body Shapes the Way We Think: A new view of intelligence*, MIT Press, Cambridge, MA
Phillips A (1970) Structure, conduct and performance – and performance, conduct and structure, in *Industrial Organization and Economic Development: [essays] in honor of E.S. Mason*, eds JW Markham, GF Papanek and ES Mason, Houghton Mifflin, Boston, MA
Porter ME (1979) The structure within industries and companies' performance, *Review of Economics and Statistics*, **61** (2), p 214, https://doi.org/10.2307/1924589 (archived at https://perma.cc/6XZV-QYXR)
Porter ME (1980) *Competitive Strategy: Techniques for analyzing industries and competitors*, Free Press, New York
Porter ME (1985) *Competitive Advantage: Creating and sustaining superior performance*, Free Press, New York
Porter ME (1996) What is strategy?, *Harvard Business Review*, **73** (6), Retrieved from https://hbr.org/1996/11/what-is-strategy (archived at https://perma.cc/8M77-4HBL)
Porter ME (1998) *The Competitive Advantage of Nations: With a new introduction*, Free Press, New York
Porter ME (2008) The five competitive forces that shape strategy, *Harvard Business Review*, **86** (1), pp 78–93
Porter ME and Heppelmann JE (2014) How smart, connected products are transforming competition, *Harvard Business Review*, **92** (11), pp 64–88
Porter ME and Kramer MR (2011) Creating shared value, *Harvard Business Review*, **89** (1/2), pp 62–77
Porter ME and Rivkin JW (2000) *Industry Transformation,* Harvard Business School Publishing, Boston, MA
Porter ME and Rivkin JW (2012a) The looming challenge to US competitiveness, *Harvard Business Review*, **90** (3), pp 54–61
Porter ME and Rivkin JW (2012b) *Restoring U.S. Competitiveness: The looming challenge to U.S. competitiveness*, Harvard Business Review, Boston, MA

Porter, M and van der Linde, C (1995) Green and competitive: Ending the stalemate, *The Dynamics of the Eco-Efficient Economy: Environmental Regulation and Competitive Advantage*, **33** (5), pp 120–134

Prahalad CK and Hamel G (2006) The core competence of the corporation, in *Strategische Unternehmungsplanung: Strategische Unternehmungsführung: Stand und Entwicklungstendenzen*, 9th ed, pp 275–292, eds B Taylor and D Hahn, Springer-Verlag, Berlin, Heidelberg

Prahalad CK and Ramaswamy V (2004) Co-creating unique value with customers, *Strategy and Leadership*, **32** (3), pp 4–9, https://doi.org/10.1108/10878570410699249 (archived at https://perma.cc/Z5UQ-XXNQ)

Priem RL, Wenzel M and Koch J (2018) Demand-side strategy and business models: Putting value creation for consumers center stage, *Long Range Planning*, **51** (1), pp 22–31, https://doi.org/10.1016/j.lrp.2017.07.007 (archived at https://perma.cc/4UEM-59C3)

Pugh DS, Hickson DJ, Hinings CR and Turner C (1968) Dimensions of organization structure, *Administrative Science Quarterly*, **13** (1), pp 65–105

Rappaport A (1998) *Creating Shareholder Value: A guide for managers and investors, revised and updated*, Free Press, New York

Rigby DK and Corbett A (2002) It takes systems, not serendipity: A blueprint for building a disruptive-innovation engine, *Ivey Business Journal Online*, pp 1–6

Ríos JP (2012) *Design and Diagnosis for Sustainable Organizations: The viable system method*, 2nd ed, Springer Berlin Heidelberg, Retrieved from http://dx.doi.org/10.1007/978-3-642-22318-1 (archived at https://perma.cc/AY7H-4T66

Ritter T and Lettl C (2018) The wider implications of business-model research, *Long Range Planning*, **51** (1), pp 1–8, https://doi.org/10.1016/j.lrp.2017.07.005 (archived at https://perma.cc/E9FL-ZSES)

Rothbard MN (1990) Concepts of the role of intellectuals in social change toward laissez faire, *Journal of Libertarian Studies*, **9** (2), pp 43–67

Rüegg-Stürm J and Grand S (2015) *Das St. Galler Management-Modell*, Haupt, Bern

Rumelt RP (1974) *Strategy, Structure, and Economic Performance*, Division of Research Graduate School of Business Administration Harvard University, Boston, MA

Rumelt RP (1979) Evaluation of strategies: Theory and models, in *Strategic Management: A new view of business policy and planning*, eds D Schendel and CW Hofer, Little, Brown, Boston

Rumelt RP (1997) Towards a strategic theory of the firm, in *Resources, Firms, and Strategies: A reader in the resource-based perspective*, ed NJ Foss, pp 131–145, Oxford University Press, New York

Rumelt RP (2012) Good strategy/bad strategy: The difference and why it matters, *Strategic Direction*, **28** (8)

Rumelt RP, Schendel D and Teece DJ (1991) Strategic management and economics, *Strategic Management Journal*, **12** (S2), pp 5–29
Rumelt RP, Schendel DE and Teece DJ (eds) (1994) *Fundamental Issues in Strategy: A research agenda*, Harvard Business School Press, Boston, MA
Sanchez R, Heene A and Thomas H (1996) *Introduction: Towards the theory and practice of competence-based competition*, Pergamon Press, Oxford
Scherer FM (1971) *Industrial Market Structure and Economic Performance*, Rand McNally, Chicago, IL
Schniederjans MJ and Cao Q (2002) *E-Commerce Operations Management*, World Scientific, Singapore
Schultz TW (1961) Investment in human capital, *American Economic Review*, **51** (1), pp 1–17
Schwaninger M (1987) A practical approach to strategy development, *Long Range Planning*, **20** (5), pp 74–85
Schwaninger M (1990a) Embodiments of organizational fitness: The viable system model (VSM) as a guide, *Systems Practice*, **3** (3), pp 249–264
Schwaninger M (1990b) Umweltverantwortung: Manager sind herausgefordert, *IO Management Zeitschrift*, **59** (1), pp 89–94
Schwaninger M (2001) System theory and cybernetics: A solid basis for transdisciplinarity in management education and research, *Kybernetes*, **30** (9/10), pp 1209–1222
Schwaninger M (2006) Design for viable organizations: The diagnostic power of the viable system model, *Kybernetes*, **35** (7/8), pp 955–966
Schwaninger M (2007) Optimal structures for social systems, *Kybernetes*, **36** (3/4), pp 307–318
Schwaninger M (2010a) Model-based management (MBM): A vital prerequisite for organizational viability, *Kybernetes*, **39** (9/10), pp 1419–1428
Schwaninger M (2010b) Reflections on a transdisciplinary workshop, *Systems Research and Behavioral Science*, **27** (4), pp 466–468
Schwaninger M and Grösser S (2008) System dynamics as model-based theory building, *Systems Research and Behavioral Science: The Official Journal of the International Federation for Systems Research*, **25** (4), pp 447–465
Schwaninger M and Scheef C (2016) A test of the viable system model: Theoretical claim vs. empirical evidence, *Cybernetics and Systems*, **47** (7), pp 544–569
Sharma SD (2009) *China and India in the Age of Globalization*, Cambridge University Press, Cambridge, Available at: https://doi.org/10.1017/CBO9780511609916 (archived at https://perma.cc/XBA3-55ZF)
Simon HA (1996) *The Sciences of the Artificial*, MIT Press, Cambridge, MA, Available at: http://search.ebscohost.com/login.aspx?direct=true&scope=site&db=nlebk&db=nlabk&AN=49230 (archived at https://perma.cc/3XGJ-R9LM)
Smith A ([1776]) *The Theory of Moral Sentiments*, 6th ed, Printed for J. Beatty and C. Jackson, Dublin

Spiegler R (2016) Choice complexity and market competition, *Annual Review of Economics*, **8** (1), pp 1–25, https://doi.org/10.1146/annurev-economics-070615-115216 (archived at https://perma.cc/9E97-6DKM)

Spohrer J and Maglio Pp (2008) The emergence of service science: Toward systematic service innovations to accelerate co-creation of value, *Production and Operations Management*, **17** (3), pp 238–246

Steer (1952) Book review. Cybernetics: Circular causal and feedback mechanisms in biological and social systems, Transactions of the Seventh Conference, March 23–24, 1950, New York. Heinz von Foerster, ed. New York: Josiah Macy, Jr. Foundation, 1951. Book review in ***Science***, 25 Jan, **115** (2978), p 100, https://science.sciencemag.org/content/115/2978/100.1.pdf-extract (archived at https://perma.cc/24QG-G4NN)

Summer CE, Bettis RA, Duhaime IH, Grant JH, Hambrick DC, Snow CC and Zeithaml CP (1990) Doctoral education in the field of business policy and strategy, *Journal of Management*, **16** (2), pp 361–398, https://doi.org/10.1177/014920639001600207 (archived at https://perma.cc/V2YW-U9N6)

Teece DJ (1992) Competition, cooperation and innovation: Oganizational arrangements for regimes of rapid technological progress, *Journal of Economic Behavior and Organization*, **18** (1), pp 1–25, https://doi.org/10.1016/0167-2681(92)90050-L (archived at https://perma.cc/BN23-JET8)

Teece DJ (1996) Firm organization, industrial structure, and technological innovation, *Journal of Economic Behavior and Organization*, **31** (2), pp 193–224, https://doi.org/10.1016/S0167-2681(96)00895-5 (archived at https://perma.cc/KS47-JBCC)

Teece DJ (2010) Business models, business strategy and innovation, *Long Range Planning*, **43** (2–3), pp 172–194, https://doi.org/10.1016/j.lrp.2009.07.003 (archived at https://perma.cc/75UM-KKU8)

Teece DJ (2018) Business models and dynamic capabilities, *Long Range Planning*, **51** (1), pp 40–49, https://doi.org/10.1016/j.lrp.2017.06.007 (archived at https://perma.cc/EDD5-VSC8)

Teece DJ, Pisano G and Shuen A (1997) Dynamic capabilities and strategic management, *Strategic Management Journal*, **18** (7), pp 509–533, https://doi.org/10.1002/(SICI)1097-0266(199708)18:7<509::AID-SMJ882>3.0.CO;2-Z (archived at https://perma.cc/H2VF-D59R)

Thanheiser HT (1972) *Strategy and Structure of German Industrial Enterprise*, Graduate School of Business Administration, Harvard University, Boston, MA

Thomas H and Pollock T (1999) From I-O economics' S-C-P paradigm through strategic groups to competence-based competition: Reflections on the puzzle of competitive strategy, *British Journal of Management*, **10** (2), pp 127–140

Ulrich H (1970) *Die Unternehmung als produktives soziales System: Grundlagen der allgemeinen Unternehmungslehre*, Haupt, Stuttgart

Ulrich H (2001) *Gesammelte Schriften: Die Unternehmung als produktives soziales System*, Haupt, Bern

Ulrich H and Krieg W (1972) *Das Sankt Galler Management-Modell*, Haupt, Bern

Varela F and Maturana H (1972) Mechanism and biological explanation, *Philosophy of Science*, **39** (3), 378–382

Varela FG, Maturana HR and Uribe R (1974) Autopoiesis: The organization of living systems, its characterization and a model, *Biosystems*, **5** (4), pp 187–196

Vargo SL and Lusch RF (2004) Evolving to a new dominant logic for marketing, *Journal of Marketing*, **68** (1), pp 1–17, https://doi.org/10.1509/jmkg.68.1.1.24036 (archived at https://perma.cc/HZ68-JVFM)

Vargo SL and Lusch RF (2014) Inversions of service-dominant logic, *Marketing Theory*, **14** (3), pp 239–248, https://doi.org/10.1177/1470593114534339 (archived at https://perma.cc/2G8Y-37FU)

Vargo SL, Maglio PP and Akaka MA (2008) On value and value co-creation: A service systems and service logic perspective, *European Management Journal*, **26** (3), pp 145–152

Vidgen R (1998) Cybernetics and business processes: using the viable system model to develop an enterprise process architecture, *Knowledge and Process Management*, **5** (2), pp 118–131, https://doi.org/10.1002/(SICI)1099-1441(199806)5:2<118::AID-KPM19>3.0.CO;2-3 (archived at https://perma.cc/7A5S-EKES)

Weiser M (2002) The computer of the 21st century, *Pervasive Computing*, (1), pp 19–25

Wernerfelt B (1984) A resource-based view of the firm, *Strategic Management Journal*, **5** (2), pp 171–180, https://doi.org/10.1002/smj.4250050207 (archived at https://perma.cc/22KR-BH6D)

Whittington R (2008) Alfred Chandler, founder of strategy: Lost tradition and renewed inspiration, *Business History Review*, **82** (2), pp 267–277

Whittington R and Mayer M (2006) *The European Corporation: Strategy, structure, and social science*, Oxford University Press, Oxford

Wiener N (1948) *Cybernetics: Or control and communication in the animal and the machine*, MIT Press, Cambridge, MA

Wirth MO and Bloch H (1995) Industrial organization theory and media industry analysis, *Journal of Media Economics*, **8** (2), pp 15–26, https://doi.org/10.1207/s15327736me0802_3 (archived at https://perma.cc/2CXE-4SY5)

Wirtz BW, Pistoia A, Ullrich S and Göttel V (2016) Business models: Origin, development and future research perspectives, *Long Range Planning*, **49** (1), pp 36–54, https://doi.org/10.1016/j.lrp.2015.04.001 (archived at https://perma.cc/9SSU-ZGCK)

Young A (2012) The African growth miracle, *Journal of Political Economy*, **120** (4), pp 696–739, https://doi.org/10.1086/668501 (archived at https://perma.cc/SM22-WWTV)

04

Global value chain management strategies and models for competitive advantage

CO-AUTHORED WITH LUKAS-ARVED EIBEN, MBA

Introduction

The importance of functioning and carefully implemented supply chains (SC) in global value chains (GVC) is undisputed, as proven by various authors (Adewole and Struthers, 2019; Elms and Low, 2013; Memedovic *et al*, 2008; Keane, 2019). However, recently no research could be found that developed actual tools for executives for the design of SC and SCM in GVCs or combined existing research to provide practitioners with hands-on advice. This is also supported by Kamran (2018), who proved in his PhD thesis that existing models (especially Porter's Five Forces Model) do not regard the viability and complexity of modern market dynamics sufficiently. Hence, he concluded that new models are needed. The theory to be proven results therefore from the novelty of this thesis and is as follows.

On the one hand, there is a large amount of theoretical research about SCs/supply chain management (SCM) and GVCs. On the other hand, there are no practical models for, and specific research, on the design of SCs in GVCs, which is leading to a lack of hands-on tools for strategic designs of SCs in GVCs. Hence a new interdisciplinary approach for the design of a holistic model is needed which can deal with the volatility and complexity of an increasingly uncertain world.

The aim and task are hence an examination of existing literature to provide an overview of research gaps, collect existing scientific approaches that could be used to fill this gap and give (proceeding from the analysed literature) recommendations to show what this model should consider.

This is done by desk research, where literature of the relevant fields (mainly logistics, SCM, value chain (VC) management and GVC) is analysed. The basic procedure for the literature review is displayed in Figure 4.1. However, this thesis is a viewpoint. Nevertheless, it does provide the reader with an indicative literature overview and covers the most important views about this multifaceted topic.

To give the reader a comprehensive overview about the relevant fields, first the historical development of logistics to modern SCM approach is described. This is followed by a short introduction to Porter's VC model, including his approach of sustainable competitive advantage and a critical review of this concept. Hereafter the basic GVC concept is outlined and an overview about current research approaches is given. This forms the basis for the discussion of SC research in GVCs. Based on this literature review, the author infers research gaps, suggests areas for future academic research and recommends aspects and trends which should be considered thereby.

The historical development: from transportation to supply chain

Transportation processes are as old as humanity. However, the simple transportation of a good from point A to B cannot be compared with the sophisticated SC networks of the modern globalized economy. The term 'logistics' was first introduced by military planners in the 19th century in France (Jomini, 1830). However, transportation processes and logistics were

FIGURE 4.1 Basic procedure for the literature analysis and evaluation

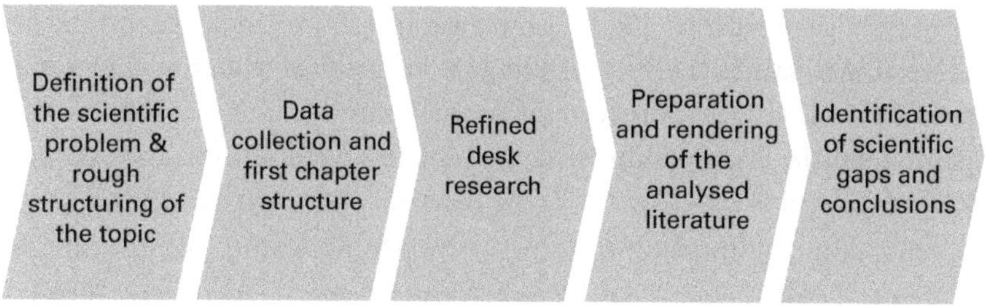

at that time mostly not seen as part of business science, and therefore remained unobserved by the first business researchers. For example, one of the standard references of historical business literature, the book 'Le Parfait Négociant' (The Perfect Merchant), written in 1675, did not discuss the transportation of goods. Until the Second World War literature about transportation was almost solely focused on railway systems (as the modern technology for that time) and analysis of freight costs. In general, transportation was seen as a single process, and a deeper integration with other activities was viewed as unnecessary (Farris, 1997).

All this changed with the end of the Second World War, as veterans returned to their old jobs and applied the knowledge they had gained about military logistics. In the military, continuous replenishment of supplies was seen as decisive for the course of the war (McGinnis, 1992). This development laid the foundation for modern logistics. However, warehousing and transportation were still mainly seen as cost drivers, which had to be minimized.

The first textbooks that were more comprehensive about logistic processes[1] were published in the 1960s. In these textbooks, the main idea was to use faster and more expensive transportation modes for inbound logistics in order to decrease capital commitment costs, as interest rates had risen sharply (Farris, 1997; McGinnis, 1992; Ballou, 1981).

This focus slowly changed in the 1970s, when continuous material flow became more important as new management techniques (such as kanban) became more popular (McGinnis, 1992). Therefore, researchers started focusing on developing new techniques for physical distribution, short lead times, depot location, and warehouse layouts that can increase the reliability of logistic networks (Scribbings, 1994).

The next trend emerged in the mid-1980s, when methods such as kanban had their final breakthrough and logistics processes became more visible to upper management. Therefore, the coordination with and the integration of transportation with other functions were enforced (holistic and connected view of logistics and adjacent activities), and partnerships with third parties were established (Farris, 1997). Companies also started focusing on improving customer satisfaction by offering more product varieties and better service. In this context, the term SCM was introduced in the 1982 article 'SCM: Logistics Catches up with Strategy' by Keith Oliver and Michael Webber (Schönberger *et al*, 2018). At the same time, Michael Porter wrote the book *Competitive Advantage: Creating and sustaining superior performance*, where he introduced the concept of a value chain (VC) and the classification of all processes into primary activities (which add direct value to a customer) and secondary activities (which support the primary activities). Two of the five primary activities were direct logistics processes (inbound and outbound logistics). The important part of Porter's model was the connection of logistics to the VC, especially to service activities, and the fact that he gave logistics such a prominent part in the model (McGinnis, 1992).

In the 1990s, new trends emerged and a continuous flow of goods and information beyond corporate boundaries became the most important. The flow was seen as critical for a company's success and a reason why some companies failed, and others flourished. Companies also began to focus on 'core competencies' and specialization. The mindset was (and partly remains) that the company should 'focus on its core business and outsource the rest'. Therefore, many companies abandoned vertical integration, sold off non-core operations, and outsourced supporting functions to external companies. However, this development changed management requirements as processes (and therefore the flow of information, goods, and labour) had to be managed through various companies, and could not be managed internally. Furthermore, suppliers had to be monitored and steered more closely, due to their deeper integration into the company's creation of value. Consequently, it was necessary to develop the management practices of logistics, operations, supply management, and additional service processes, especially since each sector has its own identity, organization and academic background (Brüning, 2018; Zinn and Goldsby, 2014; Storey *et al*, 2006). Consequently, a holistic SCM became more important, as the number of activities, which must be orchestrated and aligned to each other, increased while the qualitative requirements rose. The pioneers in this field were the automotive and consumer goods industries (Scribbings, 1994). This development marked the birth of modern SCs and SCM (Brüning, 2018; Zinn and Goldsby, 2014; Storey *et al*, 2006). The development from the first scientific approach of transportation processes to modern SCs is summarized in Figure 4.2.

To summarize, logistics research after the Second World War until the end of the 20th century developed from a functional approach, through the recognition of the interdependencies of logistics with its environment, to the acknowledgement of logistics as a strategic factor for a company's success or failure. This development led to the modern view of seeing logistics as an integrated part of a complete SC.

FIGURE 4.2 The evolution of the supply chain

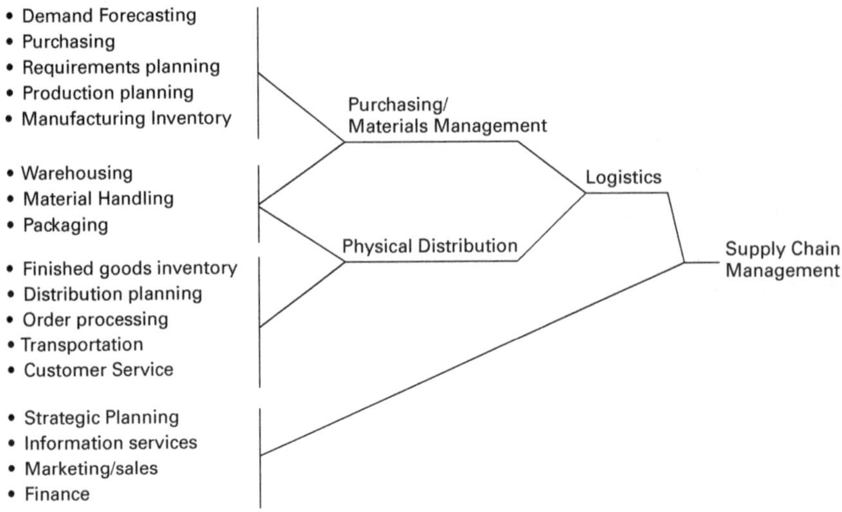

Based on Ballou (2006)

Supply chain: current state of research and approaches

As written in the previous section, the view of logistics and its interaction with other internal and external processes changed completely over the last century, and it has developed into the modern SC approach. In particular, at the beginning of the 21st century, logistics became more closely intertwined with purchasing activities, due to new concepts and trends that were mainly driven by the internet. These trends included replenishing stocks based on actual sales, 'quick response', 'efficient consumer response',[2] and product differentiation. This development was driven and inspired by the automobile industry (which was the first industry to introduce these approaches), which had extreme compartmentalization of its suppliers, to such a degree that even single suppliers had subcontractors, which had their own subcontractors, and so on. Therefore, it was not only necessary to monitor the direct contractors and suppliers (so-called tier 1), but the next and subsequent levels of suppliers also had to be monitored (tier 2, 3, and so on). To manage these sophisticated SC networks, management approaches had to change again and new KPIs and methods, such as balanced scorecards, were implemented (Storey *et al*, 2006).

The next event was the Great Recession in 2008. During and after this event, SCM and SC research focused on the connection between a company's financial performance and its SC. It was discovered that the SC is responsible for 60–70 per cent of a firm's operating cost and therefore serves as a main driver of its financial performance. Managers and researchers focused especially on these facts, as freight rates dropped dramatically and credit markets became increasingly restricted during the Great Recession (Stank *et al*, 2011: 941).

SCs have become more complex, especially in the last decade. Therefore, SCM was and continues to face new challenges. As stated above, SCs have been more deeply integrated into different functions. One of the biggest trends is the connection between SCM and operations management. Ever since the 1990s, a deep connection and a substantial overlap between these two fields has emerged, and many companies have merged these two activities. Consequently, in scientific journals, the term 'supply chain and operations management' (SCOM) is often used. The main advantage of having a harmonized SCOM department is to have a better basis for matching demand and supply, by being able to implement and operate all connected processes in the most efficient way (Schönberger *et al*, 2018). Therefore, SCOM can be seen as an integrating function to match data about demand and supply, and enable the company to use the information to plan further actions in areas like purchasing, logistics, and operations.

Consequently, steering and management have also become more complex. One of the most discussed problems is the evaluation of SCs. Due to a company's various task objectives, which occasionally conflict with each other, many trade-offs have to be made (eg low transportation costs trade off against short shipping times). Schönberger *et al* noted the following:

> In practice, SC and operations managers spend at least a half of their working time handling uncertainties and risks. That is why the control function becomes more and more important for establishing feedback between the planned and real processes (Schönberger *et al*, 2018).

There is therefore a substantial debate in research and businesses over which KPIs should be used: either reliable and classic measurements like speed, costs, reliability, and customer satisfaction, or 'soft' factors such as flexibility. Another approach is to focus on functions which actually add 'value'. The key challenge for this approach is to spot the value-adding functions and evaluate them (what is the customer actually demanding?) (Schönberger *et al*, 2018).

This leads to the next management challenge SC professionals are facing: decision problems (Lourenço and Ravetti, 2018). Decisions are becoming more complex not only because of target conflicts, but also because of an increase in the dimension and complexity of SC planning. SC planning has become more complex because of the above-mentioned developments.

Consequently, researchers and managers have introduced new management information systems, which are mainly driven by higher computing power and therefore contain possibilities for heuristic and meta-heuristic data analysis. Such data analysis is better known as its keywords, such as predictive analytics, big data analytics, or artificial intelligence. However, it is important to mention that these tools do not replace the decision-making of executives and professionals, but support their decision-making by offering solutions for foreseeable short problems. These tools basically involve a shift from purely analogue decision-making to decision-making that gains informational advantages by using (online) IT tools. These tools are especially important for SCM, not only because SCs involve connected systems and smart operations that are especially suited for data analysis, but also because SCM combines various functions and gathers data from all over the company and even external partners. Some of the key tasks of modern SCM are its integration and planning functions. Therefore, while new challenges have arisen which are more complex than the challenges in other areas, these challenges also offer the solutions despite their complexity (Lourenço and Ravetti, 2018).

Therefore, SCM and SC research has been affected by the speedy progress of IT research and digitalization in the last 10 years, to a greater extent than other business fields. The digitalization megatrend has offered former unimaginable opportunities, especially for logistics and the management of SC networks, for example through the application of predictive analytics, artificial intelligence, smart operations, e-operations or the proclamation of an 'Industry 4.0' (Schönberger *et al*, 2018).

Due to the continual and rapid succession of research breakthroughs, researchers predict that the above-mentioned applications are just the beginning of a long-lasting IT trend. In particular, fields such as data evaluation, machinery integration, and digitalization of processes will probably grow strongly over the next years and even decades (Lourenço and Ravetti, 2018). This development will be particularly advantageous for one of the current challenges facing every strategic planner: planning under uncertainty. Uncertainty is present in every part of the SC. Keeping resources available for uncertain events is one of the highest cost drivers (especially for resilient SCs), and therefore contains a large potential for optimization. Although exploiting this potential is currently difficult, it could be made more possible by improved (meta)heuristic options, which can lead to a better allocation and flexibility of existing resources (Lourenço and Ravetti, 2018).

Digitalization is also an important opportunity for another problem of modern SCs: risk reduction. Due to the enhanced connection of SCs to nearly all of an organization's processes, the globalization of trade, and the increased demands on SCs (eg low lead times, cost reductions, just-in-time delivery which leads to reduced safety stocks), SCs are currently vulnerable. Hence, any incidents to an SC can threaten a firm's existence and a solid risk management strategy is mandatory in SCM planning efforts. Consequently, researchers in the past few years have investigated how an SC can become more resilient to external shocks. Resilience here means an SC's ability to withstand sudden shocks in its environment and function properly. It is important to develop active risk management methods, especially since many companies still rely on outdated approaches, such as solely preventive or intra-organizational approaches. However, SCs require inter-organizational approaches.

One approach is so-called 'resource-sharing', which gives companies greater access to resources. During disruptions, the parties can share resources to fight the crisis. As the availability of resources is the key to higher resilience but storing resources is expensive, researchers have focused on resource-sharing as a way to gain a collaborative advantage. This not only concerns physical resources, but also human resources. It can take place between partners or even competitors, although in practice it mainly occurs within organizations, or between key customers and first-tier suppliers.

The research has confirmed that there is a positive correlation between the time it takes an SC to recover after an incident, and the firm's level of collaboration and resource-sharing with third parties (Brüning, 2018). Some of the most important factors for the success of this approach are trust, dependency, and commitment. In relationships with a high level of trust, parties can access and share external resources more quickly and the coordination is simplified. Companies have deeper commitments to resource-sharing if there is a certain level of trust, and at the same time the level of trust increases as companies deepen their commitments to resource-sharing. This process is amplified if there is a feeling of dependency on resource-sharing with third parties. Dependency in turn is strengthened if there is a high level of commitment from all partners. A successful resource-sharing network is therefore self-reinforcing (Brüning, 2018).

Another focus of literature in the last years (besides new IT solutions and new decision-making opportunities) is the so-called 'green logistics' and sustainable SCM. Due to stricter regulatory frameworks, the internalization of formerly external costs, and an increased awareness amongst the public, shareholders, and partners, nearly every company is optimizing its environmental footprint. Consequently, researchers have also focused on this development and the concomitant challenges. The Environmental Protection Agency of the United States conducted a survey where companies that had implemented green principles were compared with companies that had not implemented them. Surprisingly, the companies that had implemented green principles experienced higher savings due to their more efficient operations, as 'green thinking' is essentially an approach for waste minimization and optimization of a company's VC, by eliminating activities which do not add value (according to lean principles) (Engin *et al*, 2018).

Surprisingly, despite the consensus among stakeholders on the importance of sophisticated SC and the scientific attention it has received over the last decades, there is still no universally recognized definition of SC and SCM. In particular, the difference between logistics management and SCM is not precisely defined, as both areas naturally share overlapping functions (Lourenço and Ravetti, 2018).

The most common definition of SCM is provided by the Council of Supply Chain Management Professionals (CSCMP):

> Supply chain management encompasses the planning and management of all activities involved in sourcing and procurement, conversion, and all logistics management activities. Importantly, it also includes coordination and collaboration with channel partners, which can be suppliers, intermediaries, third party service providers, and customers. In essence, supply chain management integrates supply and demand management within and across companies (CSCMP, 2013).

Additionally, Schönberger *et al* noted: 'SCM is one of the key components of any organization and is responsible for balancing demand and supply along the entire value-adding chain' (Schönberger *et al*, 2018).

Hence, the CSCMP defines the term SC as follows:

> 1) starting with unprocessed raw materials and ending with the final customer using the finished goods, the supply chain links many companies together. 2) the material and informational interchanges in the logistical process stretching from acquisition of raw materials to delivery of finished products to the end user. All vendors, service providers and customers are links in the supply chain (CSCMP, 2013).

The indifferent definitions and the increasingly high level of overlaps with other disciplines is also raising concerns, especially about the professional and scientific identity of SC and logistics. For example, Zinn and Goldsby (2014) wrote that due to the numerous additional activities, which SCM attracted over the last years, it is uncertain if there will remain a clear focus of the discipline. Zinn and Goldsby raised the concern that the field will be dominated by new and 'bigger' tasks and the classic tasks of SCM (ensuring a continuous flow of goods and information) and especially the skills to organize these classic chores will step into the background. This shows also in the development of logistics management, which is losing its importance as a distinct management and research field but is considered more as a subdiscipline of SCM (especially in big organizations) (Zinn and Goldsby, 2014). This does not necessarily mean that logistics management is considered as unimportant, but its function in business and the research focus is changing.

Introduction to Porter's value chain theory

In 1985, Michael Porter published his book *Competitive Advantage: Creating and sustaining superior performance*. The main idea of his book was the introduction of the concept of a value chain (VC). The VC concept provides a framework for strategic thinking and encourages companies to focus on actual value-adding activities, which are the basis of a company's competitive advantage, instead of discrete supporting activities (Porter, 1985). The VC is thus the basis for a systematic analysis of all a company's activities and the interaction of them. By disaggregating a company into its strategically relevant activities, the costs of and the existing/potential sources for differentiation can be identified (Porter, 1985).

A VC is constructed for all of a company's activities in a certain business unit, as an industry-wide VC was too broad. The VC is influenced by the activity's history, strategy and economics. The sum of all the different VCs in a company is its competitive advantage or disadvantage. Buyers are willing to pay more (and therefore increase the profit margin) if a company can offer a better value than its competitors (which is the competitive advantage). Most organizations engage in hundreds, if not thousands, of activities in the process of converting inputs to outputs (Porter, 1985). Porter generally divided activities into primary and support activities.

The five primary activities are inbound logistics, operations, outbound logistics, marketing and sales, and service (Porter, 1985). Support activities are not involved directly in the value-creation process, but support the primary activities so that they can be performed better. These activities can be again divided into four categories: procurement, technology development, human resources, and firm infrastructure (Porter, 1985). Porter visualized the activities and their interaction in his famous arrow diagram, which is also a holistic summary of the VC (see Figure 4.3).

Additionally, Porter defined the activity types for primary and support activities. These types exist in both primary and supporting activities:

- **direct:** all the activities that are directly involved in creating value for the customer;
- **indirect:** activities which optimize the execution of direct activities or make them possible;
- **quality assurance** (Porter, 1985).

To which level activities are separated depends on the aim of the VC analysis and the business unit that is analysed. Some activities can be divided more finely than others, according to their importance to the company's competitive advantage. However, it is extremely important that all of a company's activities are included. The role of an activity can even change depending on the industry, or there can be overlap, which can lead to the activities being

FIGURE 4.3 Subdividing a generic value chain

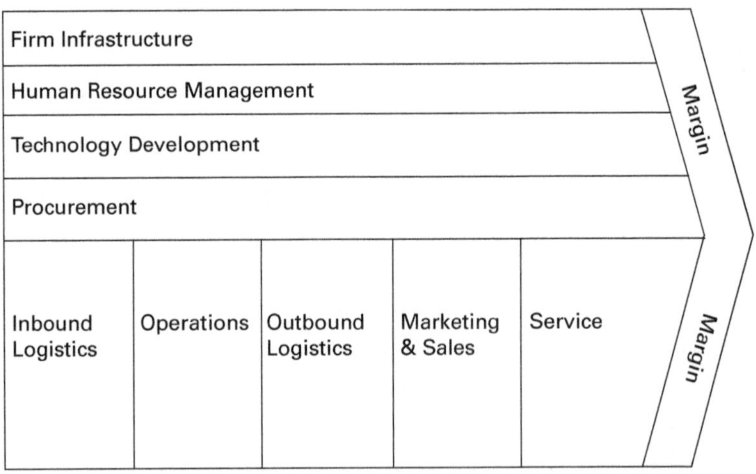

Based on Porter (1985)

reclassified (eg sales and service functions). Many companies have redefined an activity's traditional role and reclassified the activity, for example by offering outstanding customer service and using this service as part of its marketing, in order to achieve a competitive advantage (Porter, 1985). The combination of all these activities forms the VC.

Naturally, these activities must be linked to each other, as this is one of the main reasons for a company's competitive advantage or disadvantage. A proper linkage between activities leads to optimization (eg through lower inventories), or better coordination (due to better information flow). It is therefore important to observe all the linkages between all the activities (primary to supporting, supporting to supporting, and primary to primary activities). Linkages exist not only within a VC, but also between external partners and the company. These are the so-called 'vertical linkages'. The underlying principles remain the same, as optimized or better-coordinated linkages are a significant competitive advantage for all parties on all sides of the VC (suppliers and customers). It is therefore essential for every company to engage not only with its own VC, but also with its consumers' VCs, as only then can the company increase their positive impact on their customers' VCs and market that increase to them. This 'competitive scope' can be categorized into four dimensions, which shape the configuration of a VC in different ways:

- **segment scope:** differentiation through the specialization of the own VC on the VC of the buyers and their individual product needs;
- **vertical scope:** specialization according to the level of in-house-production, the level of integration with suppliers, and the degree of engagement with the buyers' industry;
- **geographic scope:** focusing the set-up of a VC on certain regions or countries (with special demands);
- **industry scope:** developing a coordinated strategy for a range of related industries, for example by specialized sales consulting or shared logistical solutions.

Setting a broad scope can increase the number of possible customers but decrease a company's competitive advantage, as their customers' special needs cannot be served in an optimal manner. However, a certain cost advantage can be generated, as the number of buyers will increase (at the expense of a higher profit margin). On the other hand, the VC can be tailored narrowly to the needs of a certain customer segment. The advantage is a higher profit margin, as the needs of these specialized customers can be fulfilled better. It can therefore be rational for a company to establish several business units with different VCs, in order to serve different markets (Porter, 1985). As setting a proper scope can be challenging for companies, they can enter into coalitions with other (independent) companies, to achieve the benefits of different VCs through collaboration. These long-term agreements between companies can broaden a company's scope without broadening its original VC. There are two types of coalitions: vertical and horizontal coalitions. Horizontal coalitions are partnerships on the same stage of the VC in which the partner companies are engaged in business in the same area. Vertical coalitions describe the collaboration between the upstream and downstream partners in a company's VC (Porter, 1985).

Hence, a VC is always embedded in a value system (VS), which is a larger stream of activities (see also Figure 4.4). The VS comprises the supplier's VC (upstream value), as the supplier delivers the inputs and channels (channel value), which influences the company's VC (eg by preventing channel conflicts or offering value-added services). Naturally (and as explained above), the customers' VCs affect the company's VC. The VCs of the various business units of a diversified company can also influence each other. Which of these VCs (competitors, suppliers, channels, or buyers) has the greatest influence depends on the company's industrial characteristics and competitive scope.

FIGURE 4.4 The value system of a diversified and a single-industry firm

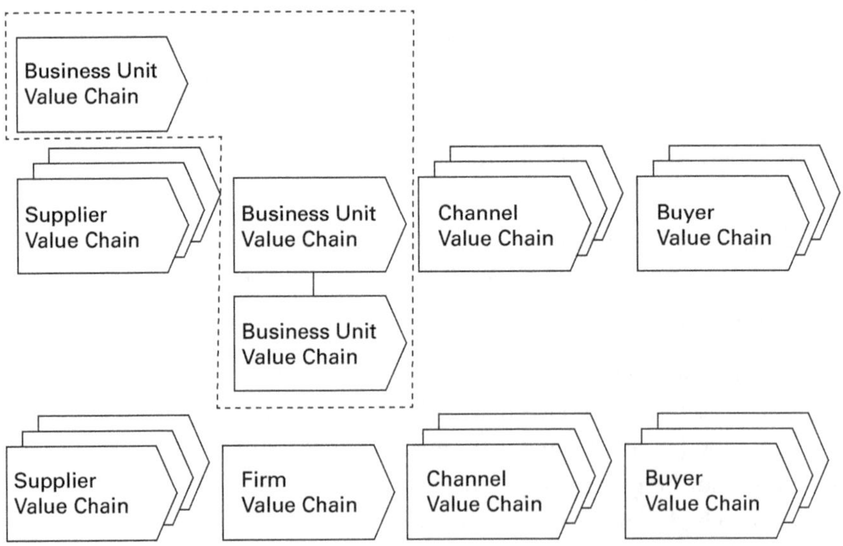

Based on Porter (1985)

It is therefore essential for every company to understand its role in the general VS (Porter, 1985).

There are various strategies and means to align the VC of a company in accordance with the overall VS. In general, a company's particular strategy should be developed relative to the most influential VC in its surroundings, so that the company can occupy a market niche and increase its profit margins.

To summarize, a VC is a combination of a company's generic activities, divided into primary and supporting activities, which must be combined in an optimal manner (through linkages) to provide significant value to the customer and consequently high profit margins to the company. The CSCMP provides the same definition of a VC: 'A series of activities, which combined, define a business process; the series of activities from manufacturers to the retail stores that define the industry supply chain' (CSCMP, 2013).

In scientific literature and elsewhere, the precise difference between VC and SC is, despite these definitions, often unclear. As mentioned in the previous section, the term 'supply chain' is usually used to describe the flow of materials and information (mainly) from their sources to the final customer. The term VC, on the other hand, refers to the complete manufacturing process (including support processes such as HR). It is used to identify the exact value of every activity (regardless of whether it is a manufacturing, primary, or supporting activity), or more precisely the value the customer places on the activity and therefore what it is willing to pay for. Hence, the two disciplines have different starting points and objectives. The VC's original purpose was to spot activities which provide value. However, the trend (as described in this section) is towards integrated value systems, which means that value-adding processes are often fragmented and scattered across different countries. Compared with traditional manufacturing systems, the number of linkages has increased drastically. This trend is also described in the following sections. Additionally, Benito *et al* noted that while Porter mentions these interdependencies and linkages between organizations, he did not sufficiently discuss their consequences, especially regarding the mode of governance, as they assume a high level of control and coordination (Benito *et al*, 2019).

A critical review of Porter's VC model and his concept of sustainable competitive advantage

Due to its popularity, Porter's VC concept is not only discussed in scientific journals, but also in popular trade magazines, such as the *Harvard Business Review* or *Forbes* magazine.

In the past few years, *Forbes* magazine has published various articles critiquing Porter's concepts. In 2012, Denning asked what had killed the Monitor Group, which was a consulting firm co-founded by Porter, as Porter is one of the most influential scholars on business strategy. He argued that 'sustainable competitive advantage simply doesn't exist' [sic.] as there is no evidence that it 'could be created in advance by studying the structure of an industry'. Denning argued that Porter's tools are excellent for storytelling and explaining certain developments in hindsight, but 'almost useless in predicting them in prospect'. Hence, companies which have become market leaders in recent years have employed strategies that are contrary to Porter's concepts. Prominent companies such as Apple, Amazon, or Zara are doing business in a rapidly changing environment. According to Denning, they are successful because they:

> focus on delivering steadily more value to customers through innovation. Thus, experimentation and innovation become an integral part of everything they do [the company does]. Companies with this mental model have shown a consistent ability to innovate and to disrupt their own businesses with innovation (Denning, 2012).

However, Denning notes that he cannot say if continuous innovation is sustainable, but notes that in the last decade these companies did much better than companies that were only focusing on shareholder value or on defeating rivals (Denning, 2012).

One year later, Denning argued that 'the uni-directional value chain – the very core of 20th Century management thinking – is now a problem, not a solution'. He stated that the original idea of the VC concept, which was about maximizing shareholder value, was the 'the dumbest idea in the world' and should be replaced with 'delighting customers profitably' (Denning, 2013). As competitive advantage is extremely volatile, coping with competitors, which was the former main driver of strategy, is now considered to be outdated. Denning argues that the new strategic paradigm is about 'adding value to customers' by operating 'multidirectional networks, in which customers (demand) play a key role' (Denning, 2013).

In one of her articles for the *Harvard Business Review*, Merchant focused on the application of the VC model in what she called 'the social era'. She stated that the VC concept was antiquated, because 'it was created at a time when being big and having scale was in itself a key aspect to competitive advantage and profitability'. However, this was only suitable for mass products, which are sold in normal retail. As the trend moves towards customized products (which was in the 1980s only available for wealthy customers), companies cannot ignore this market, especially since it is one of the most profitable markets with an increasing market share. In this market, the creation of value cannot be optimized by simply applying economies of scale and showering the consumer with mass products. Instead, companies need to become what Merchant calls 'gazelles': companies with fast, fluid, and flexible strategies (Merchant, 2012).

One of the most influential critiques of Porter's concepts came from McGrath's book *The End of Competitive Advantage: How to keep your strategy moving as fast as your business*. Published in 2013, she stated that 'virtually all strategy frameworks and tools in use today are based on a single dominant idea: that the purpose of strategy is to achieve a sustainable competitive advantage. (...) It's no longer relevant for more and more companies.' According to McGrath, competitive advantage is temporary and unsustainable, as:

> the list of once-storied organizations that are either gone or are no longer relevant is a long one. Their downfall is a predictable outcome of practices that are designed around the concept of sustainable competitive advantage. The fundamental problem is that deeply ingrained structures and systems designed to extract maximum value from a competitive advantage become a liability when the environment requires instead the capacity to surf through waves of short-lived opportunities. To compete in these more volatile and uncertain environments, you need to do things differently (McGrath, 2013).

She argued that Porter's concepts are even counterproductive, as they empower the hold of existing business models and routines.

Therefore, Porter's theory is not a given, and other theories are needed to develop new models. One possible theory is based on what McGrath calls the 'creative economy'. Companies in this economy are in a steady innovation process, in which they improve their understanding of their customers' demands and act according to their insights. It is therefore a continuous process of learning and failure (McGrath, 2013).

Furthermore, Porter's concept mainly focuses on inter-organizational or inter-industry thinking. However (as can be seen by companies like Apple and Amazon), new competitors and partners may rise in other areas. According to McGrath, the trend is not business against business, but industry or business models against other industry or business models. Additionally, the speed of change is increasing, which leads to 'big bang disruptions'. Hence, a steady optimization (according to the VC approach) is partly outdated, as customers demand change rapidly. Consequently, a new level for strategy design is needed, which reflects market segmentations, supply and demand, or geographical factors. McGrath labels this trend as 'arenas': 'Arenas are characterized by particular connections between customers and solutions, not by the conventional description of offerings that are near substitutes for one another' (McGrath, 2013).

Hence, one of the main challenges for companies will be simultaneously developing solutions for customers across multiple arenas, while maintaining a deep, intangible, and emotional customer relationship. This means that the importance of the traditional VC approach, with the goal of value optimization, will decrease, as the basic assumptions may no longer apply (McGrath, 2013).

Global value chains: the basic model

The concept of a global value chain (GVC) was introduced in the 1990s by Gary Gereffi. He based the GVC on Porter's concept of the VC. This model analysed the increased collaboration and the resulting differentiation of labour among multiple firms and regions, in the conflict between globalization and regionalization. A typical GVC is a sophisticated industrial organization, which involves stages of production worldwide that are connected by a network of trade in intermediate inputs and final goods, and steered by a lead company. It can therefore be used to analyse whole supply chains and distribution networks, by combining the various VCs of the participating companies into an extended VC (the GVC), similar to Porter's VC (Frederick, 2016).

In the late 1990s, VCs became increasingly more complex as companies started to outsource activities to suppliers around the globe and organizational fragmentation increased. Although many multinational corporations (MNCs) re-internalized their activities, the entire organizational set-up remained highly fragmented. Prominent examples of MNCs that outsourced the vast majority of their production processes are Apple, the textile industry, and parts of the automobile industry. Nevertheless, these MNCs/industries remained deeply involved in the production process, and their VCs would fail if they did not participate, due to their expertise in the complex key activities. These activities usually include governance activities, conceptualization, R&D, design, engineering, specification development, marketing, branding, and distribution. The process of outsourcing and a fragmentation of internal activities according to regional costs or quality differences has many benefits, such as a reduction in the costs of labour-intensive operations, concentration on core competencies, higher flexibility to meet fluctuations in orders, fewer regulations, or better access to specialized suppliers. However, at the same time, the process brings about many new challenges and risks, which must be managed. First of all, companies lose control over the processes (such as compliance with quality standards and delivery schedules), if they outsource them to external partners. Another challenge is the increased complexity of steering linkages between the activities, as the number of directly involved organizations increases, activities are performed in various countries, and the number of logistical processes consequently becomes higher (Strange and Humphrey, 2018).

GVCs are generally characterized by four dimensions (Gereffi and Fernandez-Stark, 2011):

1. **An input-output structure:** the transformation of inputs into the final products (which includes services) (Gereffi and Fernandez-Stark, 2011).
2. **The geographical scope:** due to ongoing globalization, companies are using regional differences as leverage to increase their competitive advantage (Gereffi and Fernandez-Stark, 2011).
3. **Governance structure:** VC governance refers to the control and direction of the relationship of all activities within the GVC. It also describes the distribution of power between the various actors in the GVC. Gereffi and Humphrey identified five basic VC governance patterns. These are presented later in this section (Gereffi and Fernandez-Stark, 2011).
4. **An institutional context:** this dimension describes the general setting in which the GVC is embedded, especially the economic, social and institutional dynamics (Gereffi and Fernandez-Stark, 2011).

This list of dimensions is not final as the important variables differ from industry to industry, and even from company to company. It is therefore vital for a holistic analysis to be performed for the strategic planning of a GVC, in which the main role of every participant in the GVC must be explained (Gereffi and Fernandez-Stark, 2011). These roles were observed in 2014 by Gereffi and Luo, who stated that GVCs consist of lead firms (which are usually MNCs) that are in control of the lead activities, and suppliers which produce the goods or provide services, but are closely steered by the lead firms (Gereffi and Luo, 2014). Strange and Humphrey additionally noted that GVCs are becoming increasingly more complex, dispersed, and fragmented. Therefore, modern GVCs are usually extremely sophisticated and involve hundreds or thousands of suppliers and distributors (Strange and Humphrey, 2018).

As with normal VCs, every GVC is also different, because of their historical development, and the industry or geographical differences. It is therefore difficult to find studies that focus on generic GVCs (similar to Porter's generic VC), as most studies focus on the GVC of certain industries or geographic locations. However, Gereffi *et al* identified three important variables to observe when studying GVCs in a certain industry or place:

1 **The complexity of transactions:** the more complex the transactions, the greater the need for closer interaction between the actors. Hence, a strong governance system must be implemented.
2 **The codifiability of transactions:** information (especially in complex transactions) is often codified to ensure efficient and standardized communication. This often comes along with advanced IT systems, but also includes technical terms or an assumption that users have basic knowledge of certain concepts. If suppliers have the competence to use such information, the GVC is most likely to be modular; if they do not, the GVC will be captive or relational.
3 **The competence of suppliers:** if the suppliers are not competent, the lead company must monitor the suppliers very closely. The monitoring can be conducted by the company itself or outsourced to a certain partner (captive suppliers) (Gereffi *et al*, 2005).

As written, various types of governance patterns exist in GVC. Gereffi introduced the term governance for the description of the various power and authority relationships between the various partners within a GVC (Gereffi, 1994). Hence Gereffi *et al* identified five typical governance patterns within GVCs:

1 **Markets:** a market is the simplest form of GVC governance, as the amount of direct governance tasks by management is low. The central governance factors are supply and demand, through the price mechanism. Direct and strategic exchanges with external partners are therefore only developed in a rudimentary manner. Therefore, strategic linkages do not exist.

2 **Modular VCs:** modular VCs are characterized through specialized suppliers (so-called 'turn-key suppliers') who focus on the supply of full modules, which simplify the interactions by reducing component variation. Although this seems at first glance similar to the market pattern, it is different as the degree of shared information is much greater and therefore the linkages between both companies are deeper. However, because of the modulization of the products, the switching costs (if a new supplier or customer can be found) remain low and also the degree of explicit coordination remains rather low compared with the following governance patterns.
3 **Relational VCs:** in this pattern, regulation is achieved through reputation, social and spatial proximity, and family or ethnic ties. As trust takes a long time to build and is limited to a relatively small group (especially in social structures), the costs of switching to new partners are extraordinarily high (not considering the emotional aspects).
4 **Captive VCs:** this pattern describes GVCs, in which small suppliers are 'trapped' as they are dependent on dominant buyers. Switching costs are therefore very high for the small suppliers, while switching costs for the dominant firm are significantly lower. This dependency is increased by the lead firm, which is often enforcing an extreme specialization of the suppliers on particular products. To maintain high product standards, the dominant firm usually monitors and controls the suppliers frequently.
5 **Hierarchy:** governance by a high level of vertical integration, which leads to a high level of managerial control (to all patterns Gereffi *et al*, 2018).

In practice, the most common types of governance are market and hierarchy governance. However, a 'real' GVC governance with explicit control can be observed very infrequently. The most common types include market transactions, which are governed by a form of managerial control and contracts, which can include clauses that control behaviour. Market governance is most frequently used in areas where the partners must make transaction-specific investments, the suppliers lose reputation if they deliver insufficient products, and if it is necessary for the partners to exchange large amounts of tacit knowledge (Frederick, 2016; Strange and Humphrey, 2018). The five governance types are displayed in Figure 4.5.

FIGURE 4.5 Five global value chain governance types

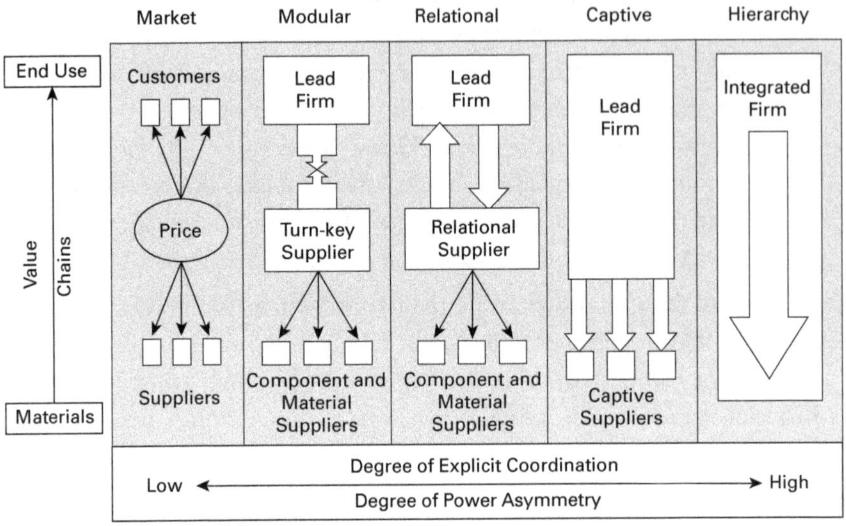

Based on Gereffi *et al* (2005)

Current trends and predictions about the development of global value chains

Just as in the ongoing discussion about Porter's concept, the GVC concept is also the subject of a continuous reassessment in business and economic research. In this section, an overview about current approaches and influencing developments of recent years is given.

In their paper 'Recent Trends in Global Trade and Global Value Chains', Degain *et al* stated that GVCs have changed dramatically since 2011, because: 'more countries joined GVCs through some of the main hubs (the United States, China, Germany, and the Republic of Korea)', and 'the relative distance between the European and Asia–Pacific communities shortened' (Degain *et al*, 2017). However, they observed that complex GVCs are declining, due to new trends such as a rising tide of protectionism, substitution of domestically produced intermediate inputs, and technological innovations which lead to a re-shoring of activities (Degain *et al*, 2017).

Contrary, Ferrantino noted that the prioritization of interventions by lawmakers have become more important, as these interventions usually involve tariff reductions and the elimination of non-tariff measures (Ferrantino, 2013).

In 2017, Strange and Zuchella examined the influence of technological innovation on GVCs. They sorted technological innovations into four main trends: Internet of Things, big data analytics, robotics, and additive manufacturing (3-D printing). Although companies have started using these innovations, their deployment and realization will probably take up to 20 years, meaning that we are currently observing the beginning of a new era. They concluded that these trends will affect strategic decision-making to a large degree and consequently will be an area for future research, particularly in the field of GVC governance, control, internalization/externalization, and their influence on trade or the role of locations (Strange and Zuchella, 2017).

Inomata stated that: 'the most pressing issue for the GVC research community is to accelerate the development of relevant data', as testing of developed models has relied on data from official merchandise trade statistics (Inomata, 2017). However, this data has various flaws, as there are overlaps in data acquisition, lack of valid data, missing information (such as the final user of goods), or a lack of clarity as to ownership (which is a problem in situations where an affiliate sells a product or service to its parent company). Inomata sums this up as 'the benefit of the datasets rests on their representativeness of various aspects of firm operations' (Inomata, 2017).

Inomata also focused on the development of GVC studies. He stated that these have evolved along three different models: sequence analysis, spot analysis, and network analysis. Consequently, the analytical framework has diverged over the last few years. Inomata concluded that due to this development:

> a wider scope of analysis is available. It is only a matter of how best to combine the relevant frameworks in an appropriate way for each research question, just as with integrating various tasks into an optimal configuration of production chains. Keeping and facilitating interdisciplinary dialogues are essential (Inomata, 2017).

In their paper 'Business Models in Global Competition', Tallmann *et al* focused on the general challenges for MNCs. However, their findings were interesting for trends in GVCs. They stated that the most important element of strategic planning is flexibility, as:

> trial and error, real options planning, and responsiveness to external change have to be included in business models. The external constraints on the viability of models are essential to cutting down the potential variability and, therefore, the observed variety of models, in any given time period (Tallmann *et al*, 2017).

Global business models are particularly influenced by these observations, as the 'pervasive use of information technologies, increased reliance on emerging markets, heightened threats from low-cost rivals, and growing pressure to be locally resilient yet globally integrated prompts business model innovations' (Tallmann *et al*, 2017). However, there are specific challenges to global business models. For example, some processes will always require local modification (eg HR functions), although other processes can be standardized. They argued that in general, there is no discussion as to the degree to which an MNC's modified business model (because of local specifications) must differ from its general business model, before it becomes a separate business model (Tallmann *et al*, 2017).

Hence, they concluded that:

> there is clearly a great deal more for researchers to work on with regard to global business models, [especially since it must be examined] what top international executives think about when employing the rhetoric of business models in global competition. Going behind the rhetoric is the task of international business and management researchers (Tallmann *et al*, 2017).

Furthermore, Tallmann *et al* argued that the 'global business model must feature sustainability, creativity, and reachability. Moreover, global competitiveness requires MNEs to constantly monitor environmental conditions that affect success of a working global business model.' Therefore, 'future research must theoretically develop and empirically verify these critical conditions that either provoke MNEs to adopt new business models or under which its existing business model will work more profitably', as the 'extensive literature on the topic is both pragmatic and acontextual in large part' (Tallmann *et al*, 2017).

One of the newest studies on GVCs was published in 2019 by the McKinsey Global Institute (Lund *et al*, 2019). The authors described five structural shifts that are already on the rise or will appear in the next few years:

1 VCs that produce goods have become less trade-intensive – as stated above, China is beginning to consume the goods it is producing, hence international trade intensity is declining. In general, consumption in emerging markets will increase drastically and exceed consumption in the 'old economies'.

2 Services play a growing but undervalued role in trade – trade in services and data is growing up to three times faster than trade in goods. Furthermore, intangible assets, such as software, branding, processes, or intellectual property are becoming more important.

3 Trade based on labour-cost arbitrage is declining in many VCs that produce goods. Unlike the last few decades, the importance of labour-intensive, particularly low-skilled, production steps are decreasing. Therefore, the effect of labour-cost arbitrage has become secondary to factors such as access to skilled workers, legal security, proximity to consumers, and good infrastructure. The authors predicted that this trend will continue, due to the improvements in automation and AI. Formerly labour-intensive production steps will transform into capital-intensive production steps.
4 Global VCs are becoming more knowledge-intensive – the share of value of the actual manufacturing steps is declining, while knowledge-intensive processes such as R&D, marketing, or services is increasing.
5 Value chains are starting to become more regionally concentrated – the intraregional consumption of goods is increasing, especially because China, the former 'workbench of the world', is starting to consume the goods which were being manufactured in China. The authors stated that given the other structural shifts, it is highly likely that this development will persist.

The study (Lund *et al*, 2019) stressed the influence of new technologies on logistics processes. Inventions such as the Internet of Things, artificial intelligence, autonomous driving, automated document processing, or blockchain technology can substantially improve logistics processes and make services more efficient. The authors calculated that by 2030, processing times could be reduced by 16–28 per cent, and overall trade could be increased by 6–11 per cent, which is particularly important for 'just in time' and 'just in sequence' manufacturing.

As a result of these findings, Lund *et al* (2019) concluded that executives need to continuously reassess where they are competing along the VC and adapt their strategy according to their observation. To summarize:

> Regardless of the strategy, a key point is to maintain control, trust, and collaboration in all parts of the value chain. For some companies, this might mean bringing more operations in-house. Those that outsource need close supplier relationships and greater visibility into lower tiers of the supply chain.

Additionally, executives must pay attention to the increasing importance of services, because 'entire business models are shifting from producing goods to delivering services. To make this shift successfully, companies need to gain insight into customer needs, invest in data' (Lund *et al*, 2019).

Consequently, a holistic observation of the whole environment is more important than ever. Transforming traditional companies and developing new ones into flexible, collaborative, and resilient organizations with a high 'speed to market' will be a major challenge for top executives.

Supply chain research and global value chains: current state, criticism and approaches

As a basic principle, SCs and GVCs are deeply connected, fluid, and may overlap. Even in Porter's VC model, inbound and outbound logistics were primary activities. In GVCs, holistic SC models are important, as they can be a crucial competitive advantage for MNCs. As Gereffi and Fernandez-Stark state: 'understanding governance and how a supply chain is controlled facilitates firm entry and development within global industries' (Gereffi and Fernandez-Stark, 2011). Additionally, Ponte and Sturgeon pointed out that: 'a group of "lead firms" play a critical role by defining the terms of supply chain membership, incorporating or excluding other actors, and allocating where, when, and by whom value is added' (Ponte and Sturgeon, 2014). They also stressed Gereffi's observation that the dominating participants not only place orders, but are involved deeply in the VC process, by 'actively helping to create, shape, and coordinate their supply chains, sometimes directly from headquarters or "overseas buying offices", and sometimes through intermediaries.' Furthermore 'global buyers sometimes specify in great detail what, how, when, where, and by whom the goods they sell are produced' (Ponte and Sturgeon, 2014).

In 2015, Cheng *et al* had already examined the papers in all the leading journals about international manufacturing networks. They discovered that research gaps and therefore potential for future research approaches exist in the management of international manufacturing networks, especially in the development of holistic models that observe interactions and relationships, as well as the implementation of such models. However, only a small number of papers focused on issues in the management of international manufacturing networks. As stated by Cheng *et al*:

> The manufacturing (strategy) management literature provides abundant insights on the management of an individual plant, but is less developed in the area of international OM with few empirical theories and models to help industrial managers address the management of the IMN (Cheng *et al*, 2015).

In their paper about the current state of global supply chain research, Ibrahim *et al* also concluded that it is a 'relatively "immature" research topic' and that 'attempts to compare strategies and practices throughout the chain is still limited, and, hence, more effort should be directed accordingly' (Ibrahim *et al*, 2015).

In 2017, Ferdows reappraised the papers published in various business journals, with a focus on global operations. He also verified that only a small number (4.5 per cent) of all papers addressed global operations (Ferdows, 2017: 392) and:

> increasing global fragmentation of supply chains creates more complexity and calls for more research, particularly from OM scholars since managing supply chains is at the core of OM discipline. (...) Many of the papers included in our count are focused only on relatively narrow topics or specific issues in this area (Ferdows, 2017).

Ferdows also argued that business research should focus more on specific strategies for managers which:

> range from specifying strategies for choosing global sites for production of each part of the firm's value chain and how it should be set up (...), as well as designing (...) supply chain network to setting strategic roles for global sites, which entails specifying the extent of involvement of each site (Ferdows, 2017).

According to Ferdows, these challenges occurred because:

> the big and strategic issues in global operations require analysis of a much larger number of independent variables and more tolerance for less exact measures for dependent variables than we are used to – at least in most of what gets published in our leading journals (Ferdows, 2017).

Hence, he concluded that research gaps exist in the development of general business strategies, choice of sites, impact of new technologies, M&A activities, quality management, allocation of critical resources, know-how transfer, and risk mitigation (Ferdows, 2017).

In their work 'Value Chain Shift: Seven Future Challenges Facing Top Executives', Cordon and Ferreiro noted that increasing internationalization will raise new challenges to managers, and therefore management practice. One issue will be increasing resource scarcity, which will force companies to develop active strategies and implement resource management for this strategic challenge. Another challenge will come from new entrants 'from the multipolar world', who will take advantage 'of new paradigms of speed, cost and flexibility they have developed in serving their initial domestic markets'. These new entrants will be a particular problem for traditional Western companies. Consequently, Western companies must participate in emerging markets in a timely manner, to gain a certain know-how in these markets and develop a higher resilience against these new competitors. This is especially important because the speed of information flows will increase, and the world will change more quickly. As a consequence:

> the winning VC2020 player [is] super-aware of the wider environment in which it operates. It is no surprise then to see the theme of corporate social responsibility also evolving from the traditional world of corporate philanthropy, image enhancement and employee engagement (all of which remain important of course) to a more strategic underpinning of the enterprise. Our businesses will succeed when they most help the societies that they work in to thrive and grow. Organizations will need to build trust to form lasting relationships with the populations they serve and the regulatory environments (Cordon and Ferreiro, 2014).

Gereffi and Fernandez-Stark made similar arguments, as they stated that because of the strong dependence of small organizations on MNCs and lead firms, solid ethical leadership is important to ensure that all partners receive a 'fair share' for their services/goods (Gereffi and Fernandez-Stark, 2011). In 2014, Gereffi and Luo put it in concrete terms when they stated that:

> GVCs are also becoming organizationally more concentrated, as the transnational lead firms in GVCs seek to 'rationalize' their global supply chains from 300–500 suppliers in the heyday of economic globalization in the 1990s to 25–30 suppliers (or less) in the current era (Gereffi and Luo, 2014).

This trend leads to competitive risks, especially for smaller market participants, who can get downgraded in the GVC (Gereffi and Luo, 2014).

In 2013, Casson performed an economic analysis of global SCs (GSC) and adopted a contrary position to Gereffi *et al.* He argued that 'it is a mistake to suppose that some firm always masterminds or orchestrates a supply chain, as it is only under specific circumstances that this is the most efficient solution' (Casson, 2013). For general decision-making, he suggested the use of SC mapping enriched by algebraic models, as:

> it is useful for the analysis of complex interactions [and] these models emphasize that intermediate product flows need to be balanced at every stage of a chain. For each intermediate product, there is a market – either notional

> or real. Demand for each intermediate product is generated downstream and supply upstream. Each market can be equilibrated by either management control or market forces (Casson, 2013).

One of the main advantages of these methods is the use of forecasts to optimize the SC configuration, by providing 'an integrated analysis of all outsourcing and offshoring decisions' and identifying 'the outcome of competition and [analysing] the role of headquarters location' (Casson, 2013). This is particularly important because the most important driver of change in SC strategies comes from 'changes in the fundamental parameters of the global economy (...) that alter the balance of costs between different supply chain configurations' (Casson, 2013). However, Casson also stated that SCs in GVCs are 'not a new phenomenon that needs a new theory to explain it, but an old phenomenon in a new guise' (Casson, 2013).

In 2017, Sturgeon *et al* published the famous article 'Scale, Distance, and Remoteness in Global Value Chains'. They argued that the role and importance of SCM in GVC is strongly dependent on the remoteness and importance of a certain country within the GVC, as distance has a strong influence on GVC participation, because of higher coordination costs and a more difficult exchange between the participating organizations (Sturgeon *et al*, 2017).

Sturgeon *et al* substantiated Dickens' argument that due to recent technological inventions GVCs have been 'offered up as the perfect example of technology overcoming geography', as they made possible 'the fragmentation and segmentation of work and its coordination and monitoring' to the needed degree of modern labour division in the process of internationalization (Dickens, 2010). However, Dickens argued that distance is still an important factor in GVCs to a certain extent, and can be a competitive disadvantage for various reasons. First, remoteness increases the cost and time required to deliver goods to their destination. Second, distance increases the administration effort, the complexity of transportation and the general disadvantage of long transit times for goods. This is aggravated by trends such as 'just-in-time' or 'lean production' manufacturing, which additionally increase the complexity of modern SC solutions for remote regions. Another issue is cultural affinities. As cultural differences and long distances decreases the efficiency of collaboration, it becomes more difficult for participants to build and maintain personal relationships with each other, which is essential. Hence remoteness affects not only the SC of physical goods, but also the SC of non-physical goods and services.

However, the view of the importance of distance in GVCs is at a turning point due to technological development. Pure distance will matter less, as monitoring and control are improving, and consequently the coordination of business processes in general, and logistics in particular, are improving as well. Additionally, the transfer of complex parameters, requirements, and instructions is becoming less complex due to new software solutions and innovative business solutions, which decrease the cost of information transfer and the loss of information when it is transferred. As a result, distance will become a non-essential factor in location selection (Sturgeon *et al*, 2017). Sturgeon *et al* concluded that consequently, in order for a region to compete in the GVC of the future, it needs different strategies for states and companies. These strategies depend on the region's size and remoteness, as well as its level of development and involvement in GVCs. As a rule of thumb, organizations in remote regions need sophisticated SC concepts to participate in GVCs (Sturgeon *et al*, 2017).

In 2013, the World Trade Organization published the report 'Global Value Chains in a Changing World', where papers about GSCs and GVCs by various well-known researchers in different disciplines from renowned institutions, such as IHEID, MIT, or the World Bank, were published.

Baldwin, a professor of international economics, argues that Porter's VC model 'is not the right framework for thinking about value chains', as Porter mainly sorts SC activities in the stages of operations, and inbound and outbound logistics. A deeper analytical focus is required because the focus of modern SCs has shifted from sectors to stages of production (Baldwin, 2012). To prove his point, he makes various basic assumptions about the SC of the future. Baldwin argues that the economics of this shift can be observed by splitting it into two phenomena: fractionalization ('unbundling of supply of chains into finer stages of production'), and dispersion ('geographic unbundling of stages') (Baldwin, 2012). Additionally, a constant trade-off is necessary between dispersion and agglomeration forces. Agglomeration forces encourage geographical clustering, as a large number of locally active companies attract more companies to the region (see also Figure 4.6).

However, Baldwin argues that 'the optimal governance solution for global supply chains would be global, not regional', which means that 'the firms conducting much of this 21st century trade find themselves faced with a

FIGURE 4.6 Equilibrium location balances agglomeration and dispersion forces

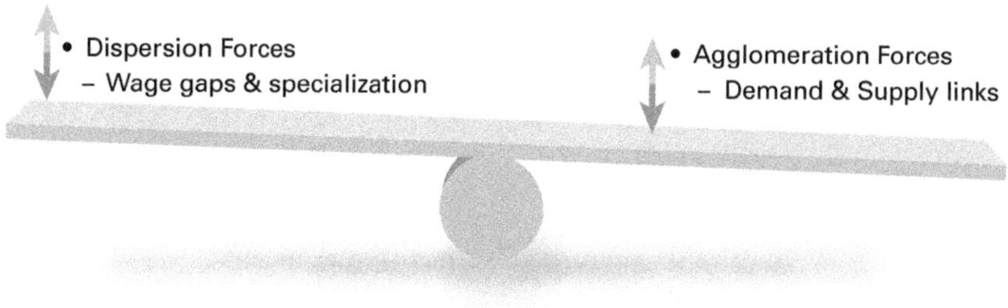

Based on Baldwin (2012)

spaghetti bowl of disciplines' (Baldwin, 2012). Baldwin phrased three questions, which allow for an estimation for how the future of SCs will be moulded (see also Figure 4.7):

1 *Will supply chains become more fractionalized?* The answer to this question is determined by the development of the gains from specialization (which come mainly from economies of scale, learning-by-doing, and the exploitation of salary differences) contrasted to the increase in coordination costs and risks (which come from the difficulties of managing versatile stages) (Baldwin, 2012).

2 *Will stages of production become more polarized in terms of skill, capital, and technology intensity?* The development of polarization is driven by the progress of research in information technologies/processes and the automation of manufacturing, which include progress in workflow organization. There will also be a cost–benefit trade-off (Baldwin, 2012).

3 *Will stages of production be further dispersed and interconnected internationally?* The advantage of dispersion again lies mainly in the exploitation of regional salary differences. The increase in dispersion is therefore dependent again on technological improvements, and shrinking transportation and travel costs. As Baldwin stated, 'unbundling along the geographic dimension will be directed by changes in these costs and benefits of dispersion' (Baldwin, 2012).

To summarize, a finer division of labour by technological inventions will allow firms to optimize their SCs by sorting stages geographically and bundling tasks, but will also lead to more complex SCs. Technological advantages can also polarize stages of production, because routine and low-skilled tasks can be easily automated, while the remaining jobs will require sophisticated skills.

FIGURE 4.7 Future of international supply chains

Based on Baldwin (2012)

Hence, 'the resulting, broader stages will involve more capital-intensive, more technology-intensive and more skill-intensive processes' (Baldwin, 2012). Baldwin concluded that the SC of the future in GVCs will be influenced by technological improvements for optimized labour coordination and computer-integrated manufacturing, resulting in the narrowing of wage gaps and reducing the costs of unbundling (Baldwin, 2012).

Elms (2013) wrote one of the few articles that focus on the role of SCs in GVCs as seen from an operational perspective. She concluded that the following factors play a key role for the design of SCs in GVCs:

- inventory management (as low inventory increases a company's flexibility and agility, and lowers costs);
- the global shifting of product manufacturing (as standardization and optimization in logistics is a significant advantage);
- outsourcing and consolidation (as disintermediation and lower cost options are significant advantages);
- transportation (as MNCs are dependent on efficient means of transportation);
- innovation (the above-mentioned influence of technological development) (Elms, 2013).

However, a GSC's precise aims depends on the company's GVC, as the above-mentioned factors emphasize the physical flow of goods, but not the flow of information, finances, and customer preferences (Elms, 2013). Elms quoted Fine *et al*, who observed that:

> competitive advantage is, at best, a fleeting commodity that must be won again and again. That requires continual disintegration and reintegration of organizations (...). A company's real core capability – perhaps its only sustainable one – is its ability to design and redesign its value chain (Fine *et al*, 2002).

Elms also stated that customers will be more aware of unethical practices, regardless of the complexity of a company's surroundings. Therefore, 'a holistic, end-to-end approach to supply chain sustainability [is] essential'. Additionally, Elms claimed that increased market transparency and higher information visibility, due to technological advantages, will lead to 'margin squeeze for intermediaries' (Elms, 2013).

Lessard, a professor at MIT who specializes in economic development, international business, and emerging markets, focused on the sources of risk for SCs. He stated that there are six main sources of risks for SCs: national

FIGURE 4.8 Sources of risk for global supply chains

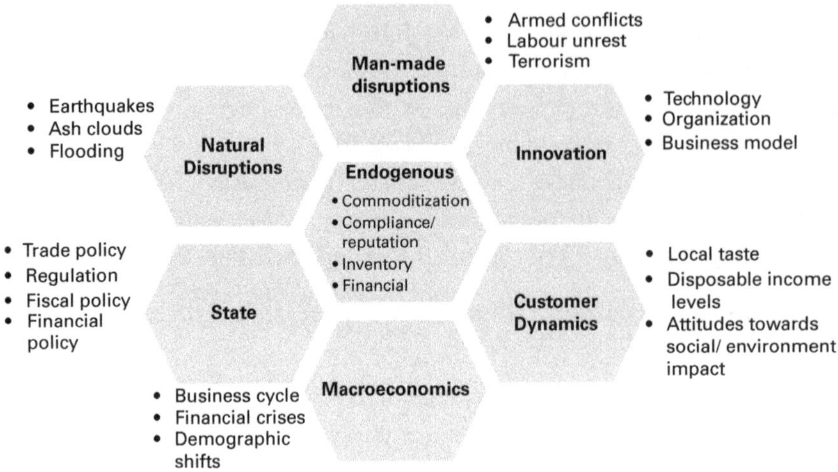

Lessard (2013)

disruptions, customer dynamics, natural and man-made disruptions, innovation, and macroeconomics (see also Figure 4.8) (Lessard, 2013).

Due to the internationalization of modern SCs, the management of these risks has become increasingly complex. Lessard classified these risks into two additional categories: inside risks and outside risks. A company can manage inside risks through good governance and management, while outside risks have to be hedged against or insured for. The problem for companies that build up GVCs and GSCs is that inside risks can no longer be controlled by traditional management processes due to the deep involvement of external partners. Another problem is that incidents often affect external stakeholders, and the impacts are more significant as GSCs are deeply connected systems. However, increasing internationalization does not only have negative outcomes on risk management, as it also leads to a greater diversification of risks, especially macro-level risks (Lessard, 2013). Lessard thus concluded that risk avoidance at all costs is not a valid strategy. Risk-taking can also be a form of competitive advantage, if the company has extensive knowledge of the risks, the ability to mitigate or shape it, and the ability to withstand the possible impacts through diversification and resilience (Lessard, 2013).

To summarize, Lessard found that risk management in GSCs involves not only the hedging against and insuring of risks, or the application of traditional management practices, but also a systematic approach at each link of the chain, which considers the interdependencies between the steps in the GSC. Additionally, solid risk management is a significant competitive advantage, but it requires risk awareness and extensive knowledge of each activity, as well as a system-wide view (Lessard, 2013).

One of the newest publications about GSCs and GVCs is from Schönberger *et al* (2018), who discussed models for the designing of GSC. However, they focused almost solely on quantitative methods for location selection and scarcity of certain resources but did not discuss classic management methods for the design and implementation of said strategies.

The missing link between existing research and hands-on models

As written in the previous sections, SCs and GVCs are a relatively new development. Porter introduced the VC model in 1985, a holistic view on SCs was developed in the 1990s, and shortly thereafter Gereffi started to develop the GVC model.

While there is a substantial amount of literature that discusses the general problems and concepts for both SCs and GVCs, they do not provide practical hands-on models for executives. There is a gap between practice (developed models and tools) and theory. As examined above, the existing literature is rich in information about developments and issues in sub-fields or in specific situations, but is missing holistic and hands-on models, especially for the development of general business strategies. Cheng *et al* (2015), Ibrahim *et al* (2015), and Ferdows (2017) all made similar findings. In particular, there is no specific research which focuses on the design of SC concepts in GVCs. This matches also with the finding of this thesis.

Hence, researchers must focus on the development of new tools for executives, and new theoretical paradigms. All the studies in the literature analysis stated that new strategic tools must be developed, and more research must be conducted in the field of general and hands-on models for strategy design. Lund *et al* (2019) summarized the consensus by stating that companies need strategies to transform into flexible, collaborative, and resilient organizations. Tallmann *et al* (2017) also stressed flexibility and responsiveness to external changes as an important element of new models. Inomata (2017) argued that these models can only be developed by using a wide scope of analysis and combining relevant frameworks through interdisciplinary dialogues, which is complicated by the fact that multi-disciplinary approaches are needed. However, logistics researchers fear that due to the high interdisciplinary overlap, knowledge of traditional logistic approaches will be lost. Consequently, although significant connections between different disciplines are required for new models to be developed, the value of every task must be clearly attributed to a certain activity or process.

Furthermore, Porter's models cannot be used in their original form, as they are regarded as outdated. Nearly all authors agreed that his theory of sustainable competitive advantage no longer applies, as holistic and flexible strategies are needed (what Merchant (2012) called 'gazelles'). Denning argued for 'multidirectional networks', which are adaptive and flexible. Additionally, Denning (2012) and almost all the authors cited emphasized the need for continuous innovation of market leaders, which contradicts Porter's concept of sustainable competitive advantages. Denning summarized this view by stating that the classic concepts of empirical investigation of the past to predict the future no longer work, as the new world is volatile and uncertain. All the authors also criticized Porter's inter-organizational theories, in particular his inter-industry thought. McGrath (2013) therefore introduced her concept of the 'arena', as a new level of strategy design is needed (across multiple arenas) and new competitors are emerging from other arenas with major disruptions. McGrath's findings match also with Baldwin's (2012) critique, that the VC theory focuses too much on the single stages and misses the links and connections between the various participants. Also, Benito *et al* (2019) argued that the VC does not sufficiently recognize the consequences of interdependencies between linkages.

Although it may seem to be obvious to apply Porter's VC concept for the development of tools, it must therefore be seen critically. Nevertheless, the criticisms of the model and certain aspects can be used as a starting point for the development of a hands-on model for SCM in GVCs, if combined with the insights of GVC research and considering SCM approaches.

As the SC is basically linked to all of a GVC's processes, and in the last few decades increased demands have been placed on SCs (as suggested above), it is highly influenced by overall developments in the GVC. It is therefore insufficient to focus solely on SC-specific tasks and trends, but those of adjacent fields must also be observed and assessed. This can only be done by involving aspects of various disciplines and considering major trends and key aspects of GVC and SCM research. Summing up the literature review, various aspects attract attention, as they are discussed in all relevant sub-fields.

One of the most considered developments is globalization. However, the further progress of this development remains questionable. Various authors mentioned the increasing protectionism in various countries, which leads to a weakening of globalization. Combined with trends such as domestically produced goods, technological innovations (such as 3D printing), declining wage differences, and the increasing domestic consumption in emerging countries, some researchers even talked about a trend towards regionalization (Degain *et al*, 2017; Ferrantino, 2013; Lund *et al*, 2019). However, Baldwin argued that SCM must be conducted globally. Van Rensburg (2009) also assumed a globalization of supply and production networks. Despite these assumptions, Degain *et al* observed that regions have become more connected because of an advanced transportation infrastructure, and more countries are joining GVCs. Lund *et al* additionally noted that the global economy is changing substantially and will become more knowledge-concentrated, service-oriented, and in general less trade-intensive. There is no answer to the question about the future of globalization, but instead the researchers are designing 'what if' scenarios. One example is Baldwin's 'three questions'. Furthermore, all researchers agreed that the trade of goods will lose its importance, but the trade of services and data will become more important. Lund *et al* (2019) predicted that the global business models of the future will be about delivering services and analysing data, but not about delivering goods. However, as Tallmann *et al* (2017) emphasized, the current approaches do not sufficiently address this development. This is problematic, especially as global organizations move between the poles of global standardization and local modification.

The handling of the mentioned uncertainty of the future of globalization corresponds with the finding of Schönberger *et al*, who stated, that the handling of uncertainties and risk is one of the most demanding tasks for executives. This is supported by Lessard (2013), who identified six main risks for global SCs from a diverse set of dimensions. He noted that this development creates various new problems for risk management, but also has positive implications such as better diversification. Therefore, a holistic approach is needed for risk management of SCM in GVC, especially since controlled risk-taking can be a form of competitive advantage. Brüning (2018) therefore suggested active risk management and resource-sharing (not just with physical resources but also with employees) in trustworthy networks as a possible solution to make SCs more resilient. However, Brüning also concluded that a new methodological framework had to be developed, as existing inter-organizational approaches were no longer sufficient. Developing new frameworks can also minimize costs, as the provision of resources is extremely expensive. Additionally, Lourenço and Ravetti (2018) stressed the importance of risk management for strategic planning, due to the high uncertainty SCM is facing and the opportunities for optimizing SCs through meta-heuristic approaches.

This development seamlessly blends into the stakeholders' higher awareness of better corporate social responsibility and sustainable/ecological business decisions, as various researchers predict that customers will sanction perceived inappropriate behaviour. In general, as Elms (2013) noted, customers have become more aware of unethical practices, which is a particular challenge for companies with large, international, volatile, and complex networks. Gereffi and Fernandez-Stark (2011) stated that this development will benefit small organizations, which may be (according to some researchers' predictions) dependent on lead companies in GVCs and prevent them from engaging in unethical business practices. According to Ponte and Sturgeon (2014), the businesses of small firms are significantly influenced by lead firms, which monitor these companies very closely. Elms noted that this is aggravated by the fact that stakeholders will have higher information visibility due to new information and communication technologies. Cordon and Ferreiro (2014) also concluded that increasing resource scarceness will force companies to adopt a more sustainable way of doing business, which will be a strategic challenge for GVCs and especially SCs. Particularly in SCM, green logistics is already considered to be a technique for cost minimization, as external costs are internalized and 'green thinking' leads to waste minimization and the elimination of activities that do not add value, as Engin *et al* (2018) noted. Brüning (2018) also argued that corporate social responsibility will become more important, as trust plays a key role in resource-sharing networks and organizations that are known for being philanthropic and helping societies will succeed. Consequently, a firmly anchored corporate social responsibility will become part of every management system. This view is also shared by Lund *et al* (2019), who indicated that maintaining trust control and collaboration in logistics will be a major success factor. However, contrary views have also been discussed and all the viewpoints must be considered. For example, Frederick (2016) concluded that more research must be done in this field.

However, the superior and most minded trend is the ongoing digitalization and the technological advantage. All the researchers assumed that we are at the beginning of what could be a new industrial revolution which will have an extensive impact on SCM. Strange and Zuchella (2017) summarized the position by saying that the application of new inventions will probably take several decades. Additionally, there is a widespread consensus that routine and low-skilled tasks will be automated, and the remaining jobs will require sophisticated skills, which will ultimately lead to more knowledge-intensive GVCs. However, as Lourenço and Ravetti (2018) stated, this development also creates new problems, which are mainly new decision problems. This problem will lead to the need for new management information systems driven by the above-mentioned meta-heuristic analyses. As authors like Casson (2013) noted, it is generally undisputed that algebraic models are needed for better decision-making. As stated above, the digitalization trend will also have a significant impact on other developments in the next few years. For example, some researchers predict that 3D printing will lead to a decline of GVCs and consequently GSCs and regional wage differences are becoming increasingly unimportant, as many tasks are being automated. On the other hand, Lund *et al* emphasized the positive influence of new technologies on logistics processes, as lead times can be drastically reduced, and administration tasks can be automated. Additionally, Ivanov *et al* (2018) noted that predictive analytics, artificial intelligence and the IoT offer incredible opportunities and are destined to be applied in logistics processes. Strange and Zuchella (2017) summarized this view by concluding that digitalization will significantly affect strategic decision-making, especially when designing applicable GVC governance.

Surprisingly, the current state of research in all these fields in relation to a holistic approach is fairly limited. Nearly all authors explicitly state that more research must be done in their fields, as common models and research does not sufficiently address or discuss the new challenges they described. This concerns also organizations which face rather specific challenges, as the location in remote destinations as described by Sturgeon *et al* (2017). Particularly in these settings, the role of a solidly designed SCM, which should be aligned to the company's GVC, is extremely important and must be assessed individually.

Conclusion and outlook

The starting point of a tool should be an analysis of the basic surrounding of the GVC (what Porter called the value system). This can be done by analysing the four dimensions as described by Gereffi and Fernandez-Stark (2011), followed by an analysis of Gereffi *et al*'s (2005) three variables. These analyses could be advanced by applying Porter's idea of 'competitive scope' on GVCs. Here it is important to consider the remarks of Tallmann *et al* (2017) about modification vs. standardization in the business model, if further research is conducted. Hereafter a deeper analysis of the influencing factors should be conducted, where also megatrends and recent developments, which influence GVCs and SCM, should be considered. However, it is difficult to group the trends, developments, and research gaps into categories, as there are significant overlaps and interdependencies. These overlaps and interdependencies are also a major challenge for designing a solid strategy for SCs in GVCs, due to the strategy's increased complexity and need to be viable.

Proceeding from the literature review, a tool for a flexible, adaptive, and continuously improving strategy design, which holistically considers the deep interdependencies between the described trends in a fast-changing world, is needed. There must be special focus placed on planning under uncertainty, risk management, the high number of linkages and interdependencies, and the changed competitive situation. Additionally, the special limitations of organizations, such as their geographical location (remoteness) or their intra-organizational characteristics (eg the ability to transform), must be considered. To make it more concrete, the tool should consider the following:

- The upcoming and long-lasting changes that will occur through technological improvements, especially digitalization and new technologies, which will cause major disruptions – the consequences for management planning should also be considered, such as possible improvements of SCs through big data analysis and data exchange between partners and competitors.
- Economic factors, not only limited to a country or a region, but also dependencies between local economies and the worldwide economy – additionally, not just direct competitors must be observed, but industries or business models which could potentially enter the 'arena' should be observed as well. Particularly the trend for companies to deliver services instead of goods must also be closely observed in the model, as this trend will also change GVCs, with the impacts on SCs being the most extreme by far. Kamran and Scheu (2018) also discussed this trend and its specific influence on logistics, such as its impact on strategy design. Additionally, local economic factors (eg the remoteness of locations and access to infrastructure) should also be assessed.
- Intra-organizational aspects, such as the culture within the company (especially its discrete ability to transform), its resources, and its collaborative networks and the current governance pattern of these networks.

- Overall societal trends, especially those of key stakeholders, which are influencing the organization – this thesis identifies a growing ecological awareness and societies' higher demand for ethical behaviours, which has regulatory consequences and should thus be considered. Therefore, the various regulatory frameworks and ecological effects must also be taken into account when designing a strategy.

Therefore, a model is needed which can not only observe every aspect on its own but also assess them in totality, with a special emphasis on the interdependencies between the various developments. Furthermore, a model must consider rapid changes in the environment. As stated, volatility and uncertainty are major challenges for SC managers. Hence, a model must develop not static, but highly viable, strategies for SCM that can be quickly adjusted to a new strategic direction of the GVC in case of a disruptive event or an external shock. Additionally, a model which primarily relies on projections from historical data or experience is insufficient, as the critiques of Porter's models have demonstrated. Therefore, a future-oriented approach, with individual and creative approaches, is needed.

Proceeding from the findings of the model, the general strategic focus of the SC within the GVC can be concluded. Based on this conclusion, a coordinated design and implementation of the single tasks and processes (which are displayed in Figure 4.2) can be performed.

Notes

1 Essays and books about transportation were also written before the 1960s; however, these were focused on single activities and did not pursue the idea of managing all these activities in a comprehensive approach.

2 **Quick response:** manufacturing approach to reduce lead times for reacting more quickly to market changes; **Efficient consumer response:** initiative to enforce collaboration between manufacturers and distributors to increase costs and better satisfaction of consumer demands, by optimizing the complete value chain.

References

Adewole A and Struthers J (2019) Trade and economic development in Africa: The interaction between logistics and global value chains, in *Logistics and Global Value Chains in Africa*, eds A Adewole and J Struthers, Palgrave, Cham

Armstrong R (2017) The Volkswagen scandal shows that corporate culture matters, https://www.ft.com/content/263c811c-d8e4-11e6-944b-e7eb37a6aa8e (archived at https://perma.cc/9SLV-J37K) (accessed on 19 March 2019)

Baldwin R (2012) Global supply chains: Why they emerged, why they matter, and where they are going, in *Global Value Chains in a Changing World*, eds P Low and D Elms, pp 13–61, WTO Publications, Geneva

Ballou R (1981) Reformulating a logistics strategy: A concern for the past, present and future, *International Journal of Physical Distribution and Materials Management*, **11** (8), pp 71–83

Ballou RH (2006) The evolution and future of logistics and supply chain management, *European Business Review*

Benito G, Petersen B and Welch L (2019) The global value chain and internalization theory, *Journal of International Business Studies*, **50**, pp 1–10

Brüning M (2018) Collaborative recovery from supply chain disruptions, in *Supply Management Research – Aktuelle Forschungsergebnisse 2018*, eds C Bode, R Bogaschewsky, M Eßig, R Lasch and W Stölzle, pp 51–69, Springer, Berlin

Casson M (2013) Economic analysis of international supply chains: An internalization perspective, *Journal of Supply Chain Management*, **49** (2), pp 8–13

Cheng Y, Farooq S and Johansen J (2015) International manufacturing network: Past, present, and future, *International Journal of Operations and Production Management*, **35** (3), pp 392–429

Cordon C and Ferreiro T (2014) *Value Chain Shift: Seven future challenges facing top executives*, IMD International, Lausanne

Council of Supply Chain Management Professionals (2013) *CSCMP Supply Chain Management Definitions and Glossary*, https://cscmp.org/CSCMP/Educate/SCM_Definitions_and_Glossary_of_Terms/CSCMP/Educate/SCM_Definitions_and_Glossary_of_Terms.aspx?hkey=60879588-f65f-4ab5-8c4b-6878815ef921 (archived at https://perma.cc/V2GA-TNYB) (accessed on 23 January 2019)

Degain C, Meng B and Wang Z (2017) Recent trends in global trade and global value chains, in *Global Value Chain Development Report 2017: Measuring and Analyzing the Impact of GVCs on Economic Development*, eds D Dollar, J Reis and Z Wang, pp 37–60, World Bank Publications, Geneva

Denning S (2012) *What Killed Michael Porter's Monitor Group? The one force that really matters*, https://www.forbes.com/sites/stevedenning/2012/11/20/what-killed-michael-porters-monitor-group-the-one-force-that-really-matters/#7e5715ee747b (archived at https://perma.cc/N4VF-QAM7) (accessed on 17 April 2019)

Denning S (2013) *The Management Revolution That's Already Happening*, https://www.forbes.com/sites/stevedenning/2013/05/30/the-management-revolution-thats-already-happening/#41879c870911 (archived at https://perma.cc/CFA6-PKS7) (accessed on 20 April 2019)

Dickens P (2010) *Global Shift: Mapping the changing contours of the world economy*, 6th ed, Lucky Duck Publishing, Chicago

Elms D (2013) Views of GVC operators, in *Global Value Chains in a Changing World*, eds P Low and D Elms, pp 161–171, WTO Publications, Geneva

Elms D and Low P (2013) Introduction, in *Global Value Chains in a Changing World*, eds P Low and D Elms, pp 1–13, WTO Publications, Geneva

Engin B, Martens M and Paksoy T (2018) Lean and green supply chain management: A comprehensive review, in *Lean and Green Supply Chain Management*, eds T Paksoy, G Weber and S Huber, pp 1–39, Springer, Berlin

Farris M (1997) Evolution of academic concerns with transportation and logistics, *Transportation Journal*, **37** (1), pp 42–50

Ferdows K (2017) Keeping up with growing complexity of managing global operations, *International Journal of Operations and Production Management*, **38** (2), pp 390–402

Ferrantino M (2013) Policies to improve the supply chain: what needs to be done?, in *Global Value Chains in a Changing World*, eds P Low and D Elms, pp 263–277, WTO Publications, Geneva

Fine C (2002) Rapid-response capability in value-chain design, *MIT Sloan Management Review*, Winter, pp 69–75

Fine C (2005) *Are you Modular or Integral? Be sure your supply chain knows*, https://www.strategy-business.com/article/05205?gko=8a29a (archived at https://perma.cc/7RCQ-8NDR) (accessed on 27 April 2019)

Frederick S (2016) *The GVC Concept and Tools*, https://globalvaluechains.org/concept-tools (archived at https://perma.cc/64QS-HZBU) (accessed on 26 February 2019)

Gereffi G (1994) The organization of buyer-driven global commodity chains: How U.S. retailers shape overseas production networks, in *Commodity Chains and Global Capitalism*, eds G Gereffi and M Korzeniwwicz, pp 95–122, Praeger, Westport, CT

Gereffi G and Fernandez-Stark K (2011) *Global Value Chain Analysis: A primer*, https://www.researchgate.net/publication/265892395 (archived at https://perma.cc/JE8U-BF76) (accessed on 26 February 2019)

Gereffi G and Luo X (2014) *Risks and Opportunities of Participation in Global Value Chains*, https://openknowledge.worldbank.org/bitstream/handle/10986/18333/WPS6847.pdf?sequence=1andisAllowed=y (archived at https://perma.cc/C2A5-JKFV) (accessed on 28 March 2019)

Gereffi G, Humphrey J and Sturgeon T (2005) The governance of global value chains, *Review of International Political Economy*, **12**, pp 78–104

Gereffi G, Humphrey J and Sturgeon TJ (2018) *Global Value Chains and Development: Redefining the contours of 21st century capitalism*, Cambridge University Press, Cambridge

Ibrahim H, Zailani A and Tan K (2015) A content analysis of global supply chain research, *Benchmarking: An International Journal*, **22** (7), pp 1429–1462

Inomata S (2017) Analytical frameworks for global value chains: An overview, in *Measuring and Analyzing the Impact of GVCs on Economic Development*, eds D Dollar, J Guilherme Reis and Z Wang, pp 15–35, The World Bank, Geneva

Ivanov D, Sethi S, Dolgui A and Sokolov B (2018) A survey on control theory applications to operational systems, supply chain management, and Industry 4.0, *Annual Reviews in Control*, **46**, pp 134–147

Jomini AH [Baron] (1830) Tableau analytique des principales combinaisons de la guerre: et de leurs rapports avec la politique des états pour servir d'introduction au Traité des grandes opérations militaires

Kamran Q (2018) *Developing a Holistic Model for Competitive Strategic Management: A critique of Porter's Five Forces Model*, University of Latvia

Kamran Q and Scheu J (2018) The service-dominant perspective to create value in the maritime business, in *Container Logistics*, ed R Neise, pp 346–373, Kogan Page, London

Keane J (2019) Logistics and value chain development: Cost and capability considerations, in *Logistics and Global Value Chains in Africa*, eds A Adewole and J Struthers, pp 217–239, Palgrave Macmillan, London

Lessard D (2013) Uncertainty and risk in global supply chains, in *Global Value Chains in a Changing World*, eds P Low and D Elms, pp 195–221, WTO Publications, Geneva

Lourenço H and Ravetti M (2018) Supply chain management, in *Handbook of Heuristics*, eds R Mart, P Pardalos and M Resende, pp 1241–1258, Springer, Berlin

Lund S, Manyika J, Woetzel J, Bughin J, Krishnan M, Seong J and Muir M (2019) *Globalization in Transition: The future of trade and value chains*, McKinsey Global Institute

McGinnis M (1992) Military logistics: Insights for business logistics, *International Journal of Physical Distribution and Logistics Management*, **22** (2), pp 22–32

McGrath R (2013) *The End of Competitive Advantage: How to keep your strategy moving as fast as your business*, Harvard Business Review Press, Boston, MA

Memedovic O, Ojala L, Rodrigue J and Naula T (2008) Fuelling the global value chains: What role for logistics capabilities?, *International Journal Technological Learning, Innovation and Development*, **1** (3), pp 353–374

Merchant N (2012) *Why Porter's Model No Longer Works*, https://hbr.org/2012/02/why-porters-model-no-longer-wo (archived at https://perma.cc/3FUG-CEXW) (accessed on 18 April 2019)

Ponte S and Sturgeon T (2014) Explaining governance in global value chains: A modular theory-building effort, *Review of International Political Economy*, **21** (1), pp 195–223

Porter M (1985) *Competitive Advantage: Creating and sustaining superior performance*, Free Press, New York

Porter M and Kramer M (2011) *Creating Shared Value*, https://hbr.org/2011/01/the-big-idea-creating-shared-value (archived at https://perma.cc/E6VX-EN7L) (accessed on 18 March 2019)

Schönberger J, Ivanov D and Tsipoulanidis A (2018) *Global Supply Chain and Operations Management*, 2nd ed, Springer, Berlin

Scribbings R (1994) The logistics response, *Logistics Information Management*, 7 (5), pp 5–9

Stallard M (2014) *3 Ways Pixar Gains Competitive Advantage from Its Culture*, https://www.foxbusiness.com/features/3-ways-pixar-gains-competitive-advantage-from-its-culture (archived at https://perma.cc/V6RM-N4JG) (accessed on 19 March 2019)

Stank T, Dittman J and Autry C (2011) The new supply chain agenda: A synopsis and directions for future research, *Logistics Information Management*, **10** (2), pp 62–67

Stank T, Autry C, Daugherty P and Closs A (2015) Reimagining the 10 megatrends that will revolutionize supply chain logistics, *Transportation Journal*, **54** (1), pp 7–32

Storey J, Emberson C, Godsell J and Harrison A (2006) Supply chain management: Theory, practice and future challenges, *International Journal of Operations and Production Management*, **26** (7), pp 754–774

Strange R and Humphrey J (2018) What lies between market and hierarchy? Insights from internalization theory and global value chain theory, *Journal of International Business Studies*, **48** (35), pp 81–89

Strange R and Zuchella A (2017) Industry 4.0, global value chains and international business, *Multinational Business Review*, **25** (3), pp 174–184

Sturgeon T, Farole T, Moncada L and Pietrobelli C (2017) Scale, distance, and remoteness in global value chains, in *Future Fragmentation Processes*, eds J Keane and R Baimbill, pp 13–24, Commonwealth Secretariat, London

Tallmann S, Luo Y and Buckley P (2017) Business models in global competition, *Global Strategy Journal*, **8**, pp 517–535

Töpfer A (2012) *Erfolgreich Forschen Ein Leitfaden für Bachelor-, Master-Studierende und Doktoranden*, 3rd ed, Springer, Berlin

Van Rensburg A (2009) *The Value Chain as an Operations Reference Model*, https://repository.up.ac.za/handle/2263/10688 (archived at https://perma.cc/ZS33-PZT3) (accessed on 13 May 2019)

Zinn W and Goldsby TJ (2014) Logistics professional identity: Strengthening the discipline as galaxies collide, *Journal of Business Logistics*, **35** (1), pp 23–28

05

Economic dimension of the six forces model and practical implications

CO-AUTHORED WITH MARYAM SEZAVAR, MIM

As a holistic and multi-disciplinary approach to strategic management, the SFM was put into action in the turbulent business environment of Iran to see if it could help companies analyse the environment and set appropriate strategies to strengthen their core competencies and gain sustainable competitive advantage in the future.

The model was applied in the Iranian partner of a German MNC. Moreover, Iranian and non-Iranian experts were surveyed to validate this effort. The results showed, although highly complicated and complex, which negatively influences its practical application, the SFM can fairly well serve companies to do trade with and in Iran. Anyway, the model and its components should be tailored to Iran's environment for better results.

Before going through the application of the SFM, the author briefly presents the current situation of Iran, so that the reader can partly familiarize themselves with the degree of environmental complexity and turbulence.

A background to the contemporary business environment of Iran

After signing the JCPOA (Joint Comprehensive Plan of Action) between Iran and the P5+1 together with the European Union in October 2015, Iran and

Europe had begun to invest in a closer commercial relationship and several important deals were struck, among which increased investments of Peugeot and Renault to set up production lines in Iran and return of Volkswagen to Iran could be named. Sadly, though, with the withdrawal of the United States in May 2018, these movements remained unfruitful and all of the foreign companies ceased operations with or in Iran, since US secondary sanctions threaten the companies of third countries with considerable fines or a ban on access to the US market should they fail to cease their Iran-related activities. Trying to keep its promises and to actively enable legitimate trade with Iran, the EU suggested the INSTEX (Instrument in Support of Trade Exchanges). Through a multinational intermediary with independent legal personality, trade through euros rather than dollars and no funds going through Iranian hands, this measure should avoid US sanctions and facilitate financial transactions with Iran. Still, big multinationals with a significant exposure to the US market fear they could be sanctioned by US authorities. Thus, the instrument is designed to encourage SMEs with little or no US exposure to stay in the Iranian market (see Adebahr, 2018: 2–14).

The US sanctions have had several impacts on Iran. From an economic viewpoint, the sanctions can generally be categorized into trade-related, financial and banking ones. Although the effects of trade-related sanctions decreased in the long run, since Iran has been able to adjust to the sanctions and find alternative sources to provide for its needs (Torbat, 2005; Askari *et al*, 2001; Aziznejad and Seyed-Noorani, 2010; Yavari and Mohseni, 2010), Iran has had to pay more for lower quality material. This leads to lower competitiveness of domestic products and higher cost and risk of transactions. (Sadrara *et al*, 2019: 6; Mohebati, 2018: 10–13).

The real cost of sanctions to Iran are indirect, such as higher financing costs, missed joint venture opportunities, impeded foreign direct investment (FDI) and broken financial relationships (Askari *et al*, 2001; Torbat, 2005; Aziznejad and Seyed-Noorani, 2010; Mohebati, 2018; Sadrara *et al*, 2019; Yavari and Mohseni, 2010). Askari *et al* (2001) discuss further that these costs are likely to accrue even after sanctions are lifted, while bilateral direct trade may be restored much more quickly. Moreover, sanctions damage Iran's economy through cutting banking transactions on an international level (Sadrara *et al*, 2019: 6; Mohebati, 2018: 10–13).

These have led to, amongst others, inflation, unemployment, investment, economic growth and exchange rate and foreign exchange reserves (Mohebati, 2018: 13–15). Sanctions cause a negative psychological atmosphere, which causes less investment, slower growth and increased inflation. The third-party countries, who do not attend in the sanctioning, worry about their relationships with the US and therefore stop investment or any other relationships with Iran (Sadrara *et al*, 2019; Mohebati, 2018).

To conclude, it should be mentioned that the long-term effects of the embargo can be significant only if the export of Iranian oil is cut off entirely. This indicates that international support to coordinate foreign policy can work better than unilateral actions (Torbat, 2005; Yavari and Mohseni, 2010).

Sanctions and MNCs in Iran

As stated earlier, in contrast to the fact that there are no legal prohibitions on doing trade with Iran (as long as the items to be related are not under sanctions, like dual-use goods), and despite efforts like INSTEX, MNCs are not willing to do trade with Iran. On the one side are the threats of the US, and on the other side is the fact that INSTEX has not yet been put into action. As dollar is the dominant currency in international trade, this leaves at the moment no or little hope for Iran in international and global business.

Although many big companies – especially those of the EU, Japan and Korea – stepped back in fear of exposure to US secondary sanctions, Chinese and Russian companies benefit from lack of competition in Iran. Nevertheless, although Chinese companies took over many projects under new US sanctions, most of them remain uncompleted.

With big foreign companies leaving the Iran market, it now remains to be seen how SMEs decide. They will perhaps be the only ones in Europe that will risk doing business with Iran. On the one hand, they do not have as considerable a bond with the US as MNCs, and on the other hand, Iran's market is an attractive one, especially with the lack of more powerful competition. Here it is just a matter of time and political games to see what will come next and how efforts like the SPV and INSTEX are going to work.

Applying the SFM in Iran

A partnership with Iran was just in the beginning stages when the US withdrew from the JCPOA. Being active under such circumstances was too risky for the German MNC and they decided to adopt a 'wait-and-see strategy'. The German MNC hopes that INSTEX (and/or other measures taken by the EU) would function in practice and the sanctions would be lifted. There exists a very good market in Iran and since the Iranian partner has the required infrastructure and capabilities, it can get active sooner than anybody else (competition), who will only be able to get started after a delay.

Meanwhile, the Iranian partner should take steps to improve itself and build on competitive advantages which could later define its success over the competition. The specifically turbulent and complex situations of Iran made it a good candidate to apply the SFM in practice and see if this model is able to function under completely different culture, infrastructure and economic aspects. Thus, a partly modified questionnaire was designed to assess how practical and helpful the SFM could be for the company, in terms of understanding the current environment and setting suitable strategies accordingly, as well as in terms of a future success to build on today. The questionnaire was also made available in other companies of the same industry to broaden the field and see how welcome it is in other Iranian companies. The results of these two field researches showed that the SFM should first be tailored to suit the culture and business environment in Iran. A strength of the SFM is that it can be tailored to each case. Yet, the problem, which was often pointed out, is that the SFM is too complicated and time-consuming – almost no CEO is going to invest that much time and effort to employ it in their organization. Below the reader can gain a more detailed view of the results of this case study.

The respondents generally believed that the SFM could help them **fairly well** to evaluate their **internal and external environments**, insofar that it is a holistic model and is based on a multi-disciplinary lens. They also believed that the SFM is **averagely to highly capable** of helping them regarding the **global and complex business environment**. The **VSM** centre of the model is highly important from the viewpoint of all respondents, while it is moderately to smoothly applicable in the companies. The **economic layer** is just rather important and almost well applicable. The **RBV layer** appropriates a higher degree of influence and importance to itself and its applicability is also considerably good. The most important aspects in this layer are human resources and information (know-how). Although the **technology and innovation layer** is highly important, it is only fairly applicable to the organizations. One reason the respondents state is that it is problematic to import new technology to Iran due to sanctions. The **stakeholder value layer** is less important: most of the respondents believe that this aspect is fairly to considerably applicable to their organizations, yet a minority believe it is not at all applicable. Some respondents believe that stakeholders make it problematic for the company to be flexible in asset investment or implementing change and such aspects. The **legal and regulatory layer** is very important but it could be applied only to some extent in the organizations due to the many changes the government brings to legal aspects, which makes it hard for the companies to stay updated. The **nature and ecology layer** is also highly important to the respondents and they all have already tried to incorporate it in their systems through, eg, waste management initiatives. **Societal aspects** are, to the contrary, important and influential only to some extent. While most of the respondents believe these concepts can be applied to their organizations without problems, a minority believe this layer is not at all applicable. Anyway, all of the respondents emphasize the cultural aspects but believe it is hard to act globally, which is again due to sanctions. The **normative layer** is seen as fairly important and fairly to considerably applicable to organizations. Core values, ethics and corporate social responsibility are the most important aspects of this layer. Finally, the **complex-strategy layer** is fairly to highly important and influential, although the applicability is a bit more difficult. Respondents point out that aspects regarding change in strategy are sensitive and time-consuming. Sometimes change happens so abrupt and fast that one cannot keep up with the pace. Thus, although this layer is applicable only to some extent in the respective organizations, it is very important.

In a next step, another similar questionnaire was sent to academics and experts, both Iranian and non-Iranian, whose field of expertise was Middle East studies and strategic management. Experts also pointed to the necessity of tailoring the SFM to Iran's environment – for instance, appropriate changes in elements of the legal and regulatory layer or more relevant aspects regarding the nature and ecological layer. Worries regarding the practicality of the SFM were also expressed and that the process of applying it in organizations would be too time-consuming.

To conclude, it should be mentioned that despite all before-mentioned concerns, it was generally confirmed that the SFM is capable of presenting organizations in turbulent and complex environments a way to better understand the situation and set more appropriate strategies. It could moreover help these companies to strengthen themselves internally and build on competitive advantages which are crucial for their success. The SFM is also flexible and, because of its holistic nature, enables the strategist to tailor it based on the specific needs and characteristics of each organization or environment.

References

Adebahr C (2018, December) *Europe and Iran: The economic and commercial dimensions of a strained relationship*, Istituto Affari Internazionali, Rome, https://www.iai.it/en/pubblicazioni/europe-and-iran-economic-and-commercial-dimensions-strained-relationship (archived at https://perma.cc/3YFR-PRGN)

Askari H, Forrer J, Teegan H and Yang J (2001) US economic sanctions: Lessons from the Iranian experience, *Business Economics*, **36** (3), pp 7–19

Aziznejad S and Seyed-Noorani M (2010) Evaluating the effects of sanctions on Iran's economy with a focus on foreign trade, *Majles-o-Pajouhesh*, **16** (61), pp 165–210

Mohebati Y (ed) (2018) Evaluating the economic sanctions and their effect on Iran's economy, *Fourth International Conference on Management, Entrepreneurship, and Economic Development*, Takestan, 18 October, Takestan Institute of Higher Education, https://www.civilica.com/Calendar-CONFME04=چهارمین-کنفرانس-بین-المللی-مدیریت-کارآفرینی-و-توسعه-اقتصادی.html (archived at https://perma.cc/KH8M-VSRD)

Sadrara M, Delzendeh M and Hoseini S (eds) (2019) Evaluating the effect of sanctions on the Iran's economy, *Third National Conference on Economy, Management and Accounting*, Ahwaz, 23 January, Chamran University of Ahwaz, https://www.civilica.com/Calendar-EMAC03=سومین-کنفرانس-ملی-سالانه-اقتصاد-مدیریت-و-حسابداری.html (archived at https://perma.cc/8QH6-3DJG)

Torbat AE (ed) (2005) *Impacts of the US Trade and Financial Sanctions on Iran*, Blackwell Publishing Ltd, Oxford

Yavari K and Mohseni R (2010) Effects of financial and monetary sanctions on Iran: A historical analysis, *Majles-o-Pajouhesh*, **16** (61), pp 9–53

Conclusion

The book has addressed and captured the essential questions of the contemporary strategic-scientific pinnacle of thinking: how to control a complex social-productive and purposive system in the century of complexity and turbulence. Never before has the word crisis so easily and irresponsibly been substituted for managerial and strategic incompetence. There are many and diverse reasons why the current state of the world's complexity increases and the rate of change accelerates – this has already outpaced our abilities to keep pace with them and has reached vast proportions of uncontrollability. The 'dot.com bubble' and recent 'advanced strategy crises of 2008' have started the wave of the next crisis. This has the making of a tsunami, hitting the shores of the strategist's island if the vanished world's concepts continue to be applied in the century of complexity.

The reader can legitimately ask the question: what do the Monitor Group, Lehman Brothers, WorldCom and Enron have in common? In Stafford Beer's words: they are disobeying the laws of effective organization, which their administrators do not know about and their mindsets are locked against (Beer, 1973). Thus, they remain with a perception of the organization's realities in terms of strategic management that is actually a sanctuary for the next catastrophic collapse.

The same goes to the additional doctrine of business administration, which fits in the Beerian notion as described above: the Chandlerian logic of observing structure as a separate entity to follow strategy. The book has established the notion that structure is strategy. There is in the dimension of structure the cognitive and executional phenomenon combined on which strategy can be founded and designed. Structure is the ethos of strategy and every dimension of strategic superiority towards a challenge can take place because of the holistic lens and viable structure. It is within the development and quality of the organization's eigen value and eigen behaviour that strategic foresight will arise. Hence, the world-view of strategy must be constructed on pillars that can take, via the craft of cybernetics, bionics and complexity sciences, the self-organizing, self-regulating and recursive structural dimensions that in the first instance have made life and systemic functions possible.

Corroborative outcomes of theoretical analysis and complexity modelling

In the current book, which is based on the cybernetic approach of general and holistic management and an in-depth strategic treatise of the field, the identification of the sixth competitive force and its attenuation and absorbance by the cultivation of the internal organizational regulatory phenomenon was established. The springboard of the work was based on the research question of enhancing Porter's five forces model, its diagnoses and reconfiguration for the contemporary turbulent times. The model proposed in this book has undergone a scientific transformation with the power of cybernetics by making it embrace a viable structure based on Beer's VSM model. This has freed its spectrum of dominance beyond the boundaries of the industry-in views and purely economic dimensions of organizational realities towards a much wider spectrum of a 'co-petition-based' alliance with the blue ocean strategy approach. Moreover, by considering the innovative lens it embeds the organization in a much wider holistic environment.

Furthermore, this book will contribute to establishing the most in-depth analysis of the Porter mindset – to the author's knowledge, this has never been conducted by a single work. The application of cybernetics and systems sciences has challenged the dominated myopia in the general scientific enquiry of reductionism, which at best must dismantle a functioning complex system in order to understand it. The book has shown that for understanding and controlling complex systems, they cannot be reduced to their smallest parts because it is within the interaction of the systems' properties that their eigen behaviour and relations to their internal parts and in the dynamics of their structures generate varieties' absorbing capacities.

Another vital aspect that will have important implications for the strategist and manager is that the Chandlerian doctrine has been challenged. Thus in complex and purposive social productive systems, not only is it the organizational structures that do not follow strategy, but it is actually the myopic boundaries of bureaucratic structures that prevent organizations from achieving their vital objectives.

Organizations must achieve the needed strategic position of homeostasis within the global and complex environments of today, whereby the equilibrium with the complexity means the essential variety-attenuating capacities to address vital customer problems and the much overdue self-transformation and adaptation to the new world is the main objective.

The book shows how the SFM can deliver a means for establishing a foundation upon which GVCs can be constructed in the turbulent contemporary era. Each individual layer of the SFM contributes to establish the needed variety in terms of Ashby's Law. Only robust models absorb complexities of this interconnected and hyper-globalized world. This book is an attempt to achieve this objective.

Exemplary application areas and recommendations

The author's model is applicable to all kinds of organizations. SMEs and smaller entrepreneurial organizations are much more encouraged to understand the laws introduced, which are universal. The cybernetic laws apply to all types of organization. Stafford Beer's translation of Wiener's insights and the application of Ashby's Law to solve the most vital problems in organizations, countries, economies and governments are too numerous to count. This work has bridged Beer's work and Porter's managerial mindset to bring a unique perspective for steering organizations in today's interconnected and global world.

In the words of von Foerster (1972):

> Cyberneticians of the world, unite! Without communication there is no regulation; without regulation there is no goal; and without a goal the concept of 'society' or 'system' becomes void. Competence implies responsibilities. A doctor must act at the scene of the accident. We can no longer afford to be the knowing spectators at a global disaster. We must share what competence we have through communication and cooperation in working together through the problems of our time. This is the only way in which we can fulfill our social and individual responsibilities as cyberneticians who should practice what they preach.

Amen to that…

References

Beer S (1973) *Designing Freedom: The future that can be demanded now*, Center for Cassette Studies, Portland, OR

Von Foerster H (1972) *Responsibilities of Competence*, Retrieved from https://sites.evergreen.edu/arunchandra/wp-content/uploads/sites/395/2018/05/competence.pdf (archived at https://perma.cc/PB8A-4VB2)

Appendix

This section attempts to connect the economic layer of the organization with the dimension of creating strategic advantages based on the collaborative enhancement of possibilities of organizations' supply chains.

The foundation of management is holistic. Therefore, the scope of embracing and observing the whole in terms of the reality in which an organization is embedded is a necessity in a rapidly changing world. The dominant resource-based view (RBV) (Barney, 1991; Teece *et al*, 1996, 1997)* has been essential to developing and enhancing organizational strategic habitus (Bourdieu, 1984) and eigen behaviour (von Foerster, 2003) in a collective sense. However, the RBV has missed and lacks additional key pillars of managerial foundations. An organization in the Bourdieuian sense is required to see the world from understanding and gaining capital resources, not only from an economic logic of capital but from a culture and relationship capital philosophy (Bourdieu, 1984). While Bourdieu's theories have been developed and applied within sociological interpretations of individuals and groups, and their structures of interpreting realities, to reproduce further realities in a societal interpretation of theories of class hierarchies (ability to access capital in the Bourdieuian sense) and ability to capture resources, it is, thus, a

* NOTE This and other references may be found in the References and further reading section on page 416 at the end of the following Appendix chapter.

good start to translate them into organizational and managerial realities. These dimensions – (1) whereby an organization makes sense of itself in terms of its structure, processes, information systems and sub-systems, whereof the organization is constructed; (2) the philosophy and habitus, whereby it structures the environmental and market realities, wherein it's embedded; and (3) the nature of strong and weak ties from the RBV lens extended by its understanding of attracting and dominating resources as operant and operand resources (Vargo *et al*, 2014) – have essential implications for designing global value chains (GVCs). The authors observe GVCs as a necessary evolution of the field under the umbrella of operations research, starting from the foundations of logistics and supply chain management to global value chain management.

Economic layer, supply chain and collaboration

CO-AUTHORED WITH DR ROLF NEISE

Introduction

This appendix will explain the importance of understanding basic economic principles and how to use these insights in relation to supply chains. We begin by defining some of the key concepts of economics which are important for supply chains, like shareholder value, the industry-in view, the red ocean perspective and the cluster approach.

Shareholder value and its importance for supply chains will be discussed in depth by explaining the influence on supply chain decisions and by outlining those factors in supply chain management which drive shareholder value.

Finally, we end with a discussion of supply chain collaboration and present a nine-step process on collaborative business-to-business (B2B) solutions in practice.

Economics

Economics is a social science that analyses and explores the production, distribution, and consumption of goods and services. Economics studies the behaviour and interaction of all private and public economic actors, like individuals, firms and business organizations, but also governments and nations. The focus of the investigations is to question how these actors allocate existing resources and efforts to satisfy their needs, and to achieve a maximum output.

The origins of this science date back to early human history – the great thinkers of antiquity and the Middle Ages are considered as ancestors of economics. A first systematic economic theory was developed by Aristotle and the term 'economics' is ascribed to him (Greek: Οίκονομικά; Latin: Oeconomica). It is composed of the terms 'oikos' (= house) and 'nomos' (= law, order).

The study of economics is generally broken down into two disciplines: microeconomics, with a focus on how individual consumers and firms make decisions; and macroeconomics, with a focus on the overall economy on both a national and international level.

The economic environment of a company refers to all those economic factors that have a bearing on the functioning of a business unit. In conjunction with the early chapters of this book, its complexity must be holistically viewed regarding the insight perspective of the company in evaluation as well as the external perspective in terms of the industry in which the company is situated. The following four components describe the economic environment of a company in its entirety: shareholder value, industry-in view, red ocean perspective, and clusters.

By taking the industry-in view combined with the shareholder value, the red ocean perspective and the possibility of defining clusters, the economic layer enables every strategist to get a clear picture of the immediate business environment of their company and to get a holistic status quo of the economic environment the firm is embedded in. Further micro- and macroeconomic aspects are considered in other layers.

Shareholder value

A *shareholder* is a person or an organization that owns shares in a company. *Shareholder value* is that value delivered to the shareholders of a company due to its capability to increase sales, earnings, and free cash flow over time, leading to the ability for companies to increase dividends and encourage capital gains for its equity owners.

Shareholder value management refers to the management practice of considering the interests of shareholders first when making management decisions. This is still today the most widespread practice of all companies, even if in public debates and academic research the concept is controversially discussed, as it is mainly focused on the short term rather than considering the long-term success of the company. This practice is still celebrated in publications like *The Economist* as the concept that 'will remain the governing principle of firms'. Even Jack Welch, CEO of General Electric from 1981 to 2001, who is regarded as the father of the shareholder value, has said it was 'a dumb idea for executives to focus so heavily on quarterly profits and share price gains'. According to him:

> the idea that shareholder value is a strategy is insane. Shareholder value is a result, not a strategy... your main constituencies are your employees, your customers and your products. Managers and investors should not set share price increases as their overarching goal... Short-term profits should be allied with an increase in the long-term value of a company.
>
> (quoted in Guerrera, 2009)

Creating *shareholder value* depends on different performance indicators that are unique from industry to industry and from company to company. These value drivers have to be defined and used to 'transfer skills or expertise among similar value chains and [...] to share activities that may create synergies that can optimize the value chain as well as building a strong relationship with [the environment]' (Porter, 1987). Creating high shareholder value, therefore, enables a sustainable competitive advantage.

Industry-in view

The industry-in view can be perceived as an additional layer of economic complexity and is based on Bain (1956) and Mason's (1939) structure, conduct and performance (SCP) paradigm, which outlines the connection between market performance and various market structure variables through the conduct of the firm within that market.

The SCP paradigm was developed in the economic field of industrial organization (IO), where the relationship between the strategic behaviour of a firm and the market structure is a key focus.

This discipline is based on the work of a group of economists at Harvard in the 1930s analysing imperfect market conditions, where market structures differ from the concept of perfect competition. In the 1950s it was the economist Joe Bain who, on the basis of extensive empirical studies, was the first to classify the various forms of imperfect competition. In 1959 he described the SCP paradigm in his book *Industrial Organization*, which became a pillar of industrial organization theory.

The paradigm can be used as an analytical framework for markets and industries to understand the relation between market structures, market conduct and market performance. It was also used in other economic fields, such as business management and controlling.

At the beginning of the 1980s, the economist Michael E. Porter applied the premise and insights of industrial organization theory to individual firms. This elaboration builds on the basics of his works on competition.

Further applications of the SCP paradigm, both in macro- and microeconomics, have been developed. Harvard Business School, for example, has developed a relation between the market concentration ratio and the harmful effects on social welfare, recognizing concentrated market power as dangerous for welfare.

In the SCP paradigm, market structure variables are considered as exogenous due to the assumption that these variables remain constant while conduct and performance-related variables are recognized as endogenous. Moreover, each variable of the three determinants of the SCP paradigm focuses on certain key aspects. Structure focuses mainly on the market, the extent to which firms create a strong corporate brand, the market entry barriers, and cost-related barriers. The focal point of conduct is the behaviour of a firm within the market, especially towards pricing, product, promoting, and research and development strategies. Performance emphasizes measurable variables, which serve as indicators for firm internal reviews, and refer to firm profitability, production and allocated efficiency, and the degree of occupancy.

Therefore, the SCP paradigm aligns a holistic competitor analysis with an internal analysis of the firm and its performance measurement tools.

ELEMENTS OF THE STRUCTURE, CONDUCT AND PERFORMANCE (SCP) PARADIGM

The elements of the SCP paradigm are described below:

- **Structure:** The structure refers to the market structure, the environment in which the firm operates and the structure of the firm. This is normally a set of variables that is relatively stable over time, like supply and demand concentration, degree of product differentiation and barriers of market entry. It is also determined by the nature of the product and available production technology.
- **Conduct:** Conduct refers to the behaviour of buyers and sellers and how they interact with each other. The variables used to capture firm behaviour include pricing strategies, collusion, advertising, research and development (R&D) and capacity investment.
- **Performance:** Performance refers to the outcome, achievements or results of a particular market or industry. The results of an individual firm are

compared with the results of other competitors of the same industry. Performance variables often used are production efficiency, product quality, product quantity, etc.

When using this model for single companies, it has to be ensured that sufficient and correct data is available. The more dynamic markets and their actors are, the higher the amount of variables to describe the market, the more difficult it is to come to sustainable results. The main problem nowadays when using this methodology to analyse a market or an industry 'is the difficulty of defining the limits or boundaries of a given industry' (Policonomics, nd).

Red ocean perspective

The concept of 'red ocean' is attributed to W. Chan Kim and Renée Mauborgne, both Professors of Strategy and Management at the INSEAD Business School. In their international bestseller *Blue Ocean Strategy*, first published in 2004, they describe a methodology for the development of permanently profitable business models in the field of strategic management. They distinguish between the red ocean perspective of existing markets today and the blue ocean perspective to create new markets and new demand.

According to Kim and Mauborgne (2004a, 2004b), the *red ocean* perspective represents all industries in existence today – the known market space in a defined market with defined competitors and a typical way to run a business in any specific industry. The framework is set and understood by every firm within this industry. Therefore, the red ocean perspective describes firms within an industry which solemnly compete for market share and seek the opportunity of outperforming their rivals. Since the competition increases steadily and the phenomenon of products turning into commodities takes place, the image of a bloody ocean is created.

In contrast to that we have the *blue ocean strategy*, which is 'the simultaneous pursuit of differentiation and low cost to open up a new market space and create new demand' (Kim and Mauborgne, 2004a). Blue ocean strategy describes the creation of new markets or industries by either a new entrant or incumbent through value or technology pioneering. Thereby it often does not matter if the industry is unattractive, attractive or non-existent, as the demand is created through operating in and establishing blue oceans, because the customers did not even imagine the product to possibly exist and therefore could not demand it. The company creating blue oceans aligns differentiation and low cost and breaks the value/cost trade-off. This is not necessarily accomplished by technology innovation, but often rather by linking technology to what buyers value.

Within red oceans we already have a number of competitors. One of the main wills to survive therefore is to fight and beat the competitor. Red ocean strategies for firms focusing on current customers have the following characteristics:

- **Focus on current customers.**
- **Compete in existing markets:** If someone wins a customer, it is assumed someone will lose a customer. The contrast to that is an uncontested market, where no one is fighting because only one firm is supplying.
- **Beat the competition by exploiting existing demand.**
- **Focus on the value/cost trade-off:** According to Michael Porter (1980/1998), there are only two strategies to choose from, either creating more value for customers, but at higher costs, or reducing costs at a reasonable value for customers. Kim and Mauborgne (2004b) have changed this concept and developed tools to create high value at low costs (blue ocean perspective).
- **Align the organization with differentiation *or* low costs:** Two strategies exist –differentiation or low costs. All activities must be aligned with one of these strategic directions. Anything that doesn't create or contribute to value has to be eliminated or reduced in the most efficient way to run the organization. This concept was also further developed by Kim and Mauborgne (2004b) to align the organization with both differentiation *and* low costs.

An example of red ocean strategy is the European airline operator Ryanair. They are able to achieve low costs in the already saturated market (red ocean) of short-haul flights by using cheaper secondary airports further away from cities, and operating all customer activities like booking and check-in online, amongst other methods. They are not really differentiated from competitors, but they run their business model on low costs.

Clusters

The theory of business clusters was developed by Michael Porter. In his ground-breaking book *The Competitive Advantage of Nations* (1990), he describes clusters as a geographic concentration of interconnected producers, suppliers, research institutions (eg universities), service providers (eg design and engineering firms), and craftsmen and associated institutions (eg chambers of commerce). According to Porter, clusters can stimulate the productivity of companies within the cluster nationally and globally by developing new business models and by driving innovation. With this theory, important insights about competitive advantage and about the microeconomics of competition can be won.

The cluster approach is considered a paradox phenomenon, as it represents the procedure of creating a local network between miscellaneous companies, suppliers, service providers, institutions, and universities which compete but also cooperate with each other at the same time. It is a paradox due to the reason that in times of globalized sourcing it is no longer necessary to build local networks. Nevertheless, Porter describes building clusters as a new form of gaining a competitive advantage as it can result in an increase in productivity and efficiency. Clustering is not only concerned with cost savings or deepening of supplier relationships, but is also related to engaging with the economy to achieve an optimal result. Therefore, these networks represent a miniature version of the economy, which makes them a competitive advantage. A study in 2000 (Porter, 2000) defined the critical success factors in cluster development, which are mainly collaboration in networking partnership and knowledge-creation for innovative technology in the cluster. This knowledge is created through various forms of local inter-organizational collaborative interaction.

Supply chain and shareholder value

There is a strong relation between supply chain management and shareholder value, which is often overlooked in daily executional activities, and this was not the traditional focus of supply chains as an operational machine to fulfil customers' orders. This misunderstanding must be overcome, and it is the obligation of supply chain managers to make their board members aware of this situation and to inform and train every employee subsequently.

The first step is often to introduce a simple performance measurement system available to everyone in the organization. This system should be supplemented by the addition of ongoing awareness courses, where every employee learns their individual influence on shareholder value.

Studies such as David Lascelles' (2018) work on how supply chains create shareholder value clearly indicate successful supply chains increase cash flow, which is the main driver of shareholder value. In a recent study by Cranfield University (Lascelles, 2018) it could be demonstrated that on average up to 20 per cent of cash flow could be released by high-performing supply chain management based on operational effectiveness and added value performance. A better supply chain performance not only improves cash flow; it also increases customer loyalty and is therefore the basis to win further market share.

But is this implicitness common sense in management boards of companies, or in the financial world? In a recent survey (Maine Pointe, 2018) of 50 private equity firm executives from all over the world who work with firms to improve financial results, supply chain functions such as logistics, operations, and procurement were surprisingly ranked by many firms as 'relatively unimportant' in driving cash and growth. This indicates a significant lack of understanding regarding the critical importance of supply chains in these areas as well as the overall appreciation of supply chains. And it clearly shows that management boards do not consider supply chains as a source to create value and differentiate advantages, but rather as an execution element.

A simple definition of shareholder value

There are different ways of calculating shareholder value. For example, one simple way is to estimate the net present value of future cash flows. Therefore we use the term 'after-tax free cash flow', which is the money left over after subtracting expenses, taxes and capital investment from revenues (net operating income), as outlined in Figure A1.1.

FIGURE A1.1 Free cash flow

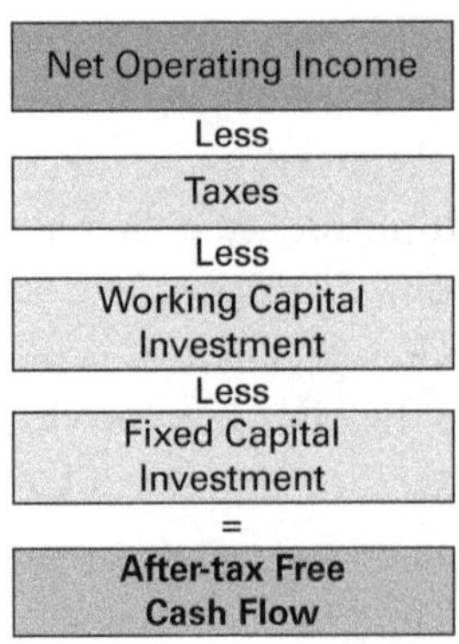

More advanced definitions have been developed, like the widely used concept of economic value added (EVA), which is the difference between operating income after taxes less the costs of capital employed to generate those profits. EVA is often also referred to as economic profit.

Another measure of a company's wealth is the market value added (MVA) concept. By multiplying the issued shares with the current stock price less the book value of the invested capital, a true measure of what the business is worth to its shareholders is available. A simple definition of MVA is shown in Figure A1.2.

FIGURE A1.2 Market value added

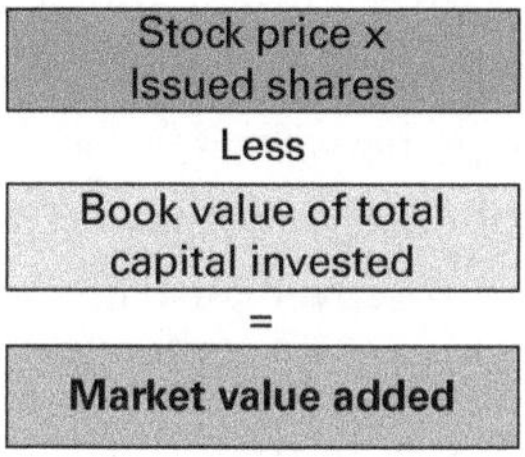

The drivers of shareholder value and the influence of supply chain

The five basic drivers of shareholder value are revenue growth, operating cost reduction, fixed capital efficiency, working capital efficiency, and tax minimization. All of these five drivers are either directly or indirectly affected by supply chain management (see Figure A1.3).

FIGURE A1.3 The drivers of shareholder value

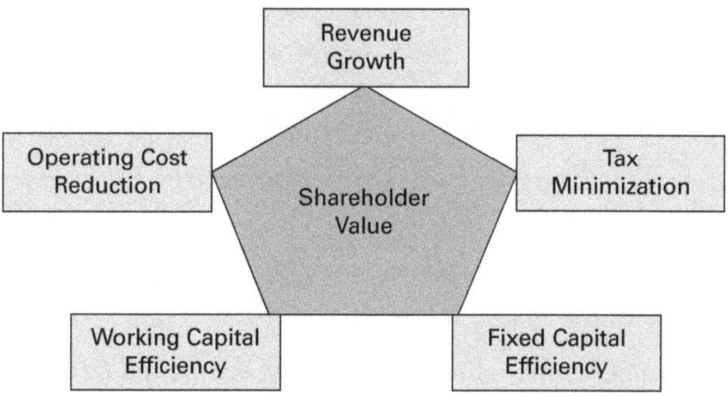

Revenue growth

The primary purpose of any supply chain is to satisfy customer needs, and in doing so to generate profits. Therefore, supply chains play a vital role in creating revenue growth, both in increasing sales volumes as well as in customer service and retention. The more a customer trusts a supplier and the longer the relationship is between the supplier and the customer, the more likely it is that the satisfied customer will make a greater portion of their purchases with that supplier.

Operating cost reduction

In general, supply chains – with all their functions mainly in logistics and production – bundle a lot of operating costs. According to several studies, total supply chain costs range between 10 and 20 per cent of a company's revenues depending on the industry (Wyman, 2019). To have a clear view of all costs, it is essential here to cover all truly 'end-to-end' costs in a cost analysis. The higher the operating costs are, the more opportunities exist to reduce them. Cost-reduction initiatives are one of the core elements of supply chain management; however, it has to be ensured that the level of customer service is not negatively impacted by these initiatives.

Fixed capital efficiency

The logistics and production functions of supply chains are by their very nature fixed assets. If production sites or distribution centres with automated handling systems are part of the company's property, considerable supply-chain-related investment decisions have to be taken.

The rapid development of third-party logistics service providers of storage facilities and trucks in recent decades is a clear method of reducing fixed asset investments by variable costs (operating costs). This tendency in the industry has even been accelerated by the trend to lease rather than buy. This is called outsourcing or 'make or buy' – and the decisions around outsourcing are typically the responsibility of supply chain managers and can influence the fixed capital efficiency.

Working capital efficiency

Supply chain management directly impacts working capital by defining the required inventory of raw materials, semi-finished and finished goods. The lower the inventory in the end-to-end pipeline, the less working capital is required. Procurement policies, like supplier payment cycles and payment terms, also affect cash flow, as order fill and invoice accuracy impact accounts receivable. A reduction can be reached through time compression and subsequently reduced order-to-cash cycle times.

Tax minimization

Globally active companies have the choice as to where they locate their assets (eg buildings, production sites, etc) and where they operate from. As tax regimes are different for each country, location decisions have an important impact on tax payments. Not only is corporate taxes a consideration, but also property tax, income tax and excise duty. Further considerations are customs regulations, tariffs and quotas as well as rules and regulations on transfer pricing. Even local decisions of building a production site can have tax implications. Supply chain decisions on where to locate a distribution centre or how to operate in a market therefore have a significant impact on the company's tax bill.

The debate about tax minimization can be a controversial topic and frequently faces public criticism. It should be common sense that companies should be transparent about their operations, make decisions based on factors other than taxation and contribute a fair amount of tax to each country in which they operate.

FIGURE A1.4 Supply chain impact of shareholder value

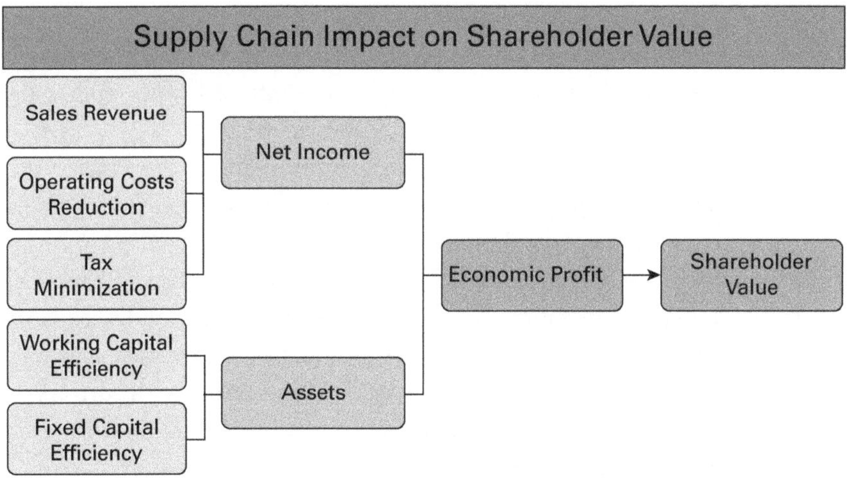

In summary, supply chains create economic profit when they:

- support higher revenue by providing flawless delivery to customers and by creating long-lasting customer relationships through outstanding customer service and engagement, thereby enabling growth;
- reduce costs by ever more efficient operations;
- reduce capital requirements with lower inventory, lower overall working capital, and streamlined physical networks.

Return on investment (ROI) and the influence of supply chain

Another important financial measurement required to take decisions is resource utilization, and specifically the use of fixed and working capital. In this regard the concept of return on investment (ROI) is used. Return on investment is the ratio between the net profit (over a period) and the cost of investment (or the capital that was used to produce that profit). When further expanding this term, ROI is the product of two ratios: profit/sales (ie margin) and sales/capital employed (ie asset turnover), as shown in Figure A1.5. With this in mind, ROI is the primary measure of how operations and therefore supply chain management add value to a company.

FIGURE A1.5 ROI formula

$$\text{ROI} = \frac{\text{Profit}}{\text{Sales}} \times \frac{\text{Sales}}{\text{Capital employed}}$$

There are several overlaps between the ROI concept and the shareholder value concept. Therefore, only new aspects are discussed in the following section or previous outlined arguments are deepened.

To improve ROI means either increasing profit margins or reducing the employed capital by a more efficient utilization. This will generate greater free cash flow and, thus, shareholder value.

Key supply chain performance indicators like effective customer service, efficiently managed operations with well-managed assets and credits, a sustainable inventory policy and an appropriate cash conversion speed all have an impact on ROI. The relationship of these indicators to the drivers of ROI is outlined in Figure A1.6, where the drivers of ROI fall into the two general categories of profitability and capital employed. Sales revenues and costs impact profit, whereas cash flow, net receivables, inventory and fixed assets impact the employed capital.

FIGURE A1.6 Supply Chain Impact on ROI

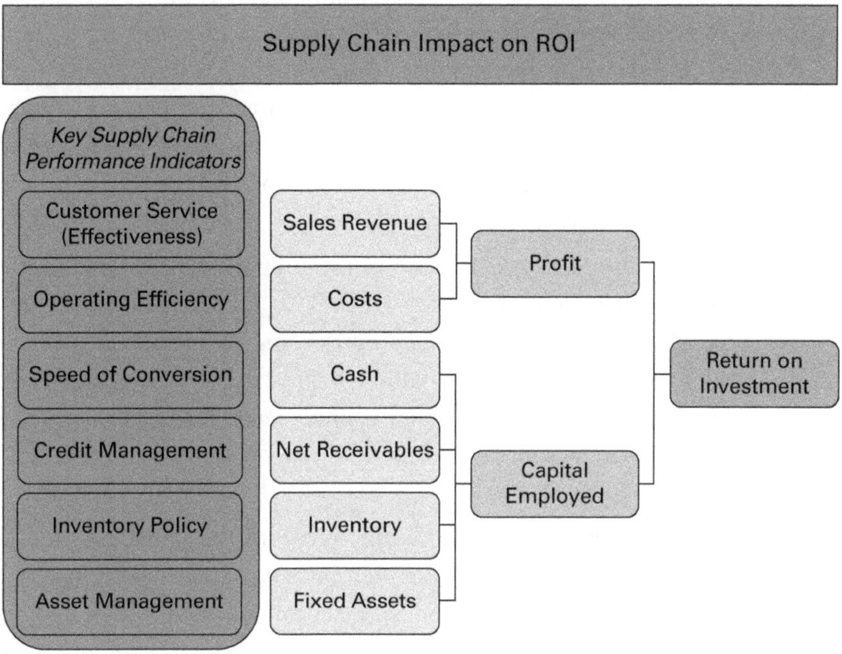

Profitability

Greater profitability can be reached by revenue growth and/or lower costs. Revenue growth through supply chain activities is strongly dependent on an efficient customer service management. This means keeping profitable customers by satisfying their needs and by developing long-lasting value-adding relationships with them. It also means acquiring new customers through outstanding service offers and sustainable customer care. Cost minimization covers the optimization of product costs as well as the costs of all supply chain management activities.

The **value levers** for supply chain management include:

- **Customer service:** Supply chain is dependent on an efficient customer service. The product availability has to be guaranteed as the price of continuing or extending your business. The quicker a business is able to shift the customer service cost curve to the right, meaning reaching the same customer service level at lower costs, the greater are the chances of growing sales revenues.

- **Customer relationships:** The target of every supply chain management should be to build long-lasting relationships with customers far beyond the service requirements they have today. The question should be how your operations and business model can add further strategic value to the business performance of your customers by, for example, exchanging further data, cooperating in planning, etc. This will not only be the base of a trustful cooperation, but will also attract the customer for a greater share of their purchase spend.
- **Product costs:** Product cost reductions are often at the centre of supply chain management activities. The target is to reduce both direct and indirect costs of a product without compromising its functionality and its perceived value. Innovative cost reduction strategies are required, which often goes beyond the responsibility of supply chain management. R&D, product design as well as suppliers have to be involved to ensure a sustainable product cost reduction.
- **Supply chain management costs:** Supply chain management costs cover all end-to-end costs incurred in the plan-buy-make-move processes of a company. The bigger the cost base is, specifically in the logistics and the production area, the more significant opportunities exist to reduce these often indirect costs.

Capital employed

A better return on capital employed can be reached by a more efficient use of the company's capital, both working capital and fixed capital. Supply chain management can influence and speed up the cash-to-cash cycle by optimizing the required time to fulfil an order and by lowering the accounts receivable dates. The impact of supply chain management on working capital is obvious as the amount of inventory is defined and managed.

The **value levers** for supply chain management include:

- **Cash-to-cash cycle:** The cash-to-cash cycle is the required time to transfer a customer order into cash. The time includes the procurement of the required materials, the production itself, up to receipt of payment from the customer. Any cut in this total time will reduce the total amount of working capital.

- **Inventory:** Inventory is the total volume of raw materials, components, semi-finished and finished products, but also all required tools and spare parts to run the operations and distribution centres in the end-to-end supply chain. This amount often accounts for more than 50 per cent of a firm's assets. The higher the amount of inventory, the more working capital is required to cover it. In addition, the costs of carrying that inventory have to be considered.
- **Asset management:** Fixed assets, like forklifts, vehicles and robots, are required to run the business and, in the end, to create a company's profit. The provision and the management of these assets is usually fulfilled by supply chain functions. The decision to be taken is the question of ownership: whether the assets are owned or leased, or whether whole parts of the business are outsourced. It should always be embedded in the overall company strategy to improve supply chain flexibility and responsiveness.
- **Throughput efficiency:** Throughput efficiency is a further aspect of asset management. The more output is created from the fixed assets in the end-to-end supply chain, the higher the capital productivity is. This requires a comprehensive optimization not only within the supply chain functions, but also in the corresponding activities, like R&D, marketing and product design, to fulfil customers' requirements in the most efficient way.

Conclusion

The evidence is overwhelming. Supply chain excellence does drive shareholder value. It can even be seen as the most important factor in determining the shareholder value in both public and private companies. All CEOs and supply chain professionals need to understand this linkage in their companies and be able to clearly explain it. To do that, supply chain leaders need to speak the language of the board of directors and the financial world. Supply chain professionals need to have a seat at the table by clearly showing how supply chain excellence enables revenue-generation, how it generates new cash flow, and, of course, a continuous reminder of how it manages the vast majority of operating cost.

Forging the connection between supply chain management and shareholder value raises the supply chain's profile in the company and provides a critical opportunity to drive home supply chain's role in the overall business.

Supply chain and collaboration

Introduction

Porter's (1980/1998) concept of *generic strategies* is based on the idea of competition. It assumes that companies try to achieve competitive advantages over other players in the markets as well as over suppliers and/or customers. New business models that characterize today's economy, such as collaborative partnerships, virtual enterprise networks and strategic alliances, are not fully considered. An extended model should therefore reflect the following:

COLLABORATION WITH CUSTOMERS

In Porter's model, *customers* are mainly seen as buyers, who are a group to squeeze profits from. This notion does not see customers as co-creators of value and collaborators. Customers and consumers provide a major collaborative force for the business and technological development of any company by giving feedback to achieve better products and services. Drucker's (1954) insight of seeing 'the purpose of a business is to create a customer' must be at the heart of every strategy today.

COLLABORATION WITH SUPPLIERS

The relationship between a company and its suppliers is similar. It is very often the case that component-makers lead the development of new products, eg in the automotive industry, and that it is not the end-product manufacturer benefiting most, as in Porter's (1987) theory. Collaborative planning, for example, emphasizes an approach by which suppliers and companies work closely together to maximize end-product opportunities in the marketplace with the right products, right pricing and right volumes. It is also of importance to rethink companies' core competencies in this context. Non-core competencies should be outsourced to specialized providers. The relationship with these suppliers should then be based on a collaborative partnership.

BALANCE OF COLLABORATION AND COMPETITION

According to Porter's model, competitive rivalry in an industry increases with the number of companies in the industry. It is not reflected in here that companies could collaborate even while competing in the marketplace.

Examples are sharing production sites, sharing marketing channels or exchanging components. Such collaboration helps companies to bring down costs and to share expertise. It can also help companies to optimize their investments by sharing resources while retaining a distinct identity.

Collaboration in practice – a nine-step guide

Collaboration is defined here as the ability to work across organizational boundaries to build and manage value-added processes. It often involves the sharing of resources – information, people, and technology – among supply chain members to create synergies for competitive advantage. It can occur in many ways and is commonly divided into two main categories: (1) *vertical*, when collaborating with customers, internally (across functions), service providers and with suppliers; and (2) *horizontal*, between different supply chains when cooperating with competitors and with non-competitors.

Collaboration is a continuous process, therefore collaborative improvement initiatives should be implemented to constantly upgrade the company's culture of collaboration. It is also important to remove resisting forces in the organization and transform a company's culture.

Collaboration goes beyond managing transactions for efficiency to managing relationships for creativity and continuous improvement. The collaborative goal is to work cooperatively together to devise and implement better approaches to solving problems and delivering value.

Partnership is always a two-way road, where each partner is responsible for the success. To do so, the ways of working and processes for the partnership should be commonly agreed.

Collaboration does not come from nothing. Just like with any other functioning process, it requires a great deal of effort and commitment from all partners involved. The more structure is behind this process, the better it works.

Learnings to create a sustainable collaboration can also be taken from several industry experiences in the past, like the introduction of **CPFR (collaborative planning, forecasting and replenishment)** tools to share information between suppliers and retailers to plan and satisfy customer demands. This approach was clearly process-driven and IT-focused; what was missing were skilled resources, joint visions, leadership, a common plan and aligned incentives between the partners.

The following nine steps (see Figure A1.7) should be taken to develop a trustful and long-lasting vertical collaboration between a company and its customers and suppliers, including service providers.

These steps are based on learnings of the author in several relationship-building exercises, both internally within a company between different functions (supply chain functions and other functions) as well as in SRM (supplier relationship management) and CRM (customer relationship management). The concept was first explained in the author's book *Container Logistics* (Neise, 2018) and is further expanded here by adding additional layers.

1. Cultural awareness – understand your partner

Every form of collaboration requires a change in strategic thinking. It is not sufficient to highlight changes on the operational level; collaboration is a clear game-changer and needs to be thoroughly embedded throughout the whole organization. Before working together, you need to better understand your partner, the thoughts and ideas that drive them, and the culture of the company. This information and knowledge is always the foundation of change and the basis of a long-lasting relationship. With this information, potential issues should be discovered along with (high-level) processes that

FIGURE A1.7 A nine-step guide to collaborative B2B – solutions in practice

1. Cultural awareness – understand your partner
2. Senior management commitment
3. Organizational commitment
4. Common objectives and targets
5. Appropriate governance
6. Effective business policies and agreements
7. A team manager driving the relationship
8. Dedicated team in a continuous improvement culture
9. Commonly defined processes and ways of working

have to be changed and adapted. Attitudes and (personal) behaviours should be identified that might prevent a trusting collaboration. This knowledge should inform managers how to best manifest collaborative activities. This is in the first instance typically a senior management task providing the basis of all B2B integration activities. It is also an ongoing process based on mutual trust between all involved employees.

2. *Senior management commitment*

One of the most crucial elements is to have management commitment for the relationship on both sides. Every initiative to share information or to integrate systems between partners has a strategic impact and therefore needs to be driven by the top management, which is tasked with defining the **vision** of the new relationship based on a business evaluation and on a solid understanding of the partner. The top management should also be responsible for developing these relationships. It is often useful to have a senior manager acting as the **sponsor** of the relationship at board level. This involves spending sufficient time with the corresponding top-level managers of the new partners. By coming together, senior managers from both sides have the potential to make sustainable, mutually beneficial changes.

3. *Organizational commitment*

The management commitment should be cascaded in the organizations and extend across functions. It should also be visible for every employee. The recognition of the need for change must be translated into managerial support for collaboration.

It is also helpful to define the importance of collaboration and its meaning for a company in **guiding principles**, which should be defined by the management board and known by the whole organization. An example here is the statement of business principles given by British American Tobacco (2010), which outlines that their relationship with supply partners should include:

- open and transparent communication; trust;
- **shared responsibility** to solve problems rapidly in the supply chain, working together to minimize and manage business risk and improve business practices;
- **a joint approach** to pursuing improvements in the supply chain, through education, training and sharing of good practice.

4. Common objectives and targets

The **objectives and targets** of a collaboration should be developed by all involved partners, based on a common vision defined by the top management. This is a multifunctional process covering all hierarchical levels involved in the relationship. It is also a regular process that needs to be reviewed annually. It should end up in the definition of tactical initiatives, such as 'improvement areas' and concrete projects the teams are working on. It should also be clear to the involved parties how they participate in the success of an initiative.

5. Appropriate governance

An appropriate **governance** is required and has to be defined. Collaborative relationships can be governed by informal understanding or written contracts. Trust is almost always a governing principle of winning collaborative relationships. The governance model includes a clear escalation-level process to deal with any misunderstandings. It is often useful to establish an **advisory board** who is in charge of the relationship; the participants should form an annual strategic meeting (see also Figure A1.8).

FIGURE A1.8 Different management layer for B2B – integrations

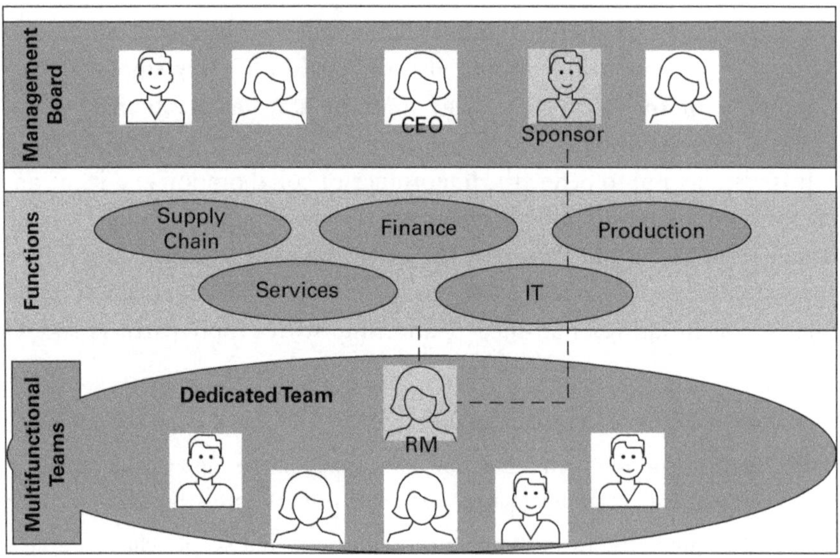

RM = relationship manager

6. *Effective business policies and agreements*

The basis of the partnership is established by formulating effective business policies, agreements and business plans that a company can use to set guidelines and rules for exchange of information with supply chain partners and for further collaborative activities. This also helps to assuage existing barriers in organizations.

7. *A team manager driving the relationship*

On all sides a person responsible for the relationship (**ownership**) has to be appointed. This could be a customer engagement manager when talking about sharing data with customers or the supplier relationship manager. It is essential that these managers have a good understanding of each other's business. They should be able to drive the relationship forward according to the commonly defined objectives. These managers also act as **advocates** for the relationship in their own organizations and share the success stories.

8. *Dedicated team working in a continuous improvement culture*

A dedicated cross-functional team with members from the partners who are dealing with the relationship should be established. The size of the team is dependent on the defined objectives and tasks. The team should be led by the appointed relationship managers of the partners and should meet regularly to discuss any progress, potential obstacles and forthcoming challenges. As this team is the regular body of driving the relationship, a **continuous improvement** culture should be established. New ideas, further options to collaborate and optimized ways of working have to be openly discussed and commonly developed. To do so, it has to be ensured that sufficient time is given to the team members to meet and understand each other. This is a prerequisite of a trusting collaboration and it includes common team events and social team-building exercises. Trust is the single most important relationship-building factor; it enables cultural transformation. It is also important to celebrate success stories. Training to develop employees and managers who know how to collaborate and are aware of opportunities to do so should be a permanent part of the relationship. Such investments keep the momentum for transformation alive and promote the behaviours that lead to a real change over the long term. It will also help to overcome resisting forces in the organization and support risk-averse employees.

9. *Commonly defined processes and ways of working*

BUSINESS CALENDAR

Between all parties a business calendar should be commonly developed that includes the following meetings (see also Figure A1.9):

- **Annual strategic meeting** – to align priorities and give business direction. This is a typical senior-level meeting with management executives from both sides. It should be led by the management sponsors of each partner.
- **Business review meetings** – on a quarterly basis and a more tactical level to prioritize activities and to review progress. This is the main meeting organized and driven by the relationship managers to understand how the collaboration is evolving.
- **Monthly operational meetings** – various monthly operational meetings might occur due to different requirements, eg a performance review meeting, a logistics executional meeting or a customs meeting. Ideally these meetings are linked with the S&OP (sales and operation planning) processes of the partners to ensure updated information is available and shared.

FIGURE A1.9 Meeting culture in a collaborative B2B environment with two companies

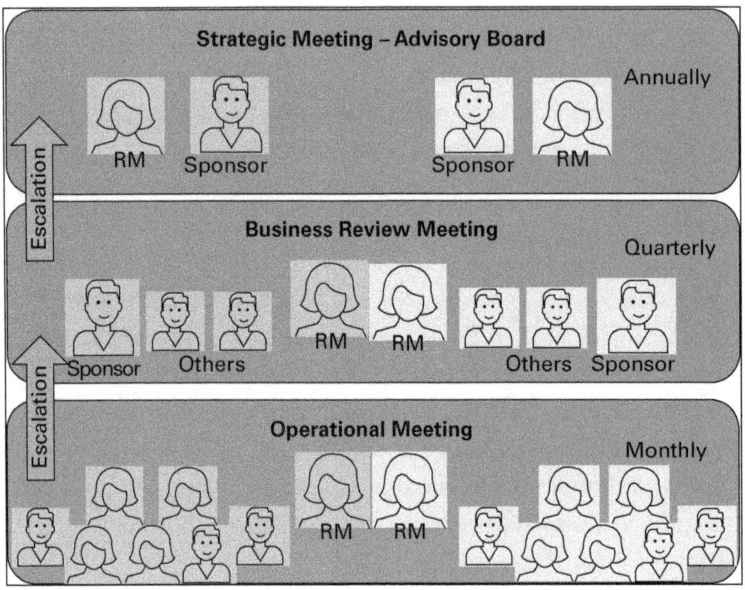

RM = relationship manager

PROCESS MAPPING

For information-sharing, the information flows between all partners have to be mapped consciously to assure consistency and timeliness. This continuous mapping is the basis of the following process adaption on each partner's side:

- **Commonly defined KPIs – measured regularly:** Based on the vision and the corresponding targets, the success of collaborative activities should be measured. This can either be in the form of realized cost savings or in the reduction of administrative workload or in improved customer service through a quicker response time. Soft aspects should also be measured in the form of regular surveys to understand which requirements are met and where improvements are necessary. It is also important to use measures which cover cross-functional results to understand all consequences of the relationship. An example here is the impact of OTIF measures on inventory levels. Performance indicators should support long-term collaboration and the benefits should be documented. The partners should have **regular, proactive communication** so that there are no surprises on either side.
- **Commonly agreed ways of working/incentives:** It is essential to have common ways of working throughout the relationship. Incentives like gain-sharing agreements will help to drive a continuous improvement culture. The benefits of collaboration should be fairly shared between the partners.

Conclusion

There is a big need for collaboration in partnership, based on mutual trust between all business partners. This is required to create sustainable solutions for all kinds of economic relationships in future. If these steps are taken, they will ultimately help mitigate the fear of information-sharing and strengthen collaborative activities. They will also improve efficiency and create new opportunities for all stakeholders. Ultimately they will prepare the organization for a successful, long-lasting relationship with partners based on mutual trust and commitment in a continuous improvement culture.

Collaboration should not only take place on an executional level; it is time to embed it in a company's strategy. The strategic framework should be adapted accordingly to be prepared for today's ever-changing world.

Further research and practical possibilities

Viable and intelligent structure as the fourth dimension of generic strategy

Porter claims that generic strategies can only embrace the aforementioned triadic understanding and hybrid interrelationships. The evolutionary process of the rise of IT is based on the foundations laid within the cybernetics movement (Wiener, 1948; Ashby, 1956; Beer, 1959, 1972, 1981, 1985, 1989, 2002). Not only is the Schumpeterian logic of creative destruction applied to product-centred innovation, but moreover, by understanding the implementation of process and business model innovation as the locus of competitive advantage, the next frontier of strategic dimension has arisen by looking at the role of organizational design, its structure and the structure of its GVCs as exploited by highly successful companies, eg Apple Inc. and Inditex (Zara Group).

The enhanced perspective of the fourth generic strategy, as constructed by the author as a viable and intelligent organizational structure, is illustrated in Figure 1.2 in Chapter 1. Thus, an organization that can adapt and sense change by having a structure that can cope with environmental turbulence in terms of fluid information, flexible structure and the capacity for self-organization, delivers an additional generic strategy. This claim is substantiated by the author's observations that strategic foresight based on logic that embraces viability, profits and performance in economic reality and capital, requires an organizational structure that actually can carry out, reshape, refocus and ubiquitously recreate itself based on organizational autopoiesis.

The role of operations research is elaborated in Figures 2.4 and 2.7 in Chapter 2. Since structure is the essence of an organization that can design and embrace, and ultimately execute, the strategy holistically, it is essential to observe the role of the viable organizational structure as the *a priori* foundation of a functioning strategy. Strategic management so far has ignored the role of execution and organizational eigen behaviour, and its role in terms of a hierarchical downplay of a separate entity. Thus execution has been left to the organization's operations, while the very embodiment of strategic thought requires executing and conceiving ever-present feedback based on the realized strategy as an emergent phenomenon, which would entail further effective leadership in the cybernetics of organizational teleology.

Pfeifer and Bongard (2007) state that embodiment expresses that intelligence always requires an executing body (operational capability), meaning that intelligence (performance) is attributed to embody real physical systems exhibiting observable behaviour during interactions with the environment. They argue that such embodied systems are confronted with various consequences of embodiment as, for example, being subject to laws of physics, implying that their survival is affected by gravity, friction and energy supply. They conclude that the essential significance of embodiment represents the interaction between physical and information processes (cf. Pfeifer and Bongard, 2007).

Kamran (2013) puts the notion of feedback, as illustrated above, at the core of organizational viability, thus it is via feedback that course and policy correction, mission-accomplishing, goal-achieving and problem-solving activities can be undertaken within an adequate timeframe, without dangerous and costly time delays, reaction gaps and organizational inabilities in terms of latency.

In order to appreciate the role of the fourth generic strategy, a radical and different philosophy in strategic thought is introduced in terms of the purpose of a system being in what it does. This lens is established by the application of the science of cybernetics (Beer, 1959, 1972, 1981). So far, the notion of capturing the future in terms of long-range planning and strategic foresight has been conducted by application of forecasting methods, linear thinking in terms of markets and their governing forces, eg the FFM, industry-based competition and the raison d'être of organizations mainly observed within an economic reality. The author challenges these dimensions based on observing the reality of an organization's function in terms of variety-lessening activity based on Ashby's Law of Requisite Variety. According to Ashby's Law, 'the variety in the control system must be equal to or larger than the variety of the perturbations in order to maintain stability', and thus 'variety can destroy variety' (Ashby, 1956). Beer rephrased it as: 'only variety can absorb variety' (Beer, 1985: 26).

From a practical point of view, the fourth generic strategy can be substantiated by the rise of giant firms within the fast response movement (eg fast food, fast fashion). For the purpose of engaging in depth with a solid example, the quick response movement of fast fashion has been observed, thus, according to Caro and Martínez-de-Albéniz (2015): 'Fast fashion is a business model that offers (the perception of) fashionable clothes at affordable prices. From an operations standpoint, fast fashion requires a highly responsive supply chain that can support a product assortment that is periodically changing.' Hence, it is the organized structure of Inditex's (Zara) organization that actually, and in contrast to other apparel brands, has enabled the firm to obtain a highly defendable source of sustainable competitive advantage. Based on the science of cybernetics, operational effectiveness is a strategy within the paradigm of the author's enhancement of the generic strategies one can establish the logic of 'embodiment' (Pfeifer and Bongard, 2007) and the author's analogy of 'structure is strategy' (Kamran, 2013), thus effective strategies require an organizational structure to execute them. This is empirically validated by the example of Inditex (Zara), delivering evidence for the fourth generic strategy. By the author's enhancement of the generic strategies, one can establish the logic of competing on operations, which is the essence of structural dynamics of viable GVCs.

References and further reading

Ashby W (1956) *An Introduction to Cybernetics*, Chapman & Hall, London

Backhouse RE and Medema S (2009) On the definitions of economics, *Journal of Economic Perspectives*, **23** (1), pp 221–33

Bain JS (1956) *Barriers to New Competition*, Harvard University Press, Cambridge, MA

Bain JS (1959) *Industrial Organization*, Wiley, New York

Barney J (1991) Firm resources and sustained competitive advantage, *Journal of Management*, **17** (1), pp 99–121

BAT (2010) *Statement of Business Principles* [Online] http://www.bat.com/group/sites/uk__9d9kcy.nsf/vwPagesWebLive/DO9EAMHQ/$FILE/medMD9G7LTW.pdf?openelement (archived at https://perma.cc/7VD3-AC5X)

Beer S (1959) *Cybernetics and Management*, John Wiley, New York

Beer S (1972) *Brain of the Firm*, 1st edn, Penguin Press, London

Beer S (1981) *Brain of the Firm: A development in management cybernetics*, 2nd edn, John Wiley & Sons, Chichester

Beer S (1985) *Diagnosing the System for Organizations*, John Wiley, Chichester, UK and New York

Beer S (1989) *The Viable System Model*, Wiley, Chichester

Beer S (2002) What is cybernetics?, *Kybernetes*, **33** (3/4), pp 499–521

Blue Ocean Strategy [Online] https://www.blueoceanstrategy.com/what-is-blue-ocean-strategy/ (archived at https://perma.cc/VZM2-UVJY)

Bourdieu P (1984) *Distinction: A social critique of the judgement of taste*, Routledge, London

Caro F and Martínez-de-Albéniz V (2015) Fast fashion: business model overview and research opportunities, in *Retail Supply Chain Management*, eds N Agrawal and SA Smith, pp 237–64, Springer, Boston, MA

Cecere L (2010) *What happened to CPFR?* [Online] http://demand-planning.com/2010/11/29/what-happened-to-cpfr/ (archived at https://perma.cc/NR3N-NV2Q)

Christopher M (2011) *Logistics and Supply Chain Management*, 4th Edn, Pearson, London

Drucker PF (1954) *The Practice of Management*, Harper & Row, New York

DTI (2005) *A Practical Guide to Cluster Development*, Report to Department of Trade and Industry and the English RDAs by Ecotec Research & Consulting

Fawcett ST, Magnan G and McCarter M (2008) A three-stage implementation model for supply chain collaboration, *Journal of Business Logistics*, **29** (1), pp 92–112

Ferguson PR and Ferguson GJ (1994) *Industrial Economics: Issues and perspectives*, 2nd edn, New York University Press, New York

Foerster H (2003) *Understanding Understanding: Essays on cybernetics and cognition*, Springer-Verlag, New York

Guerrera F (2009) Welch condemns share price focus, *Financial Times*, 12 March

Investopia (nd) *Economics: Overview, types, and economic indicators* [Online] https://www.investopedia.com/terms/e/economics.asp (archived at https://perma.cc/359E-5ZZZ)

Kamran Q (2013) *Complexity, the Sixth Competitive Force That Shapes Strategy: A cybernetics approach to 'Porter's FFM' in turbulent and complex environments*, Lambert Academic Publishing, Saarbrücken

Kaplow L (2017) The relevance of market power, *Harvard Law Review*, **130** (5), March

Kim CW and Mauborgne R (2004a) *Blue Ocean Strategy*, 15th edn, Harvard Business School Press, Boston

Kim CW and Mauborgne R (2004b) Blue ocean strategy, *Harvard Business Review*, **82** (10)

Lambert D (2008) *An Executive Summary of Supply Chain Management: Process, partnerships, performance*, The Hartley Press, Inc, Jacksonville, FL

Lascelles D (2018) *How Supply Chains Create Shareholder Value*, Supply Chain Planning UK Limited, Cranfield

Maine Pointe (2018) *2018 Private Equity Survey* [Online] https://www.maine-pointe.com/in-the-news/private-equity-firms-are-falling-short-of-their-operational-targets (archived at https://perma.cc/86L7-34CP)

Malmberg A and Power D (2005) On the role of global demand in local innovation processes, in *Rethinking Regional Innovation and Change: Path dependency or regional breakthrough*, eds G Fuchs and P Shapira, Springer, New York

Mason ES (1939) Price and production policies of large scale enterprises, *American Economic Review*, **29**, pp 61–74

Neise R (2018) *Container Logistics: The role of the container in the supply chain*, Kogan Page, London

Pfeifer R and Bongard J (2007) *How the Body Shapes the Way We Think: A new view of intelligence*, MIT Press, Boston

Policonomics (nd) *Structure, Conduct, Performance Paradigm* [Online] https://policonomics.com/structure-conduct-performance-paradigm/ (archived at https://perma.cc/X5QY-5TT2)

Porter ME (1980/1998) *Competitive Strategy: Techniques for analyzing industries and competitors*, The Free Press, New York

Porter ME (1987) From competitive advantage to corporate strategy, *Harvard Business Review*, May

Porter ME (1990) *The Competitive Advantage of Nations*, The Free Press, New York

Porter ME (2000) Location, competition, and economic development: local clusters in a global economy, *Economic Development Quarterly*, **14** (1), pp 15–34

Teece D *et al* (1996) Firm organization, industrial structure, and technological innovation, *Journal of Economic Behavior & Organization*, **31** (2), pp 193–224, doi: 10.1016/S0167-2681(96)00895-5

Teece D *et al* (1997) Dynamic capabilities and strategic management, *Strategic Management Journal*, **18** (7), pp 509–33

The Economist (2016) Shareholder value – analyse this: the enduring power of the biggest idea in business, 31 May [Online] https://www.economist.com/business/2016/03/31/analyse-this (archived at https://perma.cc/23PV-8EYQ)

Vargo SL and Lusch RF (2004) Evolving to a new dominant logic for marketing, *Journal of Marketing*, **68** (1), pp 1–17, http://doi.org/10.1509/jmkg.68.1.1.24036 (archived at https://perma.cc/3YQF-AGXQ)

Vargo SL, Lusch RF and Morgan FW (2014) Historical perspectives on service-dominant logic, in *The Service-dominant Logic of Marketing: Dialog, debate, and directions*, eds SL Vargo and RF Lusch, pp 29–42, Routledge, New York

Vrochte MB (2000) *Die ökonomische Lehre von Aristoteles - Eine Analyse der aristotelischen Theorie der Ökonomik zum Nachweis, welche Bedeutung Ökonomie heute haben könnte*, GRIN Verlag, München

Wiener N (1948) *Cybernetics: Or control and communication in the animal and the machine*, MIT Press, Cambridge, MA

Wirth, MO and Bloch, H (2009) Industrial organization theory and media industry analysis, *Journal of Media Economics*, **8** (2), pp 15–26

Wyman O (2019) *Supply-Chain Optimization: Levers for rapid EBITDA* [Online] https://www.oliverwyman.com/our-expertise/insights/2018/may/supply-chain-optimization--levers-for-rapid-ebitda.html (archived at https://perma.cc/BY8U–ZWEH)

INDEX

Note: Numbers in headings are filed as spelt out (exception being entries for VSM system numbers and theorem numbers, filed chronologically); acronyms, 'Mc' and 'St' are filed as presented. Locators in *italics* denote information in figures/tables.